COMPARATIVE EUROPEAN POLITICS

General Editors: Hans Daalder and Ken Newton

Political Data Handbook

Second Edition

COMPARATIVE EUROPEAN POLITICS

Comparative European Politics is a series for students and teachers of political science and related disciplines, published in association with the European Consortium for Political Research. Each volume will provide an up-to-date survey of the current state of knowledge and research on an issue of major significance in European government and politics.

OTHER TITLES IN THIS SERIES

Parties and Democracy: Coalition Formation and Government
Functioning in Twenty States
Ian Budge and Hans Keman

Self-Interest and Public Interest in Western Politics
Leif Lewin

Government and Politics in Western Europe: Britain,
France, Italy, West Germany (second edition)
Yves Mény with Andrew Knapp

Localism and Centralism in Europe:
The Political and Legal Bases of Local Self-Government
Edward C. Page

Electoral Systems and Party Systems: A Study
of Twenty-Seven Democracies, 1945–1990
Arend Lijphart

State Formation, Nation Building, and Mass Politics
in Europe
Stein Rokkan
(edited by Peter Flora, Stein Kuhnle, and Derek Urwin)

Parties and Their Members: Organizing for
Victory in Britain and Germany
Susan E. Scarrow

Political Data Handbook
OECD Countries

SECOND EDITION

JAN-ERIK LANE, DAVID McKAY,
AND
KENNETH NEWTON

OXFORD UNIVERSITY PRESS

1997

Oxford University Press, Walton Street, Oxford OX2 6DP

Oxford New York

Athens Auckland Bangkok Bogota Bombay
Buenos Aires Calcutta Cape Town Dar es Salaam Delhi
Florence Hong Kong Istanbul Karachi
Kuala Lumpur Madras Madrid Melbourne
Mexico City Nairobi Paris Singapore
Taipei Tokyo Toronto

and associated companies in
Berlin Ibadan

Oxford is a trade mark of Oxford University Press

Published in the United States
by Oxford University Press Inc., New York

British Library Cataloguing in Publication Data
Data available

Library of Congress Cataloging in Publication Data
Data available

ISBN 0–19–828053–X

1 3 5 7 9 10 8 6 4 2

Typeset by Pure Tech India Ltd., Pondicherry
Printed in Great Britain
on acid-free paper by
Bookcraft (Bath) Ltd
Midsomer Norton, Avon

Acknowledgements

We owe a debt of thanks to a large number of colleagues who freely gave of their time to review and comment upon individual country data. The individuals involved were Francis Castles, Margaret Clark, Eric Damgaard, Clement H. Dodd, Giorgio Freddi, André Frognier, Hannes Gissurarson, W. K. Jackson, Efthalia Kalogeropoulou, Michael Laver, Franz Lehner, Leif Lewin, Ian Neary, Richard Simeon, Ben Soetendorp, Maria José Stock, Josep Vallès, Matti Wiberg, Colette Ysmal. We would particularly like to thank Steven Studd for his work on the second edition of the book. While acknowledging the assistance of these readers we do, of course, remain responsible for any errors or misinterpretations. Above all we would like to thank Svante Ersson, Umeå University, without whom the book, both the first and second editions, could never have been completed.

Contents

Introduction

The purpose of this book is to provide, within the confines of a single and reasonably priced volume, as comprehensive and detailed a statistical guide as possible to the government and politics of the twenty-four OECD countries, together with essential social and economic back-ground information. The aim is to present essential material of a factual nature in a form which meets the needs of professional politicians, administrators, journalists, teachers, political scientists, and the interested citizen.

There is, of course, no lack of statistical data about the nations which form the OECD—the Organization for Economic Co-operation and Development. They are, by and large, the most advanced of modern societies and they generate singly and collectively a huge amount of information about themselves, but most of it is not easily available. For example, they have their own official statistical yearbooks, but complete sets of these are held by only a few of the largest and most specialized libraries. Also, various international organizations produce large amounts of statistical material dealing with such things as social trends, domestic and international trade and business, banking, public expenditure, labour markets, migration, and so on, but these figures are often difficult to understand and interpret, often contained in voluminous and very expensive publications, and rarely deal with government and politics. There are also a handful of more specialized political source books, but these tend to be expensive and sometimes difficult to find.

Those interested, therefore, usually have to plough through a fairly long list of different sources to get even the most elementary data, and even then they are likely to end up with gaps, inconsistencies, and inadequacies. To complete this book we had to comb very carefully through nearly 230 sources, and sift through 450 tables—sometimes three or four or five dealing with almost identical variables—before we could find a suitable one. Some of our sources are well known, even if they are not always readily available. Others are relatively obscure, usually costly, and invariably not held by local libraries.

Our original intention was to compile a handbook for Western Europe, because it is so sorely needed. Western Europe shows such a richness and variety of conditions and circumstances that it makes a marvellous natural laboratory for social scientists—yet it has no political handbook. But it is also the case that the major nations of Western Europe include most of the democracies of the world, and all but a few of its wealthiest and most advanced urban-industrial nations. It takes little extra effort to cover the comparable countries outside Western Europe, and it makes the volume even more useful as a source book to do so. Therefore, it was decided to cover not just the nineteen countries of Western Europe, but also the remaining five advanced democracies of the West—namely, Canada, the USA, Japan, Australia, and New Zealand. We therefore cover twenty-four nations in all, but format the statistical tables in such a way as to distinguish between the nineteen European countries, and the 'rest'. We believe that the countries are sufficiently alike to make comparison of them meaningful, and, at the same time, they provide a sufficiently large number of cases to make many forms of statistical analysis worthwhile.

The book is divided into two main sections. The first consists of comparative tables covering all countries for as much of the post-World War II period as possible. It is divided, in turn, into sections covering the following sorts of data: population structure, employment, economy, industry, public expenditure and taxation, government structure, and electoral data. Each table has notes which draw the reader's attention to the sources used, to definitions, and to various complications and observations about the figures. In the majority of cases the time period covered is 1950 to 1985, usually for five- or ten-year intervals, depending upon the nature and availability of the material to hand.

The second main part of the book consists of sections which cover the most significant features of government and politics in the twenty-four nations which cannot be easily produced in tabular form. Each section provides information about state structure and offices, parties, government, constitutions and their changes, electoral and voting systems, as well as basic material about economic interest organizations and the media.

We cannot hope to present everything that everybody ever wanted to know about the politics and society of twenty-four nations over a thirty-five-year period. Consequently we have added a third, shorter section which lists sources of further information, including both the sources which we have consulted and quoted, and other published work, and Western European data archives which typically carry an extensive array of machine readable data files covering many different aspects of government, politics, and society in Western Europe.

Although the few paragraphs above briefly outline the purposes and contents of the book, they say nothing about why it comes to have its particular contents, and something by way of general explanation should be provided on this aspect of the volume. It is both paradoxical and ironic that something as objective and statistical as a data handbook should require so many subjective judgements to be made in the process of compilation. In fact, at almost every turn we had to make difficult decisions about what to include, why, and how. There was the first intention to produce a book about Western Europe, subsequently modified to include all twenty-four OECD countries, for reasons just explained. There was then the decision about the time period covered. In theory it would be ideal to cover the twentieth century, but this is not practicable, for reasons of space, and because the further one goes back in time, the more difficult it is to find data, never mind valid and reliable data. If one then settles for the period after World War II, when good data increasingly becomes available, it would be best to include everything from 1945 to the latest year. However, information before 1950 is often thin and scattered. At the other end of the period, it usually takes sometime for statistical material to be produced, so that any book such as this one is bound to be a couple of years or more out of date. (As we go to press, West and East Germany have just been unified.) Consequently, we decided to start the statistical runs in 1950, and to end with the most recent available information, although this is often for 1985 or earlier.

Hard decisions then had to be made about what variables to cover, and which set of statistics on a given variable to include. The general policy has been to cover only basic background information on social and economic matters, so as to leave as much room as possible for political and governmental ones. There are, after all, quite a few sources of social and economic statistics, but few on political and governmental ones, and it is this deficiency which we wanted to remedy most urgently.

On some variables it is possible to assemble as many as four or five tables from different sources, and yet they rarely manage to agree entirely. It must be said, however, that the discrepancies are usually negligible, amounting to little more than rounding errors, and in these cases we opted for the set of figures which was most complete or which covered the longest time span, or both. Where the discrepancies were large, and on rare occasions they were substantial, we inspected the footnotes with extra care in order to select the figures which made most sense for this volume, and which were most compatible with other tables in it.

Finally, we had to make a basic policy decision about exactly what sort of statistics should be included: should it be basic data of a fairly 'raw' kind; should we process this data so as to produce various indices of our own design which would allow the reader to make direct comparisons between nations over a wide range of different sorts of indicators; or should we include the indices of other writers and authors who have developed them for their own particular purposes? We decided against the second on the grounds that the sort of figures which people want for their own specific purposes are usually so diverse and precise that it is best to give them the basic ingredients, with which they can work as they wish. Nevertheless, we have not provided completely raw data, but have standardized it on a 'per capita' or 'as a percentage of GDP' basis, as appropriate. This means that the tables make sense in their own right, and that the statistics can be used and manipulated in various ways for more elaborate analysis. At the same time, the social science literature does contain some indices of such general interest and importance that we have included them here. Throughout the volume we have used two abbreviations in the following way: a dash, '—', stands for information not available whereas 'n.a.' means not applicable.

We hope the resulting compilation is as useful as it is fascinating, whether it is used casually to check up on the odd fact, or for a more systematic comparison of the twenty-four most advanced political systems of the Western world. We all know that there are 'lies, damn lies, and statistics', and we all know that statistics do not speak for themselves. But if those who speak for the statistics in political life are not to be damn liars, then they—and we—must have a supply of reliable and valid data to hand. We hope that this volume provides just such a collection.

Jan-Erik Lane
David McKay
Kenneth Newton

Introduction to Revised Edition

This is a revised, expanded, and updated version of the first edition of the *Political Data Handbook* which was published in 1991. It does three main things:

It adds the most recent data to the post-war time-series—usually for 1990, but it provides more recent figures where these are available.

It revises many of the tables, or replaces some altogether with more complete, more accurate, or more satisfactory data. In this way it is a complete overhaul of the original edition.

It adds two completely new sections on political communications and on the European Union.

On 3 October 1990 East and West Germany were formally unified, but, for sake of continuity the comparative tables in the first section of this volume continues the time-series for the Federal Republic of Germany (FRG) or West Germany. However, the entry in Part II: Country Tables, deals with the newly unified Germany.

PART I

Comparative Tables

Section 1: Population

Comparative Tables

Table 1.1. Population: mid-year estimates in thousands

	1950	1960	1970	1980	1990
Aus.	6 935	7 048	7 426	7 546	7 718
Belg.	8 639	9 153	9 656	9 859	9 993
Den.	4 271	4 581	4 951	5 123	5 141
Fin.	4 009	4 430	4 606	4 779	4 986
Fr.	41 736	45 684	50 768	53 713	56 735
FRG	49 986	55 423	60 714	61 561	63 253
Gr.	7 566	8 327	8 793	9 642	10 140
Ice.	143	176	204	228	255
Ire.	2 969	2 832	2 944	3 307	3 503
It.	47 104	50 198	53 661	56 159	57 647
Lux.	296	314	339	363	380
Neth.	10 114	11 480	13 032	14 144	14 951
Norw.	3 265	3 581	3 877	4 086	4 241
Port.	8 405	8 826	9 044	9 752	9 808
Sp.	28 009	30 455	33 779	37 430	38 959
Sw.	7 047	7 480	8 043	8 311	8 559
Switz.	4 694	5 362	6 267	6 349	6 796
Turk.	20 809	27 509	35 321	44 438	56 473
UK	50 616	52 372	55 416	55 944	57 411
Can.	13 737	17 909	21 324	23 941	26 639
USA	152 271	180 671	205 052	227 658	249 925
Jap.	82 900	94 094	104 345	116 782	123 540
Austral.	8 179	10 275	12 507	14 616	17 085
NZ	1 908	2 372	2 820	3 268	3 379

Sources: 1950–80: World Bank (1984): vol. i; 1990: *OECD National Accounts 1960–1991* (1993).

TABLE 1.2. Population growth: average annual percentage changes

	1950–60	1960–70	1970–80	1980–90	1950–90
Aus.	0.16	0.58	0.11	0.22	0.27
Belg.	0.58	0.53	0.20	0.15	0.37
Den.	0.70	0.73	0.39	0.03	0.47
Fin.	1.00	0.39	0.37	0.42	0.55
Fr.	0.91	1.06	0.60	0.52	0.77
FRG	1.04	0.90	0.15	0.27	0.59
Gr.	0.98	0.55	0.93	0.51	0.74
Ice.	2.10	1.54	1.07	1.13	1.46
Ire.	−0.46	0.40	1.43	0.30	0.42
It.	0.71	0.67	0.50	0.22	0.52
Lux.	0.59	0.80	0.69	0.43	0.63
Neth.	1.28	1.28	0.82	0.55	0.98
Norw.	0.94	0.79	0.52	0.37	0.66
Port.	−0.13	0.11	1.02	0.56	0.39
Sp.	2.31	1.03	0.99	0.41	1.18
Sw.	0.65	0.73	0.33	0.29	0.50
Switz.	1.34	1.57	0.19	0.63	0.93
Turk.	2.85	2.52	2.31	2.36	2.51
UK	0.34	0.61	0.12	0.19	0.32
Can.	2.69	1.76	1.22	1.02	1.67
USA	1.72	1.27	1.06	0.93	1.25
Jap.	1.18	1.07	1.20	0.56	1.00
Austral.	2.58	1.97	1.38	1.52	1.86
NZ	2.22	1.72	1.10	0.72	1.44

Note: The date for 1950–60 are averaged over the eleven year period; data for subsequent periods are average annual percentage changes, i.e. the figures for 1950–60 are arrived at in the following way: ((Pop. 1960–Pop. 1950) × 100)/(Pop. 1950 × 11).

Sources: See Table 1.1.

Comparative Tables

TABLE 1.3. Area in km^2, population density, and inhabitants per km^2

	Area			Density		
	1955	1980	1990	1955	1980	1990
Aus.	83 849	83 849	83 859	83	90	92
Belg.	30 507	30 513	30 519	283	323	327
Den.	43 042	43 069	43 093	99	119	119
Fin.	337 009	337 032	304 623	12	14	15
Fr.	551 208	547 026	543 965	76	98	103
FRG	248 407	248 577	356 957	201	248	254
Gr.	132 526	131 944	131 957	57	73	77
Ice.	103 000	103 000	103 000	1	2	3
Ire.	70 283	70 283	68 895	42	47	50
It.	301 226	301 225	301 227	156	186	191
Lux.	2 586	2 586	2 586	114	140	147
Neth.	32 450	40 844	33 936	312	346	366
Norw.	323 917	324 219	323 877	10	13	13
Port.	92 200	92 082	92 389	91	106	107
Sp.	503 486	504 782	504 782	56	74	77
Sw.	449 682	449 964	449 964	16	18	19
Switz.	41 288	41 288	41 293	114	154	165
Turk.	776 980	780 576	779 452	27	57	72
UK	244 016	244 046	242 533	207	229	235
Can.	9 974 375	9 976 139	9 970 610	1	2	3
USA	9 357 427	9 372 614	9 372 614	16	24	27
Jap.	369 766	377 708	377 815	224	309	327
Austral.	7 704 159	7 686 848	7 682 300	1	2	2
NZ	267 995	268 676	267 844	7	12	13

Sources: 1955: UN, *Demographic Yearbook* (1957); 1980: UN, *Demographic Yearbook* (1981); 1990: OECD *OECD In Figures* (1992).

TABLE 1.4. Age structure: population aged 0 to 14 as a percentage of total population

	1950[a]	1960	1970	1980	1990
Aus.	22.9	22.1	24.4	20.4	17.4
Belg.	20.6	23.5	23.6	20.0	18.1
Den.	26.3	25.2	23.3	20.9	17.1
Fin.	30.0	30.4	24.6	20.3	19.3
Fr.	22.6	26.4	24.8	22.4	20.1
FRG	23.3	21.3	23.2	18.2	15.2
Gr.	28.4	26.5	24.6	22.8	19.4
Ice.	30.7	34.7	32.6	27.5	25.0
Ire.	28.9	31.1	31.3	30.4	27.3
It.	26.1	24.9	22.9	20.5	15.0
Lux.	19.8	21.3	22.1	18.6	17.7
Neth.	29.3	30.0	27.3	22.3	18.2
Norw.	24.4	25.9	24.5	22.2	18.9
Port.	29.4	29.2	28.8	25.3	19.3
Sp.	26.2	27.4	28.0	25.9	19.7
Sw.	23.4	22.0	20.9	19.6	17.9
Switz.	23.6	23.6	23.4	19.5	16.5
Turk.	38.3	41.2	41.8	38.5	35.8
UK	22.6	23.3	24.1	21.0	19.0
Can.	30.3	33.5	30.3	23.0	21.0
USA	25.9	31.0	28.3	22.5	21.7
Jap.	35.4	30.2	23.9	23.6	18.4
Austral.	25.2	30.1	28.8	25.3	21.9
NZ	29.4	32.9	31.9	27.2	23.2

[a] 1950 or nearest available year.

Note: Country totals for Tables 1.4 to 1.6 do not always add up to 100% because of rounding.

Sources: 1950: Mitchell (1981; 1982; 1983); UN, *Demographic Yearbook* (1949–50; 1952); 1960: World Bank (1984): vol. ii; 1970–80: OECD (1988); 1990: OECD *Labour Force Statistics 1971–1991* (1993).

TABLE 1.5. Age structure: population aged 15 to 64 as a percentage of total population

	1950	1960	1970	1980	1990
Aus.	66.5	65.8	61.6	64.2	67.5
Belg.	68.8	64.5	63.0	65.6	67.0
Den.	64.6	64.2	64.4	64.7	67.4
Fin.	63.4	62.4	66.2	67.7	67.3
Fr.	66.1	62.0	62.3	63.7	65.9
FRG	67.3	67.8	63.6	66.3	69.5
Gr.	65.0	65.3	64.3	64.0	66.8
Ice.	61.6	57.4	58.5	62.6	64.4
Ire.	60.4	57.7	57.7	58.8	61.3
It.	65.7	65.8	66.5	66.7	69.8
Lux.	70.7	67.8	65.3	67.8	68.8
Neth.	63.6	61.0	62.6	66.2	68.9
Norw.	65.9	63.0	62.6	63.1	64.7
Port.	63.3	62.9	61.9	63.3	66.6
Sp.	66.5	64.4	62.5	63.3	66.9
Sw.	66.2	66.0	65.5	64.1	64.3
Switz.	66.8	66.3	65.2	66.8	68.4
Turk.	58.4	55.2	53.8	56.6	60.0
UK	66.6	65.1	62.7	64.1	65.3
Can.	61.9	59.0	61.7	67.5	67.5
USA	62.6	59.7	61.9	66.2	65.8
Jap.	58.7	64.1	69.0	67.4	69.7
Austral.	66.8	61.4	62.8	65.1	66.9
NZ	61.3	58.5	59.6	63.1	65.7

Note and Sources: See Table 1.4.

TABLE 1.6. Age structure: population aged 65 and older as a percentage of total population

	1950	1960	1970	1980	1990
Aus.	10.6	12.0	14.1	15.4	15.1
Belg.	10.6	12.0	13.4	14.4	14.9
Den.	9.1	10.6	12.3	14.4	15.6
Fin.	6.6	7.2	9.1	12.0	13.4
Fr.	11.2	11.6	12.9	13.9	14.0
FRG	9.4	10.8	13.2	15.5	15.3
Gr.	6.6	8.3	11.1	13.1	13.8
Ice.	7.7	8.0	8.9	9.9	10.6
Ire.	10.7	11.2	11.2	10.7	11.4
It.	8.2	9.3	10.5	12.9	15.3
Lux.	9.5	10.8	12.6	13.6	13.5
Neth.	7.1	9.0	10.2	11.5	12.8
Norw.	9.7	11.1	12.9	14.8	16.3
Port.	7.3	8.0	9.3	11.5	14.1
Sp.	7.3	8.2	9.5	10.9	13.4
Sw.	10.3	12.0	13.7	16.3	17.8
Switz.	9.6	10.1	11.4	13.7	15.0
Turk.	3.3	3.5	4.4	4.8	4.2
UK	10.9	11.7	13.2	14.9	15.7
Can.	7.8	7.5	8.0	9.5	11.5
USA	11.5	9.2	9.8	11.3	12.5
Jap.	4.9	5.7	7.1	9.0	11.9
Austral.	8.0	8.5	8.3	9.6	11.2
NZ	9.2	8.6	8.4	9.7	11.1

Note and Sources: See Table 1.4.

Table 1.7.   Crude birth rate (per thousand)

	1950	1960	1970	1980	1990
Aus.	15.6	17.9	15.1	12.1	11.7
Belg.	16.9	16.9	14.7	12.6	12.4
Den.	18.6	16.6	14.3	11.2	12.3
Fin.	24.5	18.5	14.0	13.1	13.2
Fr.	20.6	17.9	16.8	14.9	13.4
FRG	16.2	17.5	13.4	10.1	11.5
Gr.	20.2	18.9	16.5	15.4	10.1
Ice.	28.7	17.5	13.4	19.9	18.8
Ire.	21.3	21.4	21.9	21.8	15.1
It.	19.6	18.1	16.8	11.4	9.9
Lux.	14.8	16.0	13.2	11.4	12.9
Neth.	22.7	20.8	18.3	12.8	13.2
Norw.	19.1	17.3	16.6	12.4	14.4
Port.	24.4	24.2	19.1	16.2	11.1
Sp.	20.2	21.7	19.4	15.1	10.2
Sw.	16.4	13.7	13.7	11.6	14.5
Switz.	18.1	17.6	15.8	11.5	12.5
Turk.	—	43.1	37.9	31.4	29.3
UK	16.2	17.5	16.3	13.5	13.9
Can.	27.1	26.7	17.4	15.4	15.2
USA	23.5	23.6	18.2	15.9	16.6
Jap.	28.2	17.3	18.7	13.5	9.9
Austral.	23.3	22.4	20.6	15.3	15.4
NZ	25.9	26.5	22.1	16.2	17.7

Note: Crude birth rate equals annual live births per thousand population.

Sources: 1950: UN, *Demographic Yearbook* (1954); 1960–70: World Bank (1984): vol. ii; 1980: World Bank (1988); 1990: *OECD Labour Force Statistics* (1993).

TABLE 1.8. Life expectancy at birth in years

	1960	1970	1980	1990
Aus.	68.6	70.5	72.5	74.8
Belg.	70.3	71.9	72.8	75.2
Den.	72.2	73.3	74.1	75.8
Fin.	68.4	70.0	72.9	75.5
Fr.	70.3	72.1	74.3	76.4
FRG	69.5	70.5	73.2	75.2
Gr.	68.8	71.3	74.2	76.1
Ice.	69.5	70.5	76.5	77.8
Ire.	69.6	71.4	72.5	74.6
It.	69.2	71.5	74.5	76.0
Lux.	68.1	70.4	72.4	74.9
Neth.	73.2	73.7	75.7	77.2
Norw.	73.4	74.2	76.1	77.1
Port.	63.3	67.1	70.1	74.0
Sp.	68.5	71.5	74.5	77.0
Sw.	73.1	74.3	76.3	77.4
Switz.	71.2	72.3	77.0	77.4
Turk.	50.5	56.6	61.7	65.1
UK	70.6	71.8	73.8	75.7
Can.	71.0	72.2	74.6	77.0
USA	69.9	70.9	73.7	75.9
Jap.	68.0	72.4	76.0	78.6
Austral.	70.9	72.1	74.6	76.5
NZ	71.7	71.8	73.3	75.2

Note: Life expectancy at birth is the number of years a newborn infant would live if prevailing patterns of mortality for all people at the time of birth were to stay the same throughout life.

Sources: 1960–70: World Bank (1984): vol. ii; 1980: World Bank (1988); 1990: *United Nations Human Development Report 1993* (1993).

Comparative Tables

TABLE 1.9. Infant mortality rates (up to one year)

	1950	1960	1970	1980	1990
Aus.	66.1	37.5	25.9	13.9	7.8
Belg.	53.4	31.2	21.1	11.0	7.9
Den.	30.7	21.5	14.2	8.4	7.5
Fin.	43.5	21.0	13.2	7.6	5.6
Fr.	52.0	27.4	18.2	10.0	7.2
FRG	55.5	33.8	23.6	12.7	7.1
Gr.	36.7	40.1	29.6	17.9	9.7
Ice.	21.7	15.2	13.2	11.1	5.9
Ire.	45.3	29.3	19.5	11.1	8.2
It.	63.8	43.9	29.6	14.3	8.2
Lux.	45.7	31.5	24.6	11.5	7.4
Neth.	25.2	17.9	12.7	8.6	7.1
Norw.	28.2	18.9	12.7	8.0	7.0
Port.	94.1	82.0	58.0	23.9	11.0
Sp.	69.8	49.6	26.5	11.1	7.8
Sw.	21.0	16.6	11.0	6.9	6.0
Switz.	31.2	21.1	15.1	8.4	6.8
Turk.	—	189.5	147.5	122.6	59.3
UK	31.4	22.5	18.4	12.1	7.9
Can.	41.3	27.3	18.8	10.4	6.8
USA	29.2	26.0	20.0	12.6	9.1
Jap.	60.1	30.4	13.1	7.5	4.6
Austral.	24.5	20.2	17.9	10.7	8.2
NZ	27.6	22.6	16.7	12.8	8.3

Note: Infant mortality rate is the number of infants who die before reaching one year of age, per thousand live births in a year.

Sources: 1950 UN, *Demographic Yearbook* (1954); 1960–70; World Bank (1984): vol. ii; 1980–5: World Bank (1988); OECD, *OECD Health Systems: Facts and Trends, 1960–1991* (1993).

TABLE 1.10. Urban concentration: largest city's percentage share of total population

		1950	1960	1970	1980	1990
Aus.	(Wien)	25	23	22	21	20
Belg.	(Bruxelles)	11	11	11	10	13
Den.	(København)	27	28	28	27	26
Fin.	(Helsinki)	9	10	11	10	10
Fr.	(Paris)	7	6	5	4	4
FRG	(Berlin West)	4	4	4	3	3
Gr.	(Athinai)	7	8	10	9	9
Ice.	(Reykjavik)	43	41	40	38	38
Ire.	(Dublin)	18	19	19	16	14
It.	(Roma)	4	4	5	5	5
Lux.	(Luxembourg)	21	23	23	22	20
Neth.	(Amsterdam)	8	8	6	5	5
Norw.	(Oslo)	13	13	13	11	11
Port.	(Lisboa)	9	9	8	8	9
Sp.	(Madrid)	6	7	9	9	8
Sw.	(Stockholm)	11	11	10	8	8
Switz.	(Zürich)	8	8	7	6	5
Turk.	(Istanbul)	5	5	6	6	6
UK	(London)	17	16	13	12	12
Can.	(Toronto)	5	4	3	3	3
USA	(New York)	5	4	4	3	3
Jap.	(Tokyo)	8	9	8	7	7
Austral.	(Sydney)	18	21	20	22	21
NZ	(Auckland)	17	17	11	10	9

Note: City refers to city proper as defined in the sources. There is a problem of comparability both between nations and over time, since city proper may be defined in various ways. The UN's *Demographic Yearbook* states that *city proper* is defined as a locality with legally fixed boundaries and an administratively recognized urban status which is usually characterized by some form of local government.

Sources: Figures for largest city 1950–70 are based on: Mitchell (1981; 1982; 1983); figures for 1980 are based on UN, *Demographic Yearbook* (1983); figures for 1990 are based on UN, *Demographic Yearbook* (1992).

Section 2: Social Structure

TABLES

TABLE 2.1. Ethno-linguistic structure: percentage of the population belonging to dominant groups

	Language group (1)	Ethno-linguistic group (2)	Language group (3)
Aus.	99	93	96
Belg.	50	59	59
Den.	97	98	97
Fin.	92	92	94
Fr.	86	82	94
FRG	100	94	94
Gr.	98	95	96
Ice.	97	99	94
Ire.	97	96	95
It.	99	96	95
Lux.	93	82	74
Neth.	95	94	96
Norw.	100	98	97
Port.	100	99	99
Sp.	73	73	72
Sw.	98	90	91
Switz.	69	63	65
Turk.	90	90	86
UK	98	79	97
Can.	58	38	61
USA	86	63	88
Jap.	99	98	99
Austral.	91	83	86
NZ	91	89	93

TABLE 2.2. Ethno-linguistic structure: fragmentation indices

	(1)	(2)	(3)	(4)	(5)	(6)
Aus.	0.04	0.01	0.13	0.02	0.02	0.13
Belg.	0.55	0.51	0.55	0.50	0.50	0.54
Den.	0.02	0.12	0.05	0.00	0.02	0.05
Fin.	0.16	0.35	0.16	0.13	0.11	0.15
Fr.	0.15	0.17	0.26	0.10	0.15	0.33
FRG	0.00	—	0.03	0.00	0.02	0.12
Gr.	0.03	0.21	0.10	0.09	0.04	0.10
Ice.	0.00	0.54	0.05	0.00	0.00	0.03
Ire.	0.22	0.44	0.04	0.04	0.18	0.07
It.	0.06	0.09	0.04	0.10	0.10	0.08
Lux.	0.00	0.12	0.15	0.00	0.14	0.32
Neth.	0.08	0.00	0.10	0.06	0.04	0.11
Norw.	0.00	0.19	0.04	0.00	0.02	0.05
Port.	0.00	0.00	0.01	0.00	0.00	0.01
Sp.	0.50	0.42	0.44	0.39	0.63	0.44
Sw.	0.00	0.12	0.08	0.00	0.02	0.19
Switz.	0.45	0.50	0.50	0.52	0.53	0.56
Turk.	—	0.24	0.25	—	0.19	0.19
UK	0.05	0.04	0.32	0.03	0.02	0.37
Can.	—	0.48	0.75	—	0.56	0.77
USA	—	0.25	0.50	—	0.31	0.58
Jap.	—	0.02	0.01	—	0.00	0.03
Austral.	—	0.03	0.32	—	0.02	0.32
NZ	—	0.07	0.37	—	0.27	0.20

Note: The index of fragmentation indicates the probabilities that two randomly sampled people will belong to different ethno-linguistic groups. The index ranges from 0 to 1, with 1 the most heterogeneous, and 0 the least.

Sources: (1): Data are for the 1920s and based on Tesnière (1928); (2): Taylor and Hudson (1972): Muller data; (3): Taylor and Hudson (1972): Atlas Narodov Mira data; (4): Data are for the 1970s and based on Stephens (1976); (5): Data are for the 1970s and based on Worldmark (1984); (6): Data are for the 1970s and based on Barrett (1982).

TABLE 2.3. Religious structure: religious affiliation by Christian denomination, other denominations, or no denomination in the mid-1970s; major religion 1990 (percentages)

	Protestants	Catholics	Other religions	No religion/ non-confession	Fragmenta-tion index	Major religious group, 1990
Aus.	7	90	0	3	0.18	84
Belg.	0	92	1	7	0.15	90
Den.	95	1	1	3	0.10	89
Fin.	94	1	0	5	0.11	88
Fr.	2	80	4	14	0.34	76
FRG	48	46	2	4	0.56	40
Gr.	0	98	2	0	0.04	98
Ice.	97	1	0	2	0.06	92
Ire.	4	96	0	0	0.08	93
It.	0	87	0	13	0.23	84
Lux.	1	94	0	5	0.11	94
Neth.	43	44	2	11	0.61	36
Norw.	98	0	0	2	0.04	88
Port.	1	96	0	3	0.08	95
Sp.	0	97	0	3	0.06	96
Sw.	71	2	0	27	0.42	89
Switz.	46	52	1	1	0.52	48
Turk.	0	1	99	0	0.02	99
UK	74	14	3	9	0.42	57
Can.	43	50	2	5	0.56	47
USA	58	31	5	6	0.56	51
Jap.	2	1	87	11	0.25	87
Austral.	57	32	1	10	0.56	26
NZ	75	18	1	6	0.40	21

Note: The fragmentation index refers to the probability that two randomly sampled people will belong to different religions. The index ranges from 0 to 1, with 0 the most homogeneous and 1 the most heterogeneous.

Sources: Barrett (1982); Major religious group reported in *Encylopaedia Brittanica* (1993).

TABLE 2.4. Income distribution: Gini-indices

	Index (Yr) (1)	Index (Yr) (2)	Index (Yr) (3)	Index (Yr) (4)	Index (Yr) (5)
Aus.	—	0.369 (67)	—	—	—
Belg.	—	—	—	—	—
Den.	0.37 (63)	0.365 (66)	—	0.38 (71)	—
Fin.	0.46 (62)	0.463 (67)	—	0.37 (71)	0.30[a] (78)
Fr.	0.50 (62)	0.421 (70)	0.416 (70)	0.414 (70)	0.43 (75)
FRG	0.45 (64)	0.392 (70)	0.396 (73)	0.383 (73)	0.31[a] (78)
Gr.	0.38 (57)	0.394 (57)	—	—	—
Ice.	—	—	—	—	—
Ire.	—	—	—	—	—
It.	0.40 (48)	0.397 (69)	—	0.398 (69)	0.37 (80)
Lux.	—	—	—	—	—
Neth.	0.42 (62)	0.393 (67)	0.385 (67)	0.354 (67)	0.31[a] (77)
Norw.	0.35 (63)	0.361 (70)	0.354 (70)	0.307 (70)	0.32[a] (79)
Port.	—	—	—	—	—
Sp.	—	0.391 (64)	—	0.355 (73)	0.39 (80)
Sw.	0.39 (63)	0.350 (72)	0.346 (72)	0.302 (72)	0.33[a] (79)
Switz.	—	0.401 (68)	—	—	0.29 (80)
Turk.	—	0.553 (68)	—	—	—
UK	0.38 (64)	0.346 (62)	0.344 (73)	0.318 (73)	0.33 (80)
Can.	—	0.383 (69)	0.382 (69)	0.354 (69)	0.36 (79)
USA	0.34 (69)	0.409 (72)	0.404 (72)	0.381 (72)	—
Jap.	0.39 (69)	0.412 (71)	0.335 (69)	0.316 (69)	0.17 (79)
Austral.	0.32 (66)	0.320 (68)	0.313 (67)	0.312 (67)	0.36 (79)
NZ	—	0.353 (72)	—	—	—

[a] Figures based on authors' computations.

Note: The Gini index ranges from 0 to 1, with 0 being maximum equality and 1 maximum inequality. See Sawyer (1976) and OECD (1986) for a discussion of the methodological problems.

Sources: (1) Paukert (1973): pre-tax; (2) Bornischer (1978): pre-tax; (3) Sawyer (1976): pre-tax; (4) Sawyer (1976): post-tax; Denmark, Finland: Uusitalo (1975); (5) OECD (1986).

TABLE 2.5. Income distribution: share of national income (pre- or post-tax) going to top 20% of the population

	Share (Yr) (1)	Share (Yr) (2)	Share (Yr) (3)	Share (Yr) (4)	Share (Yr) (5)	Share (Yr) (6)	Share (Yr) (7)
Aus.	—	—	—	—	—	—	—
Belg.	—	—	—	—	36.0 (78)	—	36.0 (78)
Den.	43.2 (63)	47.6 (68)	—	—	38.6 (81)	—	38.6 (81)
Fin.	49.3 (62)	49.3 (62)	—	—	37.6 (81)	37 (78)	37.6 (81)
Fr.	53.7 (62)	53.7 (62)	46.9 (70)	46.9 (70)	45.8 (75)	47 (75)	40.8 (79)
FRG	45.6 (70)	52.9 (64)	45.6 (70)	46.2 (73)	39.5 (78)	38 (78)	38.7 (84)
Gr.	—	49.5 (57)	—	—	—	—	—
Ice.	—	—	—	—	—	—	—
Ire.	—	—	—	—	39.4 (73)	—	—
It.	—	48.4 (48)	46.5 (70)	46.5 (69)	43.9 (77)	44 (80)	41.0 (86)
Lux.	—	—	—	—	—	—	—
Neth.	40.5 (63)	48.5 (67)	42.9 (70)	42.9 (67)	36.2 (81)	37 (77)	38.3 (83)
Norw.	—	40.5 (68)	37.3 (70)	37.3 (70)	38.2 (82)	37 (79)	36.7 (79)
Port.	—	—	—	—	49.1 (73)	—	—
Sp.	45.2 (64)	45.7 (65)	42.2 (70)	42.2 (74)	40.0 (80)	42 (80)	40.0 (80)
Sw.	42.5 (70)	44.0 (63)	37.0 (70)	37.0 (72)	41.7 (81)	37 (79)	36.9 (81)
Switz.	—	—	45.9 (70)	—	38.0 (78)	37 (78)	44.6 (82)
Turk.	60.6 (68)	60.8 (68)	56.5 (73)	56.5 (73)	56.5 (73)	—	—
UK	39.2 (68)	39.0 (68)	39.4 (70)	38.8 (73)	39.7 (79)	39 (80)	39.5 (79)

Can.	40.2 (65)	41.0 (69)	41.0 (69)	40.0 (81)	40 (79)	40.2 (87)
USA	38.8 (70)	42.8 (72)	42.8 (72)	39.9 (80)	—	41.9 (85)
Jap.	40.0 (63)	41.0 (69)	41.0 (69)	37.5 (79)	30 (79)	37.5 (79)
Austral.	38.8 (68)	38.8 (67)	38.8 (67)	47.1 (76)	42 (79)	42.2 (85)
NZ	42.0 (69)	41.4 (66)	—	44.7 (82)	—	44.7 (82)

Note: Each series for a column is based consistently on either pre- or post-tax income, but the basis of measurement may differ between the column years.

Sources: (1) Ahluwalia (1976); (2) Musgrave and Jarrett (1979); (3) Muller (1985); (4) World Bank, *World Development Report* (1979); (5) World Bank, *World Development Report* (1986; 1988); (6) OECD (1986); (7) World Bank, *World Development Report* (1993).

TABLE 2.6. Estimates of work-force unionized (percentages)

	Union density (1)					Union density (2)				Union density (3)				
	1950	1960	1970	1980	1985	1970	1975	1980	1985	1970	1975	1980	1985	1988
Aus.	62	63	62	58	58	70.4	67.0	65.3	60.8	70.4	67.0	65.3	60.8	58.2
Belg.	37	48	52	68	68	60.8	72.9	78.4	—	54.9	69.0	75.7	80.9	77.5
Den.	53	60	62	80	83	66.9	68.6	81.9	88.9	62.2	74.2	91.4	90.8	86.0
Fin.	33	35	57	81	81	58.8	78.3	85.7	86.6	58.8	78.3	85.8	86.6	90.0
Fr.	31	19	22	18	15	29.6	28.5	28.0	17.7	22.3	22.8	19.0	16.3	12.0
FRG	36	39	38	40	38	36.6	39.8	40.9	41.5	37.9	41.7	42.9	44.0	40.1
Gr.	—	—	—	—	—	—	—	—	—	—	35.8	—	36.7	(25.0)
Ice.	—	—	—	—	—	—	—	—	—	—	—	68.1	—	78.3
Ire.	39	45	54	57	48	58.1	59.0	61.1	61.2	59.0	61.3	63.4	62.2	58.4
It.	44	26	38	54	51	36.3	46.9	49.2	42.0	40.8	54.2	60.5	59.6	62.7
Lux.	—	—	—	—	—	—	—	—	—	46.8	45.8	52.2	—	49.7
Neth.	36	42	40	36	28	39.5	42.4	40.2	34.4	40.5	42.7	39.9	34.1	30.2
Norw.	46	58	57	64	64	62.4	62.2	65.5	67.9	58.1	60.4	65.3	65.4	67.7
Port.	—	—	—	—	—	—	—	—	—	59.0	52.4	58.8	51.6	(30.0)
Sp.	—	—	—	—	—	—	—	—	—	—	30.4	22.0	16.0	—
Sw.	68	72	73	88	91	80.3	82.2	87.6	94.4	74.2	82.1	89.5	94.2	96.1
Switz.	40	39	32	35	32	32.4	35.9	35.2	34.4	34.2	36.6	34.5	32.6	30.0
Turk.	—	—	—	—	—	—	—	—	—	—	18.1	—	—	19.2
UK	44	44	48	53	44	49.8	53.0	56.4	49.8	49.7	53.6	56.3	50.5	46.1

Can.	33	28	29	33	33	31.0	34.4	35.2	36.2	31.1	34.4	35.1	35.9	34.6
USA	28	29	26	20	17	30.1	28.8	24.9	17.4	30.0	29.1	24.7	—	—
Jap.	46	32	35	31	29	35.1	34.5	31.1	28.8	35.1	34.4	31.1	28.9	26.8
Austral.	56	54	49	52	51	49.8	56.3	56.4	56.7	50.2	56.0	56.4	56.5	53.4
NZ	49	45	40	46	41	52.2	56.4	61.6	54.9	—	—	—	54.1	50.5

Note: (3) Figures in parentheses for 1988 are less reliable than other figures.

Sources: (1) Western (1993); (2) Armingeon (1989); (3) Visser (1992).

Comparative Tables

TABLE 2.7. Migration

	Net migration rates			
	1970	1980	1985	1990
Aus.	2.3	1.2	1.1	3.0
Belg.	0.4	−0.4	0.1	2.0
Den.	2.4	0.2	1.8	1.6
Fin.	−7.8	−0.6	0.6	1.8
Fr.	3.5	0.8	−0.1	1.4
FRG	9.3	5.1	1.5	16.3
Gr.	−4.4	5.0	1.1	16.6
Ice.	−7.3	−2.2	−2.1	−3.9
Ire.	−1.0	−0.3	−7.3	−2.6
It.	−0.9	0.1	1.5	2.5
Lux.	3.2	3.6	2.5	7.4
Neth.	2.6	3.7	1.4	4.0
Norw.	−0.3	1.0	1.4	0.5
Port.	−16.5	−12.9	2.3	−0.3
Sp.	0.6	0.0	0.4	0.4
Sw.	6.1	1.2	1.3	4.1
Switz.	−1.0	2.7	2.2	8.5
Turk.	—	0.1	−2.0	0.0
UK	−0.5	−0.9	1.3	0.9
Can.	3.3	4.5	1.1	6.3
USA	2.1	3.7	2.7	2.7
Jap.	−0.1	0.3	0.7	−0.6
Austral.	9.8	7.1	5.2	6.5
NZ	3.9	−3.8	−4.2	2.1

Note: Net migration means immigration minus emigration.

Sources: OECD (1988); OECD (1993).

TABLE 2.8. Migration in Western Europe: minority labour force as percentage of total labour force

	1960 (1)	1970 (2)	1974 (3)	1977 (4)	1981 (5)	1982 (6)
Aus.	—	—	—	6.0	—	—
Belg.	4.8	7.1	—	8.4	8.7	8.2
Den.	—	—	—	—	—	—
Fin.	—	—	—	—	—	—
Fr.	—	6.3	8.2	7.3	6.4	6.6
FRG	1.7	6.5	10.9	9.5	9.5	9.2
Gr.	—	—	—	—	—	—
Ice.	—	—	—	—	—	—
Ire.	—	—	—	—	—	—
It.	—	—	—	—	—	—
Lux.	—	—	—	32.0	—	33.0
Neth.	1.1	2.8	3.2	3.0	4.9	3.7
Norw.	—	—	—	—	—	—
Port.	—	—	—	—	—	—
Sp.	—	—	—	—	—	—
Sw.	2.9	5.2	5.2	5.4	5.4	5.2
Switz.	21.8	25.2	25.4	16.4	22.9	19.7
UK	5.1	7.1	—	—	7.2	—

Sources: (1)–(3), (5): Castles (1984); (4): OECD, *Observer* (1979); (6): OECD, *Employment Outlook* (1985).

TABLE 2.9. Migration in Western Europe: minority population as percentage of total population

	1950 (1)	1960 (2)	1970 (3)	1975 (4)	1982 (5)	1990 (6)
Aus.	4.7	—	2.8	—	4.0	6.6
Belg.	4.3	4.9	7.2	8.5	9.0	9.1
Den.	—	—	—	—	2.0	3.1
Fin.	0.3	—	0.1	—	0.3	0.9
Fr.	4.1	5.4	5.3	7.9	6.8	6.4
FRG	1.1	1.2	4.9	6.6	7.6	8.2
Gr.	0.4	—	1.1	—	0.7	0.9
Ice.	—	—	—	—	—	—
Ire.	—	—	—	—	2.0	2.5
It.	0.1	—	—	—	0.5	1.4
Lux.	9.9	—	18.4	—	26.4	28.0
Neth.	1.1	1.0	2.0	2.6	3.9	4.6
Norw.	0.5	—	—	—	2.2	3.4
Port.	0.3	—	—	—	0.6	1.0
Sp.	0.3	—	0.9	—	1.1	1.1
Sw.	1.8	2.5	5.1	5.0	4.9	5.6
Switz.	6.1	10.8	17.2	16.0	14.7	16.3
UK	—	4.3	—	7.8	3.9	3.3

Sources: (1)–(4): Castles (1984); (5) OECD, *Employment Outlook* (1985); (1), (3), (5), (6): Fassmann and Münz (1992).

TABLE 2.10. Migration in Western Europe: estimated population and labour force living abroad

	Estimated population living abroad			Estimated labour force living abroad	
	In Europe *c.* 1970 (1)	In Europe *c.* 1982 (2)	In world *c.* 1982 (3)	In Europe *c.* 1977 (4)	In Europe *c.* 1982 (5)
Aus.	—	—	—	—	—
Belg.	—	—	—	—	—
Den.	—	—	—	—	—
Fin.	—	3.7	4.8	4.5	4.7
Fr.	—	—	—	—	—
FRG	—	—	—	—	—
Gr.	4.1	—	—	5.7	4.1
Ice.	—	—	—	—	—
Ire.	25.1	—	—	—	—
It.	3.4	4.1	9.4	4.0	4.6
Lux.	—	—	—	—	—
Neth.	—	—	—	—	—
Norw.	—	—	—	—	—
Port.	6.0	11.8	40.3	10.6	13.9
Sp.	2.9	2.3	5.6	3.2	3.1
Sw.	—	—	—	—	—
Switz.	—	—	—	—	—
UK	—	—	—	—	—

Sources: (1): Castles and Kosack (1973); (2), (3), (5): OECD, *Employment Outlook* (1985); (4): OECD, *Observer* (1979).

Comparative Tables

TABLE 2.11. Index of Social Progress

	1969–70	1979–80
Aus.	186	192
Belg.	175	178
Den.	198	201
Fin.	169	174
Fr.	172	165
FRG	179	174
Gr.	136	146
Ice.	—	—
Ire.	185	183
It.	160	158
Lux.	—	—
Neth.	187	190
Norw.	186	193
Port.	131	146
Sp.	156	129
Sw.	198	189
Switz.	164	170
Turk.	99	112
UK	171	145
Can.	157	170
USA	91	116
Jap.	149	157
Austral.	173	184
NZ	178	186

Note: The Index of Social Progress consists of 44 welfare-relevant social indicators distributed among eleven sub-indices, as follows: education, health, womens' status, defence effort, economics, demography, geography, political stability, political participation, cultural diversity, and welfare effort.

Source: (Estes, 1984).

TABLE 2.12. Human Development Index

	1960	1970	1980	1992
Aus.	0.797	0.857	0.880	0.917
Belg.	0.826	0.851	0.873	0.916
Den.	0.857	0.879	0.888	0.912
Fin.	0.811	0.855	0.880	0.911
Fr.	0.853	0.871	0.895	0.927
FRG	0.841	0.856	0.881	0.918
Gr.	0.573	0.723	0.839	0.874
Ice.	0.853	0.863	0.890	0.914
Ire.	0.710	0.829	0.862	0.892
It.	0.755	0.831	0.857	0.891
Lux.	0.826	0.843	0.869	0.908
Neth.	0.855	0.867	0.888	0.923
Norw.	0.865	0.878	0.901	0.928
Port.	0.460	0.508	0.736	0.838
Sp.	0.636	0.820	0.851	0.888
Sw.	0.867	0.881	0.889	0.928
Switz.	0.853	0.872	0.897	0.931
Turk.	0.333	0.441	0.549	0.739
UK	0.857	0.873	0.892	0.919
Can.	0.865	0.887	0.911	0.932
USA	0.865	0.881	0.905	0.925
Jap.	0.686	0.875	0.906	0.929
Austral.	0.850	0.862	0.890	0.926
NZ.	0.852	0.861	0.877	0.907

Note: Human development index (HDI) is a composite measure of human development containing indicators representing three equally weighted dimensions of human development—longevity (life expectancy at birth), knowledge (adult literacy and mean years of schooling), and income (purchasing power parity dollars per capita).

Source: UNDP, *Human Development Report 1994* (1994).

Section 3: Employment

TABLE 3.1. Labour force as a percentage of total population

	ILO figures					OECD figures			
	1950	1960	1970	1980	1990	1960	1970	1980	1990
	(1)	(2)	(3)	(4)	(5)	(6)	(7)	(8)	(9)
Aus.	47.9	48.1	41.6	45.1	45.8	47.0	42.0	43.9	45.7
Belg.	39.9	37.1	37.1	42.1	41.8	39.2	39.7	42.2	41.9
Den.	48.2	45.7	44.8	52.1	56.6	45.7	48.3	51.9	56.6
Fin.	49.3	45.7	46.1	45.9	51.7	48.6	47.7	51.7	51.7
Fr.	48.5	42.1	40.2	42.8	43.0	43.6	42.2	43.4	43.0
FRG	44.2	48.2	43.8	43.3	47.9	47.7	44.2	44.2	48.0
Gr.	37.2	42.3	36.9	36.4	39.4	43.3	37.2	35.8	39.4
Ice.	44.2	38.7	41.0	46.3	48.9	39.8	40.2	45.9	50.4
Ire.	45.1	38.4	37.6	36.9	37.3	39.4	37.9	36.7	37.3
It.	41.2	38.6	36.6	39.8	41.8	45.0	39.6	40.5	43.1
Lux.	46.4	41.2	36.6	42.0	49.9	41.9	41.2	43.6	50.1
Neth.	40.2	35.5	36.4	38.9	46.0	37.6	37.1	38.2	46.0
Norw.	42.4	39.1	37.7	49.9	50.5	40.6	40.1	47.6	50.5
Port.	39.4	37.9	38.4	43.5	50.5	37.6	39.9	46.8	48.5
Sp.	38.0	39.5	35.2	33.8	38.6	39.9	38.8	35.7	39.4
Sw.	44.2	41.8	41.6	48.2	53.5	49.0	48.7	52.0	53.5
Switz.	45.7	46.2	48.1	48.6	53.0	49.8	49.8	49.7	53.4
Turk.	60.6	47.2	42.8	42.5	37.4	48.6	41.8	39.3	36.6
UK	44.9	45.4	44.7	47.0	49.5	46.6	45.6	47.7	49.6
Can.	37.7	35.5	37.4	49.5	51.4	36.8	39.9	48.4	51.7
USA	40.0	38.8	42.0	46.3	50.6	39.9	41.9	47.7	50.6
Jap.	43.0	46.4	50.3	48.9	51.5	48.4	49.7	48.4	51.7
Austral.	44.7	40.1	41.1	45.9	49.2	40.0	43.4	45.7	49.9
NZ	38.6	37.1	38.8	42.0	47.1	36.9	38.7	41.4	47.5

Sources: (1)–(3): Mitchell (1981; 1982; 1983); Nordic Council (1984); (4): ILO, *Yearbook of Labour Statistics* (1981–5); Nordic Council (1984); (6)–(8): OECD. *Economic Outlook: Historical statistics* (1983; 1987); (5): ILO, *Yearbook of Labour Statistics* (1993); (9): OECD, *Labour Force Statistics 1971–1991* (1993).

TABLE 3.2. Female labour force as a percentage of total labour force

	1960	1970	1980	1990
Aus.	41.3	39.4	40.6	41.0
Belg.	30.2	32.0	37.7	41.6
Den.	30.9	38.6	44.1	46.1
Fin.	43.9	43.7	46.1	47.1
Fr.	32.5	35.0	39.7	42.9
FRG	37.3	35.9	37.8	40.7
Gr.	32.6	28.3	30.0	37.1
Ice.	32.6	32.5	30.0	41.5
Ire.	25.6	25.8	28.7	31.6
It.	30.7	28.8	33.3	36.8
Lux.	26.5	26.2	30.9	34.5
Neth.	21.5	23.5	30.3	39.2
Norw.	28.2	30.1	41.3	44.9
Port.	17.8	25.4	39.7	42.9
Sp.	21.7	23.4	28.5	34.8
Sw.	33.6	39.5	45.2	48.0
Switz.	34.2	34.0	36.1	38.1
Turk.	40.8	37.4	33.2	31.3
UK	32.7	35.5	39.2	42.8
Can.	26.6	33.3	39.9	44.5
USA	32.3	36.7	42.0	44.9
Jap.	40.7	39.3	38.7	40.6
Austral.	25.1	32.2	36.7	41.3
NZ	24.5	28.6	33.7	43.3

Sources: OECD *Economic Outlook: Historical statistics* (1983; 1987); 1990: OECD, *Labour Force Statistics, 1971–1991* (1993).

TABLE 3.3. Employment in agriculture as a percentage of economically active population in civilian employment

	ILO figures					OECD figures			
	1950 (1)	1960 (2)	1970 (3)	1980 (4)	1990 (5)	1960 (6)	1970 (7)	1980 (8)	1990 (9)
Aus.	32.5	22.8	13.8	8.5	7.7	22.6	14.5	9.0	7.9
Belg.	12.0	7.4	5.0	2.9	2.4	8.7	4.8	3.0	2.7
Den.	25.1	17.5	11.0	6.9	5.4	18.2	11.5	7.1	5.6
Fin.	45.9	35.5	20.3	12.3	8.3	35.2	22.6	13.5	8.4
Fr.	31.6	19.9	15.7	8.8	5.4	23.2	13.5	8.7	6.0
FRG	18.7	13.4	7.5	5.9	3.2	14.0	8.6	5.6	3.5
Gr.	48.2	55.3	40.5	28.1	22.3	57.1	40.8	30.3	23.4
Ice.	37.0	22.9	17.9	13.1	10.5	22.9	18.5	12.0	10.3
Ire.	39.6	35.2	25.4	15.6	12.8	37.3	27.1	18.3	15.0
It.	42.2	29.0	16.4	11.1	7.9	32.6	20.2	14.3	8.8
Lux.	26.0	14.9	7.5	5.0	3.7	16.6	9.3	5.4	3.3
Neth.	19.3	11.0	6.1	5.4	4.2	9.8	6.2	4.9	4.6
Norw.	25.9	19.5	11.6	8.1	6.1	21.6	13.9	8.5	6.5
Port.	48.5	43.0	30.3	19.2	17.1	43.9	30.0	27.3	17.8
Sp.	49.5	34.8	24.9	15.7	11.2	38.7	27.1	18.9	11.8
Sw.	19.1	13.8	6.8	5.6	3.3	15.7	8.1	5.6	3.3
Switz.	16.5	11.2	7.7	6.2	5.5	14.6	8.6	6.9	5.6
Turk.	85.3	75.0	67.7	57.6	43.6	75.9	67.6	60.7	46.1
UK	5.1	3.6	2.9	2.7	2.0	4.7	3.2	2.6	2.1
Can.	19.1	12.1	7.9	5.2	3.3	13.2	7.6	5.4	4.2
USA	11.9	6.5	4.3	3.0	2.8	8.5	4.5	3.6	2.8
Jap.	48.3	32.6	19.4	10.9	6.9	30.2	17.4	10.4	7.2
Austral.	13.4	10.9	7.4	6.0	5.3	11.0	8.0	6.5	5.6
NZ	17.4	14.4	12.3	10.8	8.9	14.6	12.1	10.9	10.6

Note: Agriculture includes employment in agriculture, forestry, and fishing. Tables 3.3–3.5 do not always add up to 100% due to rounding.

Sources: See Table 3.1.

TABLE 3.4. Employment in industry as a percentage of economically active population in civilian employment

	ILO figures					OECD figures			
	1950 (1)	1960 (2)	1970 (3)	1980 (4)	1990 (5)	1960 (6)	1970 (7)	1980 (8)	1990 (9)
Aus.	36.6	40.9	41.8	41.0	36.9	41.7	42.3	39.7	36.8
Belg.	48.8	47.0	43.1	34.2	25.2	45.0	42.0	34.1	28.3
Den.	33.3	36.5	37.2	31.2	27.6	36.9	37.8	30.4	27.5
Fin.	27.7	31.5	34.3	33.5	30.8	32.6	34.6	34.6	31.0
Fr.	32.9	38.4	40.4	35.9	26.5	38.4	39.2	35.9	29.9
FRG	44.9	47.2	47.9	44.6	36.6	47.0	48.5	44.1	39.8
Gr.	19.4	19.7	32.4	30.0	26.8	17.4	25.0	30.2	27.7
Ice.	30.6	33.8	38.1	37.9	29.5	34.7	36.9	38.2	29.8
Ire.	24.3	25.4	31.3	35.0	24.4	23.7	29.9	32.5	28.6
It.	32.1	40.4	42.2	39.5	28.5	33.9	39.5	37.9	32.7
Lux.	39.5	43.1	34.4	32.6	28.5	44.9	43.9	38.1	30.5
Neth.	36.9	43.4	36.7	30.6	24.0	40.5	38.9	31.4	26.3
Norw.	36.4	36.5	37.3	29.3	24.1	35.6	37.3	29.7	24.8
Port.	24.9	28.7	30.9	38.9	32.9	31.3	32.9	36.6	34.8
Sp.	25.5	35.1	37.4	35.9	31.3	30.3	35.5	36.1	33.4
Sw.	38.2	45.1	40.8	32.1	28.7	40.3	38.4	32.2	29.1
Switz.	46.7	50.5	48.2	39.0	34.0	46.5	45.9	39.7	35.0
Turk.	7.4	9.8	12.2	16.9	19.1	10.7	14.5	16.2	20.6
UK	49.1	47.4	37.9	38.1	27.1	47.7	44.7	37.7	28.8
Can.	35.5	33.2	30.8	28.1	25.2	32.7	30.9	28.5	24.6
USA	34.6	35.1	33.8	30.8	26.4	35.3	34.4	30.5	26.2
Jap.	22.6	29.7	34.4	34.2	32.7	28.5	35.7	35.3	34.1
Austral.	40.6	39.2	34.3	27.5	25.2	38.9	37.0	31.0	25.4
NZ	32.0	36.7	34.4	31.3	20.8	38.7	39.4	33.7	24.6

Note: Industry includes employment in mining and quarrying, manufacturing, electricity, gas and water, and construction. Tables 3.3–3.5 do not always add up to 100% due to rounding.

Sources: See Table 3.1.

TABLE 3.5. Employment in services as a percentage of economically active
population in civilian employment

	ILO figures					OECD figures			
	1950 (1)	1960 (2)	1970 (3)	1980 (4)	1990 (5)	1960 (6)	1970 (7)	1980 (8)	1990 (9)
Aus.	30.8	36.2	44.4	50.5	55.4	35.7	43.2	51.4	55.3
Belg.	39.2	45.5	51.9	62.9	72.4	46.4	53.2	62.9	69.0
Den.	41.6	45.9	51.7	61.9	67.0	44.8	50.7	62.4	66.9
Fin.	26.3	33.1	45.5	54.2	60.9	32.2	42.8	51.8	60.6
Fr.	35.4	41.6	43.9	55.3	68.1	38.5	47.2	55.4	64.1
FRG	36.4	39.3	44.6	49.5	60.2	39.1	42.9	50.3	56.7
Gr.	32.5	25.0	33.0	41.9	50.9	25.5	34.2	39.5	48.3
Ice.	32.4	43.3	44.0	49.0	60.0	42.4	44.6	49.8	59.8
Ire.	36.1	39.4	43.2	49.4	62.8	39.0	43.1	49.2	56.4
It.	25.7	30.6	36.6	49.4	63.6	33.5	40.3	47.8	58.5
Lux.	34.5	42.0	58.1	62.4	67.8	38.4	46.8	56.5	66.2
Neth.	43.8	48.0	57.3	64.0	71.8	49.7	54.9	63.6	69.1
Norw.	37.7	44.0	51.1	62.6	69.8	42.9	48.8	61.8	68.8
Port.	26.7	28.3	38.8	41.9	50.0	24.8	37.1	36.1	47.3
Sp.	25.0	30.1	37.7	48.4	57.5	31.0	37.4	45.1	54.8
Sw.	42.7	41.1	52.4	62.3	68.0	44.0	53.5	62.2	67.5
Switz.	37.0	38.3	43.9	54.8	60.5	38.9	45.5	53.4	59.5
Turk.	7.4	15.3	20.1	25.5	37.3	10.7	14.5	23.1	33.3
UK	45.9	48.9	59.2	59.2	70.9	47.6	52.0	59.7	69.0
Can.	45.4	54.7	61.3	66.7	71.5	54.1	61.4	66.0	71.2
USA	53.5	58.4	61.9	66.2	70.8	56.2	61.1	65.9	70.9
Jap.	29.1	37.7	46.2	54.9	60.4	41.3	46.9	54.2	58.7
Austral.	46.0	49.9	58.4	66.5	69.5	50.1	55.0	62.4	69.0
NZ	50.6	48.9	53.3	57.9	70.3	46.8	48.6	55.4	64.8

Note: Services include employment in wholesale and retail trade, restaurants and
hotels, transport, storage and communication, financing, insurance, real estate and
business services, community and social and personal services, and related services.
Tables 3.3–3.5 do not always add up to 100% due to rounding.

Sources: See Table 3.1.

TABLE 3.6. Armed forces as a percentage of total labour force

	1965	1970	1975	1980	1985	1990
Aus.	—	—	—	—	—	—
Belg.	2.8	2.5	2.2	2.2	2.1	2.1
Den.	2.1	2.0	1.3	1.1	1.1	1.2
Fin.	1.7	1.9	1.7	1.7	1.5	1.2
Fr.	2.9	2.7	2.6	2.4	2.3	2.3
FRG	1.7	1.9	2.0	2.0	1.9	1.6
Gr.	—	—	—	—	—	—
Ice.	—	—	—	—	—	—
Ire.	0.7	0.7	1.0	1.2	1.3	0.8
It.	2.5	2.7	2.4	2.5	2.6	2.2
Lux.	0.8	0.7	0.6	0.6	0.6	0.5
Neth.	2.6	2.3	2.1	2.0	1.8	1.3
Norw.	3.2	3.1	—	—	—	1.8
Port.	4.5	4.4	3.2	2.0	1.6	1.3
Sp.	3.3	3.3	3.3	3.4	2.8	2.0
Sw.	—	—	—	—	—	—
Switz.	—	—	—	—	—	—
Turk.	3.4	3.4	3.0	2.8	2.7	2.4
UK	1.7	1.5	1.3	1.2	1.2	1.1
Can.	1.5	1.1	0.8	0.6	0.6	0.6
USA	2.5	2.5	1.8	1.5	1.5	1.3
Jap.	—	—	—	—	—	—
Austral.	1.2	1.5	1.1	1.1	1.0	0.8
NZ	1.1	1.1	0.9	0.8	0.9	—

Note: The armed forces cover personnel from the metropolitan territory drawn from the total available labour force who were serving in the armed forces whether stationed in the metropolitan territory or elsewhere.

Source: 1965–1985: OECD (1988); 1990: OECD, *Labour Force Statistics, 1971–1991* (1993).

TABLE 3.7.   Public sector employment as a percentage of total civilian
employment

	Total public sector		General government		Public enterprises	
	1970–4	1975–9	1970–4	1975–9	1970–4	1975–9
Aus.	27.9	30.2	15.0	17.8	12.9	12.4
Belg.	19.5	21.6	14.3	16.3	5.1	5.2
Den.	—	27.1	19.1	23.8	—	3.3
Fin.	—	—	—	—	—	—
Fr.	18.5	19.6	14.0	15.2	4.3	4.4
FRG	20.0	22.2	12.1	14.3	7.8	7.9
Gr.	—	—	—	—	—	—
Ice.	—	—	—	—	—	—
Ire.	18.0	19.7	11.9	14.0	6.3	5.7
It.	17.6	20.3	12.0	13.9	5.6	6.4
Lux.	13.5	14.3	9.6	10.6	3.9	3.7
Neth.	—	—	—	—	—	—
Norw.	21.7	23.9	17.6	20.0	4.1	4.2
Port.	—	—	—	—	—	—
Sp.	—	—	—	—	—	—
Sw.	30.0	34.5	22.8	27.7	7.1	8.0
Switz.	—	—	—	—	—	—
Turk.	—	—	—	—	—	—
UK	27.1	29.6	19.1	21.4	7.9	8.2
Can.	24.3	24.4	19.9	19.9	4.4	4.5
USA	19.3	18.8	17.7	17.2	1.6	1.6
Jap.	—	—	—	—	—	—
Austral.	23.2	25.5	—	—	—	—
NZ	23.1	24.3	17.8	18.7	5.3	5.6

Note: Data are based on production sectors rather than institutional sectors; data for general government refer to producers of government services. Total public sector employment comprises general government employment and employment in public enterprises.

Sources: Pathirane and Blades (1982: 272–3).

TABLE 3.8. Producers of government services as a percentage of total civilian employment

	1970	1975	1980	1985	1990
Aus.	—	—	—	—	—
Belg.	13.9	15.2	18.0	19.9	19.5
Den.	16.8	23.6	28.1	29.8	30.4
Fin.	11.8	14.7	18.2	20.4	22.3
Fr.	16.5	17.5	18.1	19.6 (1984)	25.1
FRG	11.2	13.9	14.9	16.1	15.1
Gr.	—	—	—	—	—
Ice.	—	13.9	15.7	16.4 (1984)	18.4
Ire.	—	—	—	—	—
It.	11.8	14.1	15.1	15.8	15.5
Lux.	9.4	9.7	10.8	—	10.9
Neth.	12.1	13.5	14.9	16.1	13.5
Norw.	16.4	19.3	21.7	23.8	27.7
Port.	7.3	8.1	8.8	—	13.6
Sp.	—	—	9.6	12.4	15.0
Sw.	20.5	25.5	30.7	33.2	31.7
Switz.	—	—	—	—	—
Turk.	—	—	—	—	—
UK	18.0	20.9	21.3	21.8	19.9
Can.	—	—	—	—	6.6
USA	18.1	18.0	16.7	15.4	14.6
Jap.	5.8	6.5	6.6	6.4	6.0
Austral.	—	8.7	4.5	4.8	4.7
NZ	—	—	—	—	—

Note: Producers of government services mean all departments, establishments, and other bodies of central, state, and local governments which engage in different activities, i.e. 'producers of government services' is somewhat narrower than the field covered by general government.

Sources: 1970–1980: OECD, *National Accounts* (1983); 1985; OECD, *National Accounts* (1987); 1990: OECD, *National Accounts* (1993).

Comparative Tables

TABLE 3.9. Government employment as a percentage of total civilian employment

	1960	1970	1975	1980	1985	1990
Aus.	10.5	13.7	16.4	18.2	20.5	20.6
Belg.	12.2	13.9	15.7	18.6	19.9	19.5
Den.	—	16.8	23.6	28.3	29.8	30.5
Fin.	7.7	11.8	14.6	17.8	20.4	22.4
Fr.	13.1	13.4	14.3	15.6	17.8	22.6
FRG	8.0	11.2	13.9	14.9	16.0	15.1
Gr.	—	—	—	—	—	—
Ice.	—	—	13.9	15.7	16.5	17.6
Ire.	—	11.2	13.3	14.4	16.1	13.7
It.	8.7	11.8	14.0	15.0	15.8	15.5
Lux.	—	9.4	9.7	10.8	11.5	10.9
Neth.	11.7	12.1	13.5	14.9	16.1	14.7
Norw.	—	16.4	19.3	21.9	23.8	27.7
Port.	3.9	6.8	8.1	8.8	12.2	13.2
Sp.	—	7.1	10.0	11.9	14.3	14.1
Sw.	12.8	20.6	25.5	30.7	33.1	31.7
Switz.	6.4	7.9	9.5	10.7	11.2	11.0
Turk.	—	—	—	—	—	—
UK	14.8	18.0	20.7	21.1	21.8	19.2
Can.	—	19.5	20.3	18.8	19.9	19.7
USA	15.7	18.1	18.0	16.7	15.8	14.4
Jap.	—	5.8	6.5	6.6	6.4	6.0
Austral.	22.3	22.9	25.5	25.4	26.4	22.8
NZ	17.9	18.2	18.9	19.0	18.1	—

Note: Government employment is a close approximation to the institutional sector 'general government'.

Sources: 1960–80: OECD, *Economic Outlook: Historical Statistics* (1983); 1985: OECD, *Economic Outlook: Historical Statistics* (1988); 1990: OECD, *Economic Outlook: Historical Statistics* (1992).

TABLE 3.10. Unemployment as a percentage of total labour force

	1960	1970	1975	1980	1985	1990
Aus.	2.4	1.4	1.7	1.6	4.1	3.2
Belg.	3.3	1.8	4.4	7.7	12.0	8.7
Den.[a]	1.9	0.7	4.9	6.5	7.3	8.3
Fin.	1.4	1.9	2.2	4.6	4.8	3.4
Fr.	1.2	2.4	4.1	6.3	10.2	9.0
FRG	1.0	0.6	4.0	3.3	8.3	6.2
Gr.[a]	6.1	4.2	2.3	2.8	7.8	7.2
Ice.[a]	—	1.2	1.1	1.0	0.9	1.6
Ire.[a]	5.6	5.8	7.3	7.3	17.4	13.7
It.	5.5	5.3	5.8	7.5	9.9	10.8
Lux.[a]	—	0.7	0.6	0.6	1.9	1.0
Neth.	0.7	1.0	5.2	6.0	12.8	7.5
Norw.	1.2	1.6	2.3	1.7	2.5	5.2
Port.[a]	1.9	2.5	4.4	7.7	9.0	4.6
Sp.	2.3	2.5	4.3	12.3	21.5	15.9
Sw.	1.7	1.5	1.6	2.0	2.8	1.5
Switz.	—	0.0	0.3	0.2	0.9	0.5
Turk.[a]	9.2	12.0	12.9	14.4	15.9	6.9
UK	1.3	2.2	3.2	5.6	11.5	5.5
Can.	6.4	5.6	6.9	7.4	10.4	8.1
USA	5.3	4.8	8.3	7.0	7.1	5.4
Jap.	1.7	1.1	1.9	2.0	2.6	2.1
Austral.	1.4	1.6	4.8	6.0	8.2	6.9
NZ[a]	0.1	0.2	0.2	2.2	4.1	7.8

[a] Denotes a different national definition of unemployment, whereas for the other countries OECD standards are adhered to.

Sources: 1960–70: OECD, *Economic Outlook: Historical Statistics* (1983); OECD (1985*b*); 1975–85: OECD, *Economic Outlook: Historical Statistics* (1987); 1990: OECD, *Economic Outlook: Historical Statistics* (1992).

Comparative Tables

TABLE 3.11. Unemployment as a percentage of total labour force: five-year averages

	1950–4	1955–9	1960–4	1965–9	1970–4	1975–9	1980–4	1985–89
Aus.	5.2	3.6	2.1	1.9	1.3	1.7	2.9	3.4
Belg.	4.9	3.2	2.2	2.2	2.1	6.2	11.1	11.0
Den.	4.4	4.4	1.8	1.7	1.9	6.6	9.5	6.6
Fin.	1.4	1.9	1.4	2.5	2.2	5.0	5.1	4.6
Fr.	1.3	1.1	1.2	1.6	2.1	4.9	8.0	10.1
FRG	6.7	3.1	0.7	0.9	1.1	3.8	6.2	7.5
Gr.	—	—	—	5.2	2.7	1.9	5.7	7.6
Ice.	—	—	—	1.5	1.1	1.0	1.2	1.0
Ire.	6.1	5.9	5.0	4.9	5.9	8.1	11.6	16.9
It.	7.4	6.9	3.1	3.6	3.2	6.8	8.6	11.3
Lux.	—	—	—	—	—	0.6	1.2	1.5
Neth.	2.4	1.5	0.9	1.4	2.1	5.3	9.9	9.7
Norw.	0.8	1.2	1.1	0.9	0.8	1.9	2.5	3.0
Port.	—	—	—	2.5	2.3	6.8	7.9	6.9
Sp.	1.2	0.8	1.2	1.6	2.5	5.9	15.6	19.6
Sw.	2.3	2.1	1.3	1.6	1.8	1.9	2.9	2.1
Switz.	—	—	—	—	—	0.4	0.6	0.7
Turk.	—	—	—	10.1	12.1	12.4	15.1	9.4
UK	1.2	1.2	1.5	1.7	2.5	4.6	9.5	9.6
Can.	3.2	5.0	5.9	4.2	5.9	7.5	9.8	8.8
USA	3.9	4.8	5.5	3.7	5.2	6.9	8.2	6.1
Jap.	2.0	2.2	1.4	1.2	1.3	2.0	2.4	2.6
Austral.	1.1	1.5	2.9	1.5	1.9	5.5	7.5	7.5
NZ	1.1	1.0	1.2	1.2	1.5	0.9	4.1	5.0

Sources: 1950–74: Madsen and Paldam (1978); 1975–84: OECD (1988); 1985–89: OECD, *Labour Force Statistics* (1993).

TABLE 3.12. Standardized unemployment rates as a percentage of total labour force, 1965–1990

	1965	1966	1967	1968	1969	1970	1971	1972	1973	1974	1975	1976	1977	1978	1979	1980	1981	1982	1983	1984	1985	1986	1987	1988	1989	1990
Aus.	1.9	1.8	1.9	2.0	2.0	1.4	1.3	1.2	1.1	1.4	1.7	1.8	1.6	2.1	2.1	1.9	2.5	3.5	4.1	3.8	3.6	—	—	—	—	—
Belg.	1.8	2.0	2.6	3.1	2.3	2.1	2.1	2.7	2.7	3.0	5.0	6.4	7.4	7.9	8.2	8.8	10.5	12.6	13.9	14.0	13.2	11.2	11.0	9.7	8.0	7.2
Fin.	1.4	1.5	2.9	3.8	2.8	1.9	2.2	2.5	2.3	1.7	2.2	3.8	5.8	7.2	5.9	4.6	5.1	5.8	6.1	6.1	6.2	5.3	5.0	4.5	3.4	3.4
Fr.	1.5	1.8	1.9	2.6	2.3	2.4	2.6	2.7	2.6	2.8	4.0	4.4	4.9	5.2	5.9	6.3	7.3	8.1	8.3	9.7	10.1	10.4	10.5	10.0	9.4	8.9
FRG	0.3	0.2	1.3	1.5	0.9	0.8	0.9	0.8	0.8	1.6	3.7	3.6	3.6	3.5	3.2	3.0	4.4	6.1	8.0	8.5	8.6	6.4	6.2	6.2	5.6	4.8
Ire	—	—	—	—	—	—	—	—	—	—	—	—	—	—	—	—	—	—	—	—	—	17.1	16.7	16.2	14.7	13.4
It.	5.3	5.7	5.3	5.6	5.6	5.3	5.3	6.3	6.2	5.3	5.8	6.6	7.0	7.1	7.6	7.5	8.3	9.0	9.8	10.2	10.5	10.5	10.9	11.0	10.9	10.3
Neth.	0.6	0.8	1.6	1.5	1.0	1.0	1.3	2.2	2.2	2.7	5.5	5.3	5.3	5.3	5.4	6.0	8.5	11.4	13.7	14.0	13.0	9.9	9.6	9.2	8.3	7.5
Norw.	1.8	1.6	1.5	2.1	2.0	1.6	1.5	1.7	1.5	1.5	1.8	1.8	1.5	1.8	2.0	1.7	2.0	2.6	3.3	3.0	2.5	2.0	2.1	3.2	4.9	5.2
Por	—	—	—	—	—	—	—	—	—	—	—	—	—	—	—	—	—	—	—	—	—	8.5	7.0	5.7	5.0	4.6
Sp.	2.5	2.1	2.5	3.0	2.6	2.4	3.1	3.1	2.5	2.6	3.7	4.7	5.2	6.9	8.5	11.2	14.0	15.9	17.4	20.1	21.5	20.8	20.1	19.1	16.9	15.9
Sw.	1.2	1.6	2.1	2.2	1.9	1.5	2.5	2.7	2.5	2.0	1.6	1.6	1.8	2.2	2.1	2.0	2.5	3.1	3.5	3.1	2.8	2.7	1.9	1.6	1.4	1.5
Switz.	—	—	—	—	—	—	—	—	—	—	0.4	0.7	0.4	0.3	0.3	0.2	0.2	0.4	0.9	1.1	1.0	—	—	—	—	—
UK	2.3	2.3	3.4	3.4	3.1	3.0	3.7	4.0	3.0	2.9	4.3	5.7	6.1	6.0	5.1	6.6	9.9	11.4	12.6	13.0	13.1	11.2	10.3	8.6	7.2	6.8
Can.	3.6	3.3	3.8	4.4	4.4	5.6	6.1	6.2	5.5	5.3	6.9	7.1	8.0	8.3	7.4	7.4	7.5	10.9	11.8	11.2	10.4	9.5	8.8	7.7	7.5	8.1
USA	4.4	3.6	3.7	3.4	3.4	4.8	5.8	5.5	4.8	5.5	8.3	7.6	6.9	6.0	5.8	7.0	7.5	9.5	9.5	7.4	7.1	6.9	6.1	5.4	5.2	5.4
Jap.	1.2	1.3	1.3	1.2	1.1	1.1	1.2	1.4	1.3	1.4	1.9	2.0	2.0	2.2	2.1	2.0	2.2	2.4	2.6	2.7	2.6	2.8	2.8	2.5	2.3	2.1
Austral.	1.5	1.7	1.9	1.8	1.8	1.6	1.9	2.6	2.3	2.6	4.8	4.7	5.6	6.2	6.2	6.0	5.7	7.1	9.9	8.9	8.2	8.0	8.0	7.2	6.1	6.9
NZ	—	—	—	—	—	—	—	—	—	—	—	—	—	—	—	—	—	—	—	—	—	4.0	4.1	5.6	7.1	7.7

Note: By standardized unemployment rates is meant that efforts have been made to make rates for different countries comparable.

Sources: 1965–9: OECD, *Economic Outlook* (1981); 1970–85: OECD, *Economic Outlook* (1986); 1986–90: OECD, *Economic Outlook* (1993).

TABLE 3.13. Industrial disputes: workers involved per 1,000 in civilian labour force

	1960–4	1965–9	1970–4	1975–9	1980–4	1985–9
Aus.	20	18	6	0	2	3
Belg.	6	8	20	22	7[a]	4
Den.	19	9	46	31	19	11
Fin.	19	19	173	156	162	93
Fr.	108	188	102	67	12	6
FRG	3	3	9	41	7	3
Gr.	25	68[b]	—	159	196	225
Ice.	108	185	114	274	108	47
Ire.	15	39	31	33	24	39
It.	141	185	255	605	418	170
Lux.	—	—	—	—	—	0
Neth.	6	2	7	4	6	2
Norw.	5	0	4	4	8	18
Port.	—	—	—	70[c]	68	43
Sp.	6[d]	10	27	241	137	175
Sw.	1	2	6	4	41	15
Switz.	0	0	0	0	0	0
Turk.	0[d]	1	1	2	1	1
UK	61	48	62	65	49	28
Can.	12	35	48	60	29	25
USA	19	30	31	12	7	3
Jap.	28	25	42	22	5	2
Austral.	102	134	230	224	121	89
NZ	27	30	80	119	109	70

[a] 1980.
[b] 1965–7.
[c] 1977 and 1979.
[d] 1963 and 1964.

Sources: 1960–74: Mitchell (1981; 1982; 1983); OECD (1985); 1975–84: ILO, *Yearbook of Labour Statistics* (1984; 1985); OECD (1988); 1985–89: ILO, *Yearbook of Labour Statistics* (1993).

TABLE 3.14. Industrial disputes: working days lost per 1,000 in civilian labour force

	1960–4	1965–9	1970–4	1975–9	1980–4	1985–9
Aus.	55	17	14	1	1	2
Belg.	79	72	269	191	53[a]	22
Den.	230	31	356	67	86	194
Fin.	150	84	587	362	375	273
Fr.	164	297	162	165	72	32
FRG	18	6	47	41	43	2
Gr.	61	127[b]	—	297	463	1841
Ice.	1394	1179	1022	1286	938	583
Ire.	242	517	405	621	310	183
It.	400	755	972	994	611	1307
Lux.	—	—	—	—	—	0
Neth.	27	5	45	23	18	7
Norw.	103	7	47	26	53	114
Port.	—	—	—	99[c]	124	60
Sp.	11[d]	23	85	947	379	370
Sw.	5	25	54	26	218	108
Switz.	5	0	1	2	1	0
Turk.	9[d]	20	37	130	154	78
UK	129	157	566	451	397	142
Can.	180	628	723	782	535	931
USA	263	471	499	216	132	74
Jap.	97	63	113	55	10	4
Austral.	154	211	570	474	366	22
NZ	64	102	186	303	286	389

[a] 1980.
[b] 1965–7.
[c] 1977 and 1979.
[d] 1963 and 1964.

Sources: 1960–74: Mitchell (1981; 1982; 1983); OECD (1985); 1975–84: ILO, *Yearbook of Labour Statistics* (1984; 1985); OECD (1985); 1985–89: ILO, *Yearbook of Labour Statistics* (1993).

TABLE 3.15. Industrial disputes: number of persons involved in strikes per 1,000 of the non-agricultural labour force

	1919–38	1946–52	1960–7	1968–73	1974–7	1978–82
Aus.	7	5	17	3	1	1
Belg.	31	21	8	17	21	15
Den.	5	9	8	14	31	29
Fin.	6	50	18	47/230[a]	219	97
Fr.	22	94	127	135	110	27
FRG	26	5	2	4	4	5
Gr.	—	—	—	—	—	—
Ice.	—	—	—	—	—	—
Ire.	12	25	27	44	43	36
It.	6	199	135	248	371	272
Lux.	—	—	—	—	—	—
Neth.	8	3	3	5	2	2
Norw.	21	3	1	1	5	4
Port.	—	—	—	—	—	—
Sp.	—	—	—	—	—	—
Sw.	19	9	1	2	5	11
Switz.	3	0.2	0.2	0.1	0.3	0.2
Turk.	—	—	—	—	—	—
UK	24	39	39	69	41	70
Can.	12	25	19	38	56	33
USA	19	28	23	33	26	14
Jap.	3	34	35	40	40	10
Austral.	43	149	108	216	251	210
NZ	16	49	26	69	102	106

[a] Denotes a break in the statistical series for Finland.

Source: Therborn (1984).

Section 4: Economy

TABLE 4.1 GDP per capita in US $ (constant prices; US $ 1985 at 1985 exchange rate)

	1960	1965	1970	1975	1980	1985	1990
Aus.	3 823	4 537	5 718	6 831	8 088	8 623	9 813
Belg.	3 770	4 655	5 781	6 752	7 798	8 099	9 322
Den.	5 754	7 161	8 283	8 894	9 939	11 350	12 180
Fin.	4 671	5 751	7 182	8 578	9 799	11 026	12 829
Fr.	4 492	5 567	6 948	7 877	9 005	9 462	10 672
FRG	5 248	6 267	7 401	8 083	9 531	10 148	11 441
Gr.	1 138	1 631	2 246	2 793	3 245	3 366	3 582
Ice.	4 872	6 302	6 636	8 471	11 224	11 914	13 102
Ire	2 244	2 892	3 541	4 179	4 878	5 314	6 793
It.	3 128	3 891	5 098	5 660	7 020	7 431	8 560
Lux.	5 330	6 034	6 957	7 604	8 389	9 419	11 415
Neth.	4 893	5 785	7 063	7 890	8 670	8 899	9 901
Norw.	5 749	6 941	8 008	9 726	12 075	14 009	14 847
Port.	811	1 084	1 486	1 776	2 134	2 145	2 636
Sp.	1 776	2 541	3 254	3 998	4 143	4 307	5 298
Sw.	6 435	8 010	9 418	10 505	11 062	12 051	13 036
Swiz.	8 996	10 473	12 207	12 437	13 562	14 201	15 664
Turk.	527	588	713	903	934	1 042	1 248
UK	4 926	5 559	6 146	6 716	7 346	8 071	9 303
Can.	6 499	7 816	9 035	10 928	12 508	13 795	14 970
USA	10 231	12 023	13 238	14 092	15 647	16 786	18 225
Jap.	2 856	4 253	6 939	8 012	9 574	11 124	13 595
Austral.	5 622	6 452	7 673	8 562	9 238	10 163	10 918
NZ	4 650	5 372	5 525	6 211	6 130	6 863	6 761

Source: OECD, *National Accounts*, vol. ii (1993).

TABLE 4.2. Real GDP per capita in international prices (constant prices; US $ 1985 at 1985 exchange rate)

	1950	1955	1960	1965	1970	1975	1980	1985	1988
Aus.	2 533	3 437	4 476	5 437	6 781	8 164	9 616	10 291	11 201
Belg.	4 151	4 743	5 207	6 379	7 859	9 064	10 499	10 458	11 495
Den.	4 512	4 666	5 900	7 422	8 556	9 095	10 322	11 980	12 089
Fin.	3 152	4 017	4 718	5 814	7 259	8 508	9 970	11 225	12 360
Fr.	3 692	4 397	5 344	6 676	8 536	9 745	11 148	11 376	12 190
FRG	3 128	4 698	6 038	7 246	8 664	9 267	10 993	11 646	12 604
Gr.	1 225	1 541	1 889	2 766	3 798	4 742	5 478	5 712	5 857
Ice.	4 368	5 093	5 352	6 658	6 991	8 749	11 833	11 900	13 204
Ire.	2 599	2 958	3 214	3 939	4 865	5 504	6 183	6 008	6 239
It.	2 548	3 377	4 375	5 315	6 937	7 775	9 986	10 584	11 741
Lux.	6 402	6 087	6 970	7 738	8 966	9 864	11 265	12 382	13 933
Neth.	4 002	4 849	5 587	6 791	8 505	9 532	10 632	10 937	11 468
Norw.	4 263	4 932	5 443	6 702	7 761	9 357	11 956	13 495	14 976
Port.	1 050	1 334	1 618	2 121	2 919	3 659	4 500	4 535	5 321
Sp.	1 823	2 497	2 701	4 161	5 208	6 413	6 514	6 433	7 406
Sw.	4 967	5 618	6 483	8 057	9 279	10 307	10 910	12 382	12 991
Switz.	6 668	8 019	9 313	10 965	12 688	12 911	14 143	14 390	16 155
Turk.	1 097	1 462	1 669	1 875	2 293	3 035	3 003	3 204	3 598
UK	4 973	5 752	6 370	7 174	8 006	8 727	9 680	10 679	11 982
Can.	6 913	7 462	7 758	9 253	10 668	11 997	13 768	15 013	16 272
USA	8 665	9 690	9 983	11 670	12 923	13 531	15 310	16 779	18 339
Jap.	1 275	1 865	2 701	4 125	6 688	7 833	9 615	10 781	12 209
Austral.	5 929	6 619	7 204	8 122	9 978	10 719	11 715	12 550	13 321
NZ	5 608	5 925	7 222	8 068	8 581	9 533	9 189	10 138	9 864

Source: Summers and Heston (1991).

TABLE 4.3. GDP per capita at current prices and current purchasing power parities

	1970	1975	1980	1985	1990
Aus.	3 004	5 023	8 664	12 156	16 596
Belg.	3 140	5 134	8 637	11 805	16 301
Den.	3 499	5 260	8 563	12 868	16 567
Fin.	2 873	4 803	7 993	11 835	16 522
Fr.	3 499	5 552	9 247	12 785	17 301
FRG	3 678	5 623	9 660	13 535	18 307
Gr.	1 442	2 509	4 247	5 797	7 403
Ice.	2 621	4 684	9 040	12 628	16 662
Ire.	1 741	2 877	4 892	7 014	10 755
It.	2 962	4 603	8 317	11 585	16 012
Lux.	3 772	5 770	9 274	13 703	19 923
Neth.	3 534	5 526	8 847	11 949	15 951
Norw.	2 686	4 566	8 259	12 610	16 033
Port.	1 465	2 450	4 289	5 674	8 364
Sp.	2 239	3 851	5 814	7 953	11 738
Sw.	3 788	5 915	9 073	13 008	16 881
Switz.	5 088	7 257	11 527	15 884	21 020
Turk.	597	1 058	1 595	2 340	3 363
UK	3 256	4 979	7 935	11 473	15 866
Can.	3 571	6 046	10 082	14 632	19 049
USA	4 933	7 351	11 891	16 786	21 866
Jap.	2 978	4 521	7 871	12 035	17 645
Austral.	3 468	5 417	8 597	12 326	15 887
NZ	3 443	5 418	7 790	11 477	13 564

Source: OECD, *National Accounts* vol. i (1993).

TABLE 4.4. Origin of GDP by sector: agriculture (percentage)

	1950	1960	1970	1980	1990
Aus.	18	11.0	6.9	4.4	3.1
Belg.	9	6.5	3.6	2.1	1.8
Den.	21	11.2	5.6	4.5	3.9
Fin.	26	16.7	11.4	8.2	5.4
Fr.	15	10.6	6.5	4.2	3.4
FRG	10	5.7	3.4	2.2	1.5
Gr.	31	22.9	18.3	17.4	13.5
Ice.	—	—	—	•10.1	10.1
Ire.	29	—	14.4	13.3	9.0
It.	22	12.2	8.1	6.4	3.1
Lux.	—	6.6	3.8	2.5	1.4
Neth.	14	—	5.8	3.5	4.2
Norw.	14	9.0	6.4	4.5	2.9
Port.	33	24.8	18.0	12.7	5.8
Sp.	—	—	10.5	7.1	5.3
Sw.	12	—	4.1	3.2	2.6
Switz.	—	—	—	—	—
Turk.	49	40.8	26.7	21.4	16.6
UK	6	3.4	2.5	1.9	1.3
Can.	13	5.7	3.7	3.9	2.4
USA	7	4.0	2.7	2.8	2.0
Jap.	26	12.6	6.1	3.8	2.5
Austral.	24	12.0	6.1	6.8	3.3
NZ	—	—	12.6	11.3	8.6

Note: Country totals in Tables 4.4–4.6 do not always add up to 100% because of rounding.

Sources: 1950: Mitchell (1981; 1982; 1983); 1960–80: World Bank (1984): Series 1; 1985: World Bank (1988); 1990: OECD, *OECD in Figures* (1992, 1993).

Comparative Tables

TABLE 4.5. Origin of GDP by sector: industry (percentage)

	1950	1960	1970	1980	1990
Aus.	48	46.6	45.4	39.9	36.1
Belg.	44	40.9	42.3	36.7	30.1
Den.	36	31.2	29.6	23.0	24.4
Fin.	40	34.5	35.5	35.7	29.9
Fr.	48	39.1	38.8	35.8	28.6
FRG	49	53.3	53.1	47.9	38.7
Gr.	22	25.8	31.4	31.3	24.1
Ice.	—	—	—	33.8	23.4
Ire.	25	—	31.4	34.2	33.4
It.	40	41.3	42.9	42.7	33.0
Lux.	—	51.4	54.1	39.2	33.7
Neth.	40	—	37.4	32.6	31.5
Norw.	37	32.5	33.8	40.4	36.3
Port.	35	36.4	41.6	45.9	37.8
Sp.	—	—	37.1	37.9	35.0
Sw.	44	—	35.9	31.5	29.5
Switz.	—	—	—	—	—
Turk.	15	20.5	24.5	28.6	35.4
UK	48	42.8	38.1	34.6	30.0
Can.	38	34.4	31.7	33.7	29.1
USA	39	38.3	34.9	34.1	29.2
Jap.	32	44.6	46.6	42.9	41.8
Austral.	35	39.9	40.5	36.4	31.4
NZ	—	—	31.5	31.3	26.7

Note: Country totals in Tables 4.4–4.6 do not always add up to 100% because of rounding.

Sources: See Table 4.4.

TABLE 4.6   Origin of GDP by sector: services (percentage)

	1950	1960	1970	1980	1985	1990
Aus.	34	42.4	47.7	55.7	58.4	60.8
Belg.	47	52.6	54.1	61.2	64.5	68.1
Den.	43	57.6	64.8	72.5	71.6	71.7
Fin.	34	48.8	53.1	56.1	60.4	64.7
Fr.	37	50.3	54.7	60.0	62.5	68.0
FRG	41	41.0	43.5	49.9	60.9	59.8
Gr.	47	51.3	50.3	51.3	58.5	62.5
Ice.	—	—	—	56.1	60.4	66.5
Ire.	46	—	54.2	52.5	—	57.6
It.	38	46.5	49.0	50.9	62.7	63.8
Lux.	—	42.0	42.1	58.3	57.9	64.9
Neth.	46	—	56.8	63.9	62.2	64.2
Norw.	49	58.5	59.8	55.1	55.8	60.8
Port.	32	38.8	40.4	41.4	51.6	56.4
Sp.	—	—	52.4	55.0	56.5	59.7
Sw.	44	—	60.0	65.3	66.5	67.9
Switz.	—	—	—	—	—	—
Turk.	36	38.7	48.8	50.0	42.6	48.0
UK	46	53.8	59.4	63.5	61.4	68.7
Can.	49	59.9	64.6	62.4	65.5	68.5
USA	54	57.7	62.4	63.1	66.8	68.8
Jap.	42	42.8	47.3	53.3	56.0	55.7
Austral.	41	48.1	53.4	56.8	62.6	65.3
NZ	—	—	55.9	57.4	55.9	64.7

Note: Country totals in Tables 4.4–4.6 do not always add up to 100% because of rounding.

Sources: See Table 4.4.

TABLE 4.7. Inflation: average growth rates 1950—1980

	Consumer price index			Implicit GDP deflator		
	1950–60	1960–70	1970–80	1950–60	1960–70	1970–81
Aus.	5.3	3.5	6.5	5.8	3.7	6.1
Belg.	1.9	3.2	7.8	—	3.6	7.3
Den.	3.4	6.0	10.3	3.4	6.4	10.0
Fin.	5.6	3.5	12.0	6.2	6.0	12.0
Fr.	5.6	3.8	10.1	6.6	4.3	9.9
FRG	1.9	2.6	5.0	3.0	3.2	5.0
Gr.	5.8	2.2	15.4	6.2	3.2	14.8
Ice.	3.7	11.7	36.2	11.2	12.2	36.8
Ire.	3.8	4.6	14.5	3.8	5.2	14.2
It.	3.0	4.0	14.9	2.2	4.4	15.7
Lux.	1.6	2.7	7.0	—	3.7	6.8
Neth.	3.0	4.4	7.4	3.5	5.4	7.6
Norw.	4.4	4.2	8.8	4.3	4.4	8.8
Port.	1.0	9.5	19.7	1.9	3.0	17.0
Sp.	5.2	6.8	15.9	—	6.8	16.0
Sw.	3.2	4.1	9.5	4.9	4.3	10.0
Switz.	1.4	3.5	4.8	2.1	4.4	4.8
Turk.	9.5	6.1	32.9	10.1	5.6	32.7
UK	4.0	3.8	14.3	2.5	4.1	14.4
Can.	2.2	2.8	8.7	2.7	3.1	9.3
USA	2.1	2.6	8.1	2.5	2.9	7.2
Jap.	4.1	5.6	9.3	—	5.1	7.4
Austral.	6.0	2.5	11.1	3.9	3.1	11.5
NZ	4.3	3.7	13.0	4.2	3.6	12.9

Note: The consumer price index measures changes in the cost of living; the implicit GDP deflator provides a comprehensive measure of the aggregate price movements of goods and services making up the GDP.

Source: World Bank (1984): Series 1.

TABLE 4.8. Inflation: average growth rates 1960–1992

	GDP implicit price index: year to year changes				
	1960–70	1970–80	1980–90	1960–90	1985–92
Aus.	3.5	6.1	3.8	4.4	2.7
Belg.	2.8	7.1	4.7	4.9	2.6
Den.	5.5	9.5	6.5	7.1	3.6
Fin.	4.8	10.5	7.2	7.5	4.7
Fr.	4.0	9.3	7.0	6.6	3.4
FRG	2.6	5.0	2.9	3.4	2.1
Gr.	2.1	13.5	19.6	11.5	17.7
Ice.	11.1	32.3	37.0	26.2	18.0
Ire.	4.4	13.3	8.8	8.5	3.5
It.	3.8	13.3	10.8	9.1	6.1
Lux.	2.4	6.5	4.6	4.4	2.4
Neth.	4.1	7.0	2.8	4.6	1.7
Norw.	4.2	8.6	7.7	6.7	5.3
Port.	3.8	17.7	17.3	13.0	12.1
Sp.	5.7	14.5	9.9	10.0	6.6
Sw.	4.1	9.0	8.2	6.9	6.3
Switz.	3.2	4.9	3.5	3.8	3.2
Turk.	6.0	31.8	52.2	28.1	56.7
UK	3.8	13.1	7.6	7.9	5.7
Can.	2.5	7.6	6.4	5.4	4.2
USA	2.7	7.7	5.5	5.0	3.8
Jap.	5.6	8.9	2.6	5.6	1.7
Austral.	2.6	9.8	8.3	6.9	6.3
NZ	3.6	12.0	11.4	8.8	8.3

Note: The implicit GDP price index provides a comprehensive measure of the aggregate price movements of goods and services making up the GDP.

Sources: OECD, *Economic Outlook: Historical Statistics* (1987); OECD, *Economic Outlook*, Nos. 24, 32, 54 (1978, 1982, 1993).

Comparative Tables

TABLE 4.9   External dependency: exports as a percentage of GDP

	1950	1955	1960	1965	1970	1975	1980	1985	1990
Aus.	15.2	21.1	24.0	25.8	32.4	33.7	38.7	40.3	40.3
Belg.	27.8	31.9	32.8	36.3	43.9	46.1	59.9	73.9	73.9
Den.	27.1	32.9	32.8	29.8	29.6	30.1	32.7	36.9	35.3
Fin.	20.0	21.7	23.5	21.3	26.2	24.3	34.2	29.8	22.6
Fr.	15.6	15.0	15.0	13.7	16.3	19.5	22.3	25.1	22.6
FRG	11.5	20.0	20.5	19.5	21.2	25.0	27.2	32.5	32.2
Gr.	5.3	11.5	9.3	9.3	10.0	16.3	19.7	21.2	21.6
Ice.	35.1	30.4	44.5	38.6	47.7	36.3	37.1	45.1	35.9
Ire.	28.6	28.2	31.5	31.8	37.0	43.4	53.2	66.7	61.3
It.	11.7	11.0	14.7	16.9	17.8	22.8	25.1	23.7	20.9
Lux.	94.4	80.7	88.9	79.8	89.4	91.0	82.9	84.9	96.9
Neth.	41.2	47.9	50.2	45.0	47.2	52.3	52.7	64.2	54.4
Norw.	46.7	40.7	41.1	40.0	41.8	41.8	47.6	47.2	44.4
Port.	22.2	19.6	16.9	25.9	23.5	19.7	28.1	37.3	36.4
Sp.	—	—	11.2	10.6	13.5	13.3	15.5	25.9	17.1
Sw.	25.7	26.9	25.0	23.2	24.3	28.2	30.0	35.2	30.2
Switz.	25.6	28.2	30.0	30.6	32.8	31.4	36.7	39.1	36.6
Turk.	—	—	6.2	7.3	5.9	—	—	—	22.9
UK	23.2	21.9	20.2	18.5	23.6	26.6	28.3	29.4	24.5
Can.	22.2	20.3	18.5	20.5	23.4	23.3	29.4	28.8	25.6
USA	4.3	4.4	4.8	4.9	5.7	8.5	10.2	7.1	10.0
Jap.	11.8	10.7	11.1	10.8	10.8	12.8	13.9	14.7	10.8
Austral.	—	—	14.9	17.8	14.9	15.1	16.9	16.0	17.2
NZ	—	—	—	—	26.7	23.4	29.0	31.2	27.4

Note: Figures in the 1985 column refer to 1984 for Ireland and Spain and to 1982 for Luxembourg.

Sources: 1950–65: OECD, *National Accounts 1950–1968* (1968); OECD, *National Accounts 1960–1977* (1979); 1970–80: OECD, *National Accounts 1964–1981* (1981); 1985: OECD, *National Accounts 1973–1985* (1987); 1990: OECD, *National Accounts* (1993).

TABLE 4.10. External dependency: imports as a percentage of GDP

	1950	1955	1960	1965	1970	1975	1980	1985	1990
Aus.	19.5	22.5	25.4	26.8	31.4	33.0	40.6	40.1	39.0
Belg.	28.4	31.1	33.9	36.2	33.2	37.1	50.8	72.2	71.0
Den.	30.5	31.9	33.8	31.1	32.4	31.0	33.8	36.7	30.0
Fin.	18.8	20.1	24.2	23.2	27.4	30.5	34.9	28.7	24.1
Fr.	14.4	13.0	13.2	12.9	15.8	18.8	24.1	25.0	22.7
FRG	12.8	17.5	18.1	19.4	19.1	22.4	27.7	29.0	26.3
Gr.	21.1	17.8	23.9	22.0	18.4	26.9	26.4	32.8	32.6
Ice.	40.3	33.0	47.9	36.6	45.1	44.7	36.4	44.4	33.9
Ire.	43.1	40.0	36.7	40.8	45.0	48.7	66.7	64.2	53.3
It.	13.2	12.1	14.9	14.2	17.2	22.7	28.0	24.2	20.8
Lux.	74.2	74.2	76.0	81.2	77.0	88.1	86.1	88.4	97.0
Neth.	48.4	47.0	48.1	45.6	49.0	48.8	53.2	59.3	49.7
Norw.	44.9	43.6	42.8	40.2	43.1	48.5	41.4	39.3	36.8
Port.	24.7	24.0	23.2	30.9	30.4	32.2	43.4	41.4	45.4
Sp.	—	—	8.2	14.0	14.4	17.2	18.1	23.4	20.5
Sw.	25.1	27.8	25.7	24.4	24.9	28.4	31.9	32.8	29.9
Switz.	25.9	26.8	29.5	30.7	34.5	28.6	40.3	38.6	36.1
Turk.	—	—	8.5	9.6	8.6	—	—	—	23.4
UK	23.8	23.4	21.8	19.4	22.5	28.2	25.9	28.2	27.0
Can.	21.7	21.3	20.0	20.9	20.6	24.8	27.5	26.0	25.9
USA	4.1	4.5	4.4	4.5	5.5	7.8	11.0	10.1	11.5
Jap.	11.4	10.1	10.6	9.4	9.5	12.8	14.9	11.2	10.1
Austral.	—	—	17.8	17.7	15.1	14.9	19.0	19.0	17.3
NZ	—	—	—	—	25.9	30.4	30.2	34.3	28.1

Note: Figures in the 1985 column refer to 1984 for Ireland and Spain and to 1982 for Luxembourg.

Sources: See Table 4.9.

TABLE 4.11. External dependency: imports and exports as a percentage of GDP

	1950	1955	1960	1965	1970	1975	1980	1985	1990
Aus.	34.7	43.6	49.4	52.6	63.9	66.7	79.3	80.3	79.3
Belg.	56.1	63.0	66.7	72.5	77.0	83.2	110.7	146.1	145.0
Den.	57.6	64.9	66.5	60.9	62.0	61.1	66.5	73.6	65.3
Fin.	38.8	41.8	47.7	44.5	53.6	54.7	69.1	58.4	46.7
Fr.	30.0	27.9	28.2	26.6	32.2	38.4	46.4	50.1	45.3
FRG	24.3	37.4	38.6	39.0	40.3	47.4	54.8	61.5	58.4
Gr.	26.4	29.3	33.2	31.3	28.4	43.2	46.1	54.0	54.2
Ice.	75.4	63.4	92.4	75.2	92.7	81.0	73.5	89.5	69.8
Ire.	71.7	68.2	68.2	72.6	81.9	92.1	119.9	130.9	114.6
It.	24.8	23.0	29.6	31.1	35.0	45.5	53.0	47.9	41.7
Lux.	168.6	154.9	164.8	161.1	166.4	179.1	168.9	173.3	193.8
Neth.	89.6	94.9	98.3	90.6	96.2	101.0	105.9	123.4	104.1
Norw.	91.6	84.3	83.9	80.2	84.9	90.3	89.0	86.5	81.1
Port.	46.9	43.6	40.1	56.7	53.9	51.9	71.5	78.7	81.8
Sp.	—	—	19.3	24.6	27.9	0.5	33.6	49.3	37.5
Sw.	50.8	54.7	50.6	47.6	49.2	6.7	61.9	68.0	60.1
Switz.	51.4	55.0	59.5	61.3	67.2	60.0	77.0	77.8	72.8
Turk.	—	—	14.7	16.9	14.5	—	—	—	46.3
UK	47.0	45.3	42.0	37.9	46.1	54.8	54.2	57.6	51.5
Can.	43.9	41.6	38.5	41.5	44.0	48.1	56.9	54.8	51.5
USA	8.4	8.8	9.2	9.4	11.2	16.3	21.2	17.2	21.5
Jap.	23.2	20.9	21.6	20.2	20.4	35.6	28.8	25.9	20.9
Austral.	—	—	32.7	33.0	30.0	30.0	35.8	34.9	34.5
NZ	—	—	—	—	52.6	53.8	59.2	65.5	55.5

Note: Figures in the 1985 column refer to 1984 for Ireland and Spain and to 1982 for Luxembourg.

Sources: See Table 4.9.

TABLE 4.12. External dependency: trade balance as a percentage of GDP

	1950	1955	1960	1965	1970	1975	1980	1985	1990
Aus.	−4.2	−1.4	−1.4	−1.0	1.0	0.6	−1.9	0.2	1.2
Belg.	−0.6	0.8	−1.1	0.2	10.7	8.9	9.1	1.8	2.9
Den.	−3.4	1.0	−1.0	−1.3	−2.7	−0.9	−1.1	0.2	5.3
Fin.	1.2	1.7	−0.8	−1.9	−1.3	−6.2	−0.8	1.1	−1.5
Fr.	1.2	2.0	1.8	0.9	0.5	0.7	−1.7	0.2	−0.0
FRG	−1.4	2.5	2.4	0.1	2.0	2.7	−0.5	3.6	5.9
Gr.	−15.8	−6.2	−14.6	−12.7	−8.4	−10.5	−6.8	−11.6	−11.0
Ice.	−5.2	−2.6	−3.4	2.0	2.6	−8.4	0.6	0.7	2.0
Ire.	−14.5	−11.8	−5.3	− 9.0	−8.0	−5.2	−13.5	2.4	8.0
It.	−1.5	−1.1	−0.3	2.6	0.5	0.0	−2.9	−0.5	0.2
Lux.	20.2	6.6	12.9	−1.4	12.4	2.9	−3.2	−3.5	−0.1
Neth.	−7.3	0.8	2.1	−0.6	−1.8	3.5	−0.4	4.9	4.7
Norw.	1.8	−2.9	−1.7	−0.2	−1.3	−6.7	6.2	7.9	7.6
Port.	−2.4	−4.5	−6.3	−5.0	−6.8	−12.5	−15.4	−4.1	−8.9
Sp.	—	—	3.0	−3.4	−0.9	−3.9	−2.6	2.5	−3.4
Sw.	0.6	−0.9	−0.7	−1.2	−0.6	−0.2	−1.9	2.4	0.2
Switz.	−0.3	1.4	0.5	−0.1	−1.7	2.9	−3.5	0.5	0.5
Turk.	—	—	−2.4	−2.3	−2.7	—	—	—	−0.5
UK	−0.6	−1.6	−1.6	−0.9	1.0	−1.6	2.4	1.2	−2.6
Can.	0.5	−1.0	−1.5	−0.4	2.7	−1.5	1.9	2.8	−0.2
USA	0.2	−0.1	0.3	0.4	0.2	0.8	−0.8	−3.0	−1.4
Jap.	0.4	0.6	0.5	1.5	1.3	0.0	−0.9	3.4	0.7
Austral.	—	—	−2.9	−2.3	−0.2	0.2	−2.1	−3.0	−0.1
NZ	—	—	—	—	0.8	−6.9	−1.2	−3.2	−0.7

Note: Figures in the 1985 column refer to 1984 for Ireland and Spain and to 1982 for Luxembourg. By trade balance is meant exports minus imports.

Sources: See Table 4.9.

Comparative Tables

TABLE 4.13. Growth of real GDP 1960–1990 (year to year averages)

	1960–8 (1)	1968–73 (2)	1973–9 (3)	1979–85 (4)	1960–81 (5)	1970–80 (6)	1980–90 (7)	1970–90 (8)
Aus.	4.2	5.9	2.9	1.8	4.0	3.9	2.3	3.1
Belg.	4.5	5.6	2.2	1.2	3.7	3.5	2.2	2.8
Den.	4.6	4.0	1.9	1.9	3.2	2.5	1.9	2.1
Fin.	3.9	6.7	2.4	3.2	4.1	3.9	3.4	3.6
Fr.	5.4	5.9	3.1	1.1	4.4	3.9	2.2	3.0
FRG	4.1	4.9	2.3	1.3	3.6	2.9	2.0	2.5
Gr.	7.3	8.2	3.7	1.1	5.8	5.1	1.5	3.4
Ice.	4.1	6.9	5.6	1.5	4.7	6.3	2.7	4.4
Ire.	4.2	4.8	4.6	2.0	4.0	4.5	3.5	4.0
It.	5.7	4.6	2.6	1.4	4.2	4.6	2.4	3.5
Lux.	3.0	5.9	1.5	2.2	3.1	2.9	3.2	3.1
Neth.	4.8	4.9	2.7	0.7	3.8	3.3	1.8	2.6
Norw.	4.4	4.1	4.9	3.3	4.3	4.5	2.6	3.5
Port.	6.6	7.4	3.1	1.6	5.4	5.2	2.9	4.0
Sp.	7.5	6.8	2.5	1.4	5.3	3.7	2.8	3.3
Sw.	4.4	3.7	1.8	1.8	3.1	2.4	1.9	2.2
Switz.	4.4	4.5	−0.4	1.9	2.9	1.8	2.3	1.9
Turk.	5.8	5.5	6.6	4.0	5.3	5.6	4.8	5.5
UK	3.1	3.2	1.5	1.2	2.1	2.2	2.2	2.4
Can.	5.4	5.4	4.2	2.4	4.0	4.3	2.8	3.7
USA	4.4	3.2	2.4	2.5	3.3	2.6	2.7	2.8
Jap.	10.4	8.4	3.6	4.0	7.5	5.2	4.1	4.7
Austral.	5.0	5.5	2.7	2.9	4.2	3.6	3.1	3.4
NZ	3.1	5.1	0.2	2.6	2.9	2.2	1.5	1.9

Sources: (1)–(4) OECD, *Economic Outlook: Historical Statistics* (1985); (5)–(8) OECD, *Economic Outlook: Historical Statistics* (1992).

TABLE 4.14. Growth of real GDP per capita 1960–1990 (year to year averages)

	1960–8 (1)	1968–73 (2)	1973–9 (3)	1979–85 (4)	1960–81 (5)	1970–80 (6)	1980–90 (7)	1970–90 (8)
Aus.	3.6	5.4	3.0	1.8	3.7	3.8	2.1	2.9
Belg.	3.9	5.3	2.0	1.2	3.4	3.3	2.1	2.6
Den.	3.8	3.3	1.6	1.9	2.7	1.8	1.8	1.9
Fin.	3.3	6.5	2.0	2.7	3.7	3.6	3.0	3.2
Fr.	4.2	5.0	2.6	0.6	4.4	3.2	1.7	2.5
FRG	3.2	4.0	2.5	1.4	3.6	2.7	1.7	2.3
Gr.	6.7	7.8	2.6	0.4	5.0	4.2	1.0	2.7
Ice.	2.4	5.8	4.5	0.3	3.3	5.2	1.5	3.3
Ire.	3.8	3.7	3.0	1.1	3.1	3.1	3.1	3.1
It.	5.0	3.9	2.1	1.2	3.5	3.2	2.2	2.6
Lux.	2.1	5.0	0.9	2.1	2.3	2.2	2.8	2.6
Neth.	3.5	3.7	1.9	0.2	2.7	2.4	1.2	1.9
Norw.	3.6	3.3	4.4	2.3	3.6	4.0	2.3	3.1
Port.	6.5	7.7	1.5	1.1	4.9	4.3	2.3	3.3
Sp.	6.4	5.8	1.4	0.7	4.2	2.7	2.3	2.6
Sw.	3.6	3.1	1.5	1.7	2.6	2.0	1.7	1.9
Switz.	2.7	3.4	−0.1	1.4	2.1	1.5	1.7	1.5
Turk.	3.2	2.9	4.3	1.8	2.9	3.2	2.3	3.0
UK	2.4	2.9	1.5	1.1	1.8	2.0	2.0	2.2
Can.	3.5	4.1	2.9	1.3	4.0	3.0	1.8	2.5
USA	3.1	2.1	1.4	1.4	2.2	1.5	1.7	1.7
Jap.	9.3	6.8	2.5	3.3	6.4	4.0	3.0	3.8
Austral.	3.0	3.6	1.5	1.5	2.5	2.1	1.6	1.9
NZ	1.2	3.5	−0.7	2.0	1.6	1.1	0.9	1.0

Sources: See Table 4.13.

TABLE 4.15. Growth of real GDP 1950–1981 (year to year averages)

	1950–60 (1)	1960–70 (2)	1970–81 (3)
Aus.	5.9	4.6	3.5
Belg.	2.7[a]	4.7	3.0
Den.	3.2	4.7	2.1
Fin.	4.4	4.3	3.1
Fr.	4.4	5.5	3.3
FRG	7.7	4.4	2.6
Gr.	6.0	7.5	4.3
Ice.	5.5	4.5	4.3
Ire.	1.3	4.2	4.0
It.	5.5[b]	5.7	2.9
Lux.	2.7[c]	3.4	2.4
Neth.	4.6	5.3	2.7
Norw.	3.6	4.9	4.5
Port.	4.1	5.9	4.2
Sp.	3.6[d]	7.1	3.4
Sw.	3.6	4.4	1.8
Switz.	4.2	4.3	0.7
Turk.	6.3	6.0	5.2
UK	2.7	2.9	1.7
Can.	4.0	5.6	3.8
USA	2.9	4.4	2.9
Jap.	8.0[e]	10.4	4.5
Austral.	4.3[a]	5.9	2.8
NZ	2.4	3.7	2.0

[a] 1953–60.
[b] 1951–60.
[c] 1950–9.
[d] 1954–60.
[e] 1952–60.

Sources: (1): UN, *Statistical Yearbook* (1970): table 181; (2): UN, *Statistical Yearbook* (1981): table 30; (3): World Bank (1984): Series 4, table 1.

TABLE 4.16. Growth of real GDP per capita
1950–1981 (year to year averages)

	1950–60 (1)	1960–70 (2)	1970–81 (3)
Aus.	5.7	4.0	3.3
Belg.	2.0[a]	4.1	2.8
Den.	2.5	3.9	1.8
Fin.	3.3	3.8	2.7
Fr.	3.5	4.4	2.8
FRG	6.6	3.5	2.6
Gr.	5.0	6.8	3.3
Ice.	3.2	2.9	3.1
Ire.	1.8	3.8	2.7
It.	4.9[b]	5.0	2.5
Lux.	2.0[c]	2.6	1.9
Neth.	3.3	4.0	1.9
Norw.	2.7	4.0	4.0
Port.	3.7	5.9	3.4
Sp.	2.8[d]	5.9	2.3
Sw.	2.9	3.6	1.5
Switz.	2.9	2.8	0.7
Turk.	3.4	3.4	2.8
UK	2.3	2.3	1.6
Can.	1.2	3.7	2.6
USA	1.2	3.1	1.9
Jap.	6.8[e]	9.3	3.4
Austral.	2.0[a]	3.7	1.4
NZ	0.1	1.9	0.5

[a] 1953–60.
[b] 1951–60.
[c] 1950–9.
[d] 1954–60.
[e] 1952–60.

Sources: (1): UN, *Statistical Yearbook* (1970): table 181; (2): UN, *Statistical Yearbook* (1981): table 30; (3): World Bank (1984): Series 4, table 1.

TABLE 4.17. Growth of GNP per capita 1960–1991 (year to year averages)

	1960–70 (1)	1970–80 (2)	1960–80 (3)	1965–84 (4)	1973–86 (5)	1980–91 (6)
Aus.	3.9	3.4	4.1	3.5	2.4	2.1
Belg.	4.0	2.9	3.8	2.8	1.3	2.0
Den.	3.7	1.7	3.3	1.8	1.4	2.2
Fin.	3.9	2.5	4.0	3.3	2.4	2.5
Fr.	4.6	3.0	3.9	2.8	1.5	1.8
FRG	3.5	2.7	3.3	2.7	2.1	2.2
Gr.	6.6	3.7	5.8	3.6	1.4	1.1
Ice.	—	—	—	—	1.0	1.8
Ire.	3.6	2.6	3.1	2.2	1.4	3.3
It.	4.6	2.5	3.6	2.6	1.7	2.2
Lux.	—	—	—	—	2.7	3.5
Neth.	3.9	2.1	3.2	2.0	0.8	1.6
Norw.	4.1	3.8	3.5	3.3	3.4	2.3
Port.	5.3	1.2	5.0	3.3	1.1	3.1
Sp.	6.1	2.6	4.5	2.6	0.8	2.8
Sw.	3.8	1.6	2.3	1.8	1.1	1.7
Switz.	2.5	0.6	1.9	1.4	1.2	1.6
Turk.	3.9	3.0	3.6	2.6	1.4	2.9
UK	2.2	1.8	2.2	1.6	1.2	2.6
Can.	3.6	2.6	3.3	2.4	1.2	2.0
USA	3.2	2.1	2.3	1.7	1.4	1.7
Jap.	9.6	3.4	7.1	4.7	3.4	3.6
Austral.	3.1	1.3	2.7	2.0	1.4	1.6
NZ	2.1	0.3	1.8	1.4	0.7	0.7

Sources: (1): World Bank, *The World Bank Atlas 1972* (1972); (2): World Bank, *The World Bank Atlas 1983* (1983); (3): World Bank, *World Development Report 1982* (1982): table 1; (4): World Bank, *World Development Report 1987* (1987): table 1; (5): World Bank, *The 1988 Update of World Bank Atlas* (1988); (6) World Bank, *World Development Report 1993* (1993).

Section 5: Public Finance

TABLE 5.1. General government: current receipts as a percentage of GDP

	1950	1955	1960	1965	1970	1975	1980	1985	1990	1992
Aus.	27.9	29.5	31.4	36.1	39.7	42.9	46.0	47.7	46.6	48.4
Belg.	24.2	24.0	26.7	30.7	35.2	40.4	43.2	46.5	49.5	49.5
Den.	21.7	25.7	27.6	31.4	41.7	46.2	52.2	57.0	55.9	57.5
Fin.	30.3	30.2	31.6	33.5	34.9	38.8	37.8	40.5	40.8	53.2
Fr.	32.6	33.0	34.1	37.7	39.0	40.3	45.6	48.5	46.4	46.3
FRG	31.6	34.7	36.0	36.2	38.5	42.7	44.6	45.4	43.2	45.1
Gr.	15.5	18.2	20.4	23.4	26.8	27.4	30.5	34.9	34.2	40.1
Ice.	27.6	26.9	36.4	29.0	31.8	35.6	32.1	33.4	34.3	37.8
Ire.	23.4	23.8	24.6	28.0	35.3	35.2	41.7	44.3	40.3	40.1
It.	21.0	26.2	29.8	31.6	30.4	31.2	37.4	37.5	42.3	44.0
Lux.	31.7	30.0	32.5	35.2	35.0	49.0	51.5	53.0	—	—
Neth.	33.0	28.9	33.4	36.8	44.5	53.2	55.0	54.4	51.9	54.0
Norw.	29.6	30.8	34.5	37.7	43.5	49.6	54.0	56.1	56.3	55.3
Port.	20.0	19.1	17.6	20.4	24.3	24.8	31.5	35.9	37.6	—
Sp.	—	—	18.1	19.3	22.5	24.4	30.0	33.2	37.9	40.2
Sw.	26.2	32.7	35.0	42.0	47.0	50.7	56.7	59.4	63.8	59.2
Switz.	25.5	24.0	25.4	25.4	26.5	32.1	32.8	34.4	34.1	34.5
Turk.	—	—	—	19.9	23.7	—	—	—	—	—
UK	33.5	30.4	29.6	32.8	40.7	40.8	40.9	43.7	39.5	38.0
Can.	24.1	26.0	28.0	30.6	35.2	36.9	37.2	38.8	42.1	43.5
USA	24.0	25.0	27.5	27.3	30.3	30.5	32.8	31.1	31.9	31.5
Jap.	21.9	19.9	20.7	20.8	20.7	24.0	28.0	31.2	34.6	33.8
Austral.	—	—	25.4	27.3	27.8	31.0	33.4	33.7	35.2	33.1
NZ	—	—	—	—	—	—	—	—	—	—

Note: Current receipts consist mainly of direct and indirect taxes, and social security contributions paid by employers and employees. General government consists of all departments, offices, organizations, and other bodies which are agents or instruments of the central, state, or local public authorities.

Sources: 1950–65: OECD, *National Accounts 1950–1968* (1968); OECD, *National Accounts 1960–1977* (1979); 1970–80; OECD, *National Accounts 1964–1981* (1983); 1985: OECD, *National Accounts 1973–1985* (1987); OECD, *National Accounts 1975–1987* (1989); 1990: OECD, *National Accounts 1979–1991* (1993); 1992: OECD, National Accounts 1981–1993.

TABLE 5.2.   General government: taxes as a percentage of GDP

	1950	1955	1960	1965	1970	1975	1980	1985	1990	1992
Aus.	22.4	23.6	24.4	27.5	27.4	28.6	29.2	30.7	29.3	30.5
Belg.	17.9	17.4	19.2	20.8	23.9	27.5	29.9	30.7	29.3	28.7
Den.	15.5	22.5	23.8	27.4	38.2	40.6	44.4	47.1	46.6	47.5
Fin.	25.2	24.0	24.9	26.1	27.0	29.5	29.5	30.9	32.6	32.3
Fr.	20.8	21.5	22.2	23.1	22.4	21.3	23.3	24.4	23.0	22.5
FRG	22.4	23.8	24.2	24.4	24.0	24.8	25.7	25.0	23.7	25.1
Gr.	12.3	13.2	14.1	16.1	18.0	18.0	19.0	20.9	23.0	25.4
Ice.	25.0	24.1	33.8	26.2	28.3	33.6	29.7	30.2	30.5	32.0
Ire.	20.3	20.5	21.2	24.1	28.4	26.7	30.4	32.8	30.5	29.8
It.	14.2	16.8	18.4	18.8	16.7	15.4	21.2	22.3	25.0	25.6
Lux.	24.1	21.1	21.4	21.8	21.7	29.5	30.8	31.8	—	—
Neth.	26.1	22.0	22.3	22.8	25.2	27.8	27.9	23.7	28.1	28.8
Norw.	26.1	26.3	26.6	27.8	31.5	33.8	38.6	37.9	34.8	34.3
Port.	14.4	13.3	13.5	14.9	18.0	16.4	20.8	24.0	24.4	—
Sp.	—	—	13.1	11.1	11.5	11.1	13.3	17.3	21.9	22.6
Sw.	21.9	26.6	27.0	31.5	33.2	35.2	35.3	37.5	40.9	36.8
Switz.	16.1	14.4	15.9	16.8	18.2	20.9	20.7	21.2	20.8	20.4
Turk.	—	—	—	15.0	17.3	—	—	—	—	—
UK	29.7	25.7	23.8	25.2	31.5	29.9	30.3	31.4	28.6	27.4
Can.	20.0	21.6	22.6	25.0	28.2	28.6	27.5	27.6	31.3	32.7
USA	21.5	22.2	23.4	23.0	23.4	22.0	23.0	21.4	21.4	21.1
Jap.	18.6	16.0	15.8	15.6	15.3	16.1	18.5	20.1	22.0	20.9
Austral.	—	—	22.3	23.5	24.3	28.4	30.2	30.2	30.8	28.8
NZ	—	—	—	—	—	—	—	—	—	—

Note: Taxes refer to direct as well as indirect taxes. Direct taxes mean levies by public authorities at regular intervals, except social contributions, on income from employment, property, capital gains, or any other sources. Indirect taxes mean taxes assessed on producers in respect of the production, sale, purchase, or use of goods and services, which they charge to the expenses of production. General government consists of all departments, offices, organizations, and other bodies which are agents or instruments of the central, state, or local public authorities.

Sources: See Table 5.1.

TABLE 5.3. General government: social security contributions as a percentage of GDP

	1950	1955	1960	1965	1970	1975	1980	1985	1990	1992
Aus.	5.4	5.7	6.1	7.7	8.8	10.3	12.5	12.2	12.3	12.8
Belg.	5.1	5.4	6.4	9.2	10.3	12.6	12.5	14.7	15.5	16.0
Den.	1.3	1.4	1.5	1.9	1.9	0.6	0.9	1.9	1.5	1.6
Fin.	2.6	2.6	2.6	3.6	4.4	6.1	4.8	5.4	4.8	14.6
Fr.	9.3	10.8	11.2	13.8	12.9	15.3	18.4	19.9	19.3	19.5
FRG	7.7	8.2	9.7	9.7	11.6	15.0	15.5	16.2	15.8	16.0
Gr.	2.5	3.5	4.5	5.4	6.6	6.7	9.0	11.5	9.7	11.4
Ice.	2.2	2.2	2.0	2.3	2.4	0.9	1.4	1.2	1.3	2.8
Ire.	1.0	1.0	1.1	1.7	4.3	6.4	7.6	7.8	7.2	7.3
It.	4.9	6.9	8.7	10.1	10.7	13.0	12.6	11.8	12.9	13.3
Lux.	6.9	8.6	9.0	10.4	9.5	13.3	14.0	13.1	—	—
Neth.	4.3	4.7	8.1	11.3	14.6	18.4	18.2	20.5	17.0	18.6
Norw.	1.9	2.7	5.5	6.8	9.7	13.4	12.1	11.5	12.2	12.2
Port.	3.6	3.6	2.7	3.5	4.6	7.2	8.9	9.4	10.4	—
Sp.	—	—	3.5	5.0	6.6	9.4	12.0	12.0	12.2	13.1
Sw.	0.7	2.1	3.8	5.8	7.6	8.6	14.3	12.6	15.3	14.3
Switz.	4.2	4.2	4.7	4.8	5.6	8.3	9.1	9.9	9.8	10.4
Turk.	—	—	—	2.3	3.1	—	—	—	—	—
UK	3.4	3.1	3.6	4.8	5.2	6.6	6.2	6.9	6.3	6.3
Can.	1.4	1.7	2.0	1.9	2.9	3.5	3.4	4.4	4.9	4.6
USA	2.4	2.8	4.1	4.3	5.9	7.2	7.9	7.2	7.5	7.7
Jap.	1.9	2.2	2.5	3.3	4.3	6.4	7.4	8.3	9.2	9.4
Austral.	—	—	0.0	0.0	0.0	0.0	0.0	0.6	0.0	0.0
NZ	—	—	—	—	—	—	—	—	—	—

Note: Social security contributions include all compulsory contributions as payments to institutions of general government providing for social security benefits. General government consists of all departments, offices, organizations, and other bodies which are agents or instruments of the central, state, or local public authorities.

Sources: See Table 5.1.

TABLE 5.4. General government: government final consumption as a percentage of GDP

	1950	1955	1960	1965	1970	1975	1980	1985	1990	1992
Aus.	11.2	11.8	12.9	13.5	14.7	17.2	17.8	18.7	21.8	18.4
Belg.	12.6	11.4	12.6	13.1	13.7	16.8	18.5	17.7	14.5	14.7
Den.	10.2	12.9	12.7	15.4	19.8	24.6	26.7	25.4	25.2	25.7
Fin.	11.6	11.5	12.6	14.5	14.7	17.5	18.6	20.3	21.1	24.5
Fr.	12.8	13.0	12.9	12.6	13.4	14.4	15.2	16.3	17.9	18.8
FRG	14.3	13.2	13.6	15.4	15.8	20.5	20.2	19.9	18.4	17.9
Gr.	11.6	11.0	11.4	11.8	12.6	15.2	16.3	20.3	21.1	19.7
Ice.	8.6	7.9	8.0	8.0	8.7	10.0	16.4	18.2	18.8	20.2
Ire.	11.8	12.2	12.2	13.4	14.7	19.0	21.5	19.2	15.7	16.1
It.	11.6	11.8	12.1	14.1	13.8	15.4	16.4	16.6	17.4	17.6
Lux.	12.1	12.7	10.1	11.0	9.9	14.9	16.5	16.6	—	—
Neth.	12.5	14.6	13.5	15.5	16.3	18.2	18.0	16.3	14.5	14.5
Norw.	11.1	12.7	14.0	16.1	16.9	19.3	18.9	18.6	21.1	21.5
Port.	11.2	11.7	10.9	12.3	14.2	15.4	14.7	15.5	16.7	—
Sp.	—	—	8.8	7.4	8.5	9.2	11.6	13.7	15.5	17.0
Sw.	14.0	16.8	17.1	18.7	21.6	23.8	28.9	27.4	27.2	27.9
Switz.	11.4	10.5	10.2	11.6	10.5	12.6	12.7	13.2	13.4	14.3
Turk.	—	—	—	12.4	12.9	—	—	—	—	—
UK	16.4	17.1	16.8	17.2	17.7	22.0	21.5	21.1	20.0	22.2
Can.	10.3	14.3	14.3	13.9	19.2	20.0	19.6	20.1	20.2	21.9
USA	12.1	17.0	17.9	18.2	19.2	18.9	18.1	18.3	17.9	17.7
Jap.	10.8	10.4	8.9	9.3	7.4	10.1	10.0	9.7	9.1	9.3
Austral.	—	—	9.7	11.6	12.4	15.7	17.0	19.2	17.7	18.4
NZ	—	—	—	—	—	—	—	—	—	—

Note: Government final consumption consists of expenditures on goods and services for public administration, defence, health, and education. It excludes all transfer payments. General government consists of all departments, offices, organizations, and other bodies which are agents or instruments of the central, state, or local public authorities.

Sources: See Table 5.1.

TABLE 5.5. General government: social security transfers as a percentage of GDP

	1950	1955	1960	1965	1970	1975	1980	1985	1990	1992
Aus.	7.8	9.4	10.0	12.3	15.4	16.9	19.2	20.1	19.9	20.3
Belg.	9.7	9.0	10.9	12.4	14.1	18.8	21.2	22.0	22.2	24.0
Den.	5.8	6.7	7.3	8.3	11.6	13.9	16.8	16.5	18.5	19.7
Fin.	4.5	5.0	5.8	7.0	8.3	9.6	9.9	11.6	11.0	23.7
Fr.	11.2	13.1	12.9	16.1	17.2	20.6	23.3	26.6	21.5	22.4
FRG	12.3	11.4	12.6	13.0	13.4	18.4	17.3	16.6	15.9	14.8
Gr.	5.7	4.9	5.8	7.5	8.0	7.4	9.3	15.0	14.8	15.3
Ice.	6.4	5.9	7.1	7.2	8.9	10.5	4.6	5.2	5.5	6.7
Ire.	4.7	5.6	6.2	6.9	10.8	14.9	15.8	18.2	15.8	15.3
It.	6.3	9.4	10.7	13.4	12.7	16.0	16.1	16.9	18.4	19.3
Lux.	7.7	10.4	11.6	13.6	14.0	19.9	22.8	23.2	—	—
Neth.	6.7	7.2	10.3	14.0	18.4	25.6	27.4	28.5	26.1	26.5
Norw.	4.8	6.4	8.3	9.7	12.3	13.6	14.7	14.8	19.5	20.5
Port.	2.5	2.6	3.0	3.4	3.1	8.5	10.7	10.9	12.4	—
Sp.	—	—	2.3	5.7	7.5	9.3	13.8	16.0	15.9	17.6
Sw.	6.3	7.4	8.2	10.0	11.6	15.1	18.9	19.3	20.8	23.4
Switz.	4.9	5.3	6.2	7.3	6.3	10.1	10.3	13.7	13.6	15.9
Turk.	—	—	—	1.6	1.7	—	—	—	—	—
UK	5.4	5.4	6.2	7.4	9.4	10.9	12.5	14.6	12.8	14.3
Can.	5.6	6.3	8.5	8.6	8.1	10.2	10.1	12.3	12.9	15.8
USA	4.9	3.8	5.1	5.2	7.9	11.5	10.0	11.0	11.3	13.1
Jap.	2.5	4.1	3.8	4.4	4.8	8.0	10.6	11.5	12.0	11.5
Austral.	—	—	5.7	5.8	5.4	8.8	9.0	10.8	11.0	11.3
NZ	—	—	—	—	—	—	—	—	—	—

Note: Social security transfers consist of social security benefits, social assistance grants, unfunded employee pension and welfare benefits, and transfers to private non-profit institutions serving households. General government consists of all departments, offices, organizations, and other bodies which are agents or instruments of the central, state, or local public authorities.

Sources: See Table 5.1.

TABLE 5.6. General government: current disbursements as a percentage of GDP

	1950	1955	1960	1965	1970	1975	1980	1985	1990	1992
Aus.	21.2	23.0	25.4	28.9	33.1	38.6	42.7	45.2	44.7	46.4
Belg.	25.5	23.8	27.8	29.8	33.0	41.2	48.1	52.3	53.5	54.3
Den.	18.0	21.4	21.7	25.9	34.6	43.5	52.2	56.7	56.5	58.8
Fin.	19.7	20.7	21.9	25.8	28.9	32.2	34.3	37.7	37.5	56.9
Fr.	26.7	29.8	30.2	32.9	34.7	39.2	43.1	49.4	45.7	48.7
FRG	28.3	27.0	28.2	30.4	32.6	43.4	42.8	43.4	42.5	44.3
Gr.	19.6	16.3	17.8	21.3	22.4	26.7	30.4	45.3	49.6	48.9
Ice.	19.9	20.0	23.4	20.6	21.7	28.3	25.0	28.3	31.1	34.8
Ire.	22.9	23.4	24.5	27.6	34.2	42.0	48.3	50.4	41.9	41.7
It.	20.7	24.6	26.6	30.9	30.2	38.3	41.4	44.1	48.8	51.9
Lux.	22.5	26.9	25.5	29.7	28.6	41.3	45.7	47.8	—	—
Neth.	23.9	25.5	28.0	33.0	40.2	51.1	54.2	55.2	54.0	55.5
Norw.	21.9	24.4	28.0	31.9	36.5	41.8	45.1	44.0	56.3	57.7
Port.	16.3	15.9	15.2	17.7	19.5	27.2	33.8	39.4	39.4	—
Sp.	—	—	13.7	15.8	18.8	21.2	29.4	34.7	36.9	40.7
Sw.	23.5	26.4	28.7	31.9	37.2	44.9	57.1	60.8	58.5	64.3
Switz.	19.4	18.5	19.1	21.3	21.3	28.8	29.3	30.9	30.9	34.9
Turk.	—	—	—	15.5	16.4	—	—	—	—	—
UK	30.1	28.8	29.3	30.5	33.2	41.0	42.3	44.9	38.2	42.1
Can.	19.2	23.4	26.6	26.4	32.2	36.8	37.7	43.8	44.9	49.4
USA	20.0	22.5	25.0	25.2	30.3	33.6	33.5	35.3	35.1	36.6
Jap.	14.6	15.5	13.6	14.7	14.0	20.9	25.4	26.9	26.2	26.0
Austral.	—	—	18.9	21.6	21.8	27.6	30.4	35.5	34.7	36.9
NZ	—	—	—	—	—	—	—	—	—	—

Note: Current disbursements consist of final consumption expenditure, interest on the public debt, subsidies, and social security transfers to households. General government consists of all departments, offices, organizations, and other bodies which are agents or instruments of the central, state, or local public authorities.

Sources: See Table 5.1.

TABLE 5.7. Central government: current receipts as a percentage of GDP

	1950	1955	1960	1965	1970	1975	1980	1985	1990	1992
Aus.	13.2	16.6	17.2	19.1	21.0	21.0	22.0	24.1	24.3	25.4
Belg.	17.5	16.7	18.0	19.2	22.1	24.9	27.8	28.4	30.8	30.2
Den.	—	—	19.1	22.1	—	—	36.0	40.6	38.3	39.4
Fin.	—	—	21.4	22.2	22.5	22.8	22.8	24.1	25.6	26.4
Fr.	—	—	21.0	21.9	22.0	19.6	21.7	21.5	19.7	18.7
FRG	11.0	15.6	13.8	14.0	14.3	13.9	14.5	14.7	13.8	15.2
Gr.	10.5	12.4	13.1	14.3	16.1	17.4	18.1	19.3	21.9	25.0
Ice.	19.7	18.7	28.0	19.5	24.0	27.6	25.4	26.1	27.1	30.4
Ire.	19.1	19.3	20.2	23.4	29.4	28.9	35.6	37.9	33.3	33.2
It.	13.2	15.9	17.6	17.8	17.0	18.9	26.9	28.5	30.6	30.8
Lux.	21.5	18.5	19.3	19.6	20.3	28.9	29.3	32.1	—	—
Neth.	—	22.3	22.6	23.1	27.0	32.0	33.8	30.1	31.6	31.9
Norw.	22.3	22.5	26.1	28.5	35.0	40.4	49.5	36.1	34.1	33.1
Port.	14.6	13.5	13.0	15.1	17.6	16.4	22.0	25.7	—	24.1
Sp.	—	—	—	12.5	13.9	13.2	15.6	16.2	21.1	22.5
Sw.	19.9	21.9	22.9	24.9	26.8	28.7	27.7	31.3	33.2	24.7
Switz.	—	—	8.6	8.3	8.6	8.4	9.2	9.6	9.7	9.4
Turk.	—	—	—	15.4	18.1	—	—	—	—	—
UK	27.9	25.0	23.1	24.2	31.5	29.9	30.7	32.3	31.3	30.9
Can.	15.1	16.5	16.0	15.8	17.5	18.7	16.7	17.4	19.0	19.8
USA	15.5	15.8	15.6	14.6	14.5	12.7	14.6	13.6	13.6	13.0
Jap.	—	—	14.2	11.5	11.0	10.6	13.1	13.5	15.4	13.4
Austral.	—	—	20.3	21.3	21.9	23.9	26.0	27.0	26.0	23.7
NZ	—	—	—	—	—	—	—	—	—	—

Note: Current receipts consist of direct and indirect taxes, and social security contributions paid by employers and employees. Central government consists of all departments, offices, organizations, and other bodies classified under general government which are agencies or instruments of the central authority of a country, except separately organized social security funds.

Sources: See Table 5.1.

TABLE 5.8.   Central government: taxes as a percentage of GDP

	1950	1955	1960	1965	1970	1975	1980	1985	1990	1992
Aus.	13.1	16.6	16.6	18.4	17.9	18.4	19.0	20.5	20.4	21.2
Belg.	17.1	16.5	17.9	19.5	22.3	25.7	28.2	28.5	27.4	26.6
Den.	—	—	17.9	21.2	—	—	30.6	33.5	31.7	32.2
Fin.	—	—	19.7	20.4	19.4	20.6	21.1	21.8	22.9	22.6
Fr.	—	—	20.4	21.2	20.2	18.4	20.2	20.1	18.8	18.1
FRG	9.9	14.1	13.0	13.3	13.4	13.0	13.3	12.8	12.3	13.3
Gr.	10.3	11.5	12.2	13.2	15.4	16.2	17.4	18.8	21.8	23.5
Ice.	19.5	18.5	27.7	19.6	21.5	26.4	23.4	23.6	23.9	25.6
Ire.	17.0	17.0	17.5	20.7	17.5	19.8	26.8	32.0	29.5	28.9
It.	12.0	14.2	15.9	16.2	14.4	14.6	20.3	21.1	23.3	23.9
Lux.	21.5	18.2	18.1	18.4	17.9	24.6	25.1	26.8	—	—
Neth.	—	21.5	21.7	22.2	24.8	27.4	27.6	22.7	26.7	27.3
Norw.	20.9	20.9	23.5	25.9	22.5	23.7	29.7	29.3	25.0	24.6
Port.	13.0	11.8	12.0	13.6	16.2	15.6	20.3	23.4	—	20.4
Sp.	—	—	—	9.7	9.8	9.5	10.9	12.3	17.6	18.3
Sw.	18.2	20.3	20.6	20.7	22.6	23.9	20.4	23.1	25.4	18.0
Switz.	—	—	1.8	1.4	8.3	7.9	8.6	8.7	8.7	8.7
Turk.	—	—	—	14.0	16.4	—	—	—	—	—
UK	27.1	23.2	20.7	21.8	28.0	23.3	27.2	27.5	27.7	27.4
Can.	13.9	15.4	14.6	14.2	14.9	15.6	13.7	13.5	14.8	15.4
USA	15.3	15.6	15.5	14.4	14.0	12.2	13.9	11.9	11.9	11.3
Jap.	—	—	12.9	11.0	10.7	10.1	12.3	12.8	14.5	12.5
Austral.	—	—	19.3	20.2	20.9	23.1	24.9	24.6	24.6	22.2
NZ	—	—	—	—	—	—	—	—	—	—

Note: Taxes refer to direct as well as indirect taxes. Central government consists of all departments, offices, organizations, and other bodies classified under general government which are agencies or instruments of the central authority of a country, except separately organized social security funds.

Sources: See Table 5.1.

TABLE 5.9. Central government: current disbursements as a percentage of GDP

	1950	1955	1960	1965	1970	1975	1980	1985	1990	1992
Aus.	12.4	12.7	14.0	15.9	18.7	21.5	22.1	24.8	24.6	25.4
Belg.	18.8	16.9	20.0	19.5	21.3	26.5	31.7	35.1	35.1	35.4
Den.	—	—	14.4	17.8	—	—	38.7	42.3	40.4	42.2
Fin.	—	—	14.6	17.3	17.3	19.5	21.3	22.4	22.9	32.2
Fr.	—	—	18.2	18.2	19.0	19.9	20.8	23.6	20.1	21.4
FRG	10.2	11.7	10.8	12.0	11.5	14.5	14.1	14.1	14.6	15.0
Gr.	16.1	11.7	11.8	14.0	14.3	19.4	20.3	27.6	36.2	34.7
Ice.	13.4	14.1	17.7	14.4	16.8	24.9	20.6	22.9	25.9	29.2
Ire.	18.8	18.8	20.3	23.0	28.0	34.4	41.2	43.4	34.0	34.3
It.	13.4	15.3	14.9	17.3	16.7	21.4	31.5	36.0	37.5	39.8
Lux.	15.7	16.8	15.3	16.8	16.4	23.2	25.4	28.1	—	—
Neth.	—	20.1	18.5	19.7	23.6	30.0	33.1	31.7	33.9	34.2
Norw.	16.5	18.3	21.5	24.7	30.5	34.5	41.9	38.4	31.6	33.5
Port.	12.8	12.4	11.8	13.8	15.5	19.0	24.6	30.5	—	—
Sp.	—	—	—	9.5	11.4	10.8	15.3	18.4	21.1	22.5
Sw.	17.9	18.6	17.8	20.6	22.9	27.3	33.0	35.8	30.9	33.6
Switz.	—	—	5.3	5.7	6.9	7.7	8.7	9.1	8.9	9.4
Turk.	—	—	—	14.0	13.3	—	—	—	—	—
UK	25.6	23.4	22.9	22.1	24.1	31.2	31.9	33.5	29.9	34.0
Can.	11.9	16.0	16.0	14.3	17.0	20.4	19.8	23.4	22.5	23.8
USA	12.3	14.8	15.0	14.6	16.5	16.4	16.3	18.4	17.7	18.1
Jap.	—	—	5.9	5.9	8.7	11.7	15.1	15.0	13.9	13.6
Austral.	—	—	15.3	17.1	17.3	22.7	24.4	27.5	26.0	26.4
NZ	—	—	—	—	—	—	—	—	—	—

Note: Current disbursements consist of final consumption expenditure, interest on the public debt, subsidies, and social security transfers to households. Central government consists of all departments, offices, organizations, and other bodies classified under general government which are agencies or instruments of the central authority of a country, except separately organized social security funds.

Sources: See Table 5.1.

TABLE 5.10.   Central government: government final consumption as a
percentage of GDP

	1950	1955	1960	1965	1970	1975	1980	1985	1990	1992
Aus.	5.9	5.5	6.3	6.4	6.8	6.4	6.3	7.0	6.3	6.4
Belg.	9.6	8.1	9.8	10.1	10.6	12.9	13.7	13.0	9.5	9.7
Den.	—	—	5.8	7.0	—	—	8.3	7.9	7.7	7.8
Fin.	—	—	5.5	6.4	5.9	6.3	6.1	6.2	6.3	8.1
Fr.	—	—	10.0	9.5	10.2	10.6	10.9	11.4	9.9	10.3
FRG	4.3	4.3	4.1	5.0	3.9	4.3	3.9	3.8	3.1	2.4
Gr.	9.7	9.3	9.0	9.0	9.8	12.4	12.1	14.4	14.3	13.3
Ice.	7.6	5.3	5.3	5.0	5.6	6.8	9.0	10.1	11.6	12.6
Ire.	6.7	6.8	7.0	7.8	7.4	9.3	9.9	9.5	7.9	8.2
It.	8.4	8.3	8.2	9.7	7.9	8.5	9.0	8.8	9.5	9.5
Lux.	8.9	9.1	7.2	7.6	6.8	10.1	10.9	10.9	—	—
Neth.	—	8.0	6.3	6.5	7.8	8.2	8.1	7.5	6.7	6.6
Norw.	6.2	7.1	7.2	8.0	7.9	8.2	7.5	7.0	8.3	8.2
Port.	9.8	10.4	9.5	11.1	12.5	12.2	12.8	13.6	—	—
Sp.	—	—	—	5.8	6.6	6.5	7.8	6.9	6.1	6.2
Sw.	8.2	8.9	7.8	9.2	8.1	8.1	8.7	7.2	7.4	7.8
Switz.	—	—	2.8	3.2	2.9	2.9	3.0	3.3	3.1	2.9
Turk.	—	—	—	10.6	10.6	—	—	—	—	—
UK	11.6	12.3	11.3	10.8	10.5	12.4	12.7	12.9	12.1	13.6
Can.	5.2	8.7	6.6	5.4	5.2	5.0	4.6	5.0	4.6	4.7
USA	6.3	10.8	10.4	9.8	9.9	8.1	7.7	8.7	7.8	7.6
Jap.	—	—	3.8	3.7	2.1	2.4	2.4	2.4	2.2	2.2
Austral.	—	—	4.4	5.9	5.8	5.6	5.7	6.3	5.6	5.9
NZ	—	—	—	—	—	—	—	—	—	—

Note: Government final consumption consists of goods and services for public administration, defence, health, and education. It excludes all transfer payments. Central government consists of all departments, offices, organizations, and other bodies classified under general government which are agencies or instruments of the central authority of a country, except separately organized social security funds.

Sources: See Table 5.1.

TABLE 5.11. Central government: transfers to other sectors of general government as a percentage of central government disbursements

	1950	1955	1960	1965	1970	1975	1980	1985	1990	1992
Aus.	4.5	8.0	10.3	16.2	18.3	26.9	21.7	24.0	25.1	24.1
Belg.	19.8	20.3	21.8	20.9	21.6	26.6	28.0	25.1	20.4	19.8
Den.	—	—	41.5	40.1	—	—	55.6	45.1	45.2	46.3
Fin.	—	—	18.9	20.2	25.2	27.4	30.2	34.2	34.9	38.3
Fr.	—	—	7.0	8.5	12.3	13.8	15.8	15.4	8.9	8.9
FRG	15.3	24.2	36.5	32.4	25.3	28.3	28.2	24.9	23.0	23.0
Gr.	4.0	5.5	6.7	11.9	14.2	11.9	13.1	14.5	22.3	19.1
Ice.	10.3	11.4	18.4	21.2	39.5	35.6	34.0	32.0	27.8	25.9
Ire.	17.2	18.9	19.8	21.7	22.6	26.5	30.2	27.9	23.3	25.3
It.	10.0	13.4	13.8	21.9	19.8	27.4	41.4	42.7	37.2	35.9
Lux.	21.4	17.5	21.1	21.3	22.8	19.7	20.1	21.1	—	—
Neth.	—	35.0	45.9	51.0	47.1	50.0	51.4	48.1	42.2	41.8
Norw.	12.9	15.1	9.5	10.4	10.9	10.4	26.6	25.5	35.6	36.1
Port.	0.7	0.6	0.8	0.2	0.6	5.6	5.8	8.3	—	6.0
Sp.	—	—	—	1.8	4.9	5.4	13.1	26.4	40.2	42.2
Sw.	9.4	11.5	30.1	32.5	23.1	27.7	23.1	22.7	20.7	17.5
Switz.	—	—	10.3	16.5	36.7	40.0	41.6	40.2	41.2	41.8
Turk.	—	—	—	10.2	5.1	—	—	—	—	—
UK	14.1	13.1	16.6	19.8	23.5	27.2	22.6	19.9	23.7	26.9
Can.	11.5	10.3	16.9	18.9	23.1	22.5	21.7	19.7	18.0	18.3
USA	6.6	5.3	8.5	11.0	17.9	24.4	23.5	15.3	17.3	20.0
Jap.	—	—	—	—	54.2	57.3	53.1	49.3	53.3	54.7
Austral.	—	—	26.9	25.3	28.6	33.4	32.4	27.0	24.6	25.4
NZ	—	—	—	—	—	—	—	—	—	—

Note: Central government consists of all departments, offices, organizations, and other bodies classified under general government which are agencies or instruments of the central authority of a country, except separately organized social security funds.

Sources: See Table 5.1.

TABLE 5.12.   Central government: transfers to other sectors of general
government as a percentage of GDP

	1950	1955	1960	1965	1970	1975	1980	1985	1990	1992
Aus.	0.6	1.0	1.4	2.6	3.4	5.8	4.8	6.0	6.2	6.1
Belg.	3.7	3.4	4.4	4.1	4.6	7.1	8.9	8.8	7.2	7.0
Den.	—	—	6.0	7.1	—	—	21.5	19.1	18.3	19.5
Fin.	—	—	2.8	3.5	4.4	5.4	6.4	7.7	8.0	12.3
Fr.	—	—	1.3	1.6	2.3	2.7	3.3	3.6	1.8	1.9
FRG	1.6	2.8	4.0	3.9	2.9	4.1	4.0	3.5	3.4	3.5
Gr.	0.6	0.6	0.8	1.7	2.0	2.3	2.7	4.0	8.1	6.6
Ice.	1.4	1.6	3.3	3.0	6.6	8.9	7.0	7.3	7.2	7.6
Ire.	3.2	3.6	4.0	5.0	6.3	9.1	12.4	12.1	7.9	8.7
It.	1.3	2.1	2.1	3.8	3.3	5.9	13.1	15.4	13.9	14.3
Lux.	3.4	2.9	3.2	3.6	3.7	4.6	5.1	5.9	—	—
Neth.	—	7.0	8.5	10.0	11.1	15.0	17.0	15.2	14.3	14.3
Norw.	2.1	2.8	2.1	2.6	3.3	3.6	11.1	9.8	11.2	12.1
Port.	0.1	0.1	0.1	0.0	0.1	1.1	1.4	2.5	—	1.4
Sp.	—	—	—	0.2	0.6	0.6	2.0	4.9	8.5	9.5
Sw.	1.7	2.2	5.4	6.7	5.3	7.5	7.6	8.1	6.4	5.9
Switz.	—	—	0.6	1.0	2.5	3.1	3.6	3.6	3.7	3.9
Turk.	—	—	—	1.4	0.7	—	—	—	—	—
UK	3.6	3.1	3.8	4.4	5.7	8.5	7.2	6.7	7.1	9.1
Can.	1.4	1.6	2.7	2.7	3.9	4.6	4.3	4.6	4.1	4.3
USA	0.8	0.8	1.3	1.6	3.0	4.0	3.8	2.8	3.1	3.6
Jap.	—	—	—	—	4.7	6.7	8.0	7.4	7.4	7.4
Austral.	—	—	4.1	4.3	5.0	7.6	7.9	7.4	6.4	6.7
NZ	—	—	—	—	—	—	—	—	—	—

Note: Central government consists of all departments, offices, organizations, and
other bodies classified under general government which are agencies or instruments
of the central authority of a country, except separately organized social security
funds.

Sources: See Table 5.1.

TABLE 5.13. Central government: social security transfers as a percentage of GDP

	1950	1955	1960	1965	1970	1975	1980	1985	1990	1992
Aus.	4.0	4.5	4.1	4.4	6.0	6.4	7.0	6.9	6.4	6.8
Belg.	2.6	2.2	2.0	1.4	1.5	1.8	2.0	2.0	7.6	3.7
Den.	—	—	1.4	2.0	—	—	1.3	1.5	2.5	2.6
Fin.	—	—	3.0	3.3	3.3	3.6	3.9	3.5	4.1	4.9
Fr.	—	—	2.9	3.5	3.2	3.3	3.3	3.9	3.8	3.8
FRG	3.3	2.9	2.0	2.2	2.2	3.0	2.5	2.3	2.0	1.8
Gr.	3.5	1.4	1.3	1.4	0.6	0.6	0.7	1.0	1.1	1.1
Ice.	1.7	1.5	1.2	1.2	0.9	1.5	1.0	1.0	0.9	1.9
Ire.	3.3	4.0	4.1	3.8	6.2	8.1	8.0	9.0	8.7	16.1
It.	1.1	2.0	1.6	1.3	2.4	1.7	2.2	2.8	2.9	3.0
Lux.	0.9	1.2	1.4	0.9	1.4	2.2	3.0	3.4	—	—
Neth.	—	2.6	1.2	1.2	1.7	2.5	2.4	2.6	2.8	2.7
Norw.	2.4	3.4	7.0	8.6	13.0	1.6*	1.2	1.1	2.8	3.3
Port.	0.4	0.4	0.6	0.5	0.5	2.3	2.2	1.5	—	2.2
Sp.	—	—	—	1.2	1.8	1.3	1.8	2.4	2.3	2.5
Sw.	5.2	5.5	1.9	2.5	7.1	7.8	9.8	8.8	8.7	10.1
Switz.	—	—	0.4	0.3	0.0	0.0	0.0	0.3	0.3	0.4
Turk.	—	—	—	1.1	1.2	—	—	—	—	—
UK	2.3	2.1	2.1	2.1	3.4	4.0	5.2	6.5	5.5	5.6
Can.	2.7	3.5	3.9	3.6	4.7	6.4	5.5	6.7	6.4	7.8
USA	1.5	0.9	0.8	0.8	1.0	1.9	1.6	2.1	2.0	2.2
Jap.	—	—	1.4	1.3	0.5	0.6	0.7	0.8	0.6	0.4
Austral.	—	—	5.6	5.6	5.1	8.5	8.7	9.7	9.8	11.0
NZ	—	—	—	—	—	—	—	—	—	—

Note: Social security transfers consist of social security benefits, social assistance grants, unfunded employee pension and welfare benefits, and transfers to private non-profit institutions serving households. Central government consists of all departments, offices, organizations, and other bodies classified under general government which are agencies or instruments of the central authority of a country, except separately organized social security funds.

* Accounting change introduced 1975.

Sources: See Table 5.1.

TABLE 5.14.   State and local government: taxes as a
percentage of GDP

	1975	1980	1985	1990
Aus.	10.5	10.2	10.2	8.9
Belg.	1.8	1.7	2.2	1.9
Den.	—	13.8	13.8	14.9
Fin.	8.7	8.1	9.0	9.7
Fr.	2.8	3.0	4.0	4.0
FRG	11.7	12.4	12.2	11.4
Gr.	1.0	0.8	0.8	0.6
Ice.	—	6.3	6.6	6.6
Ire.	2.8	1.8	1.5	1.4
It.	0.9	1.0	1.4	1.8
Lux.	4.9	5.8	5.0	—
Neth.	0.5	0.9	1.1	1.3
Norw.	10.0	8.9	8.6	9.8
Port.	—	0.7	0.6	—
Sp.	—	2.4	4.9	4.3
Sw.	11.3	14.8	14.3	15.2
Switz.	5.9	5.2	5.5	11.9
Turk.	—	—	—	—
UK	3.8	3.6	3.9	0.9
Can.	12.6	15.8	14.1	13.0
USA	9.5	8.9	9.5	9.5
Jap.	5.8	6.8	7.5	8.1
Austral.	5.2	5.3	5.7	6.2
NZ	—	—	—	—

Note: Taxes refer to direct as well as indirect taxes. State
and local government includes all kinds of subcentral
governments.

Sources: OECD, *National Accounts 1973–1985* (1987);
OECD, *National Accounts 1979–1981* (1993).

TABLE 5.15. State and local government: final consumption as a percentage of GDP

	1975	1980	1985	1990
Aus.	7.1	7.5	7.6	7.5
Belg.	3.0	3.7	3.6	4.0
Den.	—	18.2	17.2	17.3
Fin.	10.6	11.7	13.4	14.1
Fr.	2.8	3.3	3.8	4.4
FRG	9.9	10.1	9.7	9.2
Gr.	2.0	3.8	4.1	4.9
Ice.	—	3.8	4.0	4.3
Ire.	9.2	10.5	9.4	7.5
It.	6.2	6.7	8.6	7.5
Lux.	4.0	4.6	4.6	—
Neth.	9.0	9.2	8.0	7.0
Norw.	11.0	11.3	11.4	12.6
Port.	—	1.1	1.4	—
Sp.	—	2.2	4.2	5.7
Sw.	15.5	19.8	19.9	19.4
Switz.	4.1	4.0	4.0	4.1
Turk.	—	—	—	—
UK	9.1	8.2	8.0	7.8
Can.	13.3	14.7	15.0	6.5
USA	10.5	9.9	9.6	10.1
Jap.	7.8	7.5	7.3	6.9
Austral.	11.9	12.8	12.9	12.1
NZ	—	—	—	—

Note: Government final consumption consists of goods and services for public administration, defence, health, and education. It excludes all transfer payments. State and local government includes all kinds of subcentral governments.

Sources: See Table 5.14.

TABLE 5.16. Central government: taxes as a percentage of general government taxes

	1950	1955	1960	1965	1970	1975	1980	1985	1990	1992
Aus.	58.5	70.3	67.9	67.1	65.4	64.4	65.0	66.8	69.8	69.6
Belg.	95.4	94.6	93.4	93.8	93.2	93.5	94.3	92.7	93.5	92.4
Den.	—	—	75.2	77.3	—	—	69.0	71.0	68.0	67.6
Fin.	—	—	79.0	78.2	72.0	69.9	71.7	70.7	70.3	70.1
Fr.	—	—	91.8	91.7	90.1	86.3	86.7	82.6	81.5	80.4
FRG	44.1	59.2	53.8	54.7	55.9	52.6	51.7	51.2	51.8	52.9
Gr.	84.1	87.2	86.1	82.2	85.5	89.6	91.6	90.1	94.8	92.2
Ice.	78.2	76.8	82.0	74.7	76.0	78.8	78.9	78.2	78.3	78.6
Ire.	83.8	82.8	82.5	86.2	61.4	74.0	88.0	97.4	97.0	97.0
It.	84.1	85.0	86.5	86.1	86.5	94.7	95.7	95.0	93.0	92.4
Lux.	88.9	86.5	84.9	84.5	82.9	83.3	81.5	84.2	—	—
Neth.	—	97.9	97.6	97.5	98.2	98.6	98.8	95.5	95.3	94.8
Norw.	80.3	79.7	88.5	93.0	71.5	70.3	76.9	77.3	71.8	71.6
Port.	90.2	89.1	89.5	91.2	90.1	94.6	97.5	97.3	—	91.9
Sp.	—	—	—	87.6	85.6	85.3	81.9	71.1	80.3	81.0
Sw.	83.4	76.4	76.1	65.8	68.0	67.9	57.8	61.6	62.0	48.9
Switz.	—	—	11.0	8.3	45.4	37.8	41.4	40.9	43.0	42.4
Turk.	—	—	—	93.4	94.7	—	—	—	—	—
UK	91.2	90.3	87.3	86.2	88.7	77.8	89.6	87.7	96.7	99.9
Can.	69.5	71.3	64.7	56.9	52.9	54.6	49.6	48.8	47.3	46.9
USA	71.1	70.3	66.2	62.5	59.9	55.6	60.3	55.5	55.6	53.7
Jap.	—	—	81.4	70.2	69.8	62.5	66.5	63.6	65.9	59.8
Austral.	—	—	86.4	85.7	86.1	81.5	82.5	81.3	79.8	76.9
NZ	—	—	—	—	—	—	—	—	—	—

Note: Central government consists of all departments, offices, organizations, and other bodies classified under general government which are agencies or instruments of the central authority of a country, except separately organized social security funds.

Sources: See Table 5.1.

TABLE 5.17. Central government: current receipts as a percentage of general government current receipts

	1950	1955	1960	1965	1970	1975	1980	1985	1990	1992
Aus.	47.3	56.2	54.8	52.9	52.8	49.0	47.8	50.5	52.2	52.4
Belg.	72.0	69.6	67.7	62.6	62.6	61.5	64.3	61.1	62.2	61.0
Den.	—	—	69.5	70.4	—	—	69.0	71.3	68.6	68.5
Fin.	—	—	67.5	66.0	64.4	58.9	60.4	59.5	62.6	49.5
Fr.	—	—	61.5	58.0	56.3	48.7	47.5	44.2	42.6	40.4
FRG	35.0	44.9	38.3	38.7	37.3	32.5	32.5	32.4	32.0	33.7
Gr.	67.9	68.0	64.3	61.0	60.1	63.4	59.4	55.4	64.1	62.3
Ice.	71.6	69.8	76.8	67.3	75.4	77.8	79.1	78.1	79.0	80.5
Ire.	81.4	81.1	82.0	83.8	83.4	81.7	85.3	85.6	82.6	82.7
It.	62.8	60.6	59.1	56.4	56.0	60.4	71.8	76.0	72.4	70.0
Lux.	67.7	61.6	59.4	55.6	58.1	58.7	57.0	60.5	—	—
Neth.	—	77.3	67.7	62.7	60.7	60.2	61.5	55.3	60.9	59.1
Norw.	75.5	73.2	75.5	75.6	80.3	81.3	91.7	64.4	60.6	59.9
Port.	72.8	71.0	74.2	73.9	72.4	66.3	70.0	71.5	—	66.8
Sp.	—	—	—	65.1	61.8	54.1	51.9	48.8	55.6	55.9
Sw.	76.1	67.0	65.6	59.2	56.9	56.7	48.8	52.6	52.0	41.7
Switz.	—	—	33.9	32.8	32.6	26.3	27.9	27.8	28.5	27.3
Turk.	—	—	—	77.3	76.5	—	—	—	—	—
UK	83.0	82.2	77.8	73.9	77.3	73.4	75.0	73.9	79.1	81.4
Can.	62.5	63.6	57.1	51.5	49.9	50.8	44.9	44.9	45.0	45.7
USA	64.6	63.0	56.9	53.3	47.7	41.7	44.4	43.6	42.7	41.1
Jap.	—	—	68.7	55.4	53.1	43.9	46.7	43.3	44.5	39.8
Austral.	—	—	79.9	78.0	79.0	77.2	77.8	80.2	73.8	71.5
NZ	—	—	—	—	—	—	—	—	—	—

Note: Central government consists of all departments, offices, organizations, and other bodies classified under general government which are agencies or instruments of the central authority of a country, except separately organized social security funds.

Sources: See Table 5.1.

TABLE 5.18. General government: social security contributions as a percentage of total tax revenue

	1955	1960	1965	1970	1975	1980	1985	1990
Aus.	23.8	24.2	24.9	25.4	27.7	31.3	31.8	32.9
Belg.	25.9	27.0	31.4	30.5	31.9	30.4	33.1	34.6
Den.	4.7	5.0	5.4	4.0	1.3	1.8	3.8	3.1
Fin.	7.9	6.8	2.9	4.8	8.3	8.2	9.1	7.4
Fr.	—	—	34.2	36.3	40.8	43.1	43.3	44.0
FRG	24.5	27.6	26.8	30.3	34.1	34.4	36.5	37.5
Gr.	—	—	26.9	27.1	27.2	33.6	35.7	28.4
Ice.	—	—	—	—	—	—	—	3.2
Ire.	4.6	4.9	6.5	8.2	13.8	14.3	14.8	14.6
It.	32.1	32.7	34.2	37.8	45.9	36.6	34.7	32.9
Lux.	—	—	32.3	28.6	30.3	29.2	25.5	27.7
Neth.	16.1	25.4	30.6	35.1	38.4	38.1	44.3	37.4
Norw.	4.5	8.8	12.0	16.1	24.9	21.0	20.6	26.2
Port.	17.2	18.3	21.9	23.9	34.6	29.5	26.0	27.5
Sp.	—	—	28.3	37.4	47.5	48.6	41.5	35.4
Sw.	2.1	4.3	12.1	14.9	19.5	28.6	24.8	27.6
Switz.	21.5	21.6	22.5	23.4	29.2	30.9	32.0	32.9
Turk.	5.3	7.1	5.9	6.3	9.5	5.6	14.3	19.7
UK	10.4	12.6	15.4	13.9	17.4	16.9	17.8	17.2
Can.	4.2	5.7	5.7	9.6	10.1	10.4	13.5	14.2
USA	11.0	14.4	16.4	19.3	24.5	26.1	29.4	29.5
Jap.	12.7	13.8	21.8	22.3	29.0	29.1	30.3	29.2
Austral.	0.0	0.0	0.0	0.0	0.0	0.0	0.0	0.0
NZ	22.4	20.5	0.0	0.0	0.0	0.0	0.0	0.0

Note: Social security contributions include all compulsory contributions as payments to institutions of general government providing for social security benefits. General government consists of all departments, offices, organizations, and other bodies which are agents or instruments of the central, state, or local public authorities.

Sources: OECD, *Revenue Statistics 1955—1983* (1984); OECD, *Revenue Statistics 1965—1992* (1993).

TABLE 5.19.   General government: property taxes as a percentage of total tax revenue

	1955	1960	1965	1970	1975	1980	1985	1990
Aus.	3.3	4.2	3.7	3.7	3.0	2.8	2.5	2.7
Belg.	3.9	▪ 4.1	3.7	3.0	2.4	2.4	1.7	2.6
Den.	10.1	10.7	8.0	6.0	5.9	5.7	4.3	4.2
Fin.	6.0	6.0	4.1	2.3	2.1	2.0	3.0	2.8
Fr.	—	—	4.3	3.5	3.4	3.6	4.5	5.3
FRG	9.8	7.1	5.8	4.9	3.9	3.3	3.0	3.4
Gr.	—	—	10.3	9.7	10.0	5.2	2.7	4.8
Ice.	—	—	—	—	—	—	—	8.5
Ire.	19.2	19.1	15.1	12.2	9.7	5.3	4.0	4.7
It.	8.1	7.9	7.2	6.0	3.3	3.9	2.5	2.3
Lux.	—	—	6.2	6.6	4.9	5.7	5.6	8.5
Neth.	7.0	5.6	4.9	3.3	2.6	3.9	3.5	3.6
Norw.	4.0	3.7	3.1	2.4	2.3	1.7	1.9	2.9
Port.	6.7	7.0	5.1	4.2	2.5	1.5	1.9	2.4
Sp.	—	—	6.4	6.5	6.3	4.6	2.8	5.5
Sw.	2.4	2.2	1.8	1.5	1.1	0.9	2.3	3.5
Switz.	8.9	8.5	8.8	8.8	7.1	7.3	8.2	7.8
Turk.	0.7	0.7	10.5	10.8	6.9	6.2	4.6	2.3
UK	12.9	15.2	14.5	12.4	12.7	12.0	12.0	8.8
Can.	11.3	15.6	13.2	13.0	9.4	9.1	9.4	9.2
USA	13.5	14.3	15.3	13.6	13.3	10.1	10.1	10.8
Jap.	9.9	9.3	8.1	7.6	9.1	8.2	9.7	9.0
Austral.	10.1	11.9	11.7	11.0	9.4	8.3	7.8	9.0
NZ	11.5	12.6	11.5	10.4	9.3	7.4	7.1	6.5

Note: Taxes on property cover current and non-recurrent taxes on the use, ownership, or transfer of property. General government consists of all departments, offices, organizations, and other bodies which are agents or instruments of the central, state, or local public authorities.

Sources: See Table 5.18.

TABLE 5.20.　General government: taxes on payroll and work-force as a percentage of total tax revenue

	1955	1960	1965	1970	1975	1980	1985	1990
Aus.	8.3	8.3	7.6	7.7	8.0	7.0	5.7	6.0
Belg.	0.0	0.0	0.0	0.0	0.0	0.0	0.0	0.0
Den.	0.0	0.0	0.0	0.0	0.0	0.0	0.8	0.6
Fin.	0.0	0.0	5.3	4.6	2.5	0.2	0.5	0.0
Fr.	—	—	4.6	1.2	1.9	2.1	2.1	1.9
FRG	0.8	0.7	0.6	0.6	0.8	0.2	0.0	0.0
Gr.	—	—	0.8	0.7	0.8	0.2	1.5	0.7
Ice.	—	—	—	—	—	—	—	3.6
Ire.	0.0	0.0	0.0	0.0	0.0	0.0	0.0	1.3
It.	0.0	0.0	0.0	0.0	0.0	0.6	0.6	0.3
Lux.	—	—	0.9	1.0	0.9	0.7	0.6	0.0
Neth.	4.0	0.0	0.0	0.0	0.0	0.0	0.0	0.0
Norw.	0.0	0.0	0.0	0.0	0.0	0.0	0.0	0.0
Port.	0.8	0.8	0.9	1.0	2.5	2.6	2.5	—
Sp.	—	—	0.0	0.0	0.0	0.0	0.0	0.0
Sw.	0.0	0.0	0.0	1.1	4.4	2.8	4.3	3.2
Switz.	0.0	0.0	0.0	0.0	0.0	0.0	0.0	0.0
Turk.	0.0	0.0	0.0	0.0	0.0	0.0	0.0	0.0
UK	0.0	0.0	0.0	4.4	0.0	4.2	0.1	0.0
Can.	0.0	0.0	0.0	0.0	0.0	0.0	0.0	0.0
USA	0.0	0.0	0.0	0.0	0.0	0.0	0.0	0.0
Jap.	0.0	0.0	0.0	0.0	0.0	0.0	0.0	0.0
Austral.	4.0	3.9	3.4	2.8	5.8	4.9	5.5	6.1
NZ	0.0	0.0	0.0	1.3	0.0	0.0	0.7	1.8

Note: Taxes on payroll and work-force cover taxes paid by employers, employees, or the self-employed either as a proportion of payroll or as a fixed amount per person, and which are not earmarked for social security expenditure. General government consists of all departments, offices, organizations, and other bodies which are agents or instruments of the central, state, or local public authorities.

Sources: See Table 5.18.

TABLE 5.21. General government: taxes on goods and services as a percentage of total tax revenue

	1955	1960	1965	1970	1975	1980	1985	1990
Aus.	38.9	38.8	37.4	37.4	34.5	31.3	32.6	31.5
Belg.	38.9	38.8	37.2	35.1	26.4	26.1	24.5	25.4
Den.	37.6	39.4	40.6	38.8	33.6	37.4	34.2	33.6
Fin.	43.4	46.1	43.6	40.5	34.7	40.3	36.2	37.3
Fr.	—	—	38.4	38.1	32.9	30.1	29.7	28.3
FRG	35.9	32.8	33.0	31.8	26.7	26.9	25.7	26.7
Gr.	—	—	52.2	50.2	48.3	40.1	42.6	45.7
Ice.	—	—	—	—	—	—	—	51.5
Ire.	52.4	54.8	52.6	52.4	46.5	43.7	44.4	42.3
It.	45.1	42.3	39.5	38.7	29.4	27.4	25.4	28.0
Lux.	—	—	24.8	20.5	20.8	19.8	23.9	23.5
Neth.	32.9	29.2	28.5	27.8	23.9	24.8	25.6	26.4
Norw.	44.5	42.8	41.0	42.8	37.6	35.4	37.5	35.4
Port.	40.7	39.3	44.2	44.6	40.8	44.9	42.6	43.8
Sp.	—	—	40.8	35.9	24.2	20.7	26.4	28.4
Sw.	28.6	32.3	31.2	28.2	24.4	24.0	26.4	24.6
Switz.	34.7	34.3	30.5	26.9	19.9	20.4	18.9	18.3
Turk.	59.1	53.0	54.0	49.4	41.3	29.2	36.0	27.9
UK	35.8	34.5	33.0	28.8	25.4	29.1	31.5	30.1
Can.	44.4	37.7	41.2	31.6	32.1	32.6	31.8	27.4
USA	22.1	21.5	21.9	19.2	18.5	16.7	17.8	16.5
Jap.	34.0	31.5	26.3	22.4	17.3	16.3	14.0	13.2
Austral.	36.9	37.0	34.5	32.0	29.0	30.9	32.4	27.7
NZ	32.2	31.3	27.9	27.2	24.2	22.4	23.2	33.7

Note: Taxes on goods and services cover all taxes and duties levied on the production, extraction, sale, transfer, leasing, or delivery of goods, and the rendering of services, or in respect of the use of goods or permission to use goods or to perform activities. General government consists of all departments, offices, organizations, and other bodies which are agents or instruments of the central, state, or local public authorities.

Sources: See Table 5.18.

TABLE 5.22. General government: social security contributions as a percentage of GDP

	1955	1960	1965	1970	1975	1980	1985	1990
Aus.	7.1	7.4	8.7	9.1	10.7	13.0	13.6	13.6
Belg.	6.2	7.2	9.8	10.7	13.3	13.6	15.3	15.5
Den.	1.1	1.3	1.6	1.6	0.6	0.8	1.6	1.5
Fin.	2.1	1.9	0.9	1.5	3.0	2.9	3.5	2.8
Fr.	—	—	11.9	12.7	15.3	18.3	18.9	19.3
FRG	7.6	8.6	8.5	10.0	12.3	13.0	14.0	13.8
Gr.	—	—	5.5	6.6	6.7	9.6	12.0	10.2
Ice.	—	—	—	—	—	—	—	1.0
Ire.	1.0	1.1	1.7	2.6	4.4	5.1	5.7	5.4
It.	9.8	11.3	9.3	9.1	13.3	12.2	12.4	12.9
Lux.	—	—	9.9	8.6	11.7	11.8	10.6	13.5
Neth.	4.2	7.6	10.3	13.2	16.7	17.4	19.3	16.7
Norw.	1.3	2.8	4.0	6.3	11.1	9.9	11.1	12.1
Port.	2.7	3.0	4.0	5.5	8.6	8.6	9.1	9.6
Sp.	—	—	4.2	6.4	9.3	11.7	11.9	12.2
Sw.	0.5	1.2	4.3	6.0	8.6	14.1	13.4	15.7
Switz.	4.1	4.6	4.7	5.6	8.6	9.5	10.3	10.4
Turk.	0.6	0.8	0.9	1.1	2.0	1.1	2.9	5.5
UK	3.1	3.6	4.7	5.2	6.2	6.1	7.0	6.3
Can.	0.9	1.4	1.5	3.0	3.3	3.4	4.5	5.3
USA	2.6	3.8	4.3	5.6	7.3	7.9	8.6	8.7
Jap.	2.2	2.5	4.0	4.4	6.1	7.5	8.6	9.2
Austral.	0.0	0.0	0.0	0.0	0.0	0.0	0.0	0.0
NZ	6.1	5.6	0.0	0.0	0.0	0.0	0.0	0.0

Note: Social security contributions include all compulsory contributions as payments to institutions of general government providing for social security benefits. General government consists of all departments, offices, organizations, and other bodies which are agents or instruments of the central, state, or local public authorities.

Sources: See Table 5.18.

TABLE 5.23. General government: social security expenditure as a percentage of GDP

	1960	1965	1970	1975	1980	1985
Aus.	15.4	17.7	18.6	20.2	22.4	25.2
Belg.	15.3	16.1	18.1	23.6	25.9	26.4
Den.	11.1	12.2	16.4	22.4	26.9	25.9
Fin.	8.8	10.6	12.8	16.1	18.6	22.1
Fr.	13.2	15.6	15.3	24.1	26.8	28.7
FRG	15.4	16.6	17.0	23.5	23.8	23.8
Gr.	—	9.2	10.8	10.8	12.2	19.5
Ice.	—	—	—	—	—	7.3
Ire.	9.3	10.3	11.6	19.7	21.7	2.8
It.	11.7	14.8	16.3	23.1	18.2	11.2*
Lux.	13.4	15.1	15.3	21.6	24.1	3.4
Neth.	11.1	15.5	20.0	26.8	28.6	29.1
Norw.	9.4	10.9	15.5	18.5	20.3	28.3*
Port.	5.3	5.3	5.7	11.0	10.1	10.1
Sp.	—	—	—	11.7	16.1	18.4
Sw.	10.9	13.6	18.8	26.2	32.0	30.7
Switz.	7.5	8.5	10.1	15.1	13.8	14.7
Turk.	1.4	1.7	3.2	3.5	4.3	3.9
UK	10.8	11.7	13.8	16.2	17.7	20.3
Can.	9.2	9.4	11.8	14.7	15.1	16.2
USA	6.8	7.1	9.6	13.2	12.7	12.6
Jap.	4.9	5.1	5.4	7.6	10.9	11.7
Austral.	7.7	8.3	8.0	10.7	12.1	10.0
NZ	13.1	11.5	11.5	12.5	14.4	18.0

* Not strictly comparable with previous years.

Note: Total social security expenditure includes expenditure on medical care, benefits in kind other than for medical care, and cash benefits. General government consists of all departments, offices, organizations, and other bodies which are agents or instruments of the central, state, or local public authorities.

Sources: 1960–1980: ILO (1985); 1983: ILO (1988); 1985: ILO (1992).

Comparative Tables

TABLE 5.24. General government: health expenditure as a percentage of total government expenditure

	1960	1965	1970	1975	1980	1990
Aus.	—	8.3	8.8	9.2	9.6	11.3
Belg.	8.7	9.1	9.6	9.8	9.7	12.5
Den.	—	—	12.7	12.5	10.4	9.0
Fin.	8.6	10.1	13.2	13.5	13.2	15.3
Fr.	7.4	9.5	11.3	12.8	13.4	13.2
FRG	10.0	9.7	11.4	13.9	14.0	12.9
Gr.	7.3	8.6	7.6	7.8	10.5	12.2
Ice.	—	—	—	—	—	19.2
Ire.	9.4	9.3	11.4	13.9	17.1	13.0
It.	10.7	12.1	14.3	13.9	14.2	11.8
Lux.	—	—	—	—	—	—
Neth.	4.4	8.6	12.5	11.7	11.4	11.0
Norw.	10.5	9.3	11.2	13.9	13.4	12.7
Port.	—	—	—	—	—	9.4
Sp.	—	—	—	—	—	11.6
Sw.	10.9	12.4	14.3	14.7	14.4	11.1
Switz.	—	—	15.2	16.6	—	15.7
Turk.	—	—	—	—	—	4.0
UK	10.2	10.2	10.4	11.0	11.7	12.2
Can.	8.1	10.5	14.2	14.0	13.7	14.8
USA	4.7	5.5	8.5	10.1	11.4	14.1
Jap.	7.8	14.5	15.2	15.1	15.4	15.0
Austral.	10.8	11.0	12.2	17.1	15.4	15.4
NZ	11.0	11.8	12.7	14.2	12.7	—

Note: Health expenditure includes expenditure on hospitals, clinics and medical, dental and paramedical practitioners, public health, medicaments, etc. By general government is meant central government, state or provincial government, local government, and social security funds. Total government expenditure includes current and capital outlays.

Source: 1960–80: OECD (1985*c*): annex C.; 1990: OECD, *OECD Health Systems* (1993).

TABLE 5.25.   General government: health expenditure as a percentage of GDP

	1960	1965	1970	1975	1980	1990
Aus.	2.9	3.0	3.4	4.1	4.5	5.6
Belg.	2.1	2.9	3.5	4.5	5.5	6.8
Den.	3.2	4.2	5.2	5.9	5.8	5.2
Fin.	2.3	3.2	4.1	4.9	5.0	6.3
Fr.	2.5	3.6	4.3	5.5	6.1	6.6
FRG	3.2	3.6	4.2	6.6	6.5	6.0
Gr.	1.7	2.2	2.2	2.5	3.5	4.1
Ice.	2.4	2.8	4.1	6.7	6.7	7.2
Ire.	3.0	3.3	4.3	6.3	8.1	5.2
It.	3.2	4.1	4.8	5.8	6.0	6.3
Lux.	—	—	—	5.6	6.6	6.6
Neth.	1.3	3.0	5.1	5.9	6.5	5.8
Norw.	2.6	3.2	4.6	6.4	6.7	7.1
Port.	0.9	1.2	1.9	3.8	4.2	4.1
Sp.	—	1.4	2.3	3.6	4.3	5.3
Sw.	3.4	4.5	6.2	7.2	8.8	6.9
Switz.	—	2.3	—	4.7	4.7	5.3
Turk.	—	1.2	1.3	—	1.1	1.4
UK	3.4	3.6	3.9	5.0	5.2	5.2
Can.	2.4	3.1	5.1	5.7	5.4	6.8
USA	1.3	1.6	2.8	3.7	4.1	5.2
Jap.	1.8	2.7	3.0	4.0	4.6	4.7
Austral.	2.4	2.8	3.2	5.6	4.7	5.6
NZ	3.3	3.4	3.5	4.3	4.7	5.8

Note: Public expenditure on health care equals current general government expenditure on health care. By general government is meant central government, state or provincial government, local government, and social security funds.

Source: See Table 5.24.

Comparative Tables

TABLE 5.26.   General government: total health expenditure as a percentage of GDP

	1960	1965	1970	1975	1980	1990
Aus.	4.4	4.7	5.3	6.4	7.0	8.4
Belg.	3.4	3.9	4.1	5.5	6.3	7.9
Den.	3.6	4.8	6.1	6.5	6.8	6.7
Fin.	4.2	4.9	5.6	5.8	6.3	7.8
Fr.	4.3	5.3	6.1	7.6	8.5	8.8
FRG	4.8	5.1	5.6	8.1	8.1	8.8
Gr.	2.9	3.1	3.9	4.0	4.2	4.9
Ice.	5.9	6.1	8.7	—	7.7	8.5
Ire.	4.0	4.4	5.6	7.7	8.7	7.6
It.	3.9	4.6	5.5	6.7	6.8	8.1
Lux.	—	—	4.9	5.9	6.6	7.0
Neth.	3.9	4.4	6.0	7.7	8.3	8.4
Norw.	3.3	3.9	5.0	6.7	6.8	8.0
Port.	—	—	—	6.4	6.1	6.1
Sp.	—	2.7	4.1	5.1	5.9	6.4
Sw.	4.7	5.6	7.2	8.0	9.5	8.6
Switz.	3.3	3.8	5.2	7.1	7.2	7.9
Turk.	—	—	—	—	—	3.8
UK	3.9	4.2	4.5	5.5	5.8	6.0
Can.	5.5	6.1	7.2	7.4	7.3	9.5
USA	5.3	6.1	7.6	8.6	9.5	12.2
Jap.	3.0	4.5	4.6	5.7	6.4	6.7
Austral.	5.1	5.3	5.7	7.6	7.4	8.3
NZ	4.4	—	4.5	5.2	5.7	7.1

Note: Total health expenditure equals current general government expenditure on health care and household final consumption on medical care and health expenses. By general government is meant central government, state or provincial government, local government, and social security funds.

Source: See Table 5.24.

TABLE 5.27. Central government: final consumption as a percentage of general government final consumption

	1950	1955	1960	1965	1970	1975	1980	1985	1990	1992
Aus.	52.6	46.4	49.0	47.2	46.2	37.3	35.4	37.3	29.0	34.5
Belg.	75.8	71.2	77.6	77.5	77.4	77.0	73.7	73.6	65.3	65.9
Den.	—	—	45.9	45.0	—	—	31.3	31.1	30.6	30.4
Fin.	—	—	43.8	44.2	40.3	35.8	33.0	30.5	29.8	32.4
Fr.	—	—	77.4	75.5	75.6	73.6	72.0	69.6	55.2	54.7
FRG	30.1	32.9	30.2	32.8	24.9	21.0	19.2	18.9	16.8	13.6
Gr.	83.4	84.7	79.0	76.2	77.7	82.0	74.3	71.0	67.7	67.0
Ice.	88.5	67.0	66.5	62.3	64.2	68.0	54.6	55.8	61.7	62.3
Ire.	56.7	55.4	57.6	58.3	50.8	49.1	46.2	49.3	50.2	50.7
It.	72.8	70.1	68.0	68.9	57.6	54.7	54.9	53.0	54.3	54.1
Lux.	73.0	71.6	70.7	69.1	68.7	67.5	66.0	65.8	—	—
Neth.	—	55.2	46.7	42.2	47.5	45.1	45.0	46.4	46.2	45.3
Norw.	56.1	56.2	51.4	49.2	46.4	42.4	39.9	37.4	39.2	38.4
Port.	86.8	88.6	87.3	89.8	88.0	79.0	86.7	87.6	—	—
Sp.	—	—	—	77.4	77.6	70.8	67.7	50.5	39.5	36.7
Sw.	58.9	52.9	45.4	49.1	37.4	33.9	29.9	26.1	27.3	28.0
Switz.	—	—	27.3	27.7	27.8	23.1	23.4	24.6	23.0	20.0
Turk.	—	—	—	85.5	82.5	—	—	—	—	—
UK	70.7	71.8	67.2	63.0	59.3	56.4	59.1	61.0	60.1	61.4
Can.	50.1	60.7	46.2	38.7	27.3	24.9	23.5	25.0	22.6	21.4
USA	52.4	63.7	58.0	53.6	51.4	42.9	42.3	47.4	43.7	42.9
Jap.	—	—	42.7	39.7	27.5	23.7	24.1	24.4	24.3	23.7
Austral.	—	—	45.5	50.3	46.7	35.7	33.8	32.9	31.6	32.3
NZ	—	—	—	—	—	—	—	—	—	—

Note: Central government consists of all departments, offices, organizations, and other bodies classified under general government which are agencies or instruments of the central authority of a country, except separately organized social security funds.

Sources: See Table 5.1.

TABLE 5.28. Central government: current disbursements as a percentage of general government current disbursements

	1950	1955	1960	1965	1970	1975	1980	1985	1990	1992
Aus.	58.2	55.0	55.2	55.2	56.4	55.8	51.6	54.9	54.9	54.7
Belg.	73.6	70.9	72.0	65.3	64.3	64.4	65.9	67.1	65.6	65.2
Den.	—	—	66.4	68.6	—	—	74.2	74.6	71.4	71.8
Fin.	—	—	66.6	67.1	60.1	60.7	62.2	59.5	61.2	56.5
Fr.	—	—	60.2	55.3	54.9	50.6	48.3	47.8	44.0	43.9
FRG	36.1	43.5	38.4	39.6	35.1	33.5	33.0	32.5	34.4	33.9
Gr.	82.1	71.8	66.2	65.6	63.8	72.8	66.6	60.9	73.0	70.9
Ice.	67.1	70.5	75.8	69.8	77.5	87.9	82.2	81.0	83.3	83.8
Ire.	82.0	80.4	82.6	83.3	81.8	81.9	85.2	86.2	81.3	82.3
It.	64.8	62.1	56.2	56.1	55.2	55.9	76.1	81.7	76.8	76.6
Lux.	69.8	62.5	60.0	56.6	57.3	56.1	55.4	58.8	—	—
Neth.	—	78.7	65.9	59.7	58.6	58.8	61.0	57.3	62.8	61.7
Norw.	75.4	75.0	76.9	77.6	83.5	82.6	93.0	87.3	56.0	58.1
Port.	78.1	77.8	77.4	77.9	79.3	69.6	72.8	77.4	—	68.4
Sp.	—	—	—	60.0	60.6	51.1	51.9	53.0	57.2	55.3
Sw.	76.1	70.6	62.2	64.7	61.6	60.8	57.7	58.9	52.8	52.2
Switz.	—	—	28.0	27.0	32.3	26.9	29.8	29.4	28.9	27.0
Turk.	—	—	—	90.1	80.7	—	—	—	—	—
UK	84.8	81.3	78.2	72.4	72.6	76.1	75.5	74.6	78.3	80.7
Can.	61.9	68.2	60.1	54.2	52.8	55.5	52.5	53.5	50.2	48.1
USA	61.4	65.5	60.1	57.9	54.5	48.9	48.8	52.3	50.4	49.6
Jap.	—	—	43.6	39.9	62.0	56.3	59.4	55.6	53.0	52.3
Austral.	—	—	80.9	79.5	79.3	82.5	80.3	77.6	74.9	71.5
NZ	—	—	—	—	—	—	—	—	—	—

Note: Central government consists of all departments, offices, organizations, and other bodies classified under general government which are agencies or instruments of the central authority of a country, except separately organized social security funds.

Sources: See Table 5.1.

TABLE 5.29. Central government: current disbursements minus transfers to other levels of general government as a percentage of general government current disbursements

	1950	1955	1960	1965	1970	1975	1980	1985	1990	1992
Aus.	55.6	50.6	49.5	46.3	46.1	40.8	40.4	41.7	41.1	41.5
Belg.	59.0	56.5	56.3	51.6	50.4	47.3	47.5	50.3	52.2	52.3
Den.	—	—	38.9	41.1	—	—	32.9	41.0	39.1	38.6
Fin.	—	—	54.0	53.6	44.9	44.0	43.4	39.2	39.8	34.5
Fr.	—	—	56.0	50.6	48.1	43.7	40.6	40.5	40.1	39.9
FRG	30.5	33.0	24.4	26.8	26.2	24.0	23.7	24.4	26.5	26.1
Gr.	78.8	67.9	61.8	57.8	54.8	64.1	57.9	52.1	56.8	57.4
Ice.	60.2	62.5	61.9	55.0	46.9	56.6	54.2	55.1	60.2	62.1
Ire.	67.9	65.1	66.3	65.2	63.3	60.2	59.4	62.1	62.4	61.5
It.	58.3	53.8	48.4	43.8	44.3	40.6	44.6	46.8	48.2	49.1
Lux.	54.9	51.5	47.3	44.6	44.2	45.0	44.3	46.4	—	—
Neth.	—	51.1	35.6	29.2	31.0	29.4	29.6	29.8	36.3	35.9
Norw.	65.6	63.7	69.6	69.5	74.4	74.0	68.2	65.0	36.1	37.1
Port.	77.5	77.4	76.8	77.8	78.9	65.7	68.6	71.0	—	64.3
Sp.	—	—	—	58.9	57.6	48.3	45.1	39.0	34.2	31.9
Sw.	69.0	62.5	43.4	43.7	47.4	43.9	44.4	45.6	41.9	43.1
Switz.	—	—	25.1	22.5	20.5	16.2	17.4	17.6	17.0	15.7
Turk.	—	—	—	80.9	76.6	—	—	—	—	—
UK	72.9	70.6	65.2	58.1	55.5	55.4	58.5	59.8	59.7	59.0
Can.	54.8	61.2	50.0	43.9	40.6	43.0	41.1	42.9	41.2	39.3
USA	57.3	62.2	55.0	51.5	44.7	37.0	37.3	44.3	41.7	39.7
Jap.	—	—	—	—	28.4	24.0	27.9	28.2	24.8	23.7
Austral.	—	—	59.2	59.3	56.6	54.9	54.3	56.6	55.5	53.3
NZ	—	—	—	—	—	—	—	—	—	—

Note: Central government consists of all departments, offices, organizations, and other bodies classified under general government which are agencies or instruments of the central authority of a country, except separately organized social security funds.

Sources: See Table 5.1.

TABLE 5.30. General government: expenditure by function as a percentage of GDP 1975–1990

	Defence			Education			Health		
	1975	1980	1990	1975	1980	1990	1975	1980	1990
Aus.	1.1	1.1	1.0	3.5	3.9	4.0	4.1	4.4	4.6
Belg.	2.7	2.8	—	—	—	—	—	—	—
Den.	2.5	2.5	2.0	—	6.0	5.4	5.5	5.5	4.8
Fin.	1.4	1.4	1.4	4.8	4.9	5.2	3.7	3.9	4.7
Fr.	3.2	3.3	2.9	4.9	5.1	4.6	0.4	0.5	3.0
FRG	3.1	2.7	2.2	4.0	4.1	3.5	6.1	5.9	5.6
Gr.	6.8	5.8	5.9	1.9	2.2	2.8	1.1	1.7	2.3
Ice.	—	0.0	0.0	—	3.6	3.8	—	5.4	6.8
Ire.	—	—	—	—	—	—	—	—	—
It.	1.9	1.9	1.9	4.0	4.9	4.9	3.4	3.6	3.5
Lux.	—	—	—	—	—	—	—	—	—
Neth.	3.1	3.0	—	—	—	—	—	—	—
Norw.	3.2	2.8	3.3	5.4	5.0	5.4	3.6	4.0	4.7
Port.	4.8	2.9	2.6	5.5	3.4	3.9	4.2	2.6	3.3
Sp.	1.7	—	1.8	1.3	—	2.8	1.2	—	3.4
Sw.	3.3	3.1	2.6	5.2	—	5.2	5.8	7.3	6.5
Switz.	—	—	—	—	—	—	—	—	—
Turk.	3.5[a]	—	—	3.5[a]	—	—	1.4[a]	—	—
UK	4.9	4.9	4.0	5.2	4.3	3.7	4.7	4.8	4.7
Can.	—	—	—	—	—	—	—	—	—
USA	5.7	5.3	—	5.2	4.6	—	1.2	1.0	0.21
Jap.	0.9	0.9	0.9	3.9	3.7	3.2	0.4	0.4	0.4
Austral.	2.2	2.5	2.1	4.7	4.7	3.9	3.1	4.7	3.2
NZ	—	—	—	—	—	—	—	—	—

[a] Figure for 1972.

Note: General government consists of all departments, offices, organizations, and other bodies which are agents or instruments of the central, state, or local public authorities. Expenditure refers to final consumption expenditure.

Sources: OECD, *National Accounts 1964–1981* (1983); OECD, *National Accounts 1973–1985* (1987); OECD, *National Accounts 1979–91* (1993).

TABLE 5.31.   General government: total social expenditure as a percentage of total government expenditure

	1960	1965	1970	1975	1980
Aus.	—	53.9	56.5	55.4	57.3
Belg.	57.4	65.3	68.2	76.2	72.8
Den.	—	—	63.3	68.1	61.9
Fin.	58.2	57.0	63.9	63.8	66.4
Fr.	—	—	—	56.0	61.4
FRG	65.3	63.4	63.2	68.8	66.1
Gr.	36.2	38.9	38.8	34.1	40.0
Ice.	—	—	—	—	—
Ire.	36.4	38.5	45.1	49.7	52.3
It.	56.4	60.0	64.2	62.5	63.7
Lux.	—	—	—	—	—
Neth.	54.2	65.3	71.7	73.6	62.5
Norw.	44.3	46.2	55.0	56.3	55.8
Port.	—	—	—	—	—
Sp.	—	—	—	—	—
Sw.	49.3	51.3	52.9	54.7	53.2
Switz.	—	—	59.3	65.8	—
Turk.	—	—	—	—	—
UK	42.0	46.0	48.9	49.2	49.6
Can.	41.5	46.5	52.3	53.6	52.6
USA	38.7	43.3	47.5	57.8	58.5
Jap.	47.1	50.7	47.9	53.9	56.2
Austral.	44.9	42.4	44.3	57.9	60.8
NZ	43.8	44.8	46.7	53.1	51.2

Notes: By general government is meant central government, state or provincial government, local government, and social security funds. Total government expenditure includes current and capital outlays. Total social expenditure includes expenditure on education, health, pensions, unemployment compensation, and other social expenditure such as sickness, maternity, or temporary disablement benefits.

Source: OECD (1985c): annex C.

TABLE 5.32.   General government: total social expenditure as a percentage of GDP

	1960	1965	1970	1975	1980
Aus.	17.9	19.7	21.6	24.5	27.1
Belg.	17.6	21.4	25.3	34.5	38.2
Den.	—	—	26.2	32.4	33.3
Fin.	15.4	17.7	19.9	23.3	25.4
Fr.	—	—	—	24.2	28.3
FRG	20.5	22.4	23.5	32.6	30.8
Gr.	8.5	10.1	10.9	10.6	13.4
Ice.	—	—	—	—	—
Ire.	11.7	13.9	17.1	23.1	25.7
It.	16.8	20.1	21.4	26.0	26.9
Lux.	—	—	—	—	—
Neth.	16.2	23.0	29.1	37.1	35.6
Norw.	11.7	15.8	22.5	26.2	27.2
Port.	—	—	—	—	—
Sp.	—	—	—	—	—
Sw.	15.4	18.6	23.0	26.8	32.5
Switz.	8.0	10.3	12.6	19.1	20.0
Turk.	—	—	—	—	—
UK	13.8	16.2	18.5	22.4	22.0
Can.	12.1	13.6	18.7	21.8	21.0
USA	10.9	12.3	15.7	20.8	20.7
Jap.	8.0	9.4	9.3	14.2	16.9
Austral.	10.2	11.0	11.5	18.8	18.6
NZ	13.0	12.7	12.7	16.3	19.4

Notes: By general government is meant central government, state or provincial government, local government, and social security funds. Total social expenditure includes expenditure on education, health, pensions, unemployment compensation, and other social expenditure such as sickness, maternity, or temporary disablement benefits.

Source: OECD (1985c): annex C.

TABLE 5.33. General government: educational expenditure as a percentage of total government expenditure

	1960	1965	1970	1975	1980	1991
Aus.	—	6.1	7.0	7.9	8.0	10.8
Belg.	14.6	16.2	16.2	17.2	15.2	9.5
Den.	—	—	17.1	17.1	14.3	10.4
Fin.	24.9	21.2	20.3	18.1	16.1	14.7
Fr.	—	—	—	13.5	12.4	10.6
FRG	7.6	9.8	10.8	11.4	11.0	8.0
Gr.	6.9	7.3	6.7	6.2	7.1	—
Ice.	—	—	—	—	—	—
Ire.	9.3	11.9	13.7	13.0	13.2	—
It.	12.5	11.9	13.4	11.9	13.3	—
Lux.	—	—	—	—	—	—
Neth.	15.1	16.7	16.4	15.0	12.7	9.8
Norw.	14.6	16.6	15.6	14.5	12.8	12.1
Port.	—	—	—	—	—	—
Sp.	—	—	—	—	—	—
Sw.	14.7	14.9	14.3	11.5	10.7	10.4
Switz.	—	—	19.5	19.1	—	15.9
Turk.	—	—	—	—	—	—
UK	11.0	12.8	14.0	14.9	12.7	12.5
Can.	10.3	15.9	19.3	15.7	15.1	13.8
USA	12.8	15.7	16.0	17.6	16.1	14.7
Jap.	23.3	21.1	18.5	18.6	16.5	11.4
Austral.	12.3	13.3	16.0	18.9	19.0	12.6
NZ	9.0	11.1	12.8	14.7	11.1	—

Note: By general government is meant central government, state or provincial government, local government, and social security funds. Total government expenditure includes current and capital outlays. Education includes expenditure on pre-primary, primary, secondary, tertiary, education affairs and services, and subsidiary services to education. The 1991 figures are not directly comparable with previous years.

Sources: 1960–1980: OECD (1985*c*): annex C; 1991: OECD, *Education at a Glance: OECD indicators* (1993).

TABLE 5.34. General government: educational expenditure as a percentage of GDP

	1960	1965	1970	1975	1980	1991
Aus.	2.0	2.2	2.7	3.5	3.8	—
Belg.	4.5	5.3	6.0	7.8	8.0	—
Den.	—	—	7.1	8.1	7.7	6.1
Fin.	6.6	6.6	6.3	6.6	6.2	6.6
Fr.	—	—	—	5.8	5.7	6.0
FRG	2.4	3.5	4.0	5.4	5.1	5.4
Gr.	1.6	1.9	1.9	1.9	2.4	—
Ice.	—	—	—	—	—	—
Ire.	3.0	4.3	5.2	6.1	6.5	5.9
It.	3.7	4.0	4.5	5.0	5.6	—
Lux.	—	—	—	—	—	—
Neth.	4.5	5.9	6.7	7.6	7.2	5.8
Norw.	3.9	5.7	6.4	6.7	6.3	—
Port.	—	—	—	—	—	—
Sp.	—	—	—	—	—	5.6
Sw.	4.6	5.4	6.2	5.6	6.5	6.5
Switz.	3.1	3.5	4.1	5.6	5.5	—
Turk.	—	—	—	—	—	—
UK	3.6	4.5	5.3	6.8	5.6	—
Can.	3.0	4.7	6.9	6.4	6.0	7.4
USA	3.6	4.5	5.3	6.3	5.7	7.0
Jap.	4.0	3.9	3.6	4.9	5.0	5.0
Austral.	2.8	3.5	4.2	6.2	5.8	5.5
NZ	2.7	3.1	3.5	4.5	4.2	—

Note: By general government is meant central government, state or provincial government, local government, and social security funds. Education includes expenditure on pre-primary, primary, secondary, tertiary, education affairs and services, and subsidiary services to education.

Sources: The 1991 figures are not directly comparable with previous years. See Table 5.33.

TABLE 5.35. Central government: expenditure by function as a percentage of total expenditure, 1990

	Defence	Education	Health	Social security	Housing	Economic	Other services
Aus.	2.6	9.3	12.9	45.4	2.7	9.8	17.4
Belg.	4.7	12.3	1.7	42.3	2.3	9.9	26.6
Den.	5.0	9.7	1.1	38.6	1.5	8.0	36.1
Fin.	4.7	14.8	11.2	34.6	1.9	19.0	13.7
Fr.	6.4	7.0	16.0	44.0	1.1	5.0	20.5
FRG	8.3	0.6	18.1	48.5	0.4	8.7	15.4
Gr.	—	—	—	—	—	—	—
Ice.	0.0	12.4	23.3	20.7	0.7	20.7	22.2
Ire.	3.3	12.2	13.0	26.7	2.4	12.8	29.4
It.	3.3	7.6	9.9	36.0	1.2	12.4	29.6
Lux.	2.2	9.8	2.4	47.9	4.2	16.1	17.4
Neth.	5.1	10.9	11.8	37.8	4.1	7.4	23.0
Norw.	7.8	9.2	10.1	37.3	1.2	17.1	17.2
Port.	5.2	11.9	8.0	27.1	0.8	10.4	36.6
Sp.	5.4	5.6	13.7	37.0	0.6	11.0	26.6
Sw.	6.2	8.5	0.9	50.3	4.3	7.4	22.4
Switz.	10.2	3.1	13.1	49.7	0.6	12.2	11.1
Turk.	11.7	19.2	3.6	2.1	1.5	17.8	44.2
UK	12.2	2.8	13.3	31.6	3.1	7.2	29.8
Can.	7.3	2.9	5.1	34.6	1.3	11.1	37.8
USA	22.6	1.7	13.5	25.6	2.6	10.2	23.7
Jap.	—	—	—	—	—	—	—
Austral.	8.5	6.8	12.7	28.2	1.8	7.1	34.9
NZ	4.3	13.3	11.8	36.1	1.3	8.0	25.2

Note: The central government covers all government departments, offices, establishments, and other bodies that are agencies or instruments of the central authority of a country and includes decentralized agencies, departmental enterprises, and relevant non-profit institutions attached to the central authority. Also included are social security funds, if operating nationally. Total expenditure by function comprises current expenditure and capital expenditure. Defence comprises expenditure intended mainly for military purposes. Education comprises provision, management, inspection, and support of pre-primary, primary, and secondary schools, universities and colleges, and technical, vocational, and other training institutions. Health comprises expenditures on hospitals, medical and dental centres, and clinics with a major medical component; provision of national health and medical insurance schemes. Social security and welfare comprise expenditures to compensate for temporary loss of income of the sick and temporarily disabled; to cover payments to the elderly, the permanently disabled, and the unemployed. Housing and community amenities comprise expenditure on housing, such as income-related schemes. Economic services comprise expenditure for: agriculture; industry; electricity, gas, and water; transport and communications; other economic services such as tourism, etc. 'Other' comprises expenditure on the general administration of government, etc.

Source: IMF (1993) Government Finance Statistics Yearbook.

TABLE 5.36.   General government: military expenditure as a percentage of GDP

	1950	1955	1960	1965	1970	1975	1980	1985	1990
Aus.	0.7	0.2	1.2	1.2	1.1	1.2	1.2	1.3	1.0
Belg.	—	3.8	3.6	3.2	2.9	3.1	3.3	3.0	2.4
Den.	1.7	3.2	2.7	2.8	2.4	2.4	2.4	2.2	2.0
Fin.	1.8	1.6	1.7	1.7	1.4	1.4	1.9	2.0	1.8
Fr.	5.5	6.4	6.5	5.2	4.2	3.8	4.0	4.0	3.6
FRG	4.4	4.1	4.0	4.3	3.3	3.6	3.3	3.2	2.8
Gr.	6.0	5.1	4.9	3.5	4.8	6.5	5.7	7.0	5.9
Ice.	—	—	—	—	—	—	—	—	—
Ire.	1.3	1.6	1.6	1.4	1.3	1.8	1.9	1.6	1.3
It.	4.3	3.7	3.3	3.3	2.7	2.5	2.1	2.3	2.1
Lux.	1.3	3.2	1.0	1.4	0.8	1.0	1.0	1.1	1.1
Neth.	4.8	5.7	4.1	4.0	3.5	3.4	3.1	3.1	2.7
Norw.	2.4	3.9	2.9	3.4	3.5	3.2	2.9	3.1	3.2
Port.	3.8	4.2	4.2	6.2	7.1	5.3	3.5	3.2	3.1
Sp.	—	2.2	2.2	1.8	1.6	1.7	3.1	3.3	1.8
Sw.	3.5	4.5	4.0	4.1	3.6	3.4	2.9	2.5	2.4
Switz.	2.6	2.8	2.5	2.7	2.2	2.0	1.9	1.9	1.6
Turk.	6.2	5.6	5.1	5.0	4.3	4.6	4.9	4.9	4.9
UK	6.6	8.2	6.5	5.9	4.8	5.0	4.9	5.3	3.9
Can.	2.6	6.3	4.2	2.9	2.4	1.9	1.8	2.1	2.0
USA	5.1	10.2	9.0	7.6	8.0	6.0	5.4	6.6	5.6
Jap.	—	1.8	1.1	0.9	0.8	0.9	0.9	1.0	1.0
Austral.	3.0	3.8	2.7	3.4	3.5	2.8	2.6	2.8	2.3
NZ	1.5	2.5	2.1	2.1	1.9	1.7	1.9	2.0	2.0

Note: General government consists of all departments, offices, organizations, and other bodies which are agents or instruments of the central, state, or local public authorities.

Sources: SIPRI (1980): Table 1A.4; SIPRI (1988): Table 6A.3; SIPRI (1992) Table 7A.3.

TABLE 5.37.   General government: official development assistance as a
percentage of donor GNP

	1960	1965	1970	1975	1980	1985	1990
Aus.	—	0.11	0.14	0.11	0.24	0.37	0.25
Belg.	0.88	0.63	0.47	0.68	0.49	0.52	0.45
Den.	0.09	0.13	0.47	0.76	0.82	0.91	0.93
Fin.	—	0.02	0.08	0.23	0.24	0.44	0.64
Fr.	1.35	0.76	0.62	0.66	0.64	0.71	0.79
FRG	0.31	0.40	0.35	0.41	0.43	0.42	0.42
Gr.	—	—	—	—	—	—	—
Ice.	—	—	—	—	—	—	—
Ire.	—	0.00	0.00	0.11	0.19	0.22	0.16
It.	0.22	0.08	0.13	0.09	0.16	0.26	0.32
Lux.	—	—	—	—	—	—	—
Neth.	0.31	0.36	0.62	0.84	0.99	0.85	0.94
Norw.	0.11	0.16	0.47	0.89	1.12	1.12	1.17
Port.	—	—	—	—	—	—	—
Sp.	—	—	—	—	—	—	—
Sw.	0.05	0.18	0.43	0.98	0.92	0.87	0.90
Switz.	0.04	0.09	0.15	0.23	0.24	0.29	0.31
Turk.	—	—	—	—	—	—	—
UK	0.56	0.48	0.40	0.42	0.39	0.31	0.27
Can.	0.19	0.19	0.44	0.58	0.41	0.46	0.44
USA	0.53	0.57	0.31	0.26	0.26	0.23	0.21
Jap.	0.24	0.28	0.23	0.24	0.31	0.29	0.31
Austral.	0.37	0.50	0.56	0.60	0.47	0.46	0.34
NZ	—	0.00	0.06	0.51	0.35	0.23	0.23

Note: General government consists of of all departments, offices, organizations, and other bodies which are agents or instruments of the central, state, or local public authorities.

Sources: World Bank, *World Development Report* (1984): Table 18; World Bank, *World Development Report* (1988): Table 21; World Bank, *World Development Report* (1993): Table 19.

TABLE 5.38. General government: total tax revenues as a percentage of GDP

	1955	1960	1965	1970	1975	1980	1985	1990
Aus.	30.0	30.6	34.7	35.7	38.7	41.3	42.9	41.3
Belg.	24.0	26.5	31.2	35.8	41.8	44.7	46.6	44.9
Den.	23.4	25.4	29.9	40.4	41.4	45.5	48.7	48.5
Fin.	26.8	27.7	30.1	32.2	36.2	35.3	36.8	37.9
Fr.	—	—	35.0	35.6	37.4	42.5	44.5	43.8
FRG	30.8	31.3	31.6	32.9	36.0	37.8	37.9	36.8
Gr.	—	—	20.6	24.3	24.6	28.6	35.2	36.1
Ice.	—	—	—	—	—	—	—	32.3
Ire.	22.5	21.9	26.0	31.2	32.1	35.9	39.0	36.8
It.	30.5	34.4	27.3	27.9	29.0	33.2	34.7	39.1
Lux.	—	—	30.5	30.3	38.5	40.4	42.9	48.8
Neth.	26.3	30.1	33.7	37.9	43.6	45.7	45.1	44.6
Norw.	28.3	31.2	33.2	39.2	44.8	47.1	47.4	46.3
Port.	15.4	16.3	18.5	23.1	24.8	29.3	31.5	34.8
Sp.	—	—	14.7	17.2	19.6	24.1	28.8	34.4
Sw.	25.5	27.2	35.8	40.2	43.9	49.4	50.6	56.9
Switz.	19.2	21.3	20.7	23.8	29.6	30.8	32.0	31.5
Turk.	11.9	11.5	15.0	17.7	20.7	19.0	19.7	27.8
UK	29.8	28.5	30.6	37.3	35.7	36.0	38.1	36.7
Can.	21.7	24.2	25.9	32.0	32.9	32.7	32.9	37.0
USA	23.6	26.5	26.3	29.8	29.6	30.4	29.2	29.5
Jap.	17.1	18.2	18.4	19.7	21.0	25.9	28.0	31.4
Austral.	22.5	23.4	24.3	25.3	29.0	30.3	30.8	30.8
NZ	27.0	27.4	25.0	26.9	29.6	31.0	33.8	37.3

Note: Total tax revenues include taxes on income, profits, and capital gains; social security contributions; taxes on payroll and work-force; taxes on property; taxes on goods and services; and other taxes. General government consists of all departments, offices, organizations, and other bodies which are agents or instruments of the central, state, or local public authorities.

Sources: See Table 5.18.

TABLE 5.39. General government: taxes on income and profits as a percentage of total tax revenue

	1955	1960	1965	1970	1975	1980	1985	1990
Aus.	23.8	23.5	25.7	25.2	26.2	26.7	26.4	25.5
Belg.	31.1	29.9	27.6	31.4	39.3	41.0	40.6	37.3
Den.	47.5	44.8	45.9	51.2	59.0	55.0	56.8	58.3
Fin.	42.8	41.1	44.0	47.6	52.3	49.1	51.0	52.3
Fr.	—	—	15.9	18.3	17.6	18.0	17.6	17.2
FRG	22.0	31.9	33.8	32.3	34.5	35.3	34.8	32.4
Gr.	—	—	9.8	12.3	13.7	19.3	17.4	20.4
Ice.	—	—	—	—	—	—	—	29.3
Ire.	23.8	21.3	25.7	27.1	30.0	36.5	34.5	36.9
It.	12.7	15.7	17.8	17.4	21.5	32.1	36.8	36.5
Lux.	—	—	35.8	43.3	43.1	44.6	44.5	40.3
Neth.	39.6	39.4	35.6	33.4	34.8	32.9	26.4	32.2
Norw.	46.5	44.2	43.5	38.4	34.4	41.3	39.3	34.7
Port.	27.7	27.8	24.6	23.7	17.4	19.7	25.9	25.7
Sp.	—	—	24.5	20.2	22.0	26.0	28.0	30.6
Sw.	66.9	61.3	54.9	54.2	50.5	43.5	42.0	41.0
Switz.	34.9	35.5	38.2	40.8	43.8	41.4	40.9	41.0
Turk.	34.9	39.3	29.6	33.4	42.3	59.1	37.0	33.5
UK	40.6	37.5	36.8	40.4	44.4	37.7	38.7	39.6
Can.	39.2	39.6	39.3	44.6	47.5	46.6	44.1	47.9
USA	53.4	49.9	46.3	47.9	43.8	47.1	42.8	43.2
Jap.	43.0	45.1	43.9	47.7	44.6	46.1	45.8	48.3
Austral.	49.0	47.3	50.4	54.3	55.9	55.9	54.3	57.2
NZ	33.9	35.7	60.5	61.1	66.5	70.2	69.0	58.1

Note: Taxes on income, profits, and capital gains cover taxes levied on the net income or profits of individuals and enterprises. Also covered are taxes levied on the capital gains of individuals and enterprises, and gains from gambling. General government consists of all departments, offices, organizations, and other bodies which are agents or instruments of the central, state, or local public authorities.

Sources: See Table 5.18.

TABLE 5.40. General government: deficit as a percentage of GDP

	1950	1955	1960	1965	1970	1975	1980	1985	1990	1992
Aus.	6.7	6.5	6.0	7.3	6.6	4.3	3.3	2.5	1.9	2.0
Belg.	−1.3	0.1	−1.2	0.8	2.2	−0.7	−4.9	−5.8	−4.0	−4.8
Den.	3.7	4.3	5.8	5.5	7.1	2.6	−0.0	0.3	−0.6	−1.3
Fin.	10.6	9.5	9.7	7.8	6.0	6.6	3.5	2.8	3.4	−3.7
Fr.	5.9	3.2	3.8	4.8	4.3	1.1	2.5	−0.9	0.7	−2.4
FRG	3.3	7.8	7.7	5.8	5.8	−0.7	1.8	2.0	0.6	0.8
Gr.	−4.1	1.9	2.5	2.1	4.4	0.7	0.1	−10.5	−15.4	−8.8
Ice.	7.7	6.9	13.1	8.5	10.1	7.2	7.1	5.1	3.2	3.0
Ire.	0.5	0.4	0.1	0.4	1.1	−6.7	−6.7	−6.1	−1.6	−1.6
It.	0.3	1.6	3.2	0.7	0.2	−7.1	−4.0	−6.6	−6.5	−7.9
Lux.	9.2	3.1	7.0	5.6	6.4	7.6	5.7	5.2	—	—
Neth.	9.1	3.4	5.4	3.8	4.3	2.1	0.8	−0.8	−2.1	−1.5
Norw.	7.7	6.4	6.5	5.8	7.0	7.8	8.9	12.1	0.0	−2.4
Port.	3.7	3.2	2.3	2.6	4.8	−2.5	−2.3	−3.5	−1.8	—
Sp.	—	—	4.4	3.5	3.8	3.1	0.6	−1.5	1.1	−0.4
Sw.	2.7	6.3	6.3	10.2	9.9	5.8	−0.4	−1.4	5.3	−5.1
Switz.	6.1	5.5	6.4	4.1	5.2	3.3	3.6	3.5	3.2	−0.4
Turk.	—	—	—	4.4	7.2	—	—	—	—	—
UK	3.4	1.6	0.3	2.3	7.6	−0.3	−1.4	−1.2	1.3	−4.1
Can.	4.9	2.6	1.5	4.3	3.0	0.1	−0.5	−5.0	−2.7	−5.9
USA	4.0	2.5	2.5	2.1	0.0	−3.1	−0.7	−4.2	−3.2	−5.0
Jap.	7.3	4.4	7.1	6.1	6.7	3.2	2.6	4.3	8.4	7.8
Austral.	—	—	6.5	6.7	5.9	3.4	3.0	−1.8	0.5	−3.8
NZ	—	—	—	—	—	—	—	—	—	—

Note: The deficit is current receipts minus current disbursements. General government consists of all departments, offices, organizations, and other bodies which are agents or instruments of the central, state, or local public authorities.

Sources: See Table 5.1.

TABLE 5.41. Central government: deficit as a percentage of GDP

	1950	1955	1960	1965	1970	1975	1980	1985	1990	1992
Aus.	0.9	4.0	3.2	3.2	2.3	−0.5	−0.0	−0.7	−0.2	−0.1
Belg.	−1.3	−0.2	−2.0	−0.3	0.8	−1.6	−3.9	−6.7	−4.3	−5.2
Den.	—	—	4.7	4.3	6.0	0.2	−2.7	−1.7	−2.0	−2.8
Fin.	—	—	6.8	4.8	5.1	3.3	1.5	1.7	2.6	−5.8
Fr.	—	—	2.8	3.7	2.9	−0.2	0.9	−2.2	−0.4	−2.7
FRG	0.8	3.9	2.9	2.0	2.9	−0.6	0.4	0.6	−0.9	0.1
Gr.	−5.6	0.7	1.3	0.3	1.8	−2.1	−2.1	−8.3	−14.3	−9.7
Ice.	6.4	4.7	10.3	5.2	7.2	2.8	4.8	3.2	1.2	1.2
Ire.	0.3	0.5	−0.1	0.5	1.5	−5.6	−5.6	−5.5	−0.8	−1.1
It.	−0.2	0.6	2.7	0.5	0.4	−2.6	−4.7	−7.5	−6.8	−9.0
Lux.	5.8	1.7	4.0	2.8	4.0	5.6	4.0	4.0	—	—
Neth.	—	2.3	4.1	3.4	3.5	2.0	0.7	−1.6	−2.3	−2.3
Norw.	5.8	4.3	4.5	3.8	4.5	5.9	7.6	−2.3	2.6	−0.4
Port.	1.8	1.2	1.2	1.2	2.1	−2.5	−2.6	−4.8	—	—
Sp.	—	—	—	3.1	2.6	2.3	0.3	−2.2	0.0	0.0
Sw.	2.1	3.3	5.1	4.2	3.9	1.5	−5.3	−4.5	2.3	−8.9
Switz.	—	—	3.3	2.6	1.7	0.7	0.5	0.5	0.8	0.0
Turk.	—	—	—	1.4	4.8	—	—	—	—	—
UK	2.3	1.6	0.1	2.1	7.4	−1.3	−1.3	−1.2	1.4	−3.1
Can.	3.2	0.6	0.0	1.5	0.6	−1.7	−3.1	−6.0	−3.6	−3.9
USA	3.2	1.0	0.6	−0.1	−2.0	−3.7	−1.8	−4.9	−4.1	−5.2
Jap.	—	—	8.3	5.7	2.3	−1.2	−2.0	−1.5	1.5	−0.1
Austral.	—	—	5.0	4.1	4.6	1.2	1.6	−0.5	0.0	−2.7
NZ	—	—	—	—	—	—	—	—	—	—

Note: The deficit is current receipts minus current disbursements. Central government consists of all departments, offices, organizations, and other bodies classified under general government which are agencies or instruments of the central authority of a country, except separately organized social security funds.

Sources: See Table 5.1.

TABLE 5.42.   General government debt as a percentage of nominal GDP: gross and net debt

	Gross Debt				Net Debt			
	1980	1985	1990	1995*	1980	1985	1990	1995*
Aus.	37.2	49.6	56.4	59.2	—	—	—	—
Belg.	79.9	122.3	130.7	144.8	69.3	111.9	119.4	132.2
Den.	33.5	64.1	59.5	72.1	1.8	34.4	26.5	39.1
Fin.	13.9	19.0	16.6	70.9	−6.1	0.9	−8.1	14.0
Fr.	37.3	45.5	46.6	66.3	14.3	22.9	25.0	44.7
FRG	32.8	42.5	43.5	60.0	12.8	21.8	22.8	41.3
Gr.	27.7	57.9	89.0	108.5	—	—	—	—
Ice.	—	—	—	—	—	—	—	—
Ire.	72.5	104.3	98.7	87.0	—	—	—	—
It.	59.0	84.3	100.5	118.0	53.9	81.9	99.0	116.7
Lux.	—	—	—	—	—	—	—	—
Neth.	44.8	67.9	76.5	82.8	24.4	41.5	55.9	62.0
Norw.	52.2	40.7	39.2	54.2	0.4	−16.0	−21.4	−6.4
Port.	37.5	66.5	66.6	71.4	—	—	—	—
Sp.	18.3	48.8	46.8	66.0	6.1	27.6	31.6	50.6
Sw.	44.3	67.6	44.2	91.2	−11.6	15.6	−5.6	41.4
Switz.	—	—	—	—	—	—	—	—
Turk.	—	—	—	—	—	—	—	—
UK	54.1	52.7	34.7	56.4	47.0	45.8	28.5	51.0
Can.	44.6	65.0	71.6	90.7	12.3	33.0	43.3	62.5
USA	37.7	48.1	55.4	64.1	18.8	27.1	32.8	39.8
Jap.	52.0	68.7	69.8	72.4	17.3	26.7	9.6	10.1
Austral.	25.5	11.6	—	41.3	—	—	11.6	27.4
NZ	—	—	—	—	—	—	—	—

* Estimate

Note: Gross debt of general government refers to debt and other short- and long-term liabilities of central, local, and social service sectors. Net debt is gross debt minus the financial assets of general government including cash, bank deposits, loans to the private sector, participations in private sector companies, holdings in public corporations, and foreign exchange reserves.

Source: OECD, *OECD Economic Outlook* (1995).

Section 6: Government Structures

Comparative Tables

TABLE 6.1. Chamber systems: 1990s

	Upper house	Seats	Period of office (years)	Lower house	Seats	Period of office (years)
Aus.	Bundesrat	63	5/6	Nationalrat	183	4
Belg.	Sénat	182	4	Chambre des représentants	212	4
Den.				Folketing	179	4
Fin.				Eduskunta	200	4
Fr.	Sénat	321	9	Assemblée nationale	577	5
GER	Bundesrat	69	Varies	Bundestag	662	4
Gr.				Vouli	300	4
Ice.				Alpingi	63	4
Ire.	Seanad	60	5	Dáil	166	5
It.	Senato	315	5	Camera dei deputati	630	5
Lux.				Chambre des députés	60	5
Neth.	Eerste Kamer	75	4	Tweede Kamer	150	4
Norw.				Storting	165	4
Port.				Assembleia da Republica	230	4
Sp.	Senado	251	4	Congreso de diputados	350	4
Sw.				Riksdag	349	4
Switz.	Stünderat	46	4	Nationalrat	200	4
Turk.				Büyük Millet Meclisi	450	5
UK	House of Lords	1121	Life	House of Commons	651	5 (max.)
Can.	Senate	110	Until retirement	House of Commons	195	5
USA	Senate	100	6	House of representatives	435	2
Jap.	House of councillors	252	6	House of representatives	511	4
Austral.	Senate	76	6	House of representatives	148	3
NZ				House of representatives	99	3

Sources: Mackie and Rose (1982); *Interparliamentary Union* (1986); *Encyclopaedia Britannica* (1994).

TABLE 6.2. Electoral systems: formal properties

Main Elected Assembly	General Type	Single or Two-tier districting	Electoral formula	Main assembly size	Number of districts	Legal threshold (%)
Aus. Nationalrat	PR list	2	H = d'Hondt L = LR-Hare*	185	9	SR (R)
Belg. Chambredes Représentants	PR list	2	H = d'Hondt L = LR-Hare	212	30	SR (R)
Den. Folketing	PR list	2	H = LR-Hare L = Modified Sainte-Lague	179	18	2
Fin. Eduskunta	PR list	1	d'Hondt	200	15	—
Fr. Assemblée nationale	2 ballot	1	Majority-plurality	577	577	25 (1st ballot) - (2nd ballot)
FRG Bundestag	PR Single-member and list	2	H = LR-Hare L = plurality	662	331	5 (N)
Gr. Vouli	PR list	2	H = LR-Hare L = LR-Droop*	300	56	—
Ice. Alpingi	PR list	2	H = d'Hondt L = d'Hondt	63	9	SR (N)
Ire. Dáil	PR	1	STV	166	41	—
It. Camera di deputati	PR list	2	H = LR-Hare L = LR-Hare*	630	32	—
Lux. Chambre des députés	PR list	1	d'Hondt	60	4	—
Neth. Tweede Kamer	PR list	1	d'Hondt	150	1	—
Norw. Storting	PR list	2	H = Modified Sainte-Lague L = Modified Sainte-Lague	165	20	4 (N)
Port. Assembleia da Republica	PR list	1	d'Hondt	230	20	—
Sp. Congreso de diputados	PR list	1	d'Hondt	350	60	—

Table 6.2. *(Contd.)*

Main Elected Assembly	General Type	Single or Two-tier districting	Electoral formula	Main assembly size	Number of districts	Legal threshold (%)
Sw.	Riksdag	PR list	2	d'Hondt	349	29	4 (N)
Switz.	Nationalrat	PR list	1	d'Hondt	200	26	—
UK	House of Commons	Majoritarian	1	Plurality	651	651	—
Can.	House of Commons	Majoritarian	1	Plurality	295	295	—
USA	House of Representatives	Majoritarian	1	Plurality	435	435	—
Jap.	House of Representatives	Semi-PR	1	SNTV	512	130	—
Austral.	House of Representatives	Majoritarian	1	Alternative vote	148	148	—
NZ	House of Representatives	Majoritarian	1	Plurality	99	99	—

Note: Abbreviations: PR = proportional representation; H = higher (districts); L = lower (districts); LR = largest remainders; SNTV = single non-transferable vote; STV = single transferable vote; SR = special rules; N = national; R = regional; N/A = not available. Two-tier districting, or complex districting, uses a higher electoral level made up of larger electoral districts to reduce the disproportional effects of lower and smaller electoral districts. In two-tier electoral systems the more decisive electoral formula is marked with an asterisk.

Legal threshold refers to the minimal electoral support necessary to gain representation.—signifies no threshold.

Italy—1979–1983 system.

Sources: Lijphart, (1994): 17–41; Gallagher, *et al.*, (1992): 149; *Europa World Yearbook* (1994).

TABLE 6.3. Electoral systems: operational properties

	Years	Effective threshold (%)	Disproportionality
Aus.	1971–1990	2.6	1.4
Belg.	1946–1987	4.8	6.2
Den.	1964–1988	2.0	7.5
Fin.	1945–1987	5.4	2.9
Fr.	1988	11.7	11.8
FRG	1987	5.0	1.9
Gr.	1989–1990	3.3	4.1
Ice.	1959–1987	5.8	2.9
Ire.	1948–1989	17.2	10.8
It.	1958–1987	2.0	1.1
Lux.	1945–1989	11.3	13.2
Neth.	1956–1989	1.0	4.8
Norw.	1989	4.0	3.7
Port.	1975–1987	3.0	4.2
Sp.	1977–1989	1.2	5.4
Sw.	1970–1988	4.0	1.7
Switz.	1947–1987	8.5	2.4
Turk.	N/A	—	—
UK	1945–1987	35.0*	19.5
Can.	1945–1988	35.0*	11.3
USA	1946–1990	35.0*	5.4
Jap.	1947–1990	16.4	5.8
Austral.	1984–1990	35.0*	10.2
NZ	1946–1990	35.0*	10.7

Note: The table shows the actual or operational properties of the most recent electoral systems up to 1990 for national lower-house elections, or in the case of the unicameral systems, the one chamber.

Effective thresholds are estimates of the midpoint between no representation and full representation. Falling below the effective threshold entails being substantially underrepresented, but not necessarily unrepresented.

Disproportionality is defined as the difference between the seat shares and votes shares of the parties. It is measured by means of the Gallagher least-square index of disproportionality. The higher the index the less proportional the electoral system.

Source: Lijphart (1994).

TABLE 6.4. Elections: male and female suffrage and current voting age

	Completion of		Current voting age
	male suffrage	female suffrage	
Aus.	1907	1918	19
Belg.	1893	1948	18
Den.	1901	1915	18
Fin.	1906	1906	18
Fr.	1848	1944	18
FRG	1869	1919	18
Gr.	1877	1952	20
Ice.	1915	1915	20
Ire.	1918	1918	18
It.	1912	1945	18
Lux.	1919	1919	18
Neth.	1917	1919	18
Norw.	1897	1913	18
Port.	1911	1931	18
Sp.	1869	1931	18
Sw.	1909	1921	18
Switz.	1919	1971	18
Turk.	1923	1934	20
UK	1918	1918	18
Can.	1917	1918	18
USA	1870	1920	18
Jap.	1925	1945	20
Austral.	1901	1901	18
NZ	1879	1893	18

Sources: Nohlen (1978); 37; UN, *The World's Women 1970–1990* (1991).

TABLE 6.5. Constitutional development: dates of
independence and current constitutions

	Date of independence	Date of current constitution
Aus.	1918	1920
Belg.	1830	1993
Den.	c.800	1953
Fin.	1917	1919
Fr.	843	1958
FRG	1955	1949
Gr.	1830	1975
Ice.	1944	1944
Ire.	1921	1937
It.	1861	1948
Lux.	1867	1868
Neth.	1814	1983
Norw.	1905	1814
Port.	c.1140	1976
Sp.	1492	1978
Sw.	c.836	1975
Switz.	1499	1874
Turk.	1923	1982
UK	1066	[1688]
Can.	1867	1982
USA	1776	1789
Jap.	c.660 *BC*	1947
Austral.	1901	1900
NZ	1907	1852

Source: *Encyclopaedia Britannica* (1994).

TABLE 6.6. Human rights, freedom, and democracy

| | Human rights (1) | | | Freedom (2) | | | | Democracy | | | | | |
| | | | | | | | | Bollen (3) | | | Vanhanen (4) | | |
	1980	1985	1990	1975	1980	1985	1990	1960	1965	1980	1950—9	1960—9	1970—9
Aus.	92	96	95	2	2	2	2	97.2	97.1	100	34.7	33.5	30.8
Belg.	92	96	96	2	2	2	2	99.7	99.9	100	32.0	34.2	38.0
Den.	96	98	98	2	2	2	2	99.9	99.9	100	29.7	33.6	40.3
Fin.	96	98	99	4	4	4	2	97.3	97.3	94	28.0	28.6	19.4
Fr.	88	94	94	3	3	3	3	89.7	90.8	100	28.8	17.1	33.4
FRG	91	97	98	2	3	3	3	88.0	88.6	89	31.6	30.7	32.8
Gr.	80	94	87	4	4	4	3	88.0	82.8	94	17.4	13.4	10.3
Ice.	—	—	—	2	2	2	2	100.0	100.0	100	—	—	—
Ire.	86	87	94	3	2	2	2	94.8	97.2	100	24.0	23.1	24.2
It.	88	87	90	3	4	2	2	97.0	96.8	100	32.9	36.5	38.4
Lux.	—	—	—	3	2	2	2	100.0	97.7	100	—	—	—
Neth.	94	98	98	2	2	2	2	99.9	99.7	100	35.9	37.1	39.8
Norw.	95	97	97	2	2	2	2	99.9	99.9	100	28.1	29.0	32.9
Port.	86	93	92	8	4	3	2	41.6	39.0	94	0.4	0.7	4.6
Sp.	78	86	87	10	4	3	2	10.7	10.4	83	0.0	0.0	3.0
Sw.	94	98	98	2	2	2	2	99.9	99.9	100	29.1	29.6	35.9

Switz.	92	95	96	2	2	2	99.6	99.7	100	14.7	12.9	22.3
Turk.	43	40	44	5	5	6	59.1	76.4	11	17.7	14.8	18.1
UK	95	94	93	2	2	3	99.3	99.1	100	28.0	26.9	30.0
Can.	94	96	94	2	2	2	99.9	99.5	100	20.9	22.9	24.4
USA	92	90	90	2	2	2	94.6	92.4	100	16.7	17.5	17.6
Jap.	92	88	82	3	3	3	99.3	99.8	100	22.8	20.2	26.5
Austral.	93	94	91	2	2	2	100.0	99.9	100	27.9	27.8	30.1
NZ	96	96	98	2	2	2	100.0	100.0	100	27.2	25.5	27.5

Note: (1) This index represents a rating of human rights; the higher the index, the higher the standard of human rights. (2) This index of freedom summarizes ratings on political rights and civil liberties; the higher the index, the lower the level of freedom. (3) This index of democracy incorporates measures of press freedom, freedom of group opposition, government sanctions, fairness of elections, executive selection, and legislature selection; the higher the index, the higher the level of democracy. (4) This index of democracy incorporates measures of competition multiplied with measures of participation; the higher the index, the higher the level of democracy.

Sources: (1) Humana (1983; 1986; 1992); (2) Gastil (1987) and Freedom House (1992); (3) Bollen (1980, 1993); (4) Vanhanen (1984).

TABLE 6.7. Structure of government: levels and number of units in the 1990s

Aus.	Land (9); Gemeinde (2 301)
Belg.	Communauté (3); Provins (9); Arrondissement (44); Commune (589)
Den.	Amt (14); Kommuni (273)
Fin.	Lääni (12); Kommuni (455)
Fr.	Région (22); Départment (96); Arrondissement (325); Canton (3 714); Commune (33 394)
Gr.	Nomos (52); Demos (5 922)
Ger.	Land (16); Gemeinde (16 000)
Ice.	Region (8); Syslur (23); Hreppur (196)
Ire.	Province (4); Country/Corporation (38); District/Board (75)
It.	Regione (20); Provincia (94); Commune (8 066)
Lux.	Commune (118)
Neth.	Provins (12); Gemeente (647)
Norw.	Fylke (19); Kommune (439)
Port.	Region/Distrito (20); Concelho (305); Freguesia (4 050)
Sp.	Communidad Autonoma (17); Provincia (50); Municipio (8 056)
Sw.	Län (24); Kommun (286)
Switz.	Kanton (26); Kommune (3 029)
Turk.	Il (67); İlçe; Bucak
UK	England and Wales: County (53); District (369); Parishes/Communities (10 000/1 000) Scotland: Regions (9); Island Areas (3); Districts (53)
Can.	Province (12); Municipality (3 217)
USA	State (50); County (2 992); Municipality (78 200)
Jap.	Todofuken (47); Municipality (900)
Austral.	State (6); Municipality (900)
NZ.	Region (22); County/Municipality (224)

Source: *The Statesman's Year-Book, 1989–90* (1989); Norton (1994).

TABLE 6.8. Elected governments, 1945–1994

	Number of governments	Average duration (months)	Parliamentary support (average)	Number of parties in government (average)	Average government duration (%)
Aus.	19	32.6	75.8	1.8	68.0
Belg.	32	17.7	61.6	3.1	36.5
Den.	30	20.0	40.9	2.0	41.8
Fin.	42	13.5	56.2	2.9	28.0
Fr.	47	12.3	59.0	4.1	20.5
Ger.	18	31.8	58.3	2.2	66.1
Gr.	41	11.6	62.7	1.1	24.1
Ice.	22	25.5	55.5	2.3	53.1
Ire.	21	30.2	51.2	1.6	60.9
It.	48	12.1	52.5	2.8	19.8
Lux.	13	43.2	68.2	2.0	70.8
Neth.	20	30.1	61.0	3.3	60.2
Norw.	24	25.0	46.9	1.7	52.2
Port.	15	14.2	60.0	1.6	29.2
Sp.	7	31.5	49.9	1.0	65.8
Sw.	24	25.7	47.3	1.5	64.3
Switz.	13	44.0	79.3	3.8	91.7
Turk.	30	19.9	63.8	1.7	40.1
UK	19	30.6	54.5	1.0	50.9
Can.	20	29.9	55.1	1.0	49.9
USA	15	40.6	49.6	1.0	84.6
Jap.	38	15.9	51.9	1.3	35.6
Austral.	27	22.4	58.5	1.6	62.0
NZ	22	28.5	57.4	1.0	78.5

Note: A government is identified by means of its Prime Minister or President (USA) and the participating parties. If there is a change in either of these there is a new government. A change of government always follows an election, i.e. a government cannot stay longer than an election period. Parliamentary support refers to the support (in percentage of total seats) each government has had in the lower chambers of its parliament; number of parties in government refers to the number of parties participating in government; average government duration refers to the months a government holds office as a percentage of an estimated maximum period of government. Greece did not hold democratic elections between 1967 and 1974. Portugal did not hold democratic elections in the post-war period until 1975. Spain did not hold democratic elections in the post-war period until 1977.

Sources: Paloheimo (1984); *The Europa Year Book* (various years); *Keesing's Contemporary Archives* (various years); newspaper reports for the most recent elections.

TABLE 6.9. Elected governments formed in the 1940s

	Number of governments	Average duration (months)	Parliamentary support (average)	Number of parties in government (average)	Average government duration (%)
Aus.	3	29.3	95.0	2.3	61.0
Belg.	5	10.2	57.0	2.2	21.2
Den.	2	29.0	35.8	1.0	60.5
Fin.	3	19.7	64.8	3.3	41.0
Fr.	10	5.1	64.0	4.5	8.6
Ger.	1	49.0	51.7	3.0	100.0
Gr.	6	6.7	74.6	2.0	14.0
Ice.	3	15.0	64.1	2.3	31.3
Ire.	2	42.5	50.4	3.0	88.5
It.	4	10.5	69.4	3.8	12.5
Lux.	1	52.0	65.4	2.0	87.0
Neth.	2	35.0	68.5	3.0	72.0
Norw.	2	36.0	53.7	1.0	75.0
Port.	—	—	—	—	—
Sp.	—	—	—	—	—
Sw.	3	24.7	49.6	1.0	51.3
Switz.	1	48.0	85.0	4.0	100.0
Turk.	3	19.0	84.9	1.0	39.7
UK	1	55.0	61.4	1.0	92.0
Can.	3	32.0	58.6	1.0	53.7
USA	2	44.5	53.5	1.0	92.5
Jap.	5	9.4	42.9	1.2	21.2
Austral.	3	23.3	61.7	1.3	63.7
NZ	3	31.0	54.6	1.0	83.3

Note: A government is identified by means of its Prime Minister and the participating parties. If there is a change in either of these there is a new government. A change of government always follows an election, i.e. a government cannot stay longer than an election period. Parliamentary support refers to the support (in percentage of total seats) each government had in the lower chambers of its parliament; number of parties in government refers to the number of parties participating in government; average government duration refers to the months a government holds office as a percentage of an estimated maximum period of government. See notes to Table 6.8.

Sources: Paloheimo (1984): *The Europa Year Book* (various years); *Keesing's Contemporary Archives* (various years).

TABLE 6.10. Elected governments formed in the 1950s

	Number of governments	Average duration (months)	Parliamentary support (average)	Number of parties in government (average)	Average government duration (%)
Aus.	3	32.0	92.9	2.0	66.7
Belg.	6	21.5	52.2	1.3	44.2
Den.	6	18.8	43.0	1.7	39.0
Fin.	15	10.5	49.4	2.5	18.7
Fr.	17	8.6	55.0	5.5	14.3
Ger.	2	49.0	63.1	3.0	100.0
Gr.	12	10.7	52.9	1.1	22.1
Ice.	6	27.3	47.6	1.8	56.8
Ire.	4	31.0	50.9	1.5	64.5
It.	10	12.0	48.9	1.8	20.0
Lux.	5	28.6	74.6	2.0	46.2
Neth.	4	32.5	70.0	3.8	66.0
Norw.	4	30.0	52.8	1.0	62.5
Port.	—	—	—	—	—
Sp.	—	—	—	—	—
Sw.	5	21.6	53.8	1.6	45.0
Switz.	4	36.0	74.5	3.5	75.0
Turk.	3	40.0	82.2	1.0	70.3
UK	6	25.3	53.5	1.0	42.2
Can.	3	31.3	61.8	1.0	52.3
USA	2	48.0	44.7	1.0	100.0
Jap.	9	13.6	48.3	1.0	30.9
Austral.	4	31.8	58.6	2.0	88.3
NZ	4	27.5	56.6	1.0	75.0

Note: A government is identified by means of its prime minister and the participating parties. If there is a change in either of these there is a new government. A change of government always follows an election, i.e. a government cannot stay longer than an election period. Parliamentary support refers to the support (in percentage of total seats) each government had in the lower chambers of its parliament; number of parties in government refers to the number of parties participating in government; average government duration refers to the months a government holds office as a percentage of an estimated maximum period of government. See notes to Table 6.8.

Source: See Table 6.9.

TABLE 6.11. Elected governments formed in the 1960s

	Number of governments	Average duration (months)	Parliamentary support (average)	Number of parties in government (average)	Average government duration (%)
Aus.	4	27.0	84.8	1.8	56.3
Belg.	4	32.0	67.7	2.0	65.3
Den.	6	22.5	48.5	2.0	47.0
Fin.	6	17.7	58.4	3.0	37.0
Fr.	5	24.2	66.9	2.6	40.4
FRG	5	26.6	64.9	2.0	55.4
Gr.	12	5.7	61.0	0.6	11.7
Ice.	2	40.0	53.3	2.0	83.5
Ire.	4	34.0	50.2	1.0	71.3
It.	8	15.0	48.4	1.9	25.1
Lux.	2	60.0	67.0	2.0	96.0
Neth.	4	24.0	58.0	3.3	48.5
Norw.	5	22.6	50.4	2.8	47.0
Port.	—	—	—	—	—
Sp.	—	—	—	—	—
Sw.	4	30.0	51.2	1.0	75.0
Switz.	2	48.0	85.0	4.0	100.0
Turk.	7	18.7	58.0	1.8	39.1
UK	3	26.7	55.3	1.0	44.3
Can.	5	25.2	50.0	1.0	42.0
USA	4	36.0	56.2	1.0	75.0
Jap.	6	24.0	60.4	1.0	50.8
Austral.	7	17.6	60.0	2.0	48.7
NZ	4	33.8	55.6	1.0	93.8

Note: A government is identified by means of its Prime Minister and the participating parties. If there is a change in either of these there is a new government. A change of government always follows an election, i.e. a government cannot stay longer than an election period. Parliamentary support refers to the support (in percentage of total seats) each government had in the lower chambers of its parliament; number of parties in government refers to the number of parties participating in government; average government duration refers to the months a government holds office as a percentage of an estimated maximum period of government.

Source: See Table 6.8.

TABLE 6.12. Elected government formed in the 1970s

	Number of governments	Average duration (months)	Parliamentary support (average)	Number of parties in government (average)	Average government duration (%)
Aus.	4	39.2	50.7	1.0	82.0
Belg.	7	13.6	66.6	4.3	28.1
Den.	7	17.4	36.1	1.1	36.3
Fin.	12	11.7	58.4	2.9	24.3
Fr.	5	21.2	59.3	3.4	35.4
FRG	3	31.7	53.5	2.0	66.7
Gr.	4	17.5	73.8	1.0	36.3
Ice.	5	23.0	52.0	2.2	47.8
Ire.	3	33.0	54.8	1.3	66.0
It.	12	10.3	50.1	2.7	17.0
Lux.	2	60.5	60.4	2.0	100.0
Neth.	4	30.5	55.4	4.3	59.8
Norw.	5	23.8	41.9	1.4	49.6
Port.	8	7.3	70.3	1.3	15.1
Sp.	2	21.5	47.6	1.0	45.0
Sw.	5	25.4	40.8	1.8	70.6
Switz.	3	48.0	83.3	4.0	100.0
Turk.	10	11.4	57.1	2.3	23.8
UK	5	31.4	50.7	1.0	52.4
Can.	3	30.0	47.6	1.0	50.0
USA	3	32.0	47.6	1.0	66.7
Jap.	6	18.0	52.6	1.0	41.0
Austral.	6	19.3	57.9	1.7	53.7
NZ	5	23.6	59.7	1.0	65.6

Note: A government is identified by means of its Prime Minister and the participating parties. If there is a change in either of these there is a new government. A change of government always follows an election, i.e. a government cannot stay longer than an election period. Parliamentary support refers to the support (in percentage of total seats) each government had in the lower chambers of its parliament; number of parties in government refers to the number of parties participating in government; average government duration refers to the months a government holds office as a percentage of an estimated maximum period of government.

Source: See Table 6.9.

Comparative Tables

TABLE 6.13. Elected governments formed in the 1980s

	Number of governments	Average duration (months)	Parliamentary support (average)	Number of parties in government (average)	Average government duration (%)
Aus.	3	30.3	64.8	2.0	63.3
Belg.	7	20.0	65.7	4.4	41.6
Den.	6	18.0	37.8	3.0	37.7
Fin.	4	25.8	60.6	3.8	53.5
Fr.	7	17.1	55.7	2.9	28.6
FRG	4	29.5	55.2	2.0	61.5
Gr.	5	23.6	65.0	1.6	49.0
Ice.	5	26.4	64.1	3.0	55.0
Ire.	5	25.4	49.5	1.6	48.8
It.	10	13.0	54.3	4.0	21.6
Lux.	2	60.0	65.3	2.0	100.0
Neth.	5	30.4	57.6	2.2	60.4
Norw.	6	19.7	44.6	2.0	41.0
Port.	6	23.5	53.4	2.2	48.0
Sp.	4	36.5	52.2	1.0	76.3
Sw.	5	25.0	42.5	1.2	69.4
Switz.	2	48.0	77.6	4.0	100.0
Turk.	4	32.5	60.9	1.0	67.8
UK	2	44.5	59.5	1.0	74.0
Can.	4	39.5	59.2	1.0	65.8
USA	3	48.0	40.6	1.0	100.0
Jap.	7	16.4	56.4	1.0	37.4
Austral.	4	28.3	58.2	1.3	78.5
NZ	4	26.8	57.8	1.0	73.8

Note: A government is identified by means of its Prime Minister and the participating parties. If there is a change in either of these there is a new government. A change of government always follows an election, i.e. a government cannot stay longer than an election period. Parliamentary support refers to the support (in percentage of total seats) each government had in the lower chambers of its parliament; number of parties in government refers to the number of parties participating in government; average government duration refers to the months a government holds office as a percentage of an estimated maximum period of government.

Sources: See Table 6.9.

TABLE 6.14. Elected governments formed in the 1990s.

	Number of governments	Average duration (months)	Parliamentary support (average)	Number of parties in government (average)	Average government duration (%)
Aus.	2	47.0	70.5	2.0	98.0
Belg.	3	3.0	58.8	4.0	6.0
Den.	3	22.5	42.5	3.0	44.7
Fin.	2	8.0	59.3	3.5	17.0
Fr.	3	11.0	58.9	2.0	18.0
FRG	3	24.0	55.1	2.0	50.0
Gr.	2	40.0	53.9	1.0	83.0
Ice.	1	—	56.9	2.0	—
Ire.	3	17.0	52.6	2.0	28.0
It.	4	12.0	56.0	4.0	20.0
Lux.	1	6.0	63.3	2.0	10.0
Neth.	1	—	61.3	3.0	—
Norw.	2	34.0	39.4	1.0	71.0
Port.	1	—	58.4	1.0	—
Sp.	1	—	45.4	1.0	—
Sw.	2	36.0	47.4	2.5	100.0
Switz.	1	—	73.0	4.0	—
Turk.	3	12.0	61.0	1.7	25.0
UK	2	17.0	57.1	1.0	28.0
Can.	2	5.0	56.1	1.0	8.0
USA	1	—	58.9	1.0	—
Jap.	5	13.0	49.9	3.4	29.8
Austral.	3	16.5	53.3	1.0	46.0
NZ	2	36.0	59.8	1.0	100.0

Note: A government is identified by means of its Prime Minister and the participating parties. If there is a change in either of these there is a new government. A change of government always follows an election, i.e. a government cannot stay longer than an election period. Parliamentary support refers to the support (in percentage of total seats) each government had in the lower chambers of its parliament; number of parties in government refers to the number of parties participating in government; average government duration refers to the months a government holds office as a percentage of an estimated maximum period of government.

Sources: Paloheimo (1984); *The Europa Year Book* (various years); *Keesing's Contemporary Archives* (various years); newspaper reports for the most recent elections.

TABLE 6.15. Elected governments formed 1980 to 1994

	umber of governments	Average duration (months)	Parliamentary support (average)	Number of parties in government (average)	Average government duration (%)
Aus.	5	34.5	67.0	2.0	72.0
Belg.	10	16.2	63.6	4.3	33.7
Den.	9	19.1	39.3	3.0	40.0
Fin.	6	22.2	60.2	3.7	46.2
Fr.	10	15.8	56.7	2.6	26.2
FRG	7	27.7	55.1	2.0	57.7
Gr.	7	26.3	61.9	1.4	54.7
Ice.	6	26.4	62.9	2.8	55.0
Ire.	8	23.0	50.7	1.8	42.9
It.	14	12.8	54.8	4.0	21.2
Lux.	3	41.7	64.6	2.0	70.0
Neth.	6	30.8	58.3	2.3	60.4
Norw.	8	21.7	43.3	1.8	45.3
Port.	7	23.5	54.1	2.0	48.0
Sp.	5	36.5	50.8	1.0	76.3
Sw.	7	27.0	43.9	1.6	74.5
Switz.	3	48.0	76.0	4.0	100.0
Turk.	7	25.7	61.0	1.3	53.5
UK	4	35.3	58.3	1.0	58.7
Can.	6	32.6	58.2	1.0	54.2
USA	4	48.0	45.2	1.0	100.0
Jap.	12	15.2	53.7	2.0	34.6
Austral.	7	24.3	56.1	1.1	67.7
NZ	6	28.6	58.4	1.0	79.0

Note: A government is identified by means of its Prime Minister and the participating parties. If there is a change in either of these there is a new government. A change of government always follows an election, i.e. a government cannot stay longer than an election period. Parliamentary support refers to the support (in percentage of total seats) each government had in the lower chambers of its parliament; number of parties in government refers to the number of parties participating in government; average government duration refers to the months a government holds office as a percentage of an estimated maximum period of government.

Sources: Paloheimo (1984); *The Europa Year Book* (various years); *Keesing's Contemporary Archives* (various years); newspaper reports for the most recent elections.

TABLE 6.16. Government formation and dissolution 1990–1994

	PM	Begins	Ends	Duration (months)	Parlia-mentary support	No. of parties in govern-ment	Duration
Aus.	VRANITZKY	01–87	12–90	47	85.8	2	98
	VRANITZKY	12–90	11–94	47	76.5	2	98
	VRANITZKY	11–94	—	—	64.5	2	—
Belg.	MARTENS	06–88	09–91	39	70.8	5	81
	MARTENS	09–91	11–91	2	63.3	4	4
	MARTENS	11–91	03–92	4	56.6	4	8
	DEHAENE	03–92	—	—	56.6	4	—
Den.	SCHLÜTER	12–89	12–90	12	32.6	2	25
	SCHLÜTER	12–90	01–93	25	33.7	2	52
	RASMUSSEN	01–93	09–94	20	50.9	4	42
	RASMUSSEN	09–94	—	—	42.9	3	—
Fin.	HOLKERI	04–87	08–90	40	65.5	4	83
	HOLKERI	08–90	04–91	8	61.0	3	17
	AHO	04–91	—	—	57.5	4	—
Fr.	ROCARD	06–88	05–91	35	48.4	2	58
	CRESSON	05–91	04–92	11	48.4	2	18
	BÉRÉGOVOY	04–92	03–93	11	48.4	2	18
	BALLADUR	03–93	—	—	79.9	2	—
FRG	KOHL	03–87	10–90	42	54.2	2	88
	KOHL	10–90	01–91	3	54.4	2	6
	KOHL	01–91	10–94	45	60.1	2	94
	KOHL	10–94	—	—	50.7	2	—
Gr.	ZOLOTAS	11–89	04–90	5	99.0	3	10
	MITSOTAKIS	04–90	10–93	40	51.0	1	83
	PAPANDREOU	10–93	—	—	56.7	1	—
Ice.	HERMANSSON	09–89	04–91	19	57.1	4	40
	ODDSSON	04–91	—	—	56.9	2	—
Ire.	HAUGHEY	07–89	02–92	31	50.0	2	52
	REYNOLDS	02–92	01–93	11	50.0	2	18
	REYNOLDS	01–93	12–94	23	60.8	2	38
	BRUTON	12–94	—	—	47.0	2	—
It.	ANDREOTTI	07–89	04–91	19	59.7	5	32
	ANDREOTTI	04–91	07–92	15	56.4	4	25
	AMATO	07–92	04–93	9	52.5	4	15
	CIAMPI	04–93	04–94	12	56.8	5	20
	BERLUSCONI	04–94	—	—	58.1	3	—
Lux.	SANTER	07–89	06–94	59	58.6	2	100
	SANTER	06–94	12–94	6	63.3	2	10

TABLE 6.16. *(Contd.)*

	PM	Begins	Ends	Duration (months)	Parlia-mentary support	No. of parties in govern-ment	Duration
Neth.	LUBBERS	11–89	08–94	57	68.7	2	100
	KOK	08–94	—	—	61.3	3	—
Norw.	SYSE	10–89	11–90	13	37.6	3	27
	BRUNDTLAND	11–90	09–93	34	38.2	1	71
	BRUNDTLAND	09–93	—	—	40.6	1	—
Port.	SILVA	08–87	10–91	50	60.5	2	100
	SILVA	10–91	—	—	58.4	1	—
Sp.	GONZALES	11–89	06–93	43	50.6	1	90
	GONZALES	06–93	—	—	45.4	1	—
Sw.	CARLSSON	09–88	10–91	37	44.7	1	100
	BILDT	10–91	09–94	36	48.7	4	100
	CARLSSON	10–94	—	—	46.1	1	—
Switz.	HURLIMAN	10–87	10–91	48	72.1	4	100
	FELBER	10–91	10–95	48	73.0	4	100
Turk.	AKBULUT	11–89	06–91	19	64.9	1	40
	YLIMAZ	06–91	11–91	5	64.9	1	10
	DEMIREL	11–91	06–93	19	59.1	2	40
	CILLER	06–93	—	—	59.1	2	—
UK	THATCHER	06–87	11–90	41	57.8	1	68
	MAJOR	11–90	04–92	17	57.4	1	28
	MAJOR	04–92	—	—	56.8	1	—
Can.	MULRONEY	12–88	06–93	54	57.3	1	90
	CAMPBELL	06–93	11–93	5	52.2	1	8
	CHRÉTIEN	11–93	—	—	60.0	1	—
USA	BUSH	01–89	01–93	48	39.8	1	100
	CLINTON	01–93	—	—	58.9	1	—
Jap.	KAIFU	08–89	02–90	6	58.6	1	14
	KAIFU	02–90	11–91	21	56.0	1	48
	MIYAZAWA	11–91	08–93	21	54.5	1	48
	HOSOKAWA	08–93	04–94	8	47.6	7	18
	HATA	04–94	06–94	2	31.3	5	5
	MURAYAMA	06–94	—	—	59.9	3	—
Austral.	HAWKE	07–87	04–90	33	58.1	1	92
	HAWKE	04–90	12–91	18	52.7	1	50
	KEATING	12–91	03–93	15	52.7	1	42
	KEATING	03–93	—	—	54.4	1	—
NZ	PALMER	08–89	11–90	15	60.0	1	42
	BOLGER	11–90	11–93	36	69.0	1	100
	BOLGER	11–93	—	—	50.5	1	—

Note: A government is identified by means of its Prime Minister and the participating parties. If there is a change in either of these there is a new government. A change of government always follows an election, i.e. a government cannot stay longer than an election period. Parliamentary support refers to the support (in percentage of total seats) each government had in the lower chambers of its parliament; number of parties in government refers to the number of parties participating in government; average government duration refers to the months a government holds office as a percentage of an estimated maximum period of government.

Sources: Paloheimo (1984); *The Europa Year Book* (various years); *Keesing's Contemporary Archives* (various years); newspaper reports for the most recent elections.

TABLE 6.17. Female representation in parliaments (lower house) (percentages)

	UN		Janova & Sineau				
	1975	1987	1950	1960	1970	1980	1990
Aus.	7.7	11.5	5.4	6.0	4.8	9.8	10.9
Belg.	6.6	7.5	3.3	4.2	3.7	7.5	8.5
Den.	15.6	29.1	8.0	9.5	10.6	23.4	30.7
Fin.	23.0	31.5	9.0	15.0	16.5	26.0	31.5
Fr.	1.6	6.4	6.7	1.3	1.6	3.6	5.7
FRG	5.8	15.4	6.8	9.2	6.5	9.8	20.5
Gr.	2.0	4.3	0	1.3	0.6	3.3	4.3
Ice.	5.0	20.6	3.3	3.3	5.0	5.0	20.6
Ire.	2.8	8.4	2.7	2.7	2.1	4.0	7.8
It.	3.8	12.9	7.1	4.2	2.6	8.4	12.8
Lux.	5.1	14.1	—	—	3.6	13.5	13.3
Neth.	9.3	20.0	5.0	9.3	9.3	13.3	25.3
Norw.	15.5	34.4	4.6	6.6	9.3	23.8	35.8
Port.	8.0	7.6	1.6	1.6	3.0	6.8	7.6
Sp.	—	6.4	—	—	—	6.8	13.4
Sw.	21.4	28.5	9.5	13.4	14.0	26.4	38.1
Switz.	7.5	14.0	—	—	—	10.5	14.0
Turk.	—	3.0					
UK	4.3	6.3	3.3	3.4	4.1	2.9	6.3
Can.	3.4	9.6					
USA	3.7	5.3					
Jap.	1.4	1.4					
Austral.	0.0	6.1					
NZ	4.6	14.4					

Sources: UN, *The World's Women 1970–1990* (1991); Janova and Sineau (1992).

Section 7: Political Parties and Elections

TABLE 7.1. National electoral participation: valid votes as a percentage of the electorate

	1945–9	1950–4	1955–9	1960–4	1965–9	1970–4	1975–9	1980–4	1985–9	1990–4
Aus.	94.4	94.2	93.6	92.7	92.7	91.2	91.6	91.3	88.8	82.0
Belg.	88.1	87.9	89.0	87.2	84.5	83.7	87.7	86.1	86.9	86.2
Den.	85.8	80.8	83.3	85.4	88.7	87.4	86.7	85.3	85.6	82.8
Fin.	76.1	76.8	74.6	84.8	84.6	81.5	74.3	75.4	71.7	70.8
Fr.	78.4	78.0	77.2	66.6	78.9	79.4	81.7	69.9	69.6	65.3
FRG	76.0	83.0	84.5	84.3	85.0	90.4	89.9	88.1	83.5	77.4
Gr.	—	75.9	74.9	81.7	—	78.6	80.1	77.5	82.9	79.4
Ice.	86.9	88.4	89.5	89.5	89.7	89.7	87.9	86.4	88.5	86.3
Ire.	73.5	75.2	70.6	69.9	75.3	75.7	75.7	73.7	70.2	67.5
It.	86.2	89.5	91.1	89.9	89.4	90.1	88.8	84.0	84.6	82.2
Lux.	86.7	92.6	87.9	85.1	83.2	85.2	82.7	83.4	87.3	81.8
Neth.	90.5	92.1	93.4	92.7	92.3	80.7	87.5	83.6	82.7	77.8
Norw.	78.6	78.9	77.9	78.6	84.4	80.1	82.8	81.9	83.6	75.1
Port.	—	—	—	—	—	—	84.0	79.2	70.7	59.8
Sp.	—	—	—	—	—	—	71.3	78.9	69.1	76.0
Sw.	82.4	78.7	78.1	84.5	88.7	89.4	90.8	90.6	87.0	85.4
Switz.	70.3	68.4	67.3	63.3	62.6	56.6	49.6	48.2	46.1	45.4
Turk.	—	—	—	—	—	—	—	—	88.9	—
UK	72.6	82.8	77.8	77.1	75.8	74.5	76.0	72.7	75.3	77.7
Can.	74.8	67.1	77.0	79.5	75.0	71.9	75.1	72.0	74.9	68.7
USA	53.3	63.7	61.6	64.4	62.3	57.1	55.8	55.1	52.8	55.3
Jap.	70.1	74.6	75.8	71.6	70.4	71.1	70.0	70.2	69.9	69.8
Austral.	92.9	90.7	88.9	93.4	92.4	93.5	93.1	90.9	89.2	92.6
NZ	95.1	89.7	93.0	89.9	87.2	88.5	82.6	90.0	86.6	82.8

Sources: Mackie and Rose (1982); *Keesing's Record of World Events* (various years); *European Journal of Political Research* (various years); newspapers for the most recent elections.

TABLE 7.2. National electoral participation: total votes as a percentage of the electorate

	1945–9	1950–4	1955–9	1960–4	1965–9	1970–4	1975–9	1980–4	1985–9	1990–4
Aus.	95.6	95.8	95.1	93.8	93.8	92.1	92.6	92.6	90.4	84.1
Belg.	92.4	92.9	93.6	92.3	90.8	90.5	95.0	94.6	93.5	92.7
Den.	86.1	81.1	83.7	85.6	89.0	88.0	87.2	85.8	86.3	83.5
Fin.	76.4	77.3	75.0	85.1	84.9	81.8	74.6	75.7	72.1	72.1
Fr.	79.9	80.2	79.6	68.8	80.5	81.2	83.3	70.9	71.9	68.9
FRG	78.5	85.8	87.8	87.7	86.8	91.1	90.7	88.9	84.3	78.5
Gr.	—	76.3	75.2	82.2	—	79.5	81.1	78.6	84.2	80.7
Ice.	88.2	89.9	91.0	91.1	91.4	90.9	89.8	88.9	89.5	87.6
Ire.	74.2	75.9	71.3	70.6	76.0	76.6	76.3	74.4	70.9	68.5
It.	90.7	93.9	93.7	92.9	92.8	93.1	91.9	89.0	90.5	86.7
Lux.	91.3	92.6	92.3	90.6	88.6	90.1	88.9	88.8	92.1	88.3
Neth.	93.4	95.0	95.5	95.1	94.9	81.3	88.0	84.1	82.9	78.3
Norw.	79.2	79.3	78.3	79.1	84.6	80.2	82.9	82.0	83.7	75.9
Port.	—	—	—	—	—	—	88.3	81.2	72.4	62.0
Sp.	—	—	—	—	—	—	72.5	79.5	70.4	77.3
Sw.	82.7	79.1	78.5	84.9	89.3	89.6	91.3	91.4	88.0	86.8
Switz.	71.7	69.8	68.6	64.5	63.8	56.8	50.4	48.9	46.8	46.0
Turk.	—	84.8	89.8	81.0	67.8	66.8	72.5	92.3	91.3	—
UK	—	—	—	77.2	76.0	74.7	76.3	72.8	75.4	77.8
Can.	75.6	67.9	77.8	80.2	75.8	74.1	75.8	72.5	75.5	69.6
USA	—	—	—	—	—	—	—	—	—	—
Jap.	71.4	75.3	76.5	72.3	71.3	71.8	70.7	71.4	71.4	70.3
Austral.	95.0	92.2	91.5	95.5	95.1	95.4	95.2	94.4	93.8	95.6
NZ	95.8	90.2	93.4	90.4	87.8	89.1	83.1	91.2	89.0	84.3

Source: See Table 7.1.

TABLE 7.3.   Classification of political parties, by country

Party type	Party
Austria	
Communist	Kommunistische Partei Österreichs
Environmental (Green)	Vereinte Grüne Österreichs
Environmental (Green)	Alternative Liste Österreichs
Liberal	Freiheitliche Partei Österreichs
Liberal	Liberales Forum
Protest	Demokratische Fortschrittliche Partei
Protest	Verband der Sozialversicherten
Protest	Freiheitliche Partei Österreichs (1994–)
Religious	Österreichische Volkspartei
Socialist	Sozialistische Partei Österreichs
Belgium	
Communist	Kommunistische Partij van Belgë/Parti Communiste de Belgique
Environmental (Green)	AGALEV
Environmental (Green)	Écologistes
Environmental (Green)	Regenboog
Ethnic	Christelijk Vlaamse Volksunie
Ethnic	Partei der Deutschsprächigen Belgier
Ethnic	Front Démocratique des Bruxellois Francophones
Ethnic	Front Démocratique Wallon
Ethnic	Front Wallon
Ethnic	Parti Wallon des Travailleurs
Ethnic	Rassemblement Wallon
Ethnic	Vlaams Blok
Left-Socialist	Parti du Travail de Belgique
Left-Socialist	Parti Ouvrier Socialiste
Liberal	Partij voor Vrijheid en Vooruitgang/Parti de la Liberté et du Progrès
Liberal	Partij voor Vrijheid en Vooruitgang
Liberal	Parti Réformateur Libéral
Liberal	Parti Libéral
Protest	Union Démocratique pour le Respect du Travail/Respect voor Arbeid en Demokratie
Protest	Belgïe-Europe-Belgique (BEB)
Protest	Rassemblement omniprésent social et solidaire pour l'ubiquité des masses (ROSSUM)
Religious	Parti Social Chrétien/Christelijke Volkspartij
Religious	Dissident Catholic Lists
Religious	Union Démocratique Belge
Religious	Christelijke Volkspartij
Religious	Parti Social Chrétien

Socialist	Belgische Socialistische Partij/Parti Socialiste Belge
Socialist	Belgische Socialistische Partij
Socialist	Parti Socialiste Belge
Ultra-Right	Front National
Denmark	
Agrarian	Venstre
Communist	Danmarks Kommunistiske Parti
Communist	Enhedslisten
Conservative	Konservative Folkeparti
Conservative	Uafhængige
Environmental (Green)	Grøne
Ethnic	Slesvigsk Parti/Schleswigsche Partei
Left-Socialist	Socialistisk Folkeparti
Left-Socialist	Venstresocialisterne
Left-Socialist	Fælles Kurs
Liberal	Radikale Venstre
Liberal	Retsforbundet
Liberal	Dansk Samling
Liberal	Liberalt Centrum
Liberal	Centrum-Demokraterne
Protest	Fremskridtspartiet
Religious	Kristeligt Folkeparti
Socialist	Socialdemokratiet
Finland	
Agrarian	Keskustapuolue
Agrarian	Suomen Pienviljelijäin Puolue
Communist	Suomen Kansan Demokraattinen Liitto
Communist	Demokraattinen Vaihtoehto
Communist	Vasemmistoliitto
Conservative	Kansallinen Kokomos
Conservative	Suomen Perustuslaillinen Kansanpuolue
Environmental (Green)	Green
Ethnic	Svenska Folkpartiet
Left-Socialist	Työväen ja Pienviljelijäin Sosialdemokraattinen Liitto
Liberal	Liberaalinen Kansanpuolue.
Liberal	Vapaamielisten Liitto
Protest	Suomen Maaseudun Puolue
Protest	Suomen Kansan Yhtenäisyyden Puolue
Protest	Suomen Eläkeläisten Puolue
Religious	Suomen Kristillinen Liitto
Socialist	Suomen Sosialdemokraattinen Puolue
France	
Communist	Parti Communiste Français
Conservative	Centre National des Indépendants

Conservative	Gaullistes
Conservative	Parti Républicain
Conservative	Centre Démocratie et Progrès
Environmental (Green)	Écologistes
Left-Socialist	Union des Forces Démocratiques
Left-Socialist	Parti Socialiste Unifié
Liberal	Parti Républicain Radical et Radical Socialiste
Protest	Union pour la Défense des Commerçants et Artisans
Religious	Mouvement Républicain Populaire
Religious	Centre du Progrès et de la Démocratie Moderne
Religious	Mouvement Réformateur
Religious	Centre des Démocrates Sociaux
Socialist	Parti Socialiste
Ultra-Right	Front National

Federal Republic of Germany

Communist	Kommunistische Partei Deutschlands
Communist	Deutsche Friedensunion
Communist	Aktion Demokratischer Fortschritt
Communist	Partei der Demokratischen Sozialismus
Conservative	Deutsche Partei
Conservative	Gesamtdeutsche Partei
Environmental (Green)	Die Grünen
Environmental (Green)	Bündnis 90/Grüne
Environmental (Green)	Ökologisch-Demokratische Partei
Ethnic	Bayernpartei
Ethnic	Südschleswiger Wählerverband
Ethnic	Gesamtdeutscher Block/Bund der Heimatvertriebenen und Entrechteten
Ethnic	Föderalistische Union
Liberal	Freie Demokratische Partei
Protest	Wirtschaftliche Aufbauvereinigung
Protest	Die Grauen
Religious	Zentrumspartei
Religious	Christlich Demokratische Union/Christlich Soziale Union
Socialist	Sozialdemokratische Partei Deutschlands
Socialist	Gesamtdeutsche Volkspartei
Ultra-Right	Deutsche Reichspartei
Ultra-Right	Nationaldemokratische Partei Deutschlands
Ultra-Right	Die Republikaner

Greece

Communist	Communist Party of Greece (KKE)
Communist	United Democratic Left (EDA)
Communist	Christian Democracy (CD)
Communist	Communist Party of the Interior (KKEes)

Conservative	People's Party (LK)
Conservative	National Unity Party (EEK)
Conservative	Reformist Party (MK)
Conservative	Nationalist Party (KE)
Conservative	New Party (NK)
Conservative	Greek Rally (ES)
Conservative	National Radical Union (ERE)
Conservative	Popular Social Party (LKK)
Conservative	National Democratic Union (EDE)
Conservative	New Democracy (ND)
Conservative	New Liberal Party (KN)
Conservative	Party of the Progressives (KP)
Conservative	Democratic Renewal (DIANA)
Conservative	Democratic Renewal (DIANA)
Conservative	Political Spring (POLA)
Environmental (Green)	Ecologists
Ethnic	Independent Muslims
Liberal	Liberal Party (KF)
Liberal	Republican Socialist Party (DSK)
Liberal	National Party of Greece (EKE)
Liberal	National Progressive Centre Union (EPEK)
Liberal	Farmers' and Workers' Rally (SAE)
Liberal	Democratic Party of the Working People (DKEL)
Liberal	Progressive Party (PK)
Liberal	Union of the Centre (EDHIK)
Liberal	Liberal Party (KF)
Liberal	Party for Democratic Socialism (KODISO)
Socialist	Pan-Hellenic Socialist Movement (PASOK)
Ultra-Right	National Front (EM)

Iceland

Agrarian	Progressive Party
Agrarian	National Party
Agrarian	Association for Equality and Justice
Communist	Communist Party
Conservative	Independence Party (II)
Conservative	Republic Party
Conservative	Independent Democratic Party
Conservative	Independent Party
Environmental (Green)	Women's List
Environmental (Green)	Humanist Party
Left-Socialist	National Preservation Party
Liberal	Union of Liberals and Leftists
Protest	Citizens' Party
Socialist	Social Democrats
Socialist	Social Democratic Federation
Socialist	Social Democratic Alliance

Ireland

Agrarian	Clann na Poblachta
Environmental (Green)	Green Alliance
Ethnic	Sinn Féin (II)
Ethnic	National Progressive Democrats
Ethnic	National H-Block Committee
Left-Socialist	The Workers' Party
Left-Socialist	Democratic Socialist Party
Left-Socialist	Democratic Left
Liberal	Fianna Fáil
Liberal	Clann na Talmhan
Liberal	Progressive Democrats
Religious	Fine Gael
Socialist	Irish Labour Party
Socialist	National Labour

Italy

Communist	Partito Comunista Italiano
Conservative	Partito Monarchico Popolare
Conservative	Forza Italiana
Environmental (Green)	Partito Radicale
Environmental (Green)	Lista Verde
Ethnic	Partito Sardo d'Azione
Ethnic	Movimento per l'Independenciza della Sicilia
Ethnic	Südtriroler Volkspartei
Ethnic	Union Valdotaine
Ethnic	Lista per Trieste
Ethnic	Liga Veneta
Ethnic	Lega Nord
Left-Socialist	Partito Socialista Italiano di Unità Proletaria
Left-Socialist	Manifesto/Partito di Unità Proletaria per il Communismo
Liberal	Partito Repubblicano Italiano
Liberal	Partito d'Azione
Liberal	Partito Liberale Italiano
Liberal	La Rete
Protest	Fronte dell'Uomo Qualunque
Protest	Communità
Protest	Partito Nazionale dei Pensionati
Religious	Democrazia Cristiana
Religious	Partiti Populari Italiana
Religious	Pacta Segni
Socialist	Partito Socialista Italiano
Socialist	Partito Socialista Democratico Italiano
Socialist	Partito Socialista Unificato
Ultra-Right	Movimento Sociale Italiano-Destra Nazionale
Ultra-Right	Alianza Nationale

Luxembourg

Communist	Parti Communiste Luxembourgeois
Environmental (Green)	Écologistes
Ethnic	Indépendants de l'Est
Liberal	Parti Démocratique
Protest	Parti des Classes Moyennes
Protest	Mouvement Indépendent Populaire
Protest	Enrôlés de Force
Protest	Aktiounskomitee
Protest	Lëtzebuerger National Bewegong
Religious	Parti Social-Chrétien
Socialist	Parti Ouvrier Socialiste Luxembourgeois
Socialist	Parti Social-Démocrate
Socialist	Socialistes Indépendants

The Netherlands

Communist	Communistische Partij Nederland
Environmental (Green)	Federative Groenen
Environmental (Green)	Groen Links
Ethnic	Centrumpartij
Left-Socialist	Pacifistisch-Socialistische Partij
Left-Socialist	Socialistische Partij
Liberal	Volkspartji voor Vrijheid en Democratie
Liberal	Democraten '66
Protest	Boerenpartij
Protest	Middenstands Partij
Protest	Algemeen Onderen Verbond
Protest	Unie 55+
Religious	Anti-Revolutionaire Partij
Religious	Katholieke Volkspartij
Religious	Christelijk-Historische Unie
Religious	Staatkundig Gereformeerde Partij
Religious	Katholieke Nationale Partij
Religious	Gereformeerd Politiek Verbond
Religious	Politieke Partij Radicalen
Religious	Rooms-Katholieke Partij Nederland
Religious	Christen Democratisch Appel
Religious	Reformatorische Politieke Federatie
Religious	Evangelische Volkspartij
Socialist	Partij van der Arbeid
Socialist	Democratische Socialisten '70

Norway

Agrarian	Senterpartiet
Communist	Norges Kommunistiske Parti
Communist	Rod Valgallianse
Conservative	Høyre

Conservative	Samfunnspartiet
Environmental (Green)	Green Party
Environmental (Green)	Grone
Left-Socialist	Sosialistisk Venstreparti
Liberal	Venstre
Liberal	Liberale Folkpartiet
Protest	Fremskrittspartiet
Protest	Pensionister
Religious	Kristeligt Folkeparti
Socialist	Det Norske Arbeiderparti

Portugal

Communist	Partido Comunista Português
Communist	Movimento Democrático Português
Conservative	Partido Popular Monárquico
Environmental (Green)	Partido 'Os Verdes'
Left-Socialist	Movimento de Esquerda Socialista
Left-Socialist	União Democrático Popular
Left-Socialist	Frente Socialista Popular
Left-Socialist	Partido Socialista Revolucionário
Left-Socialist	Partido Operário de Unidade Socialista
Liberal	Partido Social Democrata
Liberal	Partido Renovador Democrático
Protest	Partido de Solidariadade Nacional
Religious	Partido do Centro Democrático Social
Religious	Partido da Democracia Cristã
Socialist	Partido Socialista Português
Socialist	União de Esquerda Democrática Socialista

Spain

Communist	Partido Comunista de España
Conservative	Unión del Centro Democrático
Conservative	Alianza Popular
Conservative	Centro Democrático y Social
Environmental (Green)	Los Verdes
Ethnic	Partido Nacionalista Vasco
Ethnic	Partido Carlista
Ethnic	Partido Socialista de Andalucia
Ethnic	Unió Democràtica de Catalunya
Ethnic	Convergència Democratica de Catalunya
Ethnic	Euzkadiko Ezkerra
Ethnic	Bloque Nacional Popular Gallego
Ethnic	Partido Socialista Gallego
Ethnic	Herri Batasuna
Ethnic	Partido Aragonés Regionalista
Ethnic	Coalición Unión del Pueblo Canario
Ethnic	Unión Valenciana
Ethnic	Esquerra Republicana de Catalunya

Left-Socialist   Partido del Trabajo de España
Religious   Equipo de la Democracia Cristiana
Socialist   Partido Socialista Obrero Español
Socialist   Partido Socialista Popular
Ultra-Right   Alianza Nacional del 18 de Julio
Ultra-Right   Fuerza Nueva
Ultra-Right   Falange Española de la JONS

Sweden
Agrarian   Centerpartiet
Communist   Vänsterpartiet
Conservative   Moderata Samlingspartiet
Environmental (Green) Miljöpartiet
Liberal   Folkpartiet
Protest   Ny Demokrati
Religious   Kristdemokratiska Samhällspartiet
Socialist   Socialdemokratiska Arbetarpartiet

Switzerland
Agrarian   Schweizerische Volkspartei
Communist   Partei der Arbeit der Schweiz
Environmental (Green) Grüne
Environmental (Green) Die Andere Schweiz (DACH)
Ethnic   Entente jurassienne
Ethnic   Lega dei Ticinesi
Left-Socialist   Partito Socialista Autonomo
Left-Socialist   Progressive Organisationen der Schweiz
Liberal   Demokraten
Liberal   Liberale-konservative Partei
Liberal   Freisinnige-demokratische Partei
Liberal   Freiwirtschaftler
Liberal   Landesring der Unabhängigen
Protest   Nationale Aktion gegen die Überfremdung von
                       Volk und Heimat
Protest   Schweizerische Republikanische Bewegung
Protest   Schweizer Auto-Partei
Protest   Eidgenössisch-Demokratische Partei
Religious   Christlich Demokratische Volkspartei
Religious   Evangelische Volkspartei
Religious   Christlich-Soziale Partei
Socialist   Sozialdemokratische Partei der Schweiz

Turkey
Conservative   Justice Party
Conservative   Republican Reliance Party
Conservative   Motherland Party (ANAP) ·
Conservative   True Path Party (TPP)
Left-Socialist   Turkish Labour Party

Liberal	Turkish Unity Party
Liberal	Reformist Democracy Party
Religious	National Salvation Party
Religious	Prosperity Party (Welfare Party)
Religious	Nationalist Labour Party (NLP)
Socialist	Republican People's Party
Socialist	Social Democratic Populist Party (SDPP)
Socialist	Democratic Left Party (DLP)
Ultra-Right	National Action Party
Ultra-Right	Democratic Party
Ultra-Right	New Turkey Party
Ultra-Right	National Party
Ultra-Right	Nationalist Democrat Party

United Kingdom

Communist	Communist Party
Conservative	Conservative Party
Conservative	National Liberal Party
Environmental (Green)	Ecology Party
Ethnic	United Ireland
Ethnic	Scottish National Party
Ethnic	Plaid Cymru
Ethnic	Social Democratic and Labour Party
Ethnic	Ulster Unionists and Loyalists
Liberal	Liberal Party
Liberal	Liberal Democrats
Socialist	Independent Labour Party
Socialist	Labour Party
Socialist	Social Democratic Party
Ultra-Right	National Front

Canada

Communist	Communist Party
Conservative	Progressive Conservative Party
Environmental (Green)	Green Party
Ethnic	Parti Nationaliste du Québec
Ethnic	Confederation of Regions–Western Party
Liberal	Liberal Party
Liberal	Social Credit
Liberal	Ralliement des Créditistes du Québec
Liberal	Libertarian Party
Protest	Rhinoceros Party
Protest	Reform Party
Socialist	New Democratic Party
Socialist	Bloc Populaire Canadien

USA

| Communist | Communist Party |

Conservative	Republicans
Conservative	Independent
Liberal	Democrats
Liberal	Prohibition
Liberal	States Rights
Liberal	Libertarian Party
Protest	American Independent Party
Protest	Independent (Perot)
Socialist	Socialist Labor Party
Socialist	Socialist Party
Socialist	Progressive

Japan

Communist	Communist Party
Conservative	Democratic Liberal Party
Conservative	Hatoyama Liberal Party
Conservative	Yoshida Liberal Party
Conservative	Democratic Party
Conservative	Liberal Democratic Party
Conservative	Japan New Party
Conservative	Japan Renewal Party (Shinseito)
Conservative	New Party Harbinger (Shinto Sakigake)
Liberal	Progressive Party
Liberal	Co-operative Party
Liberal	Social Reform Party
Liberal	New Liberal Club
Liberal	Social Democratic Federation
Religious	Clean Government Party (Komeito)
Socialist	Socialist Party
Socialist	Labour-Farmer Party
Socialist	Left-Wing Socialist Party
Socialist	Right-Wing Socialist Party
Socialist	Democratic Socialist Party

Australia

Agrarian	Country Party
Agrarian	National Party
Communist	Communist Party
Conservative	Australian Liberal Party
Conservative	Country-Liberal Party
Environmental (Green)	Green
Liberal	Services Party of Australia
Liberal	Australia Party
Liberal	Liberal Movement
Liberal	National Alliance
Liberal	Australian Democrats
Socialist	Australian Labor Party

Socialist	Lang Labor Party
Socialist	Democratic Labor Party
Socialist	Queensland Labor Party
New Zealand	
Communist	Communist Party
Conservative	National Party
Environmental (Green)	Values Party
Environmental (Green)	Green Party Aotearoa
Environmental (Green)	Alliance
Ethnic	Manu Motuhake
Liberal	Social Credit Political League = Democrats
Protest	New Zealand First Party
Religious	New Zealand Party
Religious	Christian Heritage
Socialist	Labour Party
Socialist	New Labour Party

TABLE 7.4. Electoral strength of communist parties in national elections

	1945–9	1950–4	1955–9	1960–4	1965–9	1970–4	1975–9	1980–4	1985–9	1990–4
Aus.	5.3	5.3	3.9	3.0	0.4	1.2	1.1	0.7	0.7	0.3
Belg.	10.1	4.2	1.9	3.1	4.0	3.2	2.7	2.3	1.0	0.1
Den.	9.7	4.6	3.1	1.2	0.9	2.5	3.3	0.9	0.9	2.4
Fin.	21.8	21.6	23.2	22.0	21.2	16.8	18.4	13.8	13.9	10.1
Fr.	27.0	26.7	22.6	21.8	21.3	21.4	20.6	16.1	10.6	9.2
FRG	5.7	2.2	—	1.9	1.0	0.3	0.3	0.2	0.0	3.4*
Gr.	—	10.0	17.3	13.6	—	9.5	12.1	12.3	12.1	9.3
Ice.	19.5	16.0	16.8	16.0	13.9	17.7	21.3	17.3	13.3	14.4
Ire.	—	—	—	—	—	—	—	—	—	—
It.	20.6	22.6	22.7	25.3	26.9	27.2	32.4	29.9	26.6	24.1
Lux.	11.8	8.9	9.1	12.5	15.5	10.5	5.8	5.0	4.4	1.7
Neth.	9.2	6.2	3.6	2.8	3.6	4.2	1.7	2.0	0.7	—
Norw.	8.9	5.1	3.4	2.9	1.2	—	0.4	0.3	0.2	1.1
Port.	—	—	—	—	—	—	17.6	18.0	14.3	8.8
Sp.	—	—	—	—	—	—	10.1	4.1	7.4	9.6
Sw.	6.3	4.3	4.2	4.9	3.0	5.1	5.2	5.6	5.6	5.3
Switz.	5.1	2.7	2.7	2.2	2.9	2.6	2.3	0.9	0.8	0.8
Turk.	—	—	—	—	—	—	—	—	—	—
UK	0.4	0.2	0.1	0.2	0.2	0.1	0.1	0.0	0.0	—
Can.	1.4	1.1	0.1	0.1	0.1	0.1	0.1	0.1	0.1	—
USA	0.0	0.0	0.0	0.0	0.0	0.0	0.1	0.0	—	—
Jap.	5.8	2.2	2.3	3.5	5.8	10.5	10.4	9.6	8.8	7.9
Austral.	1.2	1.1	0.9	0.6	0.3	0.1	0.2	0.0	0.0	—
NZ	0.2	0.1	0.1	0.3	0.1	0.0	0.0	0.0	0.0	—

* Germany

Source: See Table 7.1.

TABLE 7.5a. Electoral strength of religious parties in national elections (CDU/CSU, ÖVP, DC included)

	1945–9	1950–4	1955–9	1960–4	1965–9	1970–4	1975–9	1980–4	1985–9	1990–4
Aus.	46.9	41.3	45.1	45.4	48.3	43.9	42.4	43.0	41.3	29.9
Belg.	44.2	44.9	46.5	44.4	33.3	31.3	36.1	26.4	28.4	24.5
Den.	—	—	—	—	—	3.0	3.8	2.5	2.2	2.1
Fin.	—	—	0.2	0.8	0.4	1.8	4.1	3.0	2.6	3.0
Fr.	26.4	12.5	11.2	8.9	11.5	16.2	5.3	5.2	—	—
FRG	34.1	46.0	50.2	45.3	46.9	44.9	48.6	46.7	44.3	42.7*
Gr.	—	—	—	—	—	—	—	—	—	0.4
Ice.	—	—	—	—	—	—	—	—	—	—
Ire.	19.8	28.9	26.6	32.0	34.1	35.1	30.5	37.7	28.2	24.5
It.	41.9	40.1	42.4	38.2	39.0	38.7	38.5	32.9	34.3	22.7
Lux.	39.2	42.4	36.9	33.3	35.3	27.9	34.5	34.9	32.4	30.3
Neth.	55.4	54.7	52.5	52.2	47.4	41.9	37.8	36.7	40.5	27.0
Norw.	8.2	10.5	10.2	9.6	8.8	12.3	12.4	9.4	8.4	7.9
Port.	—	—	—	—	—	—	14.3	22.3	8.0	4.4
Sp.	—	—	—	—	—	—	0.7	—	—	—
Sw.	—	—	—	0.9	1.5	1.8	1.4	1.9	2.7	5.6
Switz.	22.1	23.5	24.5	25.0	23.7	22.8	23.4	22.5	20.0	20.5
Turk.	—	—	—	—	—	11.9	8.6	—	7.2	16.9
UK	—	—	—	—	—	—	—	—	—	—
Can.	—	—	—	—	—	—	—	—	—	—
USA	—	—	—	—	—	—	—	—	—	—
Jap.	—	—	—	—	8.2	8.5	10.4	9.6	9.4	8.1
Austral.	—	—	—	—	—	—	—	—	—	—
NZ	—	—	—	—	—	—	—	6.2	0.3	0.3

* Germany

Source: See Table 7.1.

TABLE 7.5*b*. Electoral strength religious parties in national elections (CDU/CSU, ÖVP, DC excluded)

	1945-9	1950-4	1955-9	1960-4	1965-9	1970-4	1975-9	1980-4	1985-9	1990-4
Aus.	—	—	—	—	—	—	—	—	—	—
Belg.	44.2	44.9	46.5	44.4	33.3	31.3	36.1	26.4	28.4	24.5
Den.	—	—	—	—	—	3.0	3.8	2.5	2.2	2.1
Fin.	—	—	0.2	0.8	0.4	1.8	4.1	3.0	2.6	3.0
Fr.	26.4	12.5	11.2	8.9	11.5	16.2	5.3	5.2	—	—
FRG	—	—	—	—	—	—	—	—	—	—
Gr.	—	—	—	—	—	—	—	—	—	0.4
Ice.	—	—	—	—	—	—	—	—	—	—
Ire.	19.8	28.9	26.6	32.0	34.1	35.1	30.5	37.7	28.2	24.5
It.	—	—	—	—	—	—	—	—	—	—
Lux.	39.2	42.4	36.9	33.3	35.3	27.9	34.5	34.9	32.4	30.3
Neth.	55.4	54.7	52.5	52.2	47.4	41.9	37.8	36.7	40.5	27.0
Norw.	8.2	10.5	10.2	9.6	8.8	12.3	12.4	9.4	8.4	7.9
Port.	—	—	—	—	—	—	14.3	22.3	8.0	4.4
Sp.	—	—	—	—	—	—	0.7	—	—	—
Sw.	—	—	—	0.9	1.5	1.8	1.4	1.9	2.7	5.6
Switz.	22.1	23.5	24.5	25.0	23.7	22.8	23.4	22.5	20.0	20.5
Turk.	—	—	—	—	—	11.9	8.6	—	7.2	16.9
UK	—	—	—	—	—	—	—	—	—	—
Can.	—	—	—	—	—	—	—	—	—	—
USA	—	—	—	—	—	—	—	—	—	—
Jap.	—	—	—	—	8.2	8.5	10.4	9.6	9.4	8.1
Austral.	—	—	—	—	—	—	—	—	—	—
NZ	—	—	—	—	—	—	—	6.2	0.3	0.3

Source: See Table 7.1.

TABLE 7.6. Electoral strength of socialist parties in national elections

	1945–9	1950–4	1955–9	1960–4	1965–9	1970–4	1975–9	1980–4	1985–9	1990–4
Aus.	41.7	42.1	43.9	44.0	42.6	49.2	50.7	47.7	43.1	38.9
Belg.	31.0	37.0	37.0	36.7	28.1	27.0	26.3	25.2	29.5	25.5
Den.	36.4	40.4	39.4	42.0	36.2	31.5	35.1	32.3	29.6	36.0
Fin.	25.7	26.4	23.2	19.5	27.2	24.6	24.4	26.7	24.1	22.1
Fr.	20.9	14.5	15.3	12.7	17.7	19.7	25.0	37.8	35.2	20.3
FRG	29.2	30.0	31.8	36.2	41.0	45.8	42.6	40.6	37.0	35.0*
Gr.	—	—	—	—	—	13.6	25.3	48.1	41.9	43.0
Ice.	17.2	15.6	15.3	14.2	15.7	9.8	19.7	19.0	15.4	15.5
Ire.	11.3	11.8	9.1	12.0	16.2	13.7	11.6	9.5	7.9	19.3
It.	18.3	17.2	18.8	19.9	14.5	14.7	13.3	15.5	17.3	9.9
Lux.	32.4	35.1	34.9	37.7	32.3	38.3	32.5	36.1	26.2	25.4
Neth.	27.0	29.0	31.6	28.0	23.6	30.7	34.5	29.7	32.6	24.0
Norw.	43.4	46.7	48.3	46.8	44.8	35.3	42.3	37.2	37.6	37.0
Port.	—	—	—	—	—	—	35.4	32.9	22.1	29.3
Sp.	—	—	—	—	—	—	32.7	46.5	42.3	38.7
Sw.	46.1	46.0	45.4	47.6	50.1	44.5	43.0	45.6	44.0	41.5
Switz.	26.2	26.0	26.7	26.6	23.5	22.9	24.7	22.9	18.4	18.5
Turk.	—	37.7	40.9	36.7	28.1	33.2	41.4	30.5	33.2	31.6
UK	48.2	47.5	45.1	44.1	48.0	39.8	36.9	39.3	40.5	34.9
Can.	16.3	11.3	10.1	13.3	17.5	16.6	17.9	19.3	20.4	6.6
USA	2.8	0.2	0.1	0.1	0.1	0.1	0.1	—	—	—
Jap.	19.8	24.8	31.6	36.2	32.2	28.9	26.8	26.4	23.6	24.0
Austral.	49.0	45.3	51.0	54.8	50.2	52.8	42.6	47.7	45.8	42.2
NZ	49.3	45.0	48.3	43.6	42.8	48.4	40.0	41.0	48.0	37.5

* Germany

Source: See Table 7.1.

Table 7.7. Electoral strength of ethnic parties in national elections

	1945–9	1950–4	1955–9	1960–4	1965–9	1970–4	1975–9	1980–4	1985–9	1990–4
Aus.	—	—	—	—	—	—	—	—	—	—
Belg.	1.1	1.1	2.0	3.5	12.3	19.0	16.4	15.3	11.1	14.1
Den.	0.2	0.4	0.4	0.4	0.1	0.1	—	—	—	—
Fin.	8.1	7.3	6.7	6.4	6.0	5.6	4.8	4.9	5.6	5.5
Fr.	—	—	—	—	—	—	—	—	—	—
FRG	4.5	7.8	5.6	0.1	—	—	—	—	—	—
Gr.	—	—	—	—	—	—	—	—	—	—
Ice.	—	—	—	—	—	—	—	—	0.4	—
Ire.	—	—	5.3	2.1	—	—	—	—	1.5	2.3
It.	0.9	0.6	0.6	0.5	0.7	0.6	0.8	1.3	2.7	9.1
Lux.	0.6	—	—	—	—	—	—	—	—	—
Neth.	—	—	—	—	—	—	—	—	—	—
Norw.	—	—	—	—	—	—	—	—	—	—
Port.	—	—	—	—	—	—	—	—	—	—
Sp.	—	—	—	—	—	—	8.4	8.7	10.9	10.4
Sw.	—	—	—	—	—	—	—	—	—	—
Switz.	—	—	—	—	—	—	0.5	—	—	1.4
Turk.	—	—	—	—	—	—	—	—	—	—
UK	0.6	0.5	0.7	0.9	1.2	4.3	3.9	3.7	3.7	4.5
Can.	—	—	—	—	—	—	—	0.6	0.3	13.9
USA	—	—	—	—	—	—	—	—	—	—
Jap.	—	—	—	—	—	—	—	—	—	—
Austral.	—	—	—	—	—	—	—	—	—	—
NZ	—	—	—	—	—	—	—	0.2	0.5	0.3

Source: See Table 7.1.

TABLE 7.8. Electoral strength of agrarian parties in national elections

	1945–9	1950–4	1955–9	1960–4	1965–9	1970–4	1975–9	1980–4	1985–9	1990–4
Aus.	—	—	—	—	—	—	—	—	—	—
Belg.	—	—	—	—	—	—	—	—	—	—
Den.	22.5	22.2	25.1	21.0	19.0	14.0	15.9	11.7	11.2	19.6
Fin.	23.6	23.9	23.1	23.0	21.2	16.8	17.5	17.6	17.6	24.8
Fr.	—	—	—	—	—	—	—	—	—	—
FRG	—	—	—	—	—	—	—	—	—	—
Gr.	—	—	—	—	—	—	—	—	—	—
Ice.	23.8	21.9	22.8	28.2	28.1	25.1	20.9	18.5	21.5	20.7
Ire.	13.3	4.0	1.7	1.1	0.4	—	—	—	—	—
It.	—	—	—	—	—	—	—	—	—	—
Lux.	—	—	—	—	—	—	—	—	—	—
Neth.	—	—	—	—	—	—	—	—	—	—
Norw.	8.0	9.1	9.3	9.4	10.2	11.0	8.6	6.7	6.6	16.8
Port.	—	—	—	—	—	—	—	—	—	—
Sp.	—	—	—	—	—	—	—	—	—	—
Sw.	12.4	10.7	11.1	13.6	16.5	22.5	21.1	15.5	10.6	8.1
Switz.	12.1	12.6	11.9	11.4	11.0	11.0	10.8	11.1	11.0	11.9
Turk.	—	—	—	—	—	—	—	—	—	—
UK	—	—	—	—	—	—	—	—	—	—
Can.	—	—	—	—	—	—	—	—	—	—
USA	—	—	—	—	—	—	—	—	—	—
Jap.	—	—	—	—	—	—	—	—	—	—
Austral.	11.1	9.1	8.6	8.7	9.2	9.7	10.7	9.6	11.5	8.0
NZ	—	—	—	—	—	—	—	—	—	—

Source: See Table 7.1.

TABLE 7.9. Electoral strength of left/socialist parties in national elections

	1945–9	1950–4	1955–9	1960–4	1965–9	1970–4	1975–9	1980–4	1985–9	1990–4
Aus.	—	—	—	—	—	—	—	—	—	—
Belg.	—	—	—	—	—	—	—	—	—	0.6
Den.	—	—	—	6.0	9.5	9.1	11.7	14.1	16.9	8.7
Fin.	—	—	1.7	4.4	2.6	1.2	—	1.3	—	—
Fr.	—	—	0.7	2.4	3.1	3.3	3.3	—	—	1.8
FRG	—	—	—	—	—	—	—	—	—	—
Gr.	—	—	—	—	—	—	—	—	—	—
Ice.	—	6.0	3.5	—	—	—	—	—	—	—
Ire.	—	—	—	—	—	1.1	1.7	2.4	4.8	2.8
It.	—	—	—	—	4.4	2.6	1.5	1.5	1.7	—
Lux.	—	—	—	—	—	—	—	—	—	1.3
Neth.	—	—	0.9	3.0	2.9	1.5	0.9	2.2	1.6	7.9
Norw.	—	—	—	2.4	4.7	11.2	4.2	4.9	7.8	—
Port.	—	—	—	—	—	—	2.9	2.7	1.8	—
Sp.	—	—	—	—	—	—	1.0	—	—	—
Sw.	—	—	—	—	—	—	—	—	—	—
Switz.	—	—	—	—	—	0.3	1.7	2.7	1.8	0.8
Turk.	—	—	—	—	2.9	—	0.1	—	—	—
UK	—	—	—	—	—	—	—	—	—	—
Can.	—	—	—	—	—	—	—	—	—	—
USA	—	—	—	—	—	—	—	—	—	—
Jap.	—	—	—	—	—	—	—	—	—	—
Austral.	—	—	—	—	—	—	—	—	—	—
NZ	—	—	—	—	—	—	—	—	—	—

Source: See Table 7.1.

TABLE 7.10.　Electoral strength of liberal parties in national elections

	1945–9	1950–4	1955–9	1960–4	1965–9	1970–4	1975–9	1980–4	1985–9	1990–4
Aus.	11.7	10.6	7.1	7.0	5.4	5.5	5.8	5.0	9.7	11.2
Belg.	12.6	12.6	12.0	12.3	21.3	18.7	15.9	21.3	20.9	20.1
Den.	12.9	14.2	13.1	7.5	13.8	12.6	11.9	13.3	11.0	8.3
Fin.	4.6	7.1	6.2	6.4	6.5	5.6	4.0	—	0.9	0.8
Fr.	11.7	10.0	11.3	7.6	—	—	—	—	—	—
FRG	11.9	9.5	7.7	12.8	7.7	8.4	7.9	8.1	9.1	9.0*
Gr.	39.7	43.7	35.8	44.0	—	20.4	12.0	1.5	0.1	—
Ice.	—	—	—	—	3.7	6.8	3.3	—	—	—
Ire.	47.4	47.8	50.7	45.3	46.7	46.2	50.6	45.9	52.9	43.8
It.	9.7	4.6	4.9	8.4	7.8	6.8	4.7	8.0	5.8	5.6
Lux.	15.5	10.8	18.5	10.6	16.6	22.2	21.3	18.7	17.2	19.3
Neth.	7.2	8.8	10.5	10.3	15.2	17.9	23.3	27.9	23.0	35.4
Norw.	13.5	10.0	9.6	8.8	9.9	6.9	4.6	4.4	3.4	3.6
Port.	—	—	—	—	—	—	27.7	22.6	52.7	51.0
Sp.	—	—	—	—	—	—	—	—	—	—
Sw.	22.7	24.4	21.0	17.5	15.3	12.8	10.9	5.9	13.2	8.2
Switz.	34.0	34.8	33.7	32.9	36.0	31.5	30.9	30.3	29.8	26.8
Turk.	—	—	—	—	2.8	1.1	0.4	—	0.8	—
UK	9.0	5.9	4.3	11.2	8.5	15.0	13.8	13.7	12.8	18.0
Can.	50.0	51.2	39.9	51.2	49.7	47.2	44.7	37.2	32.0	41.6
USA	52.1	44.5	42.1	55.5	42.7	37.5	50.3	41.4	45.6	43.2
Jap.	24.9	18.6	—	—	—	—	3.6	2.7	2.6	0.8
Austral.	0.6	—	—	—	—	0.8	5.0	5.7	6.0	7.6
NZ	—	11.1	7.2	8.3	11.8	6.7	11.8	14.2	5.7	1.3

* Germany
Source: See Table 7.1.

TABLE 7.11a. Electoral strength of conservative parties in national elections (CDU/CSU, ÖVP, DC excluded)

	1945–9	1950–4	1955–9	1960–4	1965–9	1970–4	1975–9	1980–4	1985–9	1990–4
Aus.	—	—	—	—	—	—	—	—	—	—
Belg.	—	—	—	—	—	—	—	—	—	—
Den.	15.3	18.2	18.91	21.9	20.6	13.0	8.8	19.0	20.1	15.5
Fin.	16.0	13.7	15.3	14.6	13.8	17.8	21.5	22.5	23.2	19.6
Fr.	13.5	35.7	31.0	45.8	44.7	37.0	36.2	32.2	42.7	44.2
FRG	4.0	3.3	3.4	2.8	0.1	—	—	—	—	—
Gr.	58.0	43.3	46.2	41.8	—	55.5	42.9	37.6	44.1	45.9
Ice.	39.5	40.4	41.5	41.4	38.6	40.5	34.1	38.7	27.2	38.6
Ire.	—	—	—	—	—	—	—	—	—	—
It.	2.8	6.8	4.8	1.7	1.3	—	—	—	—	10.5
Lux.	—	—	—	—	—	—	—	—	—	—
Neth.	—	—	—	—	—	—	—	—	—	—
Norw.	18.1	18.6	18.9	20.0	20.4	17.4	24.8	31.7	26.3	16.9
Port.	—	—	—	—	—	—	0.5	0.5	—	0.4
Sp.	—	—	—	—	—	—	42.4	35.3	35.1	34.8
Sw.	12.3	14.4	18.3	15.7	13.7	12.9	18.0	23.6	19.8	22.2
Switz.	—	—	—	—	—	—	—	—	—	—
Turk.	—	55.1	47.7	34.8	53.0	35.1	38.8	45.2	27.7	51.0
UK	39.6	45.7	49.6	43.4	41.9	40.1	43.9	42.4	42.3	41.9
Can.	28.6	31.0	46.3	35.1	31.9	35.2	35.9	41.3	42.9	16.1
USA	45.1	55.1	57.4	44.0	43.4	60.7	48.0	58.1	53.4	37.1
Jap.	31.7	47.8	60.5	55.8	48.2	46.9	43.2	46.9	49.4	51.8
Austral.	35.9	43.1	38.5	35.4	37.5	33.5	40.0	35.4	34.5	36.0
NZ	48.4	49.2	44.2	47.4	44.4	41.5	43.7	37.4	44.0	41.5

Source: See Table 7.1.

TABLE 7.11b. Electoral strength of conservative parties in national elections (CDU/CSU, ÖVP, DC included).

	1945–9	1950–4	1955–9	1960–4	1965–9	1970–4	1975–9	1980–4	1985–9	1990–4
Aus.	46.9	41.3	45.1	45.4	48.3	43.9	42.4	43.0	41.3	29.9
Belg.	—	—	—	—	—	—	—	—	—	—
Den.	15.3	18.2	18.91	21.9	20.6	13.0	8.8	19.0	20.1	15.5
Fin.	16.0	13.7	15.3	14.6	13.8	17.8	21.5	22.5	23.2	19.6
Fr.	13.5	35.7	31.0	45.8	44.7	37.0	36.2	32.2	42.7	44.2
FRG	38.1	49.3	53.6	48.1	47.0	44.9	48.6	56.7	44.3	42.7*
Gr.	58.0	43.3	46.2	41.8	—	55.5	42.9	37.6	44.1	45.9
Ice.	39.5	40.4	41.5	41.4	38.6	40.5	34.1	38.7	27.2	38.6
Ire.	—	—	—	—	—	—	—	—	—	—
It.	44.7	46.9	47.2	39.9	40.3	38.7	38.5	32.9	34.3	33.2
Lux.	—	—	—	—	—	—	—	—	—	—
Neth.	—	—	—	—	—	—	—	—	—	—
Norw.	18.1	18.6	18.9	20.0	20.4	17.4	24.8	31.7	26.3	16.9
Port.	—	—	—	—	—	—	0.5	0.5	—	0.4
Sp.	—	—	—	—	—	—	42.4	35.3	35.1	34.8
Sw.	12.3	14.4	18.3	15.7	13.7	12.9	18.0	23.6	19.8	22.2
Switz.	—	—	—	—	—	—	—	—	—	—
Turk.	—	55.1	47.7	34.8	53.0	35.1	38.8	45.2	27.7	51.0
UK	39.6	45.7	49.6	43.4	41.9	40.1	43.9	42.4	42.3	41.9
Can.	28.6	31.0	46.3	35.1	31.9	35.2	35.9	41.3	42.9	16.1
USA	45.1	55.1	57.4	44.0	43.4	60.7	48.0	58.1	53.4	37.1
Jap.	31.7	47.8	60.5	55.8	48.2	46.9	43.2	46.9	49.4	51.8
Austral.	35.9	43.1	38.5	35.4	37.5	33.5	40.0	35.4	34.5	36.0
NZ	48.4	49.2	44.2	47.4	44.4	41.5	43.7	37.4	44.0	41.5

* Germany

Source: See Table 7.1.

TABLE 7.12. Electoral strength of protest parties in national elections

	1945–9	1950–4	1955–9	1960–4	1965–9	1970–4	1975–9	1980–4	1985–9	1990–4
Aus.	—	—	—	—	3.3	0.3	—	—	—	11.7
Belg.	—	—	—	—	—	—	0.5	2.7	0.6	3.4
Den.	—	—	—	2.2	1.0	8.0	13.1	6.3	6.9	6.4
Fin.	—	—	—	—	—	9.9	5.1	9.8	7.5	5.2
Fr.	2.9	—	6.5	—	—	—	—	—	—	—
FRG	—	—	—	—	—	—	—	—	—	0.6*
Gr.	—	—	—	—	—	—	—	—	—	—
Ice.	—	—	—	—	—	—	—	—	10.8	1.2
Ire.	—	—	—	—	—	—	—	—	—	—
It.	2.7	2.8	0.6	—	—	—	—	1.4	—	0.2
Lux.	—	—	—	6.0	0.4	—	4.5	—	10.2	11.6
Neth.	—	—	0.4	2.1	4.8	2.5	0.8	0.4	0.6	7.0
Norw.	—	—	—	—	—	5.0	1.9	4.5	8.4	7.3
Port.	—	—	—	—	—	—	—	—	—	1.7
Sp.	—	—	—	—	—	—	—	—	—	—
Sw.	—	—	—	—	—	—	—	—	—	3.9
Switz.	—	—	—	—	0.6	7.2	2.7	3.5	4.8	9.5
Turk.	—	—	—	—	—	—	—	—	—	—
UK	—	—	—	—	—	—	—	—	—	—
Can.	—	—	—	—	—	—	0.5	0.9	0.4	18.1
USA	—	—	—	—	13.5	1.4	0.2	—	0.5	18.9
Jap.	—	—	—	—	—	—	—	—	—	—
Austral.	—	—	—	—	—	—	—	—	—	—
NZ	—	—	—	—	—	—	—	—	—	4.5

* Germany

Source: See Table 7.1.

TABLE 7.13. Electoral strength of ultra-right parties in national elections

	1945–9	1950–4	1955–9	1960–4	1965–9	1970–4	1975–9	1980–4	1985–9	1990–4
Aus.	—	—	—	—	—	—	—	—	—	—
Belg.	—	—	—	—	—	—	—	—	—	1.0
Den.	—	—	—	—	—	—	—	—	—	—
Fin.	—	—	—	—	—	—	—	—	—	—
Fr.	1.8	1.1	1.0	—	0.1	0.5	0.5	0.3	9.9	12.7
FRG	—	—	—	0.8	3.2	0.6	0.3	0.2	0.6	2.2*
Gr.	—	—	—	—	—	—	6.8	—	0.3	0.1
Ice.	—	—	—	—	—	—	—	—	—	—
Ire.	—	—	—	—	—	—	—	—	—	—
It.	1.0	5.8	4.8	5.1	4.4	8.7	5.7	6.8	5.9	9.5
Lux.	—	—	—	—	—	—	—	—	—	—
Neth.	—	—	—	—	—	—	—	—	—	—
Norw.	—	—	—	—	—	—	—	—	—	—
Port.	—	—	—	—	—	—	—	—	—	—
Sp.	—	—	—	—	—	—	1.3	—	—	—
Sw.	—	—	—	—	—	—	—	—	—	—
Switz.	—	—	—	—	—	—	—	—	—	—
Turk.	—	4.1	7.2	27.7	10.3	15.8	8.2	23.3	2.9	—
UK	—	—	—	—	—	0.2	0.6	0.1	—	—
Can.	—	—	—	—	—	—	—	—	—	—
USA	—	—	—	—	—	—	—	—	—	—
Jap.	—	—	—	—	—	—	—	—	—	—
Austral.	—	—	—	—	—	—	—	—	—	—
NZ	—	—	—	—	—	—	—	—	—	—

* Germany

Source: See Table 7.1.

TABLE 7.14. Electoral strength of environmentalist/green parties in national elections

	1970–4	1975–9	1980–4	1985–9	1990–4
Aus.	—	—	3.3	4.8	6.9
Belg.	—	0.6	4.4	6.7	10.2
Den.	—	—	—	1.3	0.5
Fin.	—	—	1.4	4.0	6.8
Fr.	—	2.2	1.4	0.8	7.6
FRG	—	—	3.6	8.3	6.4*
Gr.	—	—	—	0.2	0.6
Ice.	—	—	5.5	11.7	8.6
Ire.	—	—	—	0.7	1.4
It.	—	2.3	2.2	5.1	3.4
Lux.	—	1.0	5.2	8.5	9.9
Neth.	—	—	—	0.2	3.5
Norw.	—	—	—	0.4	0.1
Port.	—	—	—	0.4	—
Sp.	—	—	—	0.7	—
Sw.	—	—	1.7	3.5	4.2
Switz.	—	—	2.9	7.8	7.4
Turk.	—	—	—	—	—
UK	—	—	0.2	0.3	0.5
Can.	—	—	—	0.4	—
USA	—	—	—	—	—
Jap.	—	—	—	—	—
Austral.	—	—	—	—	0.6
NZ	2.0	3.8	0.2	0.1	12.8

* Germany

Source: See Table 7.1.

TABLE 7.15. Electoral strength of other parties in national elections

	1945–9	1950–4	1955–9	1960–4	1965–9	1970–4	1975–9	1980–4	1985–9	1990–4
Aus.	0.4	0.4	0.1	0.5	0.0	0.1	0.0	0.3	0.3	1.1
Belg.	1.2	0.3	0.7	2.1	1.2	1.1	1.7	2.3	0.7	0.5
Den.	0.1	0.0	0.0	0.2	0.0	0.0	0.4	0.2	0.3	0.6
Fin.	0.4	0.1	0.5	0.7	0.0	0.1	0.5	0.0	0.6	2.1
Fr.	0.5	0.7	1.6	0.9	1.8	2.3	2.4	0.6	0.1	4.2
FRG	5.9	0.3	0.4	0.1	0.3	0.1	0.2	0.1	0.9	0.8*
Gr.	2.3	3.0	0.8	0.5	—	1.1	0.9	0.5	0.8	0.7
Ice.	0.1	0.0	0.0	0.2	0.0	0.2	2.4	1.0	0.0	1.0
Ire.	8.3	7.7	6.6	5.4	2.7	3.9	5.6	3.8	4.0	5.9
It.	2.3	2.2	0.5	0.9	0.8	0.9	1.0	0.5	0.7	5.0
Lux.	0.9	0.0	0.7	0.0	0.0	1.1	0.4	1.2	1.1	1.8
Neth.	1.3	1.4	0.7	1.6	2.6	1.4	0.9	1.3	0.6	1.8
Norw.	0.1	0.0	0.2	0.2	0.1	0.9	0.9	0.9	0.8	1.4
Port.	—	—	—	—	—	—	1.6	1.2	1.0	4.4
Sp.	—	—	—	—	—	—	3.6	5.5	3.9	6.5
Sw.	0.1	0.1	0.1	0.1	0.0	0.5	0.6	0.3	0.6	1.0
Switz.	0.5	0.5	0.8	1.8	2.3	1.7	2.5	3.4	4.7	2.4
Turk.	—	—	—	0.8	4.4	2.8	2.5	1.1	0.4	0.5
UK	2.2	0.3	0.2	0.2	0.2	0.5	0.7	0.6	0.3	0.2
Can.	4.8	2.4	1.7	0.3	1.0	1.0	0.9	0.8	3.6	3.7
USA	0.0	0.1	0.5	0.4	0.2	0.2	1.4	0.5	0.5	0.8
Jap.	17.8	6.7	5.7	4.8	5.7	5.3	5.8	5.1	6.0	7.4
Austral.	2.3	1.4	1.1	0.7	2.1	0.8	1.5	1.7	2.0	5.6
NZ	0.4	0.3	0.2	0.6	0.9	1.5	0.8	1.1	1.4	1.8

* Germany

Source: See Table 7.1.

TABLE 7.16. Effective number of parties in parliament

	1950–4	1955–9	1960–4	1965–9	1970–4	1975–9	1980–4	1985–9	1990–4
Aus.	2.75	2.48	2.46	2.39	2.29	2.28	2.40	2.72	3.51
Belg.	2.92	2.79	3.08	4.11	5.42	6.60	8.77	8.13	9.81
Den.	3.91	3.91	3.77	4.30	5.73	5.27	5.50	5.84	4.80
Fin.	4.97	5.18	5.78	5.21	6.06	5.80	5.46	5.81	5.91
Fr.	5.41	5.97	5.24	4.25	5.88	4.83	4.00	3.87	7.13
FRG	3.31	2.75	2.82	2.53	2.39	2.36	2.54	2.87	3.75*
Gr.	4.96	2.86	2.59	—	2.74	3.74	2.68	2.63	2.63
Ice.	4.16	3.56	3.37	3.77	3.79	4.06	4.24	5.79	4.22
Ire.	2.86	3.13	3.19	2.77	2.80	2.73	2.75	3.43	3.94
It.	4.17	3.86	4.13	3.95	4.22	3.72	4.52	4.61	7.14
Lux.	3.09	3.33	3.53	3.56	4.32	4.29	3.63	4.66	4.71
Neth.	5.00	4.36	4.78	6.21	6.97	3.97	4.41	3.84	5.66
Nor.	3.50	3.36	3.67	3.51	5.08	3.75	3.88	4.23	4.73
Port.	—	—	—	—	—	3.56	3.32	3.89	2.86
Sp.	—	—	—	—	—	4.30	3.43	3.84	3.31
Sw.	3.28	3.35	3.34	3.18	3.49	3.61	3.39	3.72	4.11
Switz.	5.10	5.02	5.00	5.52	6.06	5.64	5.99	6.84	7.37
Turk.	2.24	2.47	3.40	3.03	4.31	2.63	2.84	4.11	4.67
UK	2.29	2.22	2.53	2.42	2.91	2.87	3.12	3.33	3.03
Can.	2.86	2.72	3.22	3.14	3.11	3.09	2.84	3.04	3.92
USA	2.13	2.05	2.00	2.04	2.04	2.04	2.04	2.03	2.13
Jap.	3.96	3.15	2.52	3.23	3.44	3.93	3.56	3.39	4.40
Austral.	2.48	2.86	2.80	2.91	2.72	2.91	2.83	2.90	3.13
NZ	2.24	2.31	2.38	2.53	2.43	2.71	2.94	2.34	3.13

* Germany

Note: The effective number of parties score takes into account not just the number of parties but also their strength. The score is derived from the Laakso and Taagepera index (Laakso and Taagepera, 1979).

Sources: Computed from data provided in Mackie and Rose (1982); Bartolini and Mair (1990); Mair and Katz, eds. (1992); and recent newspaper reports.

Table 7.17. Electoral volatility in national elections

	1950–4	1955–9	1960–4	1965–9	1970–4	1975–9	1980–4	1985–9	1990–4
Aus.	3.6	4.4	1.7	4.8	4.5	0.9	4.6	6.3	11.2
Belg.	8.8	5.4	7.1	11.8	5.8	4.8	16.4	7.1	13.0
Den.	6.1	3.8	7.1	10.3	15.4	15.6	11.7	8.0	13.3
Fin.	3.5	6.3	5.6	8.4	9.4	6.5	10.3	6.9	12.4
Fr.	20.0	23.5	19.2	7.7	10.9	6.7	13.5	10.5	19.1
FRG	21.2	9.2	11.5	6.8	6.0	3.9	6.5	5.9	5.5*
Gr.	32.8	10.9	11.7	—	34.7	22.6	27.2	5.7	8.1
Ice.	9.4	9.1	4.4	6.3	9.3	15.2	10.4	23.6	13.3
Ire.	9.8	11.2	9.9	5.6	3.8	7.6	5.5	15.4	15.4
It.	14.1	5.2	8.5	7.8	5.3	7.2	8.3	8.4	28.6
Lux.	8.3	8.6	12.2	11.0	12.8	14.3	15.2	14.6	5.6
Neth.	5.6	4.6	5.0	10.8	12.1	12.8	9.1	7.8	21.5
Nor.	4.5	2.3	3.6	6.1	15.9	14.7	11.2	9.9	14.8
Port.	—	—	—	—	—	10.4	7.3	22.3	9.6
Sp.	—	—	—	—	—	7.7	39.0	7.3	10.5
Sw.	3.8	5.3	3.2	5.7	7.9	4.8	7.9	7.5	12.8
Switz.	4.0	1.9	1.6	6.0	7.6	5.8	6.1	8.0	7.4
Turk.	9.8	11.7	32.8	14.8	30.0	18.3	99.0	38.0	20.0
UK	5.6	2.9	6.0	4.3	8.2	8.5	2.9	3.9	5.1
Can.	3.5	12.1	10.8	7.8	8.3	3.6	12.9	7.8	40.6
USA	3.2	3.2	2.3	3.4	3.7	2.4	3.9	1.8	3.9
Jap.	10.0	9.5	4.5	7.2	4.1	5.3	3.2	4.9	10.3
Austral.	9.4	6.0	4.7	7.0	5.1	9.6	4.5	2.4	9.2
NZ	6.9	4.2	3.1	6.2	6.2	10.4	10.7	14.0	15.8

* Germany

Note: Volatility measures net changes in voter support for political parties in national elections. It is measured by the Pedersen volatility index (Pedersen, 1979, 1983).

Sources: See Table 7.16.

Section 8: Political Communications

TABLE 8.1. Domestic lettermail (per capita)

	1950	1955	1960	1965	1970	1975	1978
Aus.	68.7	74.1	98.6	114.3	168.8	—	222.8
Belg.	223.4	234.7	228.5	237.3	238.7	206.8	298.9
Den.	—	94.7	106.7	126.3	153.5	239.0	248.4
Fin.	33.2	45.9	62.7	84.1	127.1	132.9	135.4
Fr.	—	98.2	125.9	147.4	190.8	209.0	221.5
FRG	86.7	112.7	145.4	151.7	158.8	183.6	201.7
Gr.	16.4	20.6	22.0	30.3	24.6	26.6	31.5
Ice.	44.0	47.1	69.1	34.2	42.5	—	85.9
Ire.	70.6	86.6	—	92.8	—	—	98.8[a]
It.	53.6	70.5	98.5	101.1	—	103.6	91.5
Lux.	100.9	96.5	131.5	127.0	134.2	128.0	137.4
Neth.	137.4	151.7	160.4	194.4	225.7	253.1	279.8
Norw.	76.2	88.5	103.8	116.5	134.0	221.0	262.1
Port.	26.3	33.5	39.3	40.7	43.9	47.4	44.0
Sp.	37.0	46.3	70.3	76.6	101.8	107.0	98.4
Sw.	121.2	137.2	145.7	172.4	193.8	290.9	317.8
Switz.	194.3	220.7	254.9	245.8	263.7	422.3	476.6
Turk.	5.7	9.1	6.2	10.5	14.5	11.7	14.1[a]
UK	160.6	180.2	192.0	197.2	180.2	165.8	167.1
Can.	197.4	193.4	199.8	233.3	209.9	208.8	249.7
USA	296.0	332.9	343.5	361.1	404.3	416.5	—
Jap.	38.0	53.5	73.0	95.4	110.1	118.3	108.1[a]
Austral.	161.0	160.8	165.3	195.9	195.2	148.4	160.2
NZ	—	189.6	206.6	203.1	203.8	209.7	189.1

[a] 1977

Notes: Figures after 1978 not available. The figures cover letters (ordinary mail and registered), postcards, printed matter, merchandise samples, small packets and phonopost packets. They include mail carried without charge, but exclude ordinary parcels, and insured letters and boxes. Domestic items: items mailed for distribution within the national territory.

Figures for Canada 1950–1970 = total mail sent (domestic lettermail, foreign lettermail (sent and received)).

Sources: UN *Statistical Yearbook 1955* (1956); UN *Statistical Yearbook 1960* (1961); UN *Statistical Yearbook 1971* (1972); UN *Statistical Yearbook 1978/79* (1981).

TABLE 8.2. Foreign lettermail (sent) per capita

	1950	1955	1960	1965	1970	1975	1978
Aus.	5.3	10.8	16.4	20.1	23.6	—	28.6
Belg.	8.5	14.0	16.0	20.1	23.6	17.0	20.6
Den.	—	6.0	7.6	9.3	12.2	10.2	10.5[a]
Fin.	2.3	2.6	3.7	5.5	6.8	7.6	8.9[a]
Fr.	—	6.3	7.2	8.7	7.8	8.0	8.7[a]
FRG	3.3	5.2	8.1	11.6	8.6	7.7	7.3
Gr.	1.8	2.6	2.7	6.0	5.7	7.0	7.1
Ice.	5.0	5.5	6.4	8.9	9.6	9.0	6.9[a]
Ire.	20.9	18.8	—	23.5	—	—	26.2
It.	2.4	3.6	5.0	6.9	—	7.1	6.5
Lux.	15.2	23.0	31.5	32.9	47.5	67.4	57.5
Neth.	6.4	10.1	12.2	20.6	21.9	21.0	22.1
Norw.	5.4	6.1	7.7	10.0	9.5	8.0	9.0
Port.	2.2	5.0	8.3	9.0	10.3	5.2	4.2
Sp.	1.5	2.7	4.4	8.7	9.8	10.8	11.0
Sw.	5.2	5.8	7.3	8.7	10.3	12.9	9.2
Switz.	16.6	24.9	29.8	34.4	36.9	32.9	33.5
Turk.	0.6	0.7	0.5	1.1	1.7	2.0	1.9[a]
UK	7.4	9.3	9.9	10.4	10.3	11.2	11.1
Can.	—	—	—	—	—	4.6	5.2
USA	2.6	3.0	3.0	3.0	4.3	4.3	—
Jap.	0.1	0.3	0.5	0.8	1.1	0.8	0.9[a]
Austral.	10.4	5.9	7.6	11.1	10.7	7.4	5.7
NZ	—	17.0	16.4	11.2	11.8	13.4	12.0

[a] 1977

Notes: Figures after 1978 not available. The figures cover letters (airmail, ordinary mail and registered), postcards, printed matter, merchandise samples, small packets and phonopost packets. They include mail carried without charge, but exclude ordinary parcels, and insured letters and boxes. Foreign: items mailed for distribution outside the national territory. Mail in transit is not included.

Sources: See Table 8.1.

Comparative Tables

TABLE 8.3. Foreign lettermail (received) per capita

	1950	1955	1960	1965	1970	1975	1978
Aus.	5.3	13.4	17.2	20.0	22.4	—	29.8
Belg.	8.8	9.1	9.7	20.5	22.8	17.6	21.9
Den.	—	7.1	10.1	10.6	12.6	14.5	14.6[a]
Fin.	3.9	6.3	6.7	9.2	12.0	12.8	13.7
Fr.	—	4.1	—	7.2	6.9	6.7	8.1[a]
FRG	2.2	5.0	6.1	6.9	8.5	9.7	9.3
Gr.	—	—	—	—	—	9.1	8.4
Ice.	7.9	9.4	11.8	16.3	17.1	15.4	13.4
Ire.	20.2	22.8	—	30.8	—	24.1	24.1[a]
It.	1.8	3.4	5.1	7.5	—	7.6	7.4
Lux.	31.6	49.1	59.3	66.0	82.1	63.9	69.6
Neth.	5.5	7.3	9.2	11.0	13.4	12.5	13.4
Norw.	5.9	7.0	9.4	11.8	11.3	12.2	12.8
Port.	2.8	3.7	7.1	8.6	10.3	5.0	4.0
Sp.	2.1	3.3	5.0	9.4	8.8	9.6	9.7
Sw.	6.3	8.3	10.1	11.6	15.1	13.4	13.0
Switz.	14.6	19.7	—	28.0	29.4	27.0	27.2
Turk.	0.4	0.9	0.8	1.1	1.3	1.1	1.8[a]
UK	—	5.9	7.4	8.1	8.9	9.2	10.7
Can.	—	—	—	—	—	5.7	7.6
USA	—	4.8	5.6	10.7	7.2	8.3	—
Jap.	0.1	0.4	0.6	0.9	1.2	1.0	1.0[a]
Austral.	10.4	11.3	14.3	16.4	13.2	13.9	10.5
NZ	—	—	—	—	25.0	21.0	22.7

[a] 1977

Notes: Figures after 1978 not available. The figures cover letters (airmail, ordinary mail and registered), postcards, printed matter, merchandise samples, small packets and phonopost packets. They include mail carried without charge, but exclude ordinary parcels, and insured letters and boxes. Foreign: items received from outside the national territory. Mail in transit is not included.

Sources: See Table 8.1

TABLE 8.4. Telephones per hundred inhabitants

	1970	1975	1980	1985	1990
Aus.	19.3	28.1	40.1	49.2	58.9
Belg.	21.1	28.5	36.9	44.0	54.6
Den.	34.2	45.4	64.1	78.3	97.2
Fin.	25.7	38.9	49.6	61.7	53.0[a]
Fr.	17.2	26.2	45.9	60.8	48.2[a]
FRG	22.5	31.7	46.4	62.1	67.1
Gr.	12.0	22.1	28.9	31.3	45.8
Ice.	34.7	41.7	47.7	—	49.6
Ire.	10.4	13.8	18.7	26.5	27.9
It.	17.4	25.9	33.7	44.8	55.5
Lux.	32.6	41.2	—	—	—
Neth.	26.0	36.8	50.9	60.5	46.2[a]
Norw.	29.4	35.0	42.2	—	50.2
Port.	8.4	11.3	13.8	18.0	26.3
Sp.	13.5	—	31.5	36.3	32.3[a]
Sw.	55.7	66.1	79.6	—	68.1
Switz.	48.2	61.3	72.7	83.2	90.5
Turk.	1.6	2.5	4.2	6.7	15.1
UK	25.1	36.4	47.7	—	43.4[a]
Can.	45.4	57.5	68.6	74.9	57.0
USA	58.3	68.6	78.8	—	50.9[a]
Jap.	19.3	35.6	46.0	55.5	42.1
Austral.	31.2	39.0	48.9	55.0	—
NZ	42.7	49.6	55.0	64.0	43.0[a]

[a] Main lines only

Note: The figures relate to the number of public and private telephones installed which can be connected to a central exchange.

Sources: UN *Statistical Yearbook 1981* (1983); UN *Statistical Yearbook 1988–89* (1992); UN *Statistical Yearbook 1990–91* (1993).

TABLE 8.5. Radio broadcasting: number of receivers per thousand inhabitants

	Code	1950	1955	1960	1965	1970	1975	1980	1985	1990
Aus.	R	—	—	—	—	428	475	507	556	624
	L	190	249	279	297	269	298	317	346	—
Belg.	R	—	—	—	—	559	633	731	756	778
	L	179	241	289	320	352	397	458	459	—
Den.	R	—	—	—	—	700	914	927	952	1030
	L	283	288	332	334	332	335	380	410	—
Fin.	R	—	—	—	—	434	488	837	986	998
	L	180	241	276	334	387	445	—	—	—
Fr.	R	—	—	—	—	492	569	741	870	896
	L	165	214	241	313	315	326	334	336	—
FRG	R	—	—	—	—	824	849	893	942	952
	L	180	253	287	440	324	342	370	429	—
Gr.	R	—	—	—	104	113	276	343	403	423
	L	22	61	—	—	—	—	—	—	—
Ice.	R	—	—	—	—	613	642	711	768	787
	L	245	257	284	—	510	528	588	622	—
Ire.	R	—	—	—	—	234	285	375	577	583
	L	100	152	174	211	196	—	—	—	—
It.	R	—	—	—	—	567	586	602	648	797
	L	68	121	162	208	216	231	244	261	—
Lux.	R	—	—	—	—	463	493	548	621	630
	L	203	263	314	360	—	—	—	—	—
Neth.	R	—	—	—	—	564	565	650	829	906
	L	195	244	272	252	285	286	309	332	—
Norw.	R	—	—	—	—	633	643	661	778	798
	L	241	277	285	179	307	320	—	—	—
Port.	R	—	—	—	—	155	168	170	197	218
	L	27	55	95	128	151	166	—	—	—
Sp.	R	32	63	90	144	228	254	258	293	306
Sw.	R	—	—	—	—	466	513	842	868	888
	L	307	339	367	382	354	383	—	—	—
Switz.	R	—	—	—	—	598	710	813	838	855
	L	221	248	270	278	301	332	356	388	401
Turk.	R	—	—	—	—	101	105	113	139	161
	L	17	42	49	78	88	104	96	89	—
UK	R	—	—	—	—	624	694	950	1007	1146
	L	244	278	289	—	331	—	—	—	—
Can.	R	370	387	452	—	703	715	738	916	1026
USA	R	560	801	941	1233	1414	1857	1996	2090	2123
Jap.	R	—	—	—	209	223	520	678	786	907
	L	111	146	133	—	—	—	—	—	—
Austral.	R	—	—	—	—	578	1020	1089	1237	1280

	L	227	223	222	222	—	—	—	—	—
NZ	R	—	—	—	—	851	866	885	909	929
	L	238	240	245	—	—	—	—	—	—

Notes: This table gives information on the number of radio receivers and/or licences. Generally the data refer to the end of the year and relate to all types of receivers for radio broadcasts to the general public, including those connected to a cable distribution system (wired receivers), individual private receivers such as car radios, portable radio sets and private radio sets installed in public places as well as communal receivers. Data on receivers are estimates of the number of receivers in use. They vary widely in reliability from country to country and should be treated with caution. The number of radio licences shown in this table is composed of the number of licences for radio receivers plus the number of combined radio/television licences where applicable.

Code: R = Estimated number of receivers in use.

L = Number of licences issued or sets declared.

Sources: UNESCO *Statistical Yearbook 1965* (1966); UNESCO *Statistical Yearbook 1975* (1976); UNESCO *Statistical Yearbook 1992* (1993).

TABLE 8.6.　Television broadcasting: number of receivers per thousand inhabitants

	Code	1965	1970	1975	1980	1985	1990
Aus.	R	—	254	337	391	431	481
	L	98	190	251	295	320	—
Belg.	R	—	285	338	387	401	452
	L	163	218	260	298	302	—
Den.	R	—	372	417	498	522	535
	L	227	276	308	362	386	—
Fin.	R	—	261	352	414	469	497
	L	169	230	284	322	364	—
Fr.	R	—	236	285	353	390	406
	L	133	216	269	297	325	—
FRG	R	—	363	404	439	483	514
	L	193	275	311	337	372	403
Gr.	R	—	21	128	171	191	196
	L	—	19	116	156	173	—
Ice.	R	—	221	257	285	311	320
	L	—	201	239	281	303	324
Ire.	R	—	151	189	231	256	276
	L	114	148	167	181	211	—
It.	R	—	223	271	390	413	424
	L	117	185	218	237	254	263
Lux.	R	—	209	240	247	251	255
	L	94	—	—	—	—	—
Neth.	R	—	237	310	399	463	495
	L	172	237	267	296	320	—
Norw.	R	—	264	313	350	395	425
	L	131	220	261	293	330	355
Port.	R	—	56	95	158	174	177
	L	20	43	79	143	158	—
Sp.	R	—	122	187	254	269	396
Sw.	R	—	458	459	461	465	474
	L	270	313	355	381	390	392
Switz.	R	—	242	323	364	394	407
	L	104	207	281	316	344	—
Turk.	R	0.1	11	26	79	159	175
	L	—	11	25	77	155	—
UK	R	—	324	359	401	433	435
	L	248	293	319	329	331	—
Can.	R	271	334	405	442	553	641
USA	R	362	413	560	684	794	815
Jap.	R	183	336	359	539	579	620
	L	—	219	237	250	261	—
Austral.	R	—	220	334	381	444	486

	L	172	—	—	—	—	—
NZ	R	—	280	311	333	430	442
	L	156	235	259	277	288	—

Notes: This table gives statistics on the number of receivers and/or licences per 1,000 inhabitants. As in the case of radio receivers, data relating to television receivers is an estimate.

Code: R = Estimated number of receivers in use.

   L = Number of licences issued or sets declared.

Sources: See Table 8.5.

TABLE 8.7.   Daily newspapers (number)

	1952	1960	1965	1970	1975	1980	1985	1990
Aus.	35[a]	38	36	33	30	30	33	25
Belg.	39	47	54	49	30	26	24	33
Den.	127[a]	86	67	58	49	48	47	47
Fin.	64	64	68	67	60	58	65	66
Fr.	151	—	121	106	95	90	92	79
FRG	598[b]	473	—	—	350	329	319	315
Gr.	68	79	112	110	108	128	140	117
Ice.	5	5	5	5	5	6	6	6
Ire.	8	8	7	7	7	7	7	7
It.	107	87	92	73	78	82	72	76
Lux.	5	5	7	—	7	5	4	5
Neth.	108	—	88	95	84	84	88	86
Norw.	96	82	84	81	80	85	82	85
Port.	32	28	29	33	30	28	25	24
Sp.	104[a]	103	—	116	115	111	102	102
Sw.	145[a]	—	119	114	112	114	115	107
Switz.	127	—	132	117	95	89	97	94
Turk.	116	506	375	437	500	400	366	399
UK	114[b]	125	110	—	109	113	104	104
Can.	95	110	115	—	121	123	117	107
USA	1786	1763	1751	1773	1775	1750	1640	1611
Jap.	186	148	185	178	176	151	124	125
Austral.	54	63	61	58	70	62	62	62
NZ	43	42	—	40	40	32	33	35

   [a] 1953
   [b] 1954

Note: Daily newspapers are periodic publications (i.e. part of a continuous series of the same title) which are intended for the general public, concerned with information about current public affairs, and published at least four times a week.

Sources: See Table 8.5.

TABLE 8.8. Daily newspapers: estimated total circulation in thousands

	1952	1960	1965	1970	1975	1980	1985	1990
Aus.	1 393[a]	1 470	1 806	—	2 405	2 651	2 729	2 706
Belg.	3 343	2 500	2 701	—	2 340	2 289	2 171	3 000
Den.	1 602[a]	1 617	1 649	1 790	1 723	1 874	1 855	1 810
Fin.	1 100	1 597	—	—	2 100	2 414	2 661	2 780
Fr.	10 193	—	12 041	12 067	11 000	10 332	10 670	11 792
FRG	12 575	17 044	19 264	19 701	20 200	20 611	21 108	20 677
Gr.	550	1 000	—	705	921	1 160	1 350	1 400
Ice.	65	77	83	86	93	125	113	—
Ire.	700	691	702	686	693	799	685	591
It.	—	—	5 811	7 700	6 497	4 775	5 511	6 093
Lux.	130	140	158	—	130	135	140	145
Neth.	2 581	—	3 598	4 100	4 194	4 612	4 496	4 592
Norw.	1 317	1 353	1 431	1 487	1 657	1 892	2 120	2 588
Port.	—	4 304	622	743	612	480	413	390
Sp.	1 920	2 095	—	3 450	3 491	3 487	3 078	3 200
Sw.	3 188	—	3 909	4 324	4 413	4 386	4 389	4 499
Switz.	1 442	—	2 210	2 318	2 574	2 483	3 213	3 063
Turk.	693	1 411	—	—	2 000	2 500	3 020	4 000
UK	29 100	27 000	26 100	—	24 805	23 472	22 495	22 494
Can.	3 656[a]	3 979	4 271	—	4 900	5 425	5 566	5 993
USA	53 951	58 882	60 358	62 108	60 655	62 000	62 700	62 328
Jap.	31 998	37 039	44 480	53 304	60 728	66 258	68 296	72 524
Austral.	3 600	3 680	4 236	4 028	5 336	4 700	4 300	4 200
NZ	714	903	—	1 058	900	1 059	1 075	1 100

[a] 1953

Notes: Daily newspapers are periodic publications (i.e. part of a continuous series of the same title) which are intended for the general public, concerned with information about current public affairs, and published at least four times a week. Circulation figures for newspapers are the average daily circulation, and for non-daily publications, the average circulation per issue, including the number of copies sold directly, by subscription, and distributed free of charge nationally and abroad.

Sources: See Table 8.5.

TABLE 8.9. Daily newspapers: estimated circulation per thousand inhabitants

	1952	1960	1965	1970	1975	1980	1985	1990
Aus.	200	208	249	—	317	351	361	357
Belg.	384	285	285	—	239	232	220	305
Den.	366	353	347	364	341	366	362	352
Fin.	269	359	—	—	446	505	543	559
Fr.	239	—	246	238	209	192	193	210
FRG	242	307	326	319	327	335	346	338
Gr.	71	121	—	79	102	120	136	140
Ice.	439	438	435	410	427	548	467	—
Ire.	237	244	246	233	218	229	193	159
It.	—	—	113	144	117	85	96	107
Lux.	436	445	477	—	358	370	381	389
Neth.	249	—	293	315	307	326	310	311
Norw.	396	377	384	383	414	463	510	614
Port.	—	63	68	84	67	49	41	38
Sp.	67	70	—	104	98	93	80	82
Sw.	445	—	505	534	539	528	526	533
Switz.	300	—	376	375	406	393	497	463
Turk.	31	51	—	—	50	56	60	72
UK	114[a]	125	479	—	441	417	397	395
Can.	246	222	218	—	216	226	219	228
USA	342	326	310	302	281	272	252	250
Jap.	374	396	450	511	545	567	565	587
Austral.	416	358	373	321	392	320	273	249
NZ	358	381	—	376	292	340	331	324

[a] 1954

Notes: Daily newspapers are periodic publications (i.e. part of a continuous series of the same title) which are intended for the general public concerned with the information about current public affairs, and published at least four times a week. Circulation figures for newspapers are the average daily circulation, and for non-daily publications, the average circulation per issue, including the number of copies sold directly, by subscription, and distributed free of charge nationally and abroad.

Sources: See Table 8.5.

TABLE 8.10. Non-daily newspapers and other periodicals: number and circulation

| Country | Year | NEWSPAPERS | | | | | OTHER PERIODICALS | | |
		Total	1–3 Times a week	Issues less frequently	Estimated circulation Total (thousands)	Per thousand inhabitants	Number	Estimated circulation Total (thousands)	Per thousand inhabitants
Aus.	1964	138	137	1	—	—	2 330	—	—
	1970	116	116	—	—	—	2 541	—	—
	1975	129	129	—	—	—	2 140	—	—
	1980	142	140	2	—	—	2 172	—	—
	1984	143	143	—	—	—	2 315	—	—
	1990	124	123	1	—	—	2 619	—	—
Belg.	1960	—	—	—	—	—	3 427[a]	—	—
	1965	—	—	—	—	—	1 419	—	—
	1976	2	2	—	30	3	10 356	—	—
	1979	2	2	—	30	3	10 356	—	—
	1984	2	2	—	22	2	11 256	—	—
	1990	3	3	—	40	4	12 222	—	—
Den.	1961	—	—	—	—	—	506	9 211[a]	—
	1966	15	15	—	1 273	265	4 978	—	—
	1970	14	14	—	1 294	263	3 549	—	—
	1975	2	2	—	154	30	—	—	—
	1978	2	2	—	158	31	—	—	—
	1984	11	11	—	1 249	244	210	—	—
	1990	12	12	—	1 513	294	—	—	—
Fin.	1963	165	165	—	—	—	1 807	7 906	1 537
	1966	161	161	—	—	—	1 967	—	—

Country	Year								
Fr.	1970	173	173	—	—	—	3 351	—	—
	1975	223	223	—	—	—	2 113	—	—
	1979	234	234	—	1 108	233	3 132	—	—
	1984	311	287	24	—	—	4 432	—	—
	1990	382	330	52	—	338	5 711	—	—
FRG	1963	850	603	247	16 174	264	13 534	136 470	—
	1965	888	557	331	12 931	525	14 082	157 515	—
	1969	937	503	434	26 414	196	14 634	168 854	—
	1974	542	397	145	10 381	302	14 412	188 432	3 561
	1981	526	412	114	16 282	52	22 443	195 381	3 621
	1990	224	216	8	2 895	80	2 588	118 354	2 108
Gr.	1966	111	111	—	4 776	80	6 482[c]	151 789[c]	—
	1970	93	93	—	4 918	—	6 482[c]	151 789[c]	1 378
	1974	58[b]	58[b]	—	3 717[b]	73	867	85 305	3 596
	1978	—	49	9	2 139	72	5 268	220 466	4 477
	1986	38	29	—	4 417	—	6 908	272 733	5 049
	1989	35	35	—	4 412	—	7 831	309 041	—
	1964	789	273	516	—	—	601	—	—
	1965	790	—	355	—	—	593	—	—
	1970	541	186	431	—	—	—	—	—
	1976	642	211	619	—	—	622	—	—
	1979	871	252	—	—	—	868	—	—
	1986	—	223	—	—	—	773	—	—
	1988	1 051	236	815	—	—	309	—	—
Ice.	1957	31	—	—	—	—	122	—	—
	1967	65	9	56	—	—	196	—	—
	1970	90	6	84	—	—	176	—	—
	1975	53	9	44	—	—	302	—	—
	1990	66	15	51	—	—	562	—	—

TABLE 8.10. (*Contd.*)

| Country | Year | NEWSPAPERS | | | | | OTHER PERIODICALS | | |
| | | Total | 1–3 Times a week | Issues less frequently | Estimated circulation | | Number | Estimated circulation | |
					Total (thousands)	Per thousand inhabitants		Total (thousands)	Per thousand inhabitants
Ire.	1963	55	54	1	1 221	430	206	1 276	—
	1966	53	52	1	1 399	485	245	2 055	—
	1970	50	50	—	1 336	445	280	3 040	—
	1976	51	51	—	1 601	512	256	3 058	978
	1979	52	52	—	1 696	504	258	2 987	888
	1984	59	59	—	1 785	506	257	2 975	844
	1988	54	54	—	1 935	529	—	—	—
It.	1960	—	—	—	—	—	5 194[a]	—	—
	1963	—	—	—	—	—	6 103	—	—
	1971	147	143	4	3 350	62	7 993	—	—
	1975	111	111	—	—	—	7 325	—	—
	1979	190	150	40	—	—	7 373	—	—
	1984	264	182	82	2 052	36	8 500	75 332	1 316
	1989	235	186	49	2 223	39	9 121	79 103	1 385
Lux.	1965	3	3	—	—	—	224	—	—
	1970	1	1	—	—	—	224	—	—
	1979	—	—	—	—	—	314	—	—
	1982	4	4	—	—	—	427	—	—
	1990	1	1	—	3	8	508	—	—
Neth.	1966	154	154	—	1 001	80	1 783	16 359	—
	1971	167	162	5	1 300	99	1 800	16 000	—

	Year								
Nor.	1974	152	149	3	903	67	—	—	—
	1984	110	110	—	800	55	—	—	—
	1990	—	—	—	—	—	367	19 283	1 290
Port.	1964	99	99	—	349	94	2 412	—	—
	1970	104	104	—	356	92	2 412	—	—
	1975	73	73	—	311	78	3 855	—	—
	1979	78	78	—	374	92	4 159	—	—
	1984	81	81	—	407	99	3 881	—	—
	1990	65	65	—	347	82	6 498	—	—
Sp.	1965	265	153	112	—	—	180	2 107	—
	1967	645	183	462	2 361	250	437	—	—
	1975	307	138	169	—	—	901	—	—
	1979	—	126	—	—	—	1 123	—	—
	1984	288	115	173	1 692	167	699	5 220	514
	1990	328	112	216	—	—	937	6 359	618
Sw.	1963	68	58	10	1 933	62	4 180	4 727	—
	1970	102	84	18	3 235	97	3 685	30 695	1 261
	1975	132	94	38	3 878	109	5 163	44 739	1 523
	1977	24	23	1	1 013	28	5 508	55 352	—
	1986	85	50	35	—	—	1 998	—	—
	1988	85	50	35	3 100	79	1 998	13 020	—
Switz.	1964	45	45	—	256	33	365	—	—
	1970	53	53	—	367	46	4 061	—	—
	1974	70	—	1	477	59	4 219	4 947	—
	1977	69	68	—	512	62	3 690	18 740	—
	1990	70	70	—	416	49	46	28 994	593
	1965	341	319	22	2 023	340	1 122	31 462	—
	1971	178	164	14	890	142	1 433	—	—
	1976	160	144	16	860	134	1 460	—	4 914

TABLE 8.10. (Contd.)

| Country | Year | NEWSPAPERS | | | | | OTHER PERIODICALS | | |
| | | Total | 1–3 Times a week | Issues less frequently | Estimated circulation | | Number | Estimated circulation | |
					Total (thousands)	Per thousand inhabitants		Total (thousands)	Per thousand inhabitants
Switz.	1979	167	151	16	883	139	1 533	31 773	5 019
	1982	167	151	16	883	139	—	—	—
	1990	619	340	279	10 523	1 592	3 079	—	—
Turk.	1965	339	56	283	—	—	1 176	—	—
	1970	763	279	484	—	—	1 270	—	—
	1977	618	—	—	—	—	—	—	—
	1984	519	206	313	—	—	1 257	—	—
	1990	872	446	426	1 500	27	1 325	1 325	24
UK	1965	1 208	1 208	—	37 800^d	694^d	4 500	—	—
	1972	581	581	—	—	—	3 471	—	—
	1978	1 062	1 062	—	32 074	574	5 253	—	—
	1984	882	882	—	30 196	538	6 408	—	—
	1988	818	818	—	29 074	510	—	—	—
Can.	1965	873	873	—	—	—	864	—	—
	1968	847	—	—	—	—	895	—	—
	1975	1 095	1 005	90	7 839^c	—	988	—	—
	1979	1 268	1 101	167	13 098	553	1 015	55 110	2 326
	1984	1 229	1 085	144	14 200	565	1 382	59 071	2 348
	1990	1 425	—	—	19 719	760	1 503	39 510	1 490
USA	1966	8 012	—	—	76 159^f	387	—	427 915	—
	1967	10 109	—	—	79 834^g	401	9 400	—	—

Country	Year								
Jap.	1975	9 589	9 404	185	—	—	9 657	—	—
	1979	8 079	7 966	113	42 347	192	59 609	—	—
	1984	7 464	7 398	66	—	208	59 609	—	—
	1988	7 000	6 970	30	51 000	—	11 593	1 244 960	—
	1965	—	—	—	—	—	2 172	—	—
	1970	—	—	—	—	—	5 278	—	—
	1973	—	—	—	—	—	6 241	25 604	225
	1977	—	—	—	—	—	1 640	36 293	303
	1984	—	—	—	—	—	2 138	—	—
	1988	14	9	5	—	—	2 877	—	—
Austral.	1966	584	561	23	7 963	65	1 284	17 009	—
	1970	502	494	8	6 935	601	1 231	—	—
	1975	592	562	30	—	—	3 450	—	—
	1979	470	461	9	8 930	619	3 534	—	—
	1984	465	457	8	15 208	981	—	—	—
	1988	460	452	8	17 204	1 049	—	—	—
NZ	1964	69	62	7	1 202	463	1 452	—	—
	1970	70	66	4	1 547	549	1 576	—	—
	1976	111	78	33	—	—	4 653	—	—
	1979	111	83	28	—	—	4 653	—	—
	1984	148	118	30	—	—	5 788	—	—
	1988	139	128	11	1 100	330	—	—	—

[a] Non-daily and other periodicals

[b] Weekly newspapers only

[c] 1960

[d] Including 14 Sunday newspapers with 26 450 000 copies

[e] Circulation figure relates to 871 non-dailies

f Including circulation Sunday newspapers 49 282 000

g Including circulation Sunday newspapers 48 452 000

Notes: Non-daily newspapers are newspapers (i.e. part of a continuous series of the same title) which are intended for the general public, concerned with information about current public affairs, and published three times a week or less. Periodicals are periodic publications (i.e. part of a continuous series of the same title) which are intended for the general public and may be of very general or specialised interest. The category includes journals, reviews, magazines and other periodicals.

Sources: UNESCO *Statistical Yearbook 1965* (1966); UNESCO *Statistical Yearbook 1967* (1968); UNESCO *Statistical Yearbook 1971* (1972); UNESCO *Statistical Yearbook 1973* (1974); UNESCO *Statistical Yearbook 1976* (1977); UNESCO *Statistical Yearbook 1977* (1978); UNESCO *Statistical Yearbook 1986* (1988); UNESCO *Statistical Yearbook 1992* (1992); UNESCO *Statistical Yearbook 1993* (1993).

Section 9: The European Union

European Union

Constitutional Documents: Treaty of Rome (1958), Single European Act (1986), Maastricht Treaty (1991). The Acquis Communautaire comprise the existing obligations of membership in the EU. The European Union came into effect on January 1, 1993.

The Treaty of European Union (TEU) covers (1) the European Community, (2) Common Foreign and Security Policy and (3) Cooperation in areas of Justice and Home Affairs.

Main EU Institutions: Council of Ministers, European Commission, European Parliament and European Court of Justice.

Supportive EU Institutions: Court of Auditors, European Investment Bank, Economic and Social Committee, Consultative Committee and Committee of the Regions.

Member States: Austria (1995), Belgium (1958), Denmark (1973), Germany FR (1958), Greece (1981), Finland (1995), France (1958), Ireland (1973), Italy (1958), Luxembourg (1958), The Netherlands (1958), Portugal (1986), Spain (1986), Sweden (1995), The United Kingdom (1973).

TABLE 9.1. Own resources in 1992 by Member State (Ecu m.)

Member State	Type of resource					
	Agricultural levies	Sugar and isoglucose	Customs duties	GNP-based own resource	VAT-based own resource	Total own resources
Belg.	84.1	69.4	832.5	294.3	1 108.1	2 388.4
Den.	6.3	39.1	222.3	189.3	618.0	1 074.9
Fr.	74.7	321.8	1 548.9	1 719.0	7 505.7	11 170.2
FRG	142.0	333.0	3 546.0	2 413.3	10 162.2	16 596.5
Gr.	16.2	16.9	178.1	111.5	508.5	831.2
Ire.	2.0	12.0	153.2	54.4	248.2	469.7
It.	346.1	124.2	1 037.4	1 787.2	5 278.0	8 572.9
Lux.	0.1	—	11.5	17.4	79.2	108.2
Neth.	108.4	78.2	1 160.7	400.1	1 700.4	3 447.8
Port.	117.2	0.1	117.0	103.0	469.7	806.9
Sp.	141.3	50.0	555.8	774.2	3 531.5	5 052.8
UK	177.9	67.7	2 236.5	1 459.3	3 456.6	7 398.0
TOTAL	1 216.2	1 112.4	11 599.9	9 323.1	34 666.0	57 917.6
(% of total budget)	(2.1)	(1.9)	(20.0)	(16.1)	(60.0)	(100.0)

Source: Commission of the European Communities: 'Final Adoption of Amending and Supplementary Budget No. 3 of the European Communities for the Financial Year 1992', *Official Journal of the European Communities*, L349 (Nov.), 1–121.

TABLE 9.2. Expenditures made in 1991, by sector and recipient Member States (Ecu m.)

Member State	EAGGF Guarantee	EAGGF Guidance	Regional Fund	Social Fund	Repayment by Member States	Other	Total	a)
Belg.	1 459.4	11.3	46.4	65.3	12.5	1 039.1	2 634.0	(4.9%)
Den.	1 215.6	14.1	11.3	45.8	4.2	88.8	1 379.8	(2.6%)
Fr.	6 332.7	362.9	323.2	513.5	63.2	556.0	8 152.5	(15.2%)
FRG	4 990.5	181.0	94.8	239.7	252.9	838.5	6 597.4	(12.3%)
Gr.	2 211.8	223.4	537.2	349.1	—	367.0	3 688.5	(6.9%)
Ire.	1 628.7	153.6	411.9	403.8	101.5	110.3	2 809.7	(5.2%)
It.	5 347.0	203.8	710.8	414.5	5.7	629.5	7 311.2	(13.6%)
Lux.	2.8	5.5	18.3	1.8	—	240.2	268.5	(0.5%)
Neth.	2 469.8	15.2	34.6	122.5	211.6	146.0	2 999.8	(5.6%)
Port.	316.4	196.9	971.2	379.3	49.4	315.1	2 228.2	(4.1%)
Sp.	3 300.3	420.3	1 488.8	697.0	482.3	486.0	6 874.8	(12.8%)
UK	2 252.7	98.5	530.1	636.9	137.6	413.6	4 069.5	(7.6%)
TOTAL	31 527.8	1 886.4	5 178.6	3 869.3	1 320.8	5 231.0	49 008.5	(91.9%)

Note: a) Figures in parentheses show the percentage of the total budget allocated. The remaining 8.9% unallocated includes payments for overseas aid and administration. EAGGF enters the CAP or Common Agricultural Policy.

Source: Commission of the European Communities: 'Annual Report of the Court of Auditors Concerning the Financial Year 1991', *Official Journal of the European Communities*, C330 (Dec.), 1–496.

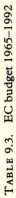

TABLE 9.3.   EC budget 1965–1992

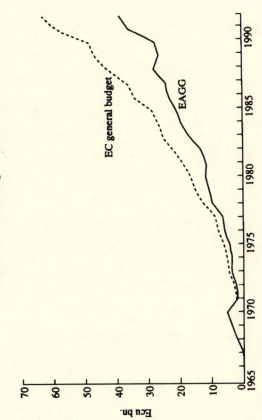

TABLE 9.4. Outline of the institutions of the European Community 1995

Country	Council of Ministers (votes)	The Commission	Parliament	Court of Justice	Economic and Social Commission	Committee of the Regions
Aus.	4	1	21	1	12	12
Belg.	5	1	25	1	12	12
Den.	3	1	16	1	9	9
FRG	10	2	99	1	24	24
Gr.	5	1	25	1	12	12
Fin.	3	1	16	1	9	9
Fr.	10	2	87	1	24	24
Ire.	3	1	15	1	19	19
It.	10	2	87	1	24	24
Lux.	2	1	6	1	6	6
Neth.	5	1	31	1	12	12
Port.	5	1	25	1	12	12
Sp.	5	2	64	1	21	21
Sw.	4	1	22	1	12	12
UK	10	2	87	1	24	24
TOTAL	87	20	626	15	222	222

There are nine Advocates-General.

TABLE 9.5. Turnout in European Parliament elections

	1979/81	1984/87	1989	1994
Belg.	80.0	82.0	83.1	90.7
Den.	46.7	51.6	45.6	52.5
FRG	65.1	55.9	61.6	58.0
Fr.	57.5	54.7	47.3	53.5
Gr.	87.3	79.8	83.4	37.0
Ire.	61.2	46.4	66.5	44.0
It.	82.9	79.1	74.4	74.8
Lux.	80.3	80.6	79.6	90.0
Neth.	57.8	50.5	47.1	35.6
Port.	—	70.3	49.5	35.7
Sp.	—	67.2	53.6	59.6
UK	32.1	32.1	36.6	36.1
N.Ire.	55.6	64.4	48.4	48.7

Note: Turnout equals valid votes as a percentage of the total electorate in each country.

Source: Curtice, J. (1989), '1989 European Elections Protest or Green Tide?' in *Electoral Studies*, vol. 8: 217–30. *Keesing's Record of World Events* (1994).

TABLE 9.6. Composition of the European Parliament 1979

	SOC	EPP	EDU	COM	LIB	EPD	TCG	NA	TOTAL
Belg.	7	10	0	0	4	0	1	2	24
Den.	4	0	3	1	3	1	4	0	16
Fr.	21	9	0	19	17	15	0	0	81
FRG	35	42	0	0	4	0	0	0	81
Ire.	4	4	0	0	1	5	1	0	15
It.	13	30	0	24	5	0	5	4	81
Lux.	1	3	0	0	2	0	0	0	6
Neth.	9	10	0	0	4	0	0	2	25
UK	18	0	61	0	0	1	0	1	81
TOTAL	112	108	64	44	40	22	11	9	410

Composition of the European Parliament 1981

	SOC	EPP	EDU	COM	LIB	EPD	TCG	NA	TOTAL
Belg.	7	10	0	0	4	0	1	2	24
Den.	4	0	3	1	3	1	4	0	16
Fr.	21	9	0	19	17	15	0	0	81
FRG	35	42	0	0	4	0	0	0	81
Gr.	10	8	0	4	0	0	0	2	24
Ire.	4	4	0	0	1	5	1	0	15
It.	13	30	0	24	5	0	5	4	81
Lux.	1	3	0	0	2	0	0	0	6
Neth.	9	10	0	0	4	0	0	2	25
UK	18	0	61	0	0	1	0	1	81
TOTAL	122	116	64	48	40	22	11	11	434

Note: SOC: Socialist group; EPP: European People's Party (Christian Democrats); EDU: European Democrats (Conservatives); COM: Communists and Allies; LIB: Liberal and Democratic Group; EPD: European Progressive Democrats (predominantly French Gaullists); TCG: Technical Co-ordination Group for the Defence of the Interests of Independent Groups and members; NA: Non- attached.

Composition of the European Parliament 1987

	SOC	EPP	EDU	COM	LIB	EPD	RBG	DR	NA	TOTAL
Belg.	9	6	0	0	5	0	4	0	0	24
Den.	3	1	4	2	2	0	4	0	0	16
Fr.	20	8	0	10	13	20	0	10	0	81
FRG	33	41	0	0	0	0	7	0	0	81
Gr.	10	9	0	4	0	0	0	1	0	24
Ire.	0	6	0	0	1	8	0	0	0	15
It.	12	27	0	27	5	0	2	5	3	81
Lux.	2	3	0	0	1	0	0	0	0	6
Neth.	9	8	0	0	5	0	2	0	1	25
Port.	7	4	0	3	10	0	0	0	0	24
Sp.	28	1	17	3	2	0	1	0	8	60
UK	33	0	45	0	0	1	0	1	1	81
TOTAL	166	114	66	49	44	29	20	17	13	518

Note: SOC: Socialist group; EPP: European People's Party (Christian Democrats); EDU: European Democrats (Conservatives); COM: Communists and Allies; LIB: Liberal and Democratic Group; EPD: European Democratic Alliance (predominantly French Gaullists); RBG: Rainbow Group (predominantly Green and Regionalist parties); DR: European Right (French FN and Italian MSI); NA: Non-attached.

Composition of the European Parliament 1989

	SOC	EPP	EDU	COM	EUL	LIB	EPD	RBG	VER	DR	NA	TOTAL
Belg.	8	7	0	0	0	4	0	1	3	1	0	24
Den.	4	2	2	0	1	3	0	4	0	0	0	16
Fr.	22	6	0	7	0	13	13	1	8	10	1	81
FRG	31	32	0	0	0	4	0	0	8	6	0	81
Gr.	9	10	0	3	1	0	1	0	0	0	0	24
Ire.	1	4	0	1	0	2	6	1	0	0	0	15
It.	14	27	0	0	22	3	0	3	7	0	5	81
Lux.	2	3	0	0	0	1	0	0	0	0	0	6
Neth.	8	10	0	0	0	4	0	0	2	0	1	25
Port.	8	3	0	3	0	9	0	0	1	0	0	24
Sp.	27	16	0	0	4	6	0	2	1	0	4	60
UK	46	1	32	0	0	0	0	1	0	0	1	81
TOTAL	180	121	34	14	28	49	20	13	30	17	12	518

Note: SOC: Socialist group; EPP: European People's Party (Christian Democrats); EDU: European Democrats (Conservatives); COM: Left Coalition (mainly French Communists); EUL: European Unity Left (mainly Italian Communists); LIB:

Note: SOC: Socialist group; EPP: European People's Party (Christian Democrats); EDU: European Democrats (Conservatives); COM: Left Coalition (mainly French Communists); EUL: European Unity Left (mainly Italian Communists); LIB: Liberal, Democratic and Reformist Group; EPD: European Democratic Alliance (predominantly French Gaullists); RBG: Rainbow Group (predominantly Regionalist parties); VER: Green Parties; DR: European Right (French FN and Italian MSI); NA: Non-attached.

Composition of the European Parliament 1994

	SOC	EPP	EUL	LIB	EPD	ERA	NE	VER	FE	NA	TOTAL
Belg.	6	7	0	6	0	1	0	2	0	3	25
Den.	3	3	0	5	0	0	4	1	0	0	16
Fr.	15	13	7	1	14	13	13	0	0	11	87
FRG	40	47	0	0	0	0	0	12	0	0	99
Gr.	10	9	4	0	2	0	0	0	0	0	25
Ire.	1	4	0	1	7	0	0	2	0	0	15
It.	18	12	5	7	0	2	0	4	27	12	87
Lux.	2	2	0	1	0	0	0	1	0	0	6
Neth.	8	10	0	10	0	0	2	1	0	0	31
Port.	10	1	3	8	3	0	0	0	0	0	25
Sp.	22	30	9	2	0	1	0	0	0	0	64
UK	63	19	0	2	0	2	0	0	0	1	87
TOTAL	198	157	28	43	26	19	19	23	27	27	567

Note: SOC: Socialist group; EPP: European People's Party (Christian Democrats and Conservatives); EUL: Confederal European United Left (mainly Italian Communists); LIB: Liberal, Democratic and Reformist Group; EPD: European Democratic Alliance (predominantly French Gaullists); ERA: European Radical Alliance (predominantly French Radicals); NE: Nations of Europe (predominantly Anti-Maastricht parties); VER: Green Parties; FE: Forza Europa; NA: Non-attached.

Source: *Keesing's Record of World Events*: (1994)

TABLE 9.7. European Parliament: 1979, 1984, 1989, 1994

Party grouping according to ideological criteria

		COM LEFT	SOC	GREEN	CHR DEM	LIB	CONS	REG NAT	FAR RIGHT	OTHER	TOTAL
Belg.	79	0	7	0	10	4	0	3	0	0	24
	84	0	9	2	6	5	0	2	0	0	24
	89	0	8	3	7	4	0	1	1	0	24
	94	0	6	2	7	6	0	1	3	0	25
Den.	79	1	4	0	0	4	2	0	0	5	16
	84	1	4	0	0	3	4	0	0	4	16
	89	1	4	0	0	5	2	0	0	4	16
	94	1	3	0	0	5	3	0	0	4	16
Fr.	79	19	22	0	0	0	40	0	0	0	81
	84	10	20	0	0	0	41	0	10	0	81
	89	7	22	9	7	0	26	0	10	0	81
	94	7	15	0	0	13	28	0	11	13	87
FRG	79	0	34	0	43	4	0	0	0	0	81
	84	0	33	7	41	0	0	0	0	0	81
	89	0	31	8	32	4	0	0	6	0	81
	94	0	40	12	47	0	0	0	0	0	99
Gr.	81	5	10	0	0	0	8	0	1	0	24
	84	4	10	0	0	0	9	0	1	0	24
	89	4	9	0	0	0	10	0	0	1	24
	94	4	10	0	0	0	11	0	0	0	25
Ire.	79	0	4	0	4	0	5	0	0	2	15
	84	0	0	0	6	0	8	0	0	1	15
	89	1	1	0	4	1	6	0	0	2	15
	94	0	1	2	4	0	7	0	0	1	15

It.	79	25	13	0	29	8	0	2	4	0	81
	84	28	12	0	26	8	0	2	5	0	81
	89	23	14	6	26	4	0	4	4	0	81
	94	21	3	3	11	4	0	7	11	27	87
Lux.	79	0	1	0	3	2	0	0	0	0	6
	84	0	2	0	3	1	0	0	0	0	6
	89	0	2	0	3	1	0	0	0	0	6
	94	0	2	1	2	1	0	0	0	0	6
Neth.	79	0	10	0	9	6	0	0	0	0	25
	84	1	9	0	10	5	0	0	0	0	25
	89	2	8	0	11	4	0	0	0	0	25
	94	0	8	1	12	10	0	0	0	0	31
Port.	79	—	—	—	—	—	—	—	—	—	—
	87	3	6	0	4	11	0	0	0	0	24
	89	4	8	0	3	9	0	0	0	0	24
	94	3	10	0	3	9	0	0	0	0	25
Sp.	79	—	—	—	—	—	—	—	—	—	—
	87	3	28	0	0	7	17	5	0	0	60
	89	4	27	0	0	5	15	9	0	0	60
	94	9	22	0	0	0	28	5	0	0	64
UK	79	0	18	0	0	0	61	1	0	1	81
	84	0	33	0	0	0	46	1	0	1	81
	89	0	46	0	0	0	33	1	0	1	81
	94	0	63	0	0	2	19	2	0	1	87

Sources: *Electoral Studies* (1984: 3; 1989: 3; 1994: 4), EP News (1994), *Keesing's Record of World Events* (1979, 1984, 1989, 1994), Mackie, T. (1990), 'Appendix: elections in Western Europe during the 1980s' in: Urwin, D. W. and W. E. Paterson (eds.), *Politics in Western Europe Today: Perspectives, Policies and Problems Since 1980* (Harlow: Longman), 270–91.

TABLE 9.8.   Decision procedures

Council of Ministers: (1) Simple majority, or more than 50% (2) more than 70% in favour of a proposal from the Commission. (3) more than 70% in favour, cast by at least two thirds of the members, in other cases. (4) Unanimity: constitutional matters, decisions overruling amendments or decisions of the EU Parliament, or amending a Commission proposal.

Commission: simple majority

European Court of Justice: simple majority

European Parliament: simple majority

EU Legislation:

Decision procedures: (a) Consultation procedure: the EU Parliament has only an advisory role in relation to the Council of Ministers. (b) Conciliation procedure: certain issues concerning free movement, the Internal Market, research frameworks, environment, consumer protection, trans-European infrastructure, education, culture and public health. (c) Cooperation procedure: remaining issues. The cooperation procedure is a double reading system involving the European Parliament, the Commission, and the Council acting in accordance with a strict time-scale for how the key players may express opinions on proposals introduced by the Commission. Under the cooperation procedure the Parliament has only a suspensive veto. The conciliation procedure involves the use of a conciliation committee where differences between the three players can be ironed out, but in this procedure the Parliament has an absolute power of veto.

Types of EU legislation: (1) Regulation: directly applicable on all states in its entirety. (2) Directive: binding on states named, who decide the form of implementation at the national level. (3) Decisions: administrative acts that are binding for only those states that are addressed. (4) Recommendations: expresses only EU preferences, not binding. (5) Opinions: not binding.

Source: Church, C. H. and Phinnemore, D. (1994), *European Union and European Community* (London: Harvester Wheatsheaf).

TABLE 9.9. Votes in the EU Council

Country	1958	1973	1981	1986	1995
Fr.	4	10	10	10	10
FRG	4	10	10	10	10
It.	4	10	10	10	10
Belg.	2	5	5	5	5
Neth.	2	5	5	5	5
Lux.	1	2	2	2	2
Den.	—	3	3	3	3
Ire.	—	3	3	3	3
UK	—	10	10	10	10
Gr.	—	—	5	5	5
Port.	—	—	—	5	5
Sp.	—	—	—	8	8
Aus.	—	—	—	—	4
Fin.	—	—	—	—	3
Sw.	—	—	—	—	4
TOTAL	17	58	63	76	87

TABLE 9.10   Voting power: Council of Ministers

Power may be tapped by a measure of different actors' degree of control over the outcomes of formal voting processes. The two most common power indices are the Shapley-Shubik and the Banzhaf power indices. Both measure the a priori ability of an actor to affect the outcome of the formal voting process. The Shapley- Shubik is based upon the probability that an actor is in a pivotal position whereas the Banzhaf index calculates the number of swings, or the probability that an actor can alter the outcome by joining or leaving a coalition. The Shapley-Shubik index and the normalized Banzhaf indices add to unity (see Stenlund, H and Lane, J.-E. (1984), 'The Structure of Voting-Power Indices' in *Quality and Quantity*, vol. 18: 367–75). In the EC or the EU actors are states or party families or groups of political parties. The data below give a systematic overview of the power scores calculated (by Reinert Maeland at Lund University) in accordance with the decision procedures described above: simple majority or more than 50%, qualified majority or more than 70% and special qualified majority.

Council of Ministers 1958: simple majority

Members	Votes	Banzhaf	Banzhaf norm.	Shapley-Shubik
Fr.	4	0.438	0.233	0.233
FRG	4	0.438	0.233	0.233
It.	4	0.438	0.233	0.233
Belg.	2	0.188	0.100	0.100
Neth.	2	0.188	0.100	0.100
Lux.	1	0.188	0.100	0.100

Council of Ministers 1973: simple majority

Members	Votes	Banzhaf	Banzhaf norm.	Shapley-Shubik
Fr.	10	0.375	0.174	0.181
FRG	10	0.375	0.174	0.181
It.	10	0.375	0.174	0.181
UK	10	0.375	0.174	0.181
Belg.	5	0.188	0.087	0.081
Neth.	5	0.188	0.087	0.081
Den.	3	0.094	0.043	0.038
Ire.	3	0.094	0.043	0.038
Lux.	2	0.094	0.043	0.038

Council of Ministers 1981: simple majority

Members	Votes	Banzhaf	Banzhaf norm.	Shapley-Shubik
Fr.	10	0.367	0.162	0.164
FRG	10	0.367	0.162	0.164
It.	10	0.367	0.162	0.164
UK	10	0.367	0.162	0.164
Belg.	5	0.180	0.079	0.076
Neth.	5	0.180	0.079	0.076
Gr.	5	0.180	0.079	0.076
Den.	3	0.086	0.038	0.038
Ire.	3	0.086	0.038	0.038
Lux.	2	0.086	0.038	0.038

Council of Ministers 1986: simple majority

Members	Votes	Banzhaf	Banzhaf norm.	Shapley-Shubik
Fr.	10	0.336	0.134	0.135
FRG	10	0.336	0.134	0.135
It.	10	0.336	0.134	0.135
UK	10	0.336	0.134	0.135
Sp.	8	0.268	0.107	0.107
Belg.	5	0.160	0.064	0.063
Neth.	5	0.160	0.064	0.063
Gr.	5	0.160	0.064	0.063
Port.	5	0.160	0.064	0.063
Den.	3	0.100	0.040	0.038
Ire.	3	0.100	0.040	0.038
Lux.	2	0.061	0.024	0.023

Council of Ministers 1995: simple majority

Members	Votes	Banzhaf	Banzhaf norm.	Shapley-Shubik
Fr.	10	0.326	0.117	0.082
FRG	10	0.326	0.117	0.082
It.	10	0.326	0.117	0.082
UK	10	0.326	0.117	0.082
Sp.	8	0.254	0.091	0.064
Belg.	5	0.156	0.056	0.038
Neth.	5	0.156	0.056	0.038
Gr.	5	0.156	0.056	0.038
Port.	5	0.156	0.056	0.038
Aus.	4	0.130	0.047	0.032
Sw.	4	0.130	0.047	0.046

Council of Ministers 1995: simple majority

Members	Votes	Banzhaf	Banzhaf norm.	Shapley-Shubik
Fin.	3	0.092	0.033	0.033
Den.	3	0.092	0.033	0.033
Ire.	3	0.092	0.033	0.033
Lux.	2	0.061	0.022	0.022

Council of Ministers 1958: qualified majority, 12 of 17

Members	Votes	Banzhaf	Banzhaf norm.	Shapley-Shubik
Fr.	4	0.312	0.238	0.233
FRG	4	0.312	0.238	0.233
It.	4	0.312	0.238	0.233
Belg.	2	0.188	0.143	0.150
Neth.	2	0.188	0.143	0.150
Lux.	1	0.000	0.000	0.000

Council of Ministers 1973: qualified majority, 41 of 58

Members	Votes	Banzhaf	Banzhaf norm.	Shapley-Shubik
Fr.	10	0.207	0.167	0.179
FRG	10	0.207	0.167	0.179
It.	10	0.207	0.167	0.179
UK	10	0.207	0.167	0.179
Belg.	5	0.113	0.091	0.081
Neth.	5	0.113	0.091	0.081
Den.	3	0.082	0.066	0.051
Ire.	3	0.082	0.066	0.051
Lux.	2	0.020	0.016	0.010

Council of Ministers 1981: qualified majority, 45 out of 63

Members	Votes	Banzhaf	Banzhaf norm.	Shapley-Shubik
Fr.	10	0.195	0.158	0.174
FRG	10	0.195	0.158	0.174
It.	10	0.195	0.158	0.174
UK	10	0.195	0.158	0.174
Belg.	5	0.102	0.082	0.071
Neth.	5	0.102	0.082	0.071
Gr.	5	0.102	0.082	0.071
Den.	3	0.051	0.041	0.030
Ire.	3	0.051	0.041	0.030
Lux.	2	0.051	0.041	0.030

Council of Ministers 1986: qualified majority, 54 out of 76

Members	Votes	Banzhaf	Banzhaf norm.	Shapley-Shubik
Fr.	10	0.140	0.129	0.134
FRG	10	0.140	0.129	0.134
It.	10	0.140	0.129	0.134
UK	10	0.140	0.129	0.134
Sp.	8	0.118	0.109	0.111
Belg.	5	0.072	0.067	0.064
Neth.	5	0.072	0.067	0.064
Gr.	5	0.072	0.067	0.064
Port.	5	0.072	0.067	0.064
Den.	3	0.050	0.046	0.043
Ire.	3	0.050	0.046	0.043
Lux.	2	0.020	0.018	0.012

Council of Ministers 1995: qualified majority, 62 out of 87

Members	Votes	Banzhaf	Banzhaf norm.	Shapley-Shubik
Fr.	10	0.113	0.112	0.116
FRG	10	0.113	0.112	0.116
It.	10	0.113	0.112	0.116
UK	10	0.113	0.112	0.116
Sp.	8	0.093	0.092	0.095
Belg.	5	0.059	0.059	0.055
Neth.	5	0.059	0.059	0.055
Gr.	5	0.059	0.059	0.055
Port.	5	0.059	0.059	0.055
Aus.	4	0.048	0.048	0.045
Swe.	4	0.048	0.048	0.045
Fin.	3	0.036	0.036	0.035
Den.	3	0.036	0.036	0.035
Ire.	3	0.036	0.036	0.035
Lux.	2	0.023	0.023	0.021

Council of Ministers 1958: qualified majority with at least 4 members

Members	Votes	Banzhaf	Banzhaf norm.	Shapley-Shubik
Fr.	4	0.281	0.214	0.217
FRG	4	0.281	0.214	0.217
It.	4	0.281	0.214	0.217
Belg.	2	0.219	0.167	0.167
Neth.	2	0.219	0.167	0.167
Lux.	1	0.031	0.024	0.017

Council of Ministers 1973: qualified majority with at least 6 members

Members	Votes	Banzhaf	Banzhaf norm.	Shapley-Shubik
Fr.	10	0.188	0.154	0.171
FRG	10	0.188	0.154	0.171
It.	10	0.188	0.154	0.171
UK	10	0.188	0.154	0.171
Belg.	5	0.125	0.103	0.087
Neth.	5	0.125	0.103	0.087
Den.	3	0.094	0.077	0.063
Ire.	3	0.094	0.077	0.063
Lux.	2	0.031	0.026	0.016

Council of Ministers 1981: qualified majority with at least 7 members

Members	Votes	Banzhaf	Banzhaf norm.	Shapley-Shubik
Fr.	10	0.156	0.134	0.158
FRG	10	0.156	0.134	0.158
It.	10	0.156	0.134	0.158
UK	10	0.156	0.134	0.158
Belg.	5	0.105	0.091	0.077
Neth.	5	0.105	0.091	0.077
Gr.	5	0.105	0.091	0.077
Den.	3	0.074	0.064	0.045
Ire.	3	0.074	0.064	0.045
Lux.	2	0.074	0.064	0.045

Council of Ministers 1986: qualified majority with at least 8 members

Members	Votes	Banzhaf	Banzhaf norm.	Shapley-Shubik
Fr.	10	0.128	0.121	0.130
FRG	10	0.128	0.121	0.130
It.	10	0.128	0.121	0.130
UK	10	0.128	0.121	0.130
Sp.	8	0.111	0.104	0.109
Belg.	5	0.075	0.070	0.066
Neth.	5	0.075	0.070	0.066
Gr.	5	0.075	0.070	0.066
Port.	5	0.075	0.070	0.066
Den.	3	0.056	0.053	0.046
Ire.	3	0.056	0.053	0.046
Lux.	2	0.027	0.025	0.016

Council of Ministers 1995: qualified majority with at least 10 members

Members	Votes	Banzhaf	Banzhaf norm.	Shapley-Shubik
Fr.	10	0.098	0.101	0.111
FRG.	10	0.098	0.101	0.111
It.	10	0.098	0.101	0.111
UK	10	0.098	0.101	0.111
Sp.	8	0.083	0.085	0.092
Belg.	5	0.059	0.061	0.056
Neth.	5	0.059	0.061	0.056
Gr.	5	0.059	0.061	0.056
Port.	5	0.059	0.061	0.056
Aus.	4	0.051	0.052	0.048
Sw.	4	0.051	0.052	0.048
Fin.	3	0.042	0.043	0.039
Den.	3	0.042	0.043	0.039
Ire.	3	0.042	0.043	0.039
Lux.	2	0.030	0.031	0.025

TABLE 9.11.   Seats in the EU Parliament

Countries	1979	1981	1986	1994	1995
Fr.	81	81	81	87	87
FRG.	81	81	81	99	99
It.	81	81	81	87	87
Belg.	24	24	24	25	25
Neth.	25	25	25	31	31
Lux.	6	6	6	6	6
Den.	16	16	16	16	16
Ire.	15	15	15	15	15
UK	81	81	81	87	87
Gr.	—	24	24	25	25
Port.	—	—	24	25	25
Sp.	—	—	60	64	64
Aus.	—	—	—	—	21
Fin.	—	—	—	—	16
Sw.	—	—	—	—	22
TOTAL	410	434	518	567	626

TABLE 9.12.   Voting power: European Parliament 1981: States

Members	Votes	Banzhaf	Banzhaf norm.	Shapley-Shubik
Fr.	81	0.375	0.170	0.179
FRG.	81	0.375	0.170	0.179
It.	81	0.375	0.170	0.179
UK	81	0.375	0.170	0.179
Neth.	25	0.164	0.074	0.067
Belg.	24	0.141	0.064	0.057
Gr.	24	0.141	0.064	0.057
Den.	16	0.117	0.053	0.048
Ire.	15	0.117	0.053	0.048
Lux.	6	0.023	0.011	0.010

Voting power: European Parliament 1986: States: Simple Majority

Members	Votes	Banzhaf	Banzhaf norm.	Shapley-Shubik
Fr.	81	0.368	0.166	0.166
FRG.	81	0.368	0.166	0.166
It.	81	0.368	0.166	0.166
UK	81	0.368	0.166	0.166
Sp.	60	0.298	0.134	0.126
Neth.	25	0.081	0.037	0.038
Belg.	24	0.081	0.037	0.038
Gr.	24	0.081	0.037	0.038
Port.	24	0.081	0.037	0.038
Den.	16	0.060	0.027	0.028
Ire.	15	0.056	0.025	0.025
Lux.	6	0.009	0.004	0.004

Voting power: European Parliament 1995: States

Members	Votes	Banzhaf	Banzhaf norm.	Shapley-Shubik
Fr.	87	0.351	0.144	0.145
FRG.	99	0.405	0.166	0.168
It.	87	0.351	0.144	0.145
UK	87	0.351	0.144	0.145
Sp.	64	0.259	0.106	0.101
Neth.	31	0.108	0.044	0.045
Belg.	25	0.090	0.037	0.037
Gr.	25	0.090	0.037	0.037
Port.	25	0.090	0.037	0.037
Aus.	22	0.079	0.032	0.032
Sw.	21	0.075	0.031	0.030

Voting power: European Parliament 1995: States

Members	Votes	Banzhaf	Banzhaf norm.	Shapley-Shubik
Fin.	16	0.058	0.024	0.023
Den.	16	0.058	0.024	0.023
Ire.	15	0.053	0.022	0.021
Lux.	6	0.021	0.009	0.008

Voting power: European Parliament 1981: Party Groups

Members	Votes	Banzhaf	Banzhaf norm.	Shapley-Shubik
SOC	122	0.531	0.293	0.310
EPP	116	0.469	0.259	0.281
EDU	64	0.312	0.172	0.162
COM	48	0.188	0.103	0.095
LIB	40	0.188	0.103	0.095
EPD	22	0.062	0.034	0.029
TCG	11	0.031	0.017	0.014
NA	11	0.031	0.017	0.014

Note: For explanation of abbreviations see Table 9.6.

Voting power: European Parliament 1987: Party Groups: Simple Majority

Members	Votes	Banzhaf	Banzhaf norm.	Shapley-Shubik
SOC	166	0.688	0.374	0.388
EPP	114	0.312	0.170	0.200
EDU	66	0.250	0.136	0.128
LIB	44	0.141	0.077	0.071
COM	49	0.164	0.089	0.082
EPD	29	0.102	0.055	0.051
RBG	20	0.070	0.038	0.032
DR	17	0.062	0.034	0.028
NA	13	0.047	0.026	0.021

Voting power: European Parliament 1989: Party Groups

Members	Votes	Banzhaf	Banzhaf norm.	Shapley-Shubik
SOC	180	0.750	0.404	0.407
EPP	121	0.250	0.135	0.175
LIB	49	0.203	0.109	0.106
EDU	34	0.137	0.074	0.068
COM	14	0.053	0.028	0.024
EUL	28	0.105	0.057	0.049
EPD	20	0.084	0.045	0.040

Voting power: European Parliament 1989: Party Groups

Members	Votes	Banzhaf	Banzhaf norm.	Shapley-Shubik
RBG	13	0.047	0.025	0.022
VER	30	0.117	0.063	0.057
DR	17	0.066	0.036	0.032
NA	12	0.043	0.023	0.020

Voting power: European Parliament 1994: Party Groups

Members	Votes	Banzhaf	Banzhaf norm.	Shapley-Shubik
SOC	198	0.707	0.362	0.376
EPP	157	0.293	0.150	0.194
LIB	43	0.207	0.106	0.098
KUL	28	0.113	0.058	0.051
EPD	26	0.113	0.058	0.051
ERA	19	0.098	0.050	0.043
NE	19	0.098	0.050	0.043
VER	23	0.098	0.050	0.043
FE	27	0.113	0.058	0.051
NA	27	0.113	0.058	0.051

TABLE 9.13.   The EU Parliament 1995: Party Groups

Party groups	Seats	Voting Power
Left Unity Group (LU)	31	0.044
Greens	25	0.044
Rainbow Group (RBW)	19	0.044
European Socialist Party (PES)	221	0.377
Independents	79	0.167
Liberal Democratic and Reformist Group (LDR)	52	0.096
European People's Party (EPP)	173	0.184
European Democratic Alliance (EDA)	26	0.044

Note: Banzhaf normalized scores.

Source: *The Economist*, 15 Apr. 1995.

TABLE 9.14.   The European Parliament 1995: Party Groups

Members	Votes	Banzhaf	Banzhaf norm.	Shapley-Shubik
Group of Party of Europeant Socialists (PES)	217	0.699	0.361	0.375
European People's Party (Cristian-Democrats) (EPP)	172	0.301	0.155	0.197
Group of the European Liberal, Democratic and Reformist Party (ELDR)	52	0.230	0.119	0.110
Confederal Group of the United Left – Northern Green Left (GUE)	33	0.121	0.062	0.054
Forza Europa Group (FE)	29	0.105	0.054	0.048
Group of European Democratic Alliance (EDA)	26	0.098	0.050	0.044
Green Group in the European Parliament (GRN)	28	0.105	0.054	0.048
Group of European Radical Alliance (ERA)	19	0.082	0.042	0.037
Europe of Nations Group (EN)	19	0.082	0.042	0.037
Non-attached members (NI)	31	0.113	0.058	0.051

TABLE 9.15a.   The European Parliament 1979: Member States

Members	Votes	Banzhaf	Banzhaf norm.	Shapley-Shubik
Germany	81	0.375	0.174	0.181
France	81	0.375	0.174	0.181
Italy	81	0.375	0.174	0.181
United Kingdom	81	0.375	0.174	0.181
Netherlands	25	0.188	0.087	0.081
Belgium	24	0.188	0.087	0.081
Denmark	16	0.094	0.043	0.038
Ireland	15	0.094	0.043	0.038
Luxembourg	6	0.094	0.043	0.038

TABLE 9.15b.   The European Parliament 1979: Party Groups

Members	Votes	Banzhaf	Banzhaf norm.	Shapley-Shubik
SOC	112	0.523	0.289	0.306
EPP	108	0.477	0.263	0.285
EDU	64	0.320	0.177	0.165
COM	44	0.180	0.099	0.092
LIB	40	0.180	0.099	0.092
EPD	22	0.070	0.039	0.032
TCG	11	0.039	0.022	0.018
NA	9	0.023	0.013	0.011

PART II
Country Tables

1. Austria

State Structure: Federal.

Form of State: Republic.

Parliament (bicameral): Federal council (Bundesrat): 63 seats, 5/6 years;
National council (Nationalrat): 183 seats, 4 years.

Electoral System: Proportional representation: Hare quota.

Main Language: German (98%).

Population: 7,812,100.

Constitutional Development: Present constitution dates from 1920;
amended 1929; also of importance is the state treaty concluded in 1955.

Heads of State:

K. Renner (SPÖ)	Dec. 1945–Dec. 1950
T. Körner (SPÖ)	May 1951–Jan. 1957
A. Schärf (SPÖ)	May 1957–Feb. 1965
F. Jonas (SPÖ)	May 1965–Apr. 1974
B. Kreisky (SPÖ) (interim)	Apr. 1974–July 1974
R. Kirchschläger (SPÖ)	July 1974–June 1986
K. Waldheim (ÖVP)	June 1986–Apr. 1992
T. Klestil (ÖVP)	July 1992–

Capital City: Wien   (1985): 1,489,200.

Ministries:

Office of the Federal Chancellor

Agriculture and Forestry	Foreign Affairs
Economic Affairs	Interior
Education and the Arts	Justice
Employment and Social Affairs	National Defence
Environment, Youth and Family	Public Sector and Transport
Finance	Science and Research

Governments:

	Prime Minister	Parties represented in government
Apr. 1945–Dec. 1945	Renner (SPÖ)	SPÖ, ÖVP, KPÖ
Dec. 1945–Nov. 1947	Figl I (ÖVP)	SPÖ, ÖVP, KPÖ
Nov. 1947–Nov. 1949	Figl II (ÖVP)	SPÖ, ÖVP
Nov. 1949–Oct. 1952	Figl III (ÖVP)	SPÖ, ÖVP
Oct. 1952–Apr. 1953	Figl IV (ÖVP)	SPÖ, ÖVP
Apr. 1953–June 1956	Raab I (ÖVP)	SPÖ, ÖVP
June 1956–July 1959	Raab II (ÖVP)	SPÖ, ÖVP
July 1959–Nov. 1960	Raab III (ÖVP)	SPÖ, ÖVP
Nov. 1960–Apr. 1961	Raab IV (ÖVP)	SPÖ, ÖVP
Apr. 1961–Mar. 1963	Gorbach I (ÖVP)	SPÖ, ÖVP
Mar. 1963–Apr. 1964	Gorbach II (ÖVP)	SPÖ, ÖVP
Apr. 1964–Apr. 1966	Klaus I (ÖVP)	SPÖ, ÖVP
Apr. 1966–Apr. 1970	Klaus II (ÖVP)	ÖVP
Apr. 1970–Nov. 1971	Kreisky I (SPÖ)	SPÖ
Nov. 1971–Oct. 1975	Kreisky II (SPÖ)	SPÖ
Oct. 1975–May 1979	Kreisky III (SPÖ)	SPÖ
May 1979–May 1983	Kreisky IV (SPÖ)	SPÖ
May 1983–June 1986	Sinowatz (SPÖ)	SPÖ, FPÖ
June 1986–Jan. 1987	Vranitzky I (SPÖ)	SPÖ, FPÖ
Jan. 1987–Dec. 1990	Vranitzky II (SPÖ)	SPÖ, ÖVP
Dec. 1990–Nov. 1994	Vranitzky III (SPÖ)	SPÖ, ÖVP
Nov. 1994	Vranitzky IV (SPÖ)	SPÖ, ÖVP

Provinces (Länder):

	Population (1991)	Capital
Burgenland	273 541	Eisenstadt
Kärnten	552 421	Klagenfurt
Niederösterreich	1 480 927	Sankt Pölten
Oberösterreich	1 340 076	Linz
Salzburg	483 880	Salzburg
Steiermark	1 184 593	Graz
Tirol	630 358	Innsbruck
Vorarlberg	333 128	Bregenz
Wien	1 533 176	(Wien)

Media:

(*a*) Major newspapers:

Name	Location	Circulation
Neue Kronen-Zeitung	Vienna	577 197
Kurier	Vienna	391 239
Kleine Zeitung	Graz	268 283
Oberösterreichische Nachrichten	Linz	108 777
Tiroler Tageszeitung	Innsbruck	97 325
Der Standard	Vienna	95 000
Salzburger Nachrichten	Salzberg	84 636
Die Presse	Vienna	70 807

(*b*) Radio and television: *Österreichischer Rundfunk* (ORF), controls all three channels.

Education:

(1991/92 figures)	No. Staff	No. Students
Primary	34 902	399 374
Secondary	52 028	414 875
Vocational	26 322	333 177
Universities	12 034	201 615

Economic Interest Organizations:

Employers' organization: Bundeskammer der gewerblichen Wirtschaft, founded 1946.

Central trade union peak organization: Österreichischer Gewerkschafts-bund (ÖGB), founded 1945; membership: 638 179 (Dec. 1991).

National or Central Bank: Öesterreichische Nationalbank.

Central Statistical Office:
Austrian Central Statistical Office
Hintere Zollamtsstr. 2B
A-1033 Vienna

National Income and Expenditure:

Federal Budget: (1991)—in 1992 US dollars ($1 = 9.949 Schilling)—millions

Revenue	
Direct taxes on income and wealth	17 973
Social security contributions	2 719
Indirect taxes	17 739
Current transfers	2 423
Sales and charges	1 628
Interest, shares of profit	2 869
Sales of assets	295
Repayments of loans granted	44
Capital transfers	67
Borrowing	12 236
Other revenue	1 831
Total	59 824

Expenditure	
Expenditure on goods/services	11 994
Interest on public debt	7 457
Current transfers to:	
Regional and local authorities	4 232
Other public bodies	7 529
Households	9 850
Other	5 957
Deficits of Government enterprises	1 124
Gross capital formation	1 106
Capital transfers	3 015
Acquisition of assets	455
Loans granted	100
Debt redemption	5 934
Other expenditure	1 073
Total	59 824

Further Information:

Fischer, H. (1982) (ed.), *Das politische System Österreichs*. Wien: Europa. Verlag.

Jelavich, B. (1987), *Modern Austria*. Cambridge: Cambridge U. P.

Luther, K. R., and Muller, W. C. (1992) (eds.), *Politics in Austria*. London: Frank Cass.

Muller, W. C. (1992), 'Austria', in *European Journal of Political Research* 22: 357–61.

Nick, R., and Pelinka, A. (1983), *Bürgerkrieg–Sozialpartnerschaft: Das politische System Österreichs 1. und 2. Republik: Ein Vergleich*. Wien: Jugend und Volk.

Pelinka, A., and Plasser, F. (1987) (eds.), *Das Österreichischen Parteinsystem*. Wien: Böhlau.

Pulzer, P. (1992), 'The Austrian Presidential Election of 1992', in *Electoral Studies* 11: 347–51.

Steiner, K. (1981) (ed.), *Modern Austria*. Palo Alto: SPOSS.

Sully, M. A. (1981), *Political Parties and Elections in Austria*. London: Hurst.

Sully. M. A. (1990). *A Contemporary History of Austria*. London: Routledge.

Sweeney, J., *et al.* (1988), *Austria: A Study in Modern Achievement*. Aldershot: Avebury.

Wright, W. E. (1982) (ed.), *Austria Since 1945*. Minneapolis: University of Minnesota Center for Austrian Studies.

2. Belgium

State Structure: Quasi-unitary (with regional and community levels of government).

Form of State: Constitutional monarchy.

Parliament (bicameral): Chamber of representatives (Chambre des représentants/Kamer van Volksvertegenwoordigers): 212 seats, 4 years; Senate (Sénat/Senaat): 183 seats, 4 years.

Electoral System: Proportional representation: Hare quota.

Main Languages: Dutch (59%); French (34%); German (1%).

Population: 10,021,997 (1991).

Constitutional Development: Present constitution dates from 1830 but has been amended several times; changes were introduced in 1971, 1980, and 1988 with regard to the country's different cultural entities.

Heads of State:

Regency	Sept. 1944–July 1950
King Leopold III (abdication)	July 1950–July 1951
King Baudouin	July 1951–1993
King Albert	1993–

Capital City: Bruxelles (1985): 976, 536.

Ministries:

Prime Minister

Brussels Region	Internal Affairs and the Civil Service
Budget	Justice
Defence	Pensions
Development Co-operation	Scientific Policy
Economic Affairs	Small and Medium-Sized
Employment	Enterprises and Agriculture
Finance	Social Affairs
Foreign Affairs	Social Integration, Public Health
Foreign Trade and European	and the Environment
Affairs	Transport and Public Enterprises

Governments:

	Prime Minister	Parties represented in government
Feb. 1945–Aug. 1945	Van Acker I (BSP/PSB)	BSP/PSB CVP/PSC PVV/PLP PCB/BCP
Aug. 1945–Mar. 1946	Van Acker II (BSP/PSB)	BSP/PSB PVV/PLP UDB PCB/BCP
Mar. 1946–Apr. 1946	Spaak I (BSP/PSB)	BSP/PSB
Apr. 1946–Aug. 1946	Van Acker III (BSP/PSB)	BSP/PSB PVV/PLP PCB/BCP
Aug. 1946–Mar. 1947	Huysmans (BSP/PSB)	BSP/PSB PVV/PLP PCB/BCP
Mar. 1947–Nov. 1948	Spaak II (BSP/PSB)	BSP/PSB CVP/PSC
Nov. 1948–Aug. 1949	Spaak III (BSP/PSB)	BSP/PSB CVP/PSC
Aug. 1949–June 1950	Eyskens I (CVP/PSC)	CVP/PSC PVV/PLP
June 1950–Aug. 1950	Duvieusart (CVP/PSC)	CVP/PSC
Aug. 1950–Jan. 1952	Pholien (CVP/PSC)	CVP/PSC
Jan. 1952–Apr. 1954	Van Houtte (CVP/PSC)	CVP/PSC
Apr. 1954–June 1958	Van Acker (BSP/PSB)	BSP/PSB PVV/PLP
June 1958–Nov. 1958	Eyskens II (CVP/PSC)	CVP/PSC
Nov. 1958–Sept. 1960	Eyskens III (CVP/PSC)	CVP/PSC PVV/PLP
Sept. 1960–Apr. 1961	Eyskens IV (CVP/PSC)	CVP/PSC PVV/PLP
Apr. 1961–July 1965	Lefèvre (CVP/PSC)	CVP/PSC BSP/PSB
July 1965–Mar. 1966	Harmel (CVP/PSC)	CVP/PSC BSP/PSB
Mar. 1966–June 1968	Vanden Boeynants (CVP/PSC)	CVP/PSC PVV/PLP

	Prime Minister	Parties represented in government
June 1968–Jan. 1972	Eyskens V (CVP/PSC)	CVP/PSC BSP/PSB
Jan. 1972–Jan. 1973	Eyskens VI (CVP)	PSB, BSP CVP, PSC
Jan. 1973–Apr. 1974	Leburton (PSB)	PSB, BSP CVP, PSC PVV, PLP
Apr. 1974–June 1974	Tindemans I (CVP)	CVP, PSC PVV, PLP
June 1974–June 1977	Tindemans II (CVP)	CVP, PSC PVV, PLP RW
June 1977–Oct. 1978	Tindemans III (CVP)	CVP, PSC PSB, BSP FDF, VU
Oct. 1978–Apr. 1979	Vanden Boeynants II (CVP) (PSC)	CVP, PSC PSB BSP, FDF VU
Apr. 1979–Jan. 1980	Martens I (CVP)	CVP, PSC PSB, BSP FDF
Jan. 1980–May 1980	Martens II (CVP)	CVP, PSC PSB, BSP
May 1980–Oct. 1980	Martens III (CVP)	CVP, PSC PSB, BSP PVV, PLP
Oct. 1980–Apr. 1981	Martens IV (CVP)	CVP, PSC PSB, BSP
Apr. 1981–Sept. 1981	Eyskens I (CVP)	CVP, PSC PSB, BSP
Sept. 1981–Dec. 1981	Eyskens II (CVP)	caretaker
Dec. 1981–Nov. 1985	Martens V (CVP)	CVP, PSC PVV, PRL
Nov. 1985–May 1988	Martens VI (CVP)	CVP, PSC PVV, PRL

	Prime Minister	Parties represented in government
May 1988–Sept. 1991	Martens VII (CVP)	CVP, PSC PS, SP VU
Sept. 1991–Nov. 1991	Martens VIII (CVP)	CVP, PSC, PSB, BSP
Nov. 1991–Mar. 1992	Martens IX (CVP)	CVP, PSC, PSB, BSP
Mar. 1992–	Dehaene (CVP)	CVP, PSC, PSB, BSP

Provinces:

	Population (1991)	Capital
Antwerp	1 610 695	Antwerp
Brabant	2 253 794	Brussels
Flanders (East)	1 340 056	Ghent
Flanders (West)	1 111 557	Bruges
Hainaut	1 283 252	Mons
Liège	1 006 081	Liège
Limburg	755 593	Hasselt
Luxembourg	234 664	Arlon
Namur	426 305	Namur

Media:
(*a*) Major newspapers:

Name	Location	Circulation
De Standaard	Brussels	375 240
Nieuwsbald	Brussels	
De Gentenaar	Ghent	
Het Laatste Nieuws	Brussels	287 738
De Nieuwe Gazet	Antwerp	
Gazet van Antwerpen	Antwerp	189 250
Gazet van Mechelen	Mechelen	
Le Soir	Brussels	181 635
Het Volk	Ghent	179 437
De Nieuwe Gids	Brussels	
La Muese	Liege	129 119

Name	Location	Circulation
La Lanterne	Brussels	
La Derniere Heure	Brussels	92 926
La Libre Belgique	Brussels	85 352

(*b*) Radio and television: Public: *Radio-Télévision Belge de la Communauté Culturelle Française* (French); *Belgische Radio en Televisie* (Dutch); Belgisches Rundfunk-und Fernsehzentrum der *Deutschsprachigen Gemeinschaft* (BRF). Private: *Radio Télé Luxembourg* (RTL) (French); *VTM* (Dutch); *Canal Plus Belgique* (Cable).

Education:

(1990/91 figures)	No. Staff	No. Students*
Pre-Primary and Primary	71 064 (1987)	1 118 626
Secondary	114 628 (1987)	793 322
Higher education		
(non-uni.)	14 548 (1987)	137 179
University	5 349 (1986)	111 845

* French, German, and Dutch speakers combined.

Economic Interest Organizations:
Employers' organization: Fédération des Entreprises de Belgique.

Central trade union peak organizations: Fédération Génerale du Travail de Belgique/Algemeen Belgisch Vakverbond (FGTB/ABVV), founded 1898, reorganized 1937; membership: 1 036 028 (1986); Confédération des Syndicats Chrétiens (CSC), founded 1909; membership 1 336 000 (1987).

National or Central Bank: Banque Nationale de Belgique.

Central Statistical Office:
Institut National de Statistique
44 rue du Louvain,
B-Brussels 1000

Federal Budget: (1991)—in 1992 US dollars ($1 = 29.20 francs)—millions

Revenue	
National Government	
Direct taxation	24 879
Customs and excise	5 133
VAT, stamp, registration etc. duties	6 412
Other current revenue	3 946
Capital revenues	356
Regions and communities	24 276
Total	65 002

Expenditure	
National Government	
Government departments	19 708
Public debt	21 139
Pensions	8 178
Defence	3 476
Other expenditure	457
Regions and Communities	26 562
Total	79 521

Further Information:
Albareuol *et al.* (1987), 'Belgique', in *Cahiers du CACEF*, 130. CACEF.
Boudart, M., and Bryssinck. R. (1990). *Modern Belgium*. Palo Alto: Sposs.
Delruelle *et al.* (1983), *Regioscope I & IV: 1979–1982*. Bruxelles: CRISP.
Economist Intelligence Unit Country Profiles. (1987) *Belgium and Luxembourg*. London.
Fitzmaurice, J. (1983), *The Politics of Belgium: Crisis and Compromise in a Plural Society*. London: Hurst.
Kossman, E.H. (1978) *The Low Countries 1780–1940*. Oxford: Clarendon Press.
Lijphart, A. (1981) (ed.), *Conflict and Coexistence in Belgium: The Dynamics of a Culturally Divided Society*. Berkeley: Institute of International Studies.
Mabille, X. (1985), *Histoire politique de la Belgique: Facteurs et acteurs de changement*. Bruxelles: CRISP.
McRae, K. D. (1983), *Conflict and Compromise in Multilingual Societies: Belgium*. Waterloo, Ont.: Wilfred Laurier U. P.

3. Denmark

(NB: All figures exclude the Faroe Islands and Greenland.)

State Structure: Unitary.

Form of State: Constitutional monarchy.

Parliament (unicameral): Folketing: 179 seats, 4 years.

Electoral System: Proportional representation: modified Sainte Lague.

Main Language: Danish (98%).

Population: 5,162,126 (official estimate, 1992).

Constitutional Development: The constitutional charter (Grundloven) was adopted in 1953. The previous constitution dates from 1849 (changed 1866 and 1915).

Heads of State:

King Christian X	May 1912–Apr. 1947
King Frederik IX	Apr. 1947–Jan. 1972
Queen Margrethe II	Jan. 1972–

Capital City: København (1985): 1,358,540.

Ministries:

Office of Prime Minister

Agriculture	Foreign Affairs
Cultural Affairs	Health
Defence	Housing and Building
Ecclesiastical Affairs	Industry and Energy
Economic and Fiscal Affairs	Interior
Education and Research	Justice
Environment	Labour
Finance	Social Affairs
Fisheries	Transport

Governments:

	Prime Minister	Parties represented in government
May 1945–Nov. 1945	Buhl (SD)	SD, V, RV, KF, DKP
Nov. 1945–Nov. 1947	Kristensen (V)	V
Nov. 1947–Sept. 1950	Hedtoft I (SD)	SD
Sept. 1950–Oct. 1950	Hedtoft II (SD)	SD
Oct. 1950–Sept. 1953	Eriksen (V)	V, KF
Sept. 1953–Feb. 1955	Hedtoft III (SD)	SD
Feb. 1955–May 1957	Hansen I (SD)	SD
May 1957–Feb. 1960	Hansen II (SD)	SD, RV, RFB
Feb. 1960–Nov. 1960	Kampmann I (SD)	SD, RV, RFB
Nov. 1960–Sept. 1962	Kampmann II (SD)	SD, RV
Sept. 1962–Sept. 1964	Krag I (SD)	SD, RV
Sept. 1964–Nov. 1966	Krag II (SD)	SD
Nov. 1966–Feb. 1968	Krag III (SD)	SD
Feb. 1968–Oct. 1971	Baunsgaard (RV)	RV, V, KF
Oct. 1971–Oct. 1972	Krag IV (SD)	SD
Oct. 1972–Dec. 1973	Anker Jörgensen I (SD)	SD
Dec. 1973–Feb. 1975	Hartling (V)	V
Feb. 1975–Feb. 1977	Anker Jörgensen II (SD)	SD
Feb. 1977–Aug. 1978	Anker Jörgensen III (SD)	SD
Aug. 1978–Oct. 1979	Anker Jörgensen IV (SD)	SD, V
Oct. 1979–Dec. 1981	Anker Jörgensen V (SD)	SD
Dec. 1981–Sept. 1982	Anker Jörgensen VI (SD)	SD
Sept. 1982–Jan. 1984	Schlüter I (KF)	KF, V, KRF, CD
Jan. 1984–Sept. 1987	Schlüter II (KF)	KF, V, KRF, CD
Sept. 1987–June 1988	Schlüter III (KF)	KF, V, KRF, CD
June 1988–Dec. 1989	Schlüter IV (KF)	KF, V, RV
Dec. 1989–Dec. 1990	Schlüter V (KF)	KF, V
Dec. 1990–Jan. 1993	Schlüter VI (KF)	KF, V
Jan. 1993–Sept. 1994	Rasmussen (SD)	SD, RV, CD, KRF
Sept. 1994–	Rasmussen (SD)	SD, RV, CD

Provinces (Amt):

	Population (1983)	Capital
Københavns kommune	486 593	—
Frediksborg	88 409	—
Københavns amtskommune	619 687	—
Fredriksborg amtskommune	331 349	Hillerød
Roskilde amtskommune	205 414	Roskilde
Vestsjælland amtskommune	277 914	Sorø
Storstrøm amtskommune	258 670	Nykøbing
Bornholm amtskommune	47 313	Rønne
Fyn amtskommune	453 773	Odense
Sønderjylland amtskommune	249 970	Åbenrå
Ribe amtskommune	214 700	Ribe
Vejle amtskommune	327 102	Vejle
Ringkøbing amtskommune	264 103	Ringkøbing
Århus amtskommune	578 149	Århus
Viborg amtskommune	230 909	Viborg
Nordjylland amtskommune	482 409	Ålborg

Media:

(*a*) Major newspapers:

Name	Location	Circulation
Ekstra Bladet	Copenhagen	202 984
B.T.	Copenhagen	195 009
Politiken	Copenhagen	150 949
Jyllands-Posten	Viby	141 919
Berlingske Tidende	Copenhagen	128 775
Erhvervs-Bladet	Copenhagen	108 682
Jydske Vestkysten	Esbjerg	79 402
Ålborg Stiftstidende	Ålborg	72 918
Århus Stiftstidende	Århus	64 396

(*b*) Radio and television: Radio Denmark, Radio Denmark-TV, TV2, a private station began broadcasts in Oct. 1988.

Education:

(1991/92 figures)	No. Staff	No. Students
Pre-primary, primary and 1st stage secondary	59 800	613 329
2nd stage secondary:		
General	7 500	74 000

Education: (*Cont.*)

(1991/92 figures)	No. Staff	No. Students
Vocational	n.a.	149 000
Teacher training, technical education, universities, other university level	n.a.	156 000

Economic Interest Organizations:
Employers' organization: Dansk arbejdsgiverforening.

Central trade union peak association: Landsorganisationen i Danmark (LO), founded 1898; membership: 1,446,354 (Jan. 1992) Funktionærernes og Tjenestemændens Fællesråd (FTF), founded 1952; membership: 350,000 (1984).

National or Central Bank: Danmarks Nationalbank.

Central Statistical Office:
Danmarks Statistik
Sejrøgade 11
DK-2100 København Ø

Budget: (1991)—in 1992 US dollars ($1 = 5.480 kroner)—millions

Revenue	
Income and property taxes	23 287
Customs and excise duties	22 124
Other revenue	5 657
Interest (net)	
Total	51 068

Expenditure	
Ministry of Social Affairs	13 804
Ministry of Education	3 737
Ministry of Defense	2 886
Public Corporations	212
Ministry of Agriculture	323
Ministry of Justice	1 280
Ministry of Finance	1 008
Other expenditure	34 812
Total	58 062

Further Information:

Abrahamson, (1988) (ed.), *Welfare States in Crisis: The Crumbling of the Scandinavian Model?* Copenhagen: Forlaget Sociologi.

Billie, Lars (1990), 'Denmark: The Osscillating Party System', in *West European Politics*, 185–210.

Daalder, H. (1987) (ed.), *Party Systems in Denmark, Austria, Switzerland, The Netherlands and Belgium*. London: Pinter.

Elder, N., *et al.* (1988), *The Consensual Democracies: The Government and Politics of the Scandinavian States*. Rev. edn. Oxford: Blackwell.

Eliassen, K., and Pedersen, M. N. (1985), *Nordiske politiske fakta*. Oslo: Tiden.

Fitzmaurice, J. (1981), *Politics in Denmark*. London: Hurst.

Fulerton, B., and Knowles, R. (1991), *Scandinavia*, London: Paul Chapman Publishing Ltd.

Jones, W. Glyn (1986), *Denmark: A Modern History*. Beckenham: Croom Helm.

4. Finland

State Structure: Unitary.

Form of State: Republic.

Parliament (unicameral): Eduskunta: 200 seats, 4 years.

Electoral System: Proportional representation: d'Hondt divisor.

Main Languages: Finnish (94%); Swedish (6%).

Population: 5,029,002 (1991 estimate).

Constitutional Development: Present constitution dates from 1919.

Heads of State:

J. Paasikivi (KOK)	Mar. 1945–Feb. 1956
U. Kekkonen (KESK)	Mar. 1956–Jan. 1982
M. Koivisto (SDP)	Jan. 1982–
Harri Holkeri (KOK)	Apr. 1987–March 1991
Esko Aho (Kesk)	March 1991–

Capital City: Helsinki (1985): 484,263.

Ministries:

Office of the Prime Minister

Agriculture and Forestry	Interior
Defence	Justice
Education	Labour
Environment	Social Affairs and Health
Finance	Trade and Industry
Foreign Affairs	Transport and Communications

Governments:

	Prime Minister	Parties represented in government
Apr. 1945–Mar. 1946	Paasikivi III (Indep.)	SKDL, SDP, KESK, SFP, LKP
Mar. 1946–July 1948	Pekkala (SKDL)	SKDL, SDP, KESK, SFP
July 1948–Mar. 1950	Fagerholm I (SDP)	SDP
Mar. 1950–Jan. 1951	Kekkonen I (KESK)	KESK, LKP, SFP
Jan. 1951–Sept. 1951	Kekkonen II (KESK)	SDP, KESK, LKP, SFP
Sept. 1951–July 1953	Kekkonen III (KESK)	SDP, KESK, LKP, SFP
July 1953–Nov. 1953	Kekkonen IV (KESK)	KESK, SFP
Nov. 1953–May 1954	Tuomioja (Indep.)	LKP, SFP, KOK
May 1954–Oct. 1954	Törngren (SFP)	SDP, KESK, SFP
Oct. 1954–Mar. 1956	Kekkonen V (KESK)	SDP, KESK
Mar. 1956–May 1957	Fagerholm II (SDP)	SDP, KESK, LKP, SFP
May 1957–Nov. 1957	Sukselainen (KESK)	KESK, LKP, SFP
Nov. 1957–Apr. 1958	von Fieandt (Indep.)	KESK
Apr. 1958–Aug. 1958	Kuuskoski (Indep.)	KESK, TPSL, LKP
Aug. 1958–Jan. 1959	Fagerholm III (SDP)	SDP, KESK, LKP, SFP, KOK
Jan. 1959–July 1961	Sukselainen II (KESK)	KESK, SFP
July 1961–Apr. 1962	Miettunen I (KESK)	KESK
Apr. 1962–Dec. 1963	Karjalainen I (KESK)	KESK, LKP, SFP, KOK
Dec. 1963–Sept. 1964	Lehto (Indep.)	SDP
Sept. 1964–May 1966	Virolainen (KESK)	KESK, SFP, LKP, KOK
May 1966–Mar. 1968	Paasio I (SDP)	KESK, SDP, TPSL, SKDL
Mar. 1968–May 1970	Koivisto I (SDP)	SDP, KESK, TPSL, SFP, SKDL
May 1970–July 1970	Aura I (LKP)	SDP, KESK, LKP, SFP, KOK
July 1970–Oct. 1971	Karjalainen II (KESK)	KESK, SDP, LKP, SFP, SKDL
Oct. 1971–Feb. 1972	Aura II (LKP)	SDP, KESK, LKP, SFP, KOK

	Prime Minister	Parties represented in government
Feb. 1972–Sept. 1972	Paasio II (SDP)	SDP
Sept. 1972–June 1975	Sorsa I (SDP)	SDP, KESK, LKP, SFP
June 1975–Nov. 1975	Liinamaa (SDP)	SDP, KESK, LKP, KOK, SFP
Nov. 1975–Sept. 1976	Miettunen II (KESK)	SDP, KESK, LKP, SFP, SKDL
Sept. 1976–May 1977	Miettunen III (KESK)	KESK, LKP, SFP
May 1977–Mar. 1978	Sorsa II (SDP)	SDP, KESK, LKP, SFP, SKDL
Mar. 1978–May 1979	Sorsa III (SDP)	SDP, KESK, LKP, SKDL
May 1979–Feb. 1982	Koivisto II (SDP)	SDP, KESK, SFP, SKDL
Feb. 1982–Dec. 1982	Sorsa IV (SDP)	SDP, KESK, SFP, SKDL
Dec. 1982–May 1983	Sorsa V (SDP)	SDP, KESK, SFP
May 1983–Apr. 1987	Sorsa VI (SDP)	SDP, KESK, SFP, SMP
Apr. 1987–Aug. 1990	Holkeri I (KOK)	SDP, KOK, RKP, FRP
Aug. 1990–Apr. 1991	Holkeri II (KOK)	SDP, KOK, RKP
Apr. 1991–	Aho (KESK)	KESK, KOK, SFP, SKL

Provinces: (Läänit)

	Population (1991)	Capital
Uudenmaan	1 264 048	Helsinki
Turun-Porin	730 076	Turku
Ahvenanmaan	24 847	Maarianhamina
Hämeen	685 220	Hämeenlinna
Kymen	335 298	Kouvala
Mikkelin	207 936	Mikkeli
Kuopion	257 808	Kuopio
Pohjois-Karjalan	177 449	Joensuu
Vaasan	447 022	Vaasa
Keski-Suomen	254 732	Jyväskylä

Provinces (Läänit): (*Cont.*)

	Population (1991)	Capital
Oulun	442 914	Oulu
Lapin	201 652	Rovaniemi

Media:
(*a*) Major newspapers

Name	Location	Circulation
Iltalehti	Helsinki	1 113 544
Helsingin Sanomat	Helsinki	482 944
Ilta-Sanomat	Helsinki	218 642
Aamulehti	Tampere	140 236
Turun Sanomat	Turku	127 850
Kaleva	Oulu	97 149
Savon Sanomat	Kuoppio	90 609
Kauppalehti	Helsinki	84 068
Keskisuomalainen	Jyväskylä	82 080
Etela-Suomen Sanomat	Lahti	71 252
Hufvudstadsbladet	Helsinki	63 649

(*b*) Radio and television: *Öy Yleisradio AB* (YLE) (Finnish Broadcasting Company) operates five national radio and three television channels, and broadcasting time is leased from them by commercial companies, e.g. MTV. There are also commercial local radios and local cable television companies have their own programmes.

Education:

1990/91 figures	No. Staff	No. Students
First level	48 786	394 299
Secondary, general		315 686
Secondary, vocational	18 082	123 296
Universities, and third level	7 802	174 985

Economic Interest Organizations:
Employers' organization: Suomen Työnantajain Keskusliitto (Finnish Employers' Confederation).

Central trade union peak association: Suomen Ammattiliittojen Keskusjärjestö (Central Organization of Finnish Trade Unions) (SAK), first founded 1907, reunited 1969; membership: 1,086,590 (1991); Toimihenkilö-ja Virkamiesjärjestöjen Keskusliitto (Confederation of Salaried Employees) (TVK), founded 1927; membership: 359,000 (1984).

National or Central Bank: Suomen Pankki/Finlands Bank.

Central Statistical Office:
Central Statistical Office of Finland
POB 504
SF-00101 Helsinki

Budget: (1991)—in 1992 US dollars ($1 = 4.470 markkaa)— millions

Revenue	
Direct taxes	9 184
Indirect taxes	16 583
Other	11 807
Total	37 575

Expenditure	
Education	6 601
Social Security, Health	11 614
Agriculture and forestry	2 980
Transport and communications	2 356
Defence	1 984
Public debt	1 358
Other	11 770
Total	37 575

Allinson, R. (1985), *Finland's Relation with the Soviet Union 1944–84*. Brighton: Wheatsheaf.

Anckar, D. (1990), 'Democracy in Finland: The Constitutional Framework', in J. Sundelberg and S. Berglund (eds.), *Finnish Democracy*. Helsinki: The Finnish Political Science Association.

—— (1992), 'Finland: Dualism and Consensual Rule', in E. Damgaard (ed.), *Parliamentary Change in the Nordic Countries*. Oslo: Scandinavian University Press.

Arter, D. (1987), *Politics and Policy-Making in Finland*. Brighton: Wheatsheaf.

Granberg, L. (1986), 'Small Production and State Intervention in Agriculture' in *Acta Sociologica*, 3.

Kirby, D. G. (1979), *Finland in the Twentieth Century*. London: Hurst.

Lindström, U., and Karvonen, L. (1987) (eds.), *Finland: En politisk loggbok*. Stockholm: Almqvist & Wiksell International.

5. France

State Structure: Unitary.

Form of State: Republic.

Parliament (bicameral): National assembly (Assemblée nationale): 577 seats, 5 years; Senate (Sénat): 319 seats, 9 years.

Electoral System: First round: majority formula; second round: plurality formula.

Main Languages: French (93%); Arabic (3%).

Population: 56,614,493 (1990 census).

Constitutional Development: The present constitution of the Fifth French Republic dates from 1958, with modification in 1962 (election of the President).

Heads of State:

A. Auriol (SFIO)	Jan. 1947–Dec. 1953
R. Coty (Moderate Indep.)	Dec. 1953–Oct. 1958
C. de Gaulle (RPR)	Jan. 1959–Apr. 1969
A. Poher (Interim)	Apr. 1969–June 1969
G. Pompidou (UDR)	June 1969–Apr. 1974
A. Poher (Interim)	Apr. 1974–May 1974
V. Giscard d'Estaing (PR)	May 1974–May 1981
F. Mitterrand (PS)	May 1981–May 1994
J. Chirac (RPR)	May 1994–

Capital City: Paris (1982): 2,188,960.

Ministries:
(As of Jan 1993)

Office of the President
Office of the Prime Minister

Agriculture and Forestry	Interior
Civil Service and Administrative Reform	Justice
Co-operation and Development	Labour, Employment and Professional Training
National Education and Culture	Youth and Sport
Defence	Overseas Departments and Territories
Industry and Regional Planning	

Economy, Finance and the Budget
Equipment, Housing, Transport
  and the Sea
European Affairs
Foreign Affairs
Foreign Trade

Postal Services,
  Telecommunications and Space
Relations with Parliament
Research and Technology
Social Affairs and Solidarity

Governments:

	Prime Minister	Parties represented in government
Nov. 1944–Nov. 1945	de Gaulle I	PCF, SFIO, MRP, Rad. Soc.
Nov. 1945–Jan. 1946	de Gaulle II	PCF, MRP, SFIO, UDSR, Rad. Soc.
Jan. 1946–June 1946	Gouin (SFIO)	SFIO, MRP, PCF
June 1946–Dec. 1946	Bidault I (MRP)	SFIO, MRP, PCF, UDSR
Dec. 1946–Jan. 1947	Blum (SFIO)	SFIO
Jan. 1947–Nov. 1947	Ramadier (SFIO)	SFIO, MRP, PCF, UDSR, Soc. Ind., Rad. Soc.
Nov. 1947–July 1948	Schuman I (MRP)	MRP, SFIO, Rad. Soc., UDSR, Soc. Ind.
July 1948–Aug. 1948	Marie (Rad. Soc.)	SFIO, MRP, UDSR, PRL, Rad. Soc., Soc. Ind.
Aug. 1948–Sept. 1948	Schuman II (MRP)	MRP, Rad. Soc., Soc. Ind., UDSR
Sept. 1948–Oct. 1949	Queuille I (Rad. Soc.)	SFIO, MRP, Rad. Soc., UDSR, Indep., PRL
Oct. 1949–Feb. 1950	Bidault II (MRP)	MRP, Rad. Soc., SFIO, UDSR, Indep.
Feb. 1950–July 1950	Bidault III (MRP)	MRP Rad. Soc., UDSR, Indep.
July 1950–July 1950	Queuille II (Rad. Soc.)	MRP, Rad. Soc., Indep., UDSR
July 1950–Mar. 1951	Pleven I (UDSR)	MRP, UDSR, SFIO, Indep., Rad. Soc.
Mar. 1951–Aug. 1951	Queuille III (Rad. Soc.)	MRP, UDSR, SFIO, Rad. Soc., Indep.
Aug. 1951–Jan. 1952	Pleven II (UDSR)	MRP, Indep., Rad. Soc., UDSR, Paysan, RGR

	Prime Minister	Parties represented in government
Jan. 1952–Mar. 1952	Faure I (Rad. Soc.)	Rad. Soc., MRP, UDSR, Indep., Paysan
Mar. 1952–Jan. 1953	Pinay (Indep.)	Rad. Soc., Indep., MRP, Paysan, UDSR
Jan. 1953–June 1953	Mayer (Rad. Soc.)	Rad. Soc., MRP, Indep., Paysan, UDSR, ARS
June 1953–June 1954	Laniel (Indep.)	Indep., MRP, Rad. Soc., Paysan, UDSR, ARS, URAS
June 1954–Feb. 1955	Mendes-France (Rad. Soc.)	Rad. Soc., Gaull., Indep., UDSR, MRP, RGR
Feb. 1955–Jan. 1956	Faure II (Rad. Soc.)	Rad. Soc., Gaull., Indep., MRP, Paysan, UDSR
Jan. 1956–June 1957	Mollet (SFIO)	SFIO, Rad. Soc., UDSR
June 1957–Nov. 1957	Bourges-Maunoury (Rad. Soc.)	Rad. Soc., SFIO, UDSR, RGR
Nov. 1957–May 1958	Gaillard (Rad. Soc.)	Rad. Soc., MRP, SFIO, Indep., UDSR, RGR
May 1958–June 1958	Pflimlin (MRP)	MRP, UDSR, RGR, Indep., Rad. Soc.
June 1958–Jan. 1959	de Gaulle III (UNR)	SFIO, MRP, UDSR, Indep., Gaull., Rad. Soc.
Jan. 1959–Apr. 1962	Debré (UNR)	UNR, MRP, Indep., Rad. Soc.
Apr. 1962–Dec. 1962	Pompidou I (UNR)	UNR, MRP, Indep.
Dec. 1962–Jan. 1966	Pompidou II (UNR-UDT)	UNR-UDT, Rep. Ind.
Jan. 1966–Apr. 1967	Pompidou III (UNR-UDT)	UNR-UDT, Rep. Ind., GD
Apr. 1967–May 1968	Pompidou IV (UNR-UDT)	UNR-UDT, Rep. Ind.
May 1968–July 1968	Pompidou V (UNR-UDT)	UNR-UDT, Rep. Ind.
July 1968–June 1969	Couve de Murville (UDR)	UDR, Rep. Ind.
June 1969–July 1972	Chaban-Delmas (UDR)	UDR, Rep. Ind., PDM
July 1972–Apr. 1973	Messmer I (UDR)	UDR, Rep. Ind., CDP

	Prime Minister	Parties represented in government
Apr. 1973–Mar. 1974	Messmer II (UDR)	UDR, Rep. Ind., CDP
Mar. 1974–May 1974	Messmer III (UDR)	UDR, Rep. Ind., CDP
May 1974–Aug. 1976	Chirac I (UDR)	UDR, Rep. Ind., MRG
Aug. 1976–Mar. 1978	Barre I (UDR)	UDR, Rep. Ind., CDS, Rad. Soc.
Mar. 1978–May 1981	Barre II (RPR)	RPR, Rep. Ind., CDS, Rad. Soc.
May 1981–June 1981	Mauroy I (PS)	PS, MRG
June 1981–Mar. 1983	Mauroy II (PS)	PS, PCF, MRG
Mar. 1983–July 1984	Mauroy III (PS)	PS, PCF MRG, PSU
July 1984–Mar. 1986	Fabius (PS)	PS (39), MRG, PSU
Mar. 1986–May 1988	Chirac II (RPR)	RPR, PR, CDS
May 1988–June 1988	Rocard I (PS)	PS, MRG, UDF, Indep.
June 1988–May 1991	Rocard II (PS)	PSF, MRG
May 1991–Apr. 1992	Cresson (PS)	PSF, MRG
Apr. 1992–Mar. 1993	Beregovoy (PS)	PSF, MRG
Mar. 1993–	Balladur (RPR)	RPR, UDR

Regions (Régions):

	Population (1990 census)
Île-de-France	10 660 600
Champagne-Ardenne	1 347 800
Picardie	1 810 700
Haute-Normandie	1 737 200
Centre	2 371 000
Basse-Normandie	1 391 300
Bourgogne	1 609 700
Nord-Pas-de-Calais	3 965 100
Lorraine	2 305 700
Alsace	1 624 400
Franche-Comté	1 097 300
Pays de la Loire	3 059 100
Bretagne	2 795 600
Poitou-Charentes	1 595 100
Aquitaine	2 795 800
Midi-Pyrenees	2 430 700
Limousin	722 900
Rhône-Alpes	5 350 700

	Population (1990 census)
Auvergne	1 321 200
Languedoc-Roussillon	2 115 000
Provence-Alpes-Cote d'Azur	4 257 900
Corse	249 700

Media:

(a) Major newspapers:

Name	Location	Circulation
Le Figaro	Paris	433 496
Le Progrès	Chassieu	411 000
Le Parisien	Paris	402 085
La Voix du Nord	Lille	374 050
Sud-Ouest	Bordeaux	366 387
Le Monde	Paris	362 443
France-Soir	Paris	301 716
L'Équipe	Paris	300 940
La Dauphiné Libéré	Grenoble	294 200
L'Est Republicain	Heillecourt	267 588
La Nouvelle Republique du Centre-Ouest	Tours	267 064
Nice-Martin	Nice	265 104
La Montagne	Clermont-Ferrand	252 691
Dépêche Du Midi	Toulouse	241 514
Dernieres Nouvelles d'Alsace	Strasbourg	220 082
Le Republicain Lorrain	Metz	192 853
International Herald Tribune	Paris	178 000
Libération	Paris	256 324

(*b*) Radio and television: *Commission Nationale de la Communication et des Libertés* (*CNCL*) supervises all French broadcasting, allocates concessions for privatized channels, distributes cable networks and frequencies. In 1987 there were two state-run channels (*A2* and *FR3*) and four private channels (*Canal Plus, La 5, M6*, and *TF1*).

Education:

1991/92 figures	No. Staff	No. Students
Pre-Primary and Primary	373 004	6 704 800
Secondary	358 500	5 523 400
Higher:		
Universities	46 200	1 080 200
Other	40 200	620 600

NB. Figures for number of staff are 1990/91.

Economic Interest Organizations:
Employers' organization: Conseil National du Patronat Français (CNPF).

Central trade union peak associations: Confédération Générale du Travail (CGT), founded 1895; membership: 1,600,000; Force Ouvrière (FO), founded 1947; membership: 1,100,000; Confédération Française Démocratique du Travail (CFDT), founded 1964; membership: 558,000, Confédération Générale des Cadres (CGC), founded 1944; membership: 300,000, Fédération de l'Éducation Nationale (FEN), founded 1948; membership: 395,000.

National or Central Bank: Banque de France.

Central Statistical Office:
Institut National de la Statistique et des Études Économiques
18, boulevard Adolphe-Pinard
F-75675 PARIS CEDEX 14

Budget: US 1989(—in 1992) dollars ($1 = 4.7825)—millions

Revenue	
Tax Revenue	276 251
Income tax	50 884
Corporation tax	32 305
Value-added tax	122 732
Stamp duty	15 280
Petroleum revenue	23 753
Other taxes	42 342
Non-tax Revenue	20 786
Sub-Total	297 037
Tax relief and reinbursements	−32 013
Other deductions, eg. EC	−38 756
Total	226 268

Expenditure	
Public authorities, general administration	30 935
Education and culture	58 048
Social Services, health and employment	46 665
Agriculture and rural areas	5 088
Housing and town planning	11 360
Transport and communications	9 937
Industry and services	7 273
Foreign affairs	11 178
Defence	39 898
Other	25 721
Total	246 145

Further Information:

Ardagh, J. (1987), *France Today*. London: Secker & Warburg.

Chambers, F. (1980), *France*. Oxford: Clio Press World Bibliographic Series, Vol. 13.

Flockton, C., and Kofman, E. (1989), *France*. London: Chapman.

Hall, P. A., J. Hayward, and Machin, H. (1990) (eds.), *Developments in French Politics*. London: Macmillan.

Hayward, J. (1983), *Governing France: The One and Indivisible French Republic*. London: Weidenfeld & Nicolson.

Larkin, M. (1988), *France since the Popular Front: Government and People 1936–86*. Oxford: Oxford U.P.

OECD Country Reports. Annual. *France* (Paris).

Ross, G. *et al.* (1987) (eds.), *The Mitterrand Experiment*. Oxford: Polity Press.

Stevens, A. (1992), *The Government and Politics of France*. London: Macmillan.

Wright, V. (1983), *The Government and Politics of France*. London: Hutchinson.

6.   Federal Republic of Germany[1]

State Structure: Federal.

Form of State: Republic.

Parliament (bicameral): Bundestag (Federal Assembly) now has 656 seats, 4 years: The Bundesrat (Federal Council) represents the states and has 68 seats, various no. of years.

Electoral System: The electoral system is half a party list system, and half a majority plurality system.

Main Languages: German (94%); Turkish (2%).

Population: 79,753,227 (1990 official estimate).

Constitutional Development: The Federal Republic of Germany was established in October 1990, uniting the Federal Republic of Germany (West Germany) with the German Democratic Republic (East Germany).

Heads of State:

T. Heuss (FDP)	Sept. 1949–July 1959
H. Lubke (CDU)	July 1959–June 1969
G. Heinemann (SPD)	July 1969–June 1974
W. Scheel (FDP)	July 1974–June 1979
K. Carstens (CDU)	July 1979–June 1984
R. von Weizäcker (CDU)	July 1984–

Capital City: Bonn (1985): 292,600.

Ministries:
(As of Jan. 1993)

Office of the Federal President
Federal Chancellery
Office of the Head of the Press and Information Office of the Federal
Government

Defence	Health
Economic Co-operation	Interior
Economics	Justice
Education and Science	Posts and Telecommunications

[1] These data refer to the Federal Republic before reunification.

Environment   Regional Planning, Construction
Family Affairs and Senior Citizens   and Urban Development
Finance   Research and Technology
Food, Agriculture and Forestry   Transport
Foreign Affairs   Women and Youth
Labour and Social Affairs

Governments:

	Prime Minister	Parties represented in government
Sept. 1949–Sept. 1953	Adenauer I (CDU)	CDU/CSU, FDP, DP
Oct. 1953–Oct. 1957	Adenauer II (CDU)	CDU/CSU, FDP, DP, BHV
Oct. 1957–Nov. 1961	Adenauer III (CDU)	CDU/CSU, DP
Nov. 1961–Dec. 1962	Adenauer IV (CDU)	CDU/CSU, FDP
Dec. 1962–Oct. 1963	Adenauer V (CDU)	CDU/CSU, FDP
Oct. 1963–Oct. 1965	Erhard I (CDU)	CDU/CSU, FDP
Oct. 1965–Dec. 1966	Erhard II (CDU)	CDU/CSU, FDP
Dec. 1966–Oct. 1969	Kiesinger (CDU)	CDU/CSU, SPD
Oct. 1969–Dec. 1972	Brandt I (SPD)	SPD, FDP
Dec. 1972–May 1974	Brandt II (SPD)	SPD, FDP
May 1974–Dec. 1976	Schmidt I (SPD)	SPD, FDP
Dec. 1976–Nov. 1980	Schmidt II (SPD)	SPD, FDP
Nov. 1980–Oct. 1982	Schmidt III (SPD)	SPD, FDP
Oct. 1982–Mar. 1983	Kohl I (CDU)	CDU/CSU, FDP
Mar. 1983–Mar. 1987	Kohl II (CDU)	CDU/CSU, FDP
Mar. 1987–Oct. 1990	Kohl III (CDU)	CDU/CSU, FDP
Oct. 1990–Jan. 1991	Kohl IV (CDU)	CDU/CSU, FDP
Jan. 1991–Oct. 1994	Kohl V (CDU)	CDU/CSU, FDP
Oct. 1994–	Kohl VI (CDU)	CDU/CSU, FDP

States (Länder):

	Population, 000s (1990)
Baden-Württemberg	9 822
Bayern	11 449
Berlin	3 434
Brandenburg	2 578
Bremen	682
Hamburg	1 652
Hessen	5 763

	Population, 000s (1990)
Mecklenburg-Vorpommern	1 924
Niedersachsen	7 387
Nordrhein-Westfalen	17 350
Rheinland-Pfalz	3 764
Saarland	1 073
Sachsen	4 764
Sachsen-Anhalt	2 874
Schleswig-Holstein	2 626
Thuringen	2 611

Media:

(*a*) Major newspapers:

Name	Place	Circulation
Bild-Zeitung	Hamburg	4 892 400
Westdeutsche Allgemeine Zeitung	Essen	1 209 400
Freie Presse	Chemnitz	560 000
Mitteldeutsche Zeitung	Halle	510 000
Sachsische Zeitung	Dresden	470 000
Rheinische Post	Düsseldorf	390 000
Augsburger Allgemeine	Augsburg	360 000
Berliner Zeitung	Berlin	330 000
BZ	Berlin	367 100
Super!	Berlin	370 000
Die Welt	Bonn	225 200

(*b*) Radio and television: *Arbeitsgemeinschaft der öffentlich-rechtlichen Rundfunkanstalten der Bundesrepublik Deutschland* (ARD) is the co-ordinating body of the Federal German Radio and Television organizations (nine autonomous regional organizations as well as broadcast programmes for Europe and overseas).

Education: Education is still organised on a slightly different basis in the former East Germany. Therefore aggregate data are not yet available.

The former East Germany:

1990/91 figures	No. Institutions	No. Students
Infant schools	18 766	2 218 550
General and Extended polytechnic schools	742	109 542
Vocational schools	983	280 058
Technical schools	232	115 631
Universities	54	133 602

The former West Germany:

1991 figures	Institutions	No. Staff	No. Students
Pre-primary and primary	41 556	n.a.	4 122 000
General secondary	12 695	294 997	4 070 000
Vocational secondary	5 821	83 028	2 001 000
Special	2 704	41 666	259 000
Higher:			
Non-university	2 842	17 837	232 000
University	249	163 138	1 539 000

Economic Interest Organizations:
Employers' organization: Bundesvereinigung der Deutschen Arbeitsgeber-verbände.

Central trade union peak association: Deutscher Gewerkschaftsbund (DGB), first founded 1868, reorganized 1949; membership: 10,500,000. After unification the trade unions of East Germany were absorbed into the 16 unions affiliated to the DGB.

National or Central Bank: Deutsche Bundesbank.

Central Statistical Office:
Statistiches Bundesamt,
Gustav-Stresemann-Ring 11,
Postfach 5528,
D-6200 Wiesbaden 1

Budget: (1992)—in 1992 US dollars ($1 = 1.4135 DM)—millions

Revenue	
Current Receipts	564 249
Taxes and similar revenue	489 602
Income from economic activity	29 535

Revenue	
Interest	2 845
Allocations and grants	112 500
Other receipts	32 244
Less deductible payments	102 477
Capital Receipts	15 026
Sale of Property	6 200
Loans and grants for investment	20 778
Repayment of loans	5 815
Public sector borrowing	959
Less deductible payments	18 725
Sub-total	579 274
Adjustment	729
Total	580 004

Expenditure	
Current expenditure	552 398
Personnel expenses	170 039
Goods and services	83 489
Interest	63 053
Allocations and grants	338 294
Less deductible payments	102 477
Capital expenditure	110 608
Construction	38 587
Purchase of property	10 263
Allocations and grants for investment	56 819
Loans	19 677
Sale of shares	2 913
Repayment expenses	1 075
Less deductible payments	18 725
Sub-total	663 005
Adjustment	−446
Total	662 560

Further Information:
Ardagh, J. (1987), *Germany and the Germans*. London: Hamish Hamilton.
Beyme, K. von (1979), *Das politische System der Bundesrepublik Deutschland: Eine Einführung*. München: Piper.

Dalton, R. J. (1988), *Politics in West Germany*. Boston: Little, Brown.

Padgett, S., and Burkett, T. (1987), *Political Parties and Elections in Germany: The Search for a New Stability*. London: Hurst.

Paterson, W., and Southern, D. (1991), *Governing Germany*. Oxford: Blackwell.

——, and Spence, D. (1993), *German Unification*. Oxford: Blackwell.

Smith, G. (1986), *Democracy in Western Germany: Parties and Politics in the Federal Republic*. Aldershot: Avebury.

——, Paterson, W., Merkl, P. H., and Padgett, S. (1992), *Developments in German Politics*. Basingstoke: Macmillan.

7.   Greece

State Structure: Unitary.

Form of State: Republic.

Parliament (unicameral): Parliament (Vouli): 300 seats, 4 years.

Electoral System: Proportional representation: Hagenbach quota.

Main Language: Greek (96%).

Population: 10,020,000 (official 1989 estimate).

Constitutional Development: Present constitution dates from 1975 introducing a republican constitution. The military governed Greece from April 1967 to July 1974.

Heads of State:

King Georg II	Sept. 1946–Apr. 1947
King Paul I	Apr. 1947–Mar. 1964
King Kostantinos II	Mar. 1964–Dec. 1967
K. Zoitakis	Dec. 1967–Mar. 1972
G. Papadopoulos	Mar. 1972–Nov. 1973
F. Gizikis	Nov. 1973–Dec. 1974
M. Stasinopoulos	Dec. 1974–June 1975
C. Tsatsos	June 1975–May 1980
C. Karamanlis	May 1980–Mar. 1985
C. Sartzetakis	Mar. 1985–Feb. 1990
C. Karamanlis	May 1990–

Capital City: Athinai (1981): 885, 737.

Ministries:
(As of Jan. 1993)

Ministry to the Prime Minister

Agriculture	Interior
Culture	Justice
Education and Religion	Labour
Environment, Physical	Macedonia and Thrace
Finance	Merchant Marine

Foreign Affairs   Transport and Communications
Health, Welfare and the   National Defence
    Social Services   National Economy
Industry and Commerce   Planning and Public Works
                                                    Public Order

Governments:

	Prime Minister	Parties represented in government
Apr. 1946–Apr. 1946	Poulitsas (Indep.)	
Apr. 1946–Jan. 1947	Tsaldaris I (Prog.)	
Jan. 1947–Aug. 1947	Maximos (Indep.)	
Aug. 1947–Sept. 1947	Tsaldaris II (Prog.)	
Sept. 1947–June 1949	Sophoulis (Lib.)	
June 1949–Jan. 1950	Diomidis (Lib.)	
Jan. 1950–Mar. 1950	Theotokis (Indep.)	
Mar. 1950–Apr. 1950	Venizelos I (Lib.)	
Apr. 1950–Aug. 1950	Plastiras I (Prog.)	
Aug. 1950–Sept. 1950	Venizelos II (Lib.)	
Sept. 1950–Oct. 1951	Venizelos III (Lib.)	Lib., People's, Soc. Dem.
Oct. 1951–Oct. 1952	Plastiras II (Prog.)	Prog. Lib.
Oct. 1952–Nov. 1952	Kioussopoulos (Indep.)	Indep. (caretaker)
Nov. 1952–Oct. 1955	Papagos (ERE)	ERE
Oct. 1955–Feb. 1956	Karamanlis I (ERE)	ERE
Feb. 1956–Mar. 1958	Karamanlis II (ERE)	ERE
Mar. 1958–May 1958	Georgakopoulos (Indep.)	Indep. (caretaker)
May 1958–Nov. 1961	Karamanlis III (ERE)	ERE
Nov. 1961–June 1963	Karamanlis IV (ERE)	ERE
June 1963–Nov. 1963	Pipinellis (ERE)	Indep. (caretaker)
Nov. 1963–Feb. 1964	Papandreou I (EDHIK)	EDHIK
Feb. 1964–July 1965	Papandreou II (EDHIK)	EDHIK
July 1965–Aug. 1965	Athanasiadis-Novas (EDHIK)	EDHIK
Aug. 1965–Sept. 1965	Tsirimokos (EDHIK)	EDHIK
Sept. 1965–Dec. 1966	Stephanopoulos (EDHIK)	EDHIK, ERE
Dec. 1966–Apr. 1967	Paraskevopoulos (Indep.)	Indep.

	Prime Minister	Parties represented in government
Apr. 1967–Dec. 1967	Kollias	Civilian
Dec. 1967–Aug. 1971	Papadopoulos I	Military
Aug. 1971–July 1972	Papadopoulos II	Military
July 1972–Oct. 1973	Papadopoulos III	Military
Oct. 1973–Nov. 1973	Markezinis	Civilian
Nov. 1973–July 1974	Androutsopoulos	Civilian
July 1974–Oct. 1974	Karamanlis V (ND)	ND EDHIK, Indep.
Oct. 1974–Nov. 1974	Karamanlis VI (ND)	Indep. (caretaker)
Nov. 1974–Nov. 1977	Karamanlis VII (ND)	ND
Nov. 1977–May 1980	Karamanlis VIII (ND)	ND
May 1980–Oct. 1981	Rallis (ND)	ND
Oct. 1981–June 1985	Papandreou I (Pasok)	Pasok
June 1985–June 1989	Papandreou II (Pasok)	Pasok
June 1989–Oct. 1989	Tzannetakis (ND)	ND, KKE
Oct. 1989–Nov. 1989	Grivas	ND, Pasok, KKE
Nov. 1989–Apr. 1990	Zolotas	ND, Pasok, KKE
Apr. 1990–Oct. 1993	Mitsotakis (ND)	ND
Oct. 1993–	Papandreou III (Pasok)	Pasok

Regions (Provinces):

	Population (1981)
Greater Athens	3 027 331
Rest of Central Greece and Euboea	1 099 841
Peloponnesos	1 012 528
Ionian Islands	182 651
Epirus	324 541
Thessaly	695 654
Macedonia	2 120 481
Thrace	345 220
Aegean Islands	428 533
Crete	502 165

Media:

(*a*) Major newspapers:

Name	Location	Circulation
Eleftheros Typos	Athens	167 186
Ta Nea	Athens	150 664
Estia	Athens	85 000
Ethnos	Athens	84 735
Apogevmatini	Athens	72 911
Vradyni	Athens	71 914

(*b*) Radio and television: *Elliniki Radiophonia Tileorasi* (Hellenic National Radio Television) has been state controlled since 1939 and operates radio and television.

1987 saw the emergence of 10 municipal radio stations, therefore loosening the central states monopoly of radio.

1990 saw two private TV stations begin to broadcast, therefore breaking the state monopoly; Mega-Channel and Antenna TV.

Education:

1987/88 figures	No. Teachers	No. Students
Pre-primary and primary	47 065	868 490
Secondary:		
General	44 887	708 549
Vocational	9 286	131 471
Higher:		
Universities	7 435	117 193
Other	5 325	71 980

Economic Interest Organizations:

Employers' organization: Union of Greek Industrialists (EEB).

Central trade union peak association: General Confederation of Greek Workers (GSEE), founded 1918; membership: 600,000 (no date available)

National or Central Bank: Bank of Greece.

Central Statistical Office:
National Statistical Service of Greece
Odos Likourgou 14–16
Athens

Budget: (1989 estimates) in 1992 US dollars ($ = 181. 175 drachmae)—
millions

Revenue

Ordinary Budget:	
Direct taxes	3 400
Excise duty	2
Indirect taxes	8 290
European Community	372
Credit receipts	5 805
Other	686
Sub-total	18 556
Extraordinary Budget:	
Revenue from investments	50
Aid and loans from abroad	1 104
Revenue from NATO works	110
Increase in national debt	773
Receipts from EC	447
Total	21 043

Expenditure

Ordinary Budget:	
Political ministries	15 324
Defence	1 932
European Community	561
Police and other sectors	463
Sub-total	18 280
Provision for increase	276
Sub-total	18 556
Extraordinary Budget:	
Expenditure on NATO works	110
Investments	2 377
Total	21 043

Further Information:
Clogg, R. (1979), *A Short History of Modern Greece*. Cambridge: Cambridge
U.P.
—— (1983) (ed.), *Greece in the 1980s*. London: Macmillan.

Featherstone, K., and Katsoudas, D. (1987) (eds.), *Political Change in Greece: Before and after the Colonels*. London: Croom Helm.

Freris, A. F. (1986). *The Greek Economy in the Twentieth Century*. London: Croom Helm.

Kourvetaris, Y. A. and Dobratz, B. A. (1988), *Parties and Elections in Greece: The Search for Legitimacy*. Oxford: Clarendon Press.

Mavrogordatos, G. (1983), *Stillborn Republic*. Berkeley, Calif.: University of California Press.

Mouzelis, N. (1978), *Modern Greece: Facets of Underdevelopment*. London: Macmillan.

Spoundalakis, M. (1988), *The Rise of the Greek Socialist Party*. London: Routledge.

Yannopoulos, G. N. (1987), *Greece and the EEC: Integration and Convergence*. London: Macmillan.

8. Iceland

State Structure: Unitary.

Form of State: Republic

Parliament (unicameral): Alpingi: 60 seats, 4 years. Two-chamber substitute: one-third of lower house elected by Alpingi to constitute upper house.

Electoral System: Proportional representation: d'Hondt divisor.

Main Language: Icelandic (97%).

Population: 259,577 (official estimate, 1991).

Constitutional Development: Its present constitution dates from 1944, the year of its independence.

Heads of State:

S. Björnssen	June 1944–July 1952
A. Asgeirsson	July 1952–Aug. 1968
K. Eldjarn	Aug. 1968–Aug. 1980
V. Finnbogadottir	Aug. 1980–

Capital City: Reykjavik (1986): 91,394.

Ministries:

Prime Minister's Office

Agriculture	Fisheries
Commerce	Foreign Affairs
Communications	Health
Education and Culture	Industry
Environment	Justice and Ecclesiastical Affairs
Finance	Social Affairs

Governments:

	Prime Minister	Parties represented in government
Oct. 1944–Feb. 1947	Thors II (IP)	IP, SDP, SP
Feb. 1947–Dec. 1949	Stefansson (SDP)	SDP, IP, PP
Dec. 1949–Mar. 1950	Thors III (IP)	IP
Mar. 1950–Sept. 1953	Steinthorsson (PP)	PP, IP
Sept. 1953–July 1956	Thors IV (IP)	IP, PP
July 1956–Dec. 1958	Jonasson (PP)	PP, PA, SDP
Dec. 1958–Nov. 1959	Jonsson (SDP)	SDP
Nov. 1959–Nov. 1963	Thors V (IP)	IP, SDP
Nov. 1963–July 1970	Benediktsson (IP)	IP, SDP
July 1970–June 1971	Hafstein (IP)	IP, SDP
June 1971–Aug. 1974	Johannesson I (PP)	PP, PA, ULL
Aug. 1974–Aug. 1978	Hallgrimsson (IP)	IP, PP
Aug. 1978–Oct. 1979	Johannesson II (PP)	PP, SDP, PA
Oct. 1979–Feb. 1980	Grondal (SDP)	SDP
Feb. 1980–May 1983	Thoroddsen (IP)	IP, PP, PA
May 1983–July 1987	Hermannsson I (PP)	IP, PP
July 1987–Sept. 1988	Palsson (IP)	IP, PP, SDP
Sept. 1988–Sept. 1989	Hermannsson II (PP)	PP, SDP, PA
Sept. 1989–Apr. 1991	Hermansson III (PP)	PP, SDP, CP, PA
Apr. 1991–	Oddsson (IP)	PP, SDP

Regions (Sýslur):

	Population (1986)
Austurland	13 131
Norðurland eystra	25 764
Norðurland vestra	10 676
Rekjavíkursvæði og Reykjanessvæði	148 883
Suðurland	20 065
Vestfirðir	10 193
Vesturland	14 940

Media:

(*a*) Major newspapers:

Name	Location	Circulation
Mogunbladið	Reykjavik	52 000
Dagbladið-Visir (DV)	Reykjavik	39 000
Timinn	Reykjavik	15 000
Thjodviljinn	Reykjavik	12 000
Althydubladid	Reykjavik	8 500
Dagur	Akureyri	6 200

(*b*) Radio and Television: *Ríkisútvarpið* (Icelandic State Broadcasting Service) ran radio and television until 1986. In 1986 its monopoly was abolished. There is now a privately owned TV station, Station Two, and several private radio stations.

Education:

1988 figures	No. Institutions	No. Staff	No. Students*
Pre-primary, primary and lower secondary	211	3 200	41 908
Higher secondary	54	n.a.	17 874
Tertiary (universities and colleges)	4	n.a.	6 161

NB:* = 1991 figures.

Economic Interest Organizations:

Employers' organization: Vinnuveitendasamband Islands (Employers' Federation).

Central trade union peak organization: Alþýðussamband Islands (Icelandic Federation of Labour) (ASI), founded 1918; membership: 70,000.

National or Central Bank: Sedlabanki Islands.

Budget: (1991)—in 1992 US dollars ($1 = 53.82 kronur)—millions

Revenue	
Direct taxes	840
Indirect taxes	1 478
Non-tax revenue	185
Total	2 503

Expenditure	
General administration	152
Education	374
Health and Welfare	979
Subsidies	210
Agriculture	198
Fisheries	17
Manufacturing	10
Power	15
Communications	213
Other purposes	815
Total	2 982

Central Statistical Office:
Statistical Bureau of Iceland
Reykjavik

Further Information:
Griffiths, J. C. (1969), *Modern Iceland*. London: Pall Mall.
Grimsson, O. R. (1977), *The Icelandic Multilateral Coalition System*. London: University College.
Horton, J. J. (1983), *Iceland*, Oxford: Clio Press, World Bibliographical Series, Vol. 37.
Iceland 1996 (1996), The Central Bank of Iceland.
Morgunbladid. Monthly. *News from Iceland*. Reykjavik.
National Economic Institute. *Briefs on the Icelandic Economy. Statistical Reports*.
Tomasson, R. F. (1980), *Iceland: The First New Society*. Minneapolis: University of Minnesota Press.

9. Ireland

State Structure: Unitary.

Form of State: Republic.

Parliament (bicameral): Oireachtas: Seanad Éireann (Upper house): 60 seats, 5 years; Dáil Éireann (Lower house): 166 seats, 5 years.

Electoral System: Proportional representation: single transferable vote.

Main Languages: English (95%); Irish (5%).

Population: 3,523,401 (Preliminary population figures from the 1991 census).

Constitutional Development: The original constitution dates from 1922 and it was renewed in 1937. From 1937 presidents have been elected in Ireland.

Heads of State:

S. T. O'Kelly	June 1945–June 1959
E. de Valera	June 1959–June 1973
E. Childers	June 1973–Nov. 1974
C. O'Dalaigh	Dec. 1974–Oct. 1976
P. Hillery	Oct. 1976–
P. Hillery	Dec. 1976–Dec. 1990
M. Robinson	Dec. 1990–

Capital City: Dublin (1981): 915,115.

Ministries:
(Ministries are known as Department's in Ireland)
Office of the President

Department of the Taoiseach	Finance
Agriculture, Food and Forestry	Foreign Affairs
Arts, Culture and the Gaeltacht	Health
Defence	Justice
Education	Marine
Energy	Social Welfare
Enterprise and Employment	Tourism and Trade
Environment	Transport, Energy and
Equality and Law	Communications

Governments:

	Prime Minister	Parties represented in government
June 1944–Feb. 1948	de Valera I (FF)	FF
Feb. 1948–May 1951	Costello I (FG)	FG, CP, CT
May 1951–June 1954	de Valera II (FF)	FF
June 1954–Mar. 1957	Costello II (FG)	FG, Lab. CT
Mar. 1957–June 1959	de Valera III (FF)	FF
June 1959–Oct. 1961	Lemass I (FF)	FF
Oct. 1961–Apr. 1965	Lemass II (FF)	FF
Apr. 1965–Nov. 1966	Lemass III (FF)	FF
Nov. 1966–July 1969	Lynch I (FF)	FF
July 1969–Mar. 1973	Lynch II (FF)	FF
Mar. 1973–July 1977	Cosgrave (FG)	FG
July 1977–Dec. 1979	Lynch III (FF)	FF
Dec. 1979–June 1981	Haughey I (FF)	FF
June 1981–Mar. 1982	Fitzgerald I (FG)	FG, Lab.
Mar. 1982–Dec. 1982	Haughey II (FF)	FF
Dec. 1982–Mar. 1987	Fitzgerald II (FG)	FG, Lab.
Mar. 1987–July 1989	Haughey III (FF)	FF
July 1989–Feb. 1992	Haughey IV (FF)	FF, PD
Feb. 1992–Jan. 1993	Reynolds I (FF)	FF, PD
Jan. 1993–Dec. 1994	Reynolds II (FF)	FF, Lab.
Dec. 1994–	Bruton (FF)	FF, Lab.

Provinces:

Name	Population (1991 preliminary census results)
Connaught	422 909
Leinster	1 860 037
Munster	1 008 443
Ulster (part)	232 012

Media:
(a) Major newspapers:

Name	Location	Circulation
Irish Independent	Dublin	150 121
Evening Herald	Dublin	132 314
Evening Press	Dublin	101 962
The Irish Times	Dublin	93 187
Irish Press	Dublin	86 655
Cork Examiner	Cork	63 560

(b) Radio and television: *Raidio Telfís Éireann* (RTE) is the Irish national broadcasting organization. [1988 Radio and Television Act provided for an independent national radio service and 23 regional stations, and an independent TV station.]

RTE (the state controlled station) now broadcasts on 3 channels; Radio 1, Radio 2 and FM3 Music. Raidio na Gaeltachta still broadcasts in Gaelic and is financed by RTE.

RTE still broadcasts RTE-1 and RTE-2.

TV3 broadcast as an independent station from April 1989, but had its franchise removed in Nov 1991.

RTE broadcasts on two channels (Radio 1 and Radio 2) and transmits two programmes on television (RTE-1 and RTE-2). In addition *Raidio na Gaeltachta* broadcasts in Gaelic.

Education:

1990/91 figures	No. Institutions	No. Staff	No. Students
State primary	3 352	20 430	543 744
Secondary	476	11 550	212 966
Vocational	248	4 836	86 428
Comprehensive	16	512	8 861
Community	52	1 946	34 080
Primary teacher training	5	n.a. [combined = 125]	821
Preparatory colleges	1	n.a.	21
Technical colleges	9	1 236	16 801
Technology colleges	11	779	10 470
Universties and institutions	7	2 046	39 837

Economic Interest Organizations:
Employers' organization: Federated union of employers.

Federation of Irish Employers–3,500 members.

Central trade union peak association: Irish Congress of Trade Unions (ICTU), founded 1894; membership: 672,600 (199).

National or Central Bank: Bank Ceannais nahEireann (Central Bank of Ireland).

Central Statistical Office:
Central Statistics Office
St Stephen's Green House
Earlsfort Terrace
Dublin 2

Budget: (1992 estimates) US—in 1992 dollars ($1 = 53.85 pence)— millions

Revenue	
Customs	238
Excise	3 190
Capital taxes	143
Income tax	6 325
Corporation tax	1 259
Motor vehicle duties	403
Stamp duties	483
VAT	4 141
Employment and training levy	264
EC agricultural levies	19
Total	17 293

Expenditure	
Debt service	4 477
Agriculture, fisheries and forestry	531
Defence	691
Justice and police	877
Education	2 494
Social welfare	3 605
Health	2 604
Housing	9
Industry and labour	490
Total (inc. others)	17 916

Further Information:

Brown, T. (1981), *Ireland: A Social and Cultural History 1922–79*. London: Fontana.

Carter, R. W., and Parker, A. J. (1988), *Ireland: A Contemporary Geographical Perspective*. London: Routledge.

Chubb, B. (1982), *The Government and Politics of Ireland*. London: Longman.

—— (1992), *The Government and Politics of Ireland*. London: Longman.

—— (1991), *The Politics of the Irish Constitution*. Dublin: Institute of Public Administration.

Gallagher, M. (1985), *Political Parties in the Republic of Ireland*. Manchester: Manchester U.P.

MacDonagh, O. (1977), *Ireland: The Union and its Aftermath*. London: Allen & Unwin.

Mair, P. (1987), *The Changing Irish Party System*. London: Pinter.

O'Halloran, C. (1988), *Partition and the Limits of Irish Nationalism*. Dublin: Gill & Macmillan.

Peillon, M. (1982), *Contemporary Irish Society: An Introduction*. Dublin: Gill & Macmillan.

10. Italy

State Structure: Unitary.

Form of State: Republic since 1946.

Parliament (bicameral): Chamber of deputies (Camera dei deputati): 630 seats, 5 years; Senate (Senato): 323 seats, 5 years.

The 1994 elections were the first under new rules, determined by a series of referenda in August 1993, which are intended to strengthen parliamentary democracy whilst destroying the corrupt patronage of the old system.

The new arrangements: Three quarters of the seats in the Chamber of Deputies and in the Senate are directly elected by a simple majority in each constituency. The remaining one quarter of seats are proportionally divided.

Electoral System: Proportional representation: imperiali quota.

Main Language: Italian (99%).

Population: 57,746,163 (1990 official estimate).

Constitutional Development: The present constitution dates from 1948.

Heads of State:

L. Einaudi	May 1948–Apr. 1955
G. Gronchi	Apr. 1955–May 1962
A. Segni	May 1962–Dec. 1964
G. Saragat	Dec. 1964–Dec. 1971
G. Leone	Dec. 1971–June 1978
A. Fanfani (acting)	June 1978–July 1978
S. Pertini	July 1978–July 1985
F. Cossiga	July 1985–Apr. 1992
O. L. Scalfaro	May 1992–

Capital City: Roma (1985): 2,826,488.

Ministries:
(As of March 1993)

Office of the President
Office of the Prime Minister

Agriculture	Cultural and Environmental
Budget	Heritage
Industry	Health

Interior

Defence

Environment

Education

Employment and Social Welfare

Finance

Foreign Affairs

Foreign Trade

Justice

Merchant Navy

Posts and Telecommunications

Public Works

State Participation

Tourism

Transport

Treasury

Governments:

	Prime Minister	Parties represented in government
July 1946–Feb. 1947	De Gasperi II (DC)	DC, PSI, PCI, PRI
Feb. 1947–May 1947	De Gasperi III (DC)	DC, PSI, PCI
May 1947–May 1948	De Gasperi IV (DC)	DC, PRI, PSLI, PLI
May 1948–Jan. 1950	De Gasperi V (DC)	DC, PSLI, PRI, PLI
Jan. 1950–July 1951	De Gasperi VI (DC)	DC, PSLI, PRI
July 1951–Nov. 1952	De Gasperi VII (DC)	DC, PRI
Nov. 1952–July 1953	De Gasperi VIII (DC)	DC, PRI
July 1953–Aug. 1953	De Gasperi IX (DC)	DC
Aug. 1953–Jan. 1954	Pella (DC)	DC
Jan. 1954–Feb. 1954	Fanfani I (DC)	DC
Feb. 1954–Mar. 1955	Scelba I (DC)	DC, PSDI, PLI
Mar. 1955–July 1955	Scelba II (DC)	DC, PSDI, PLI
July 1955–Mar. 1957	Segni I (DC)	DC, PSDI, PLI
Mar. 1957–May 1957	Segni II (DC)	DC, PSDI, PLI
May 1957–July 1958	Zoli (DC)	DC
July 1958–Feb. 1959	Fanfani II (DC)	DC, PSDI
Feb. 1959–Mar. 1960	Segni III (DC)	DC
Mar. 1960–July 1960	Tambroni (DC)	DC
July 1960–Feb. 1962	Fanfani III (DC)	DC
Feb. 1962–June 1963	Fanfani IV (DC)	DC, PSDI, PRI
June 1963–Dec. 1963	Leone I (DC)	DC
Dec. 1963–July 1964	Moro I (DC)	DC, PSI, PSDI, PRI
July 1964–Feb. 1966	Moro II (DC)	DC, PSI, PSDI, PRI
Feb. 1966–June 1968	Moro III (DC)	DC, PSI, PSDI, PRI
June 1968–Dec. 1968	Leone II (DC)	DC
Dec. 1968–Aug. 1969	Rumor I (DC)	DC, PSU, PRI
Aug. 1969–Mar. 1970	Rumor II (DC)	DC
Mar. 1970–Aug. 1970	Rumor III (DC)	DC, PSI, PSDI, PRI
Aug. 1970–Feb. 1972	Colombo (DC)	DC, PSI, PSDI, PRI

	Prime Minister	Parties represented in government
Feb. 1972–June 1972	Andreotti I (DC)	DC
June 1972–July 1973	Andreotti II (DC)	DC, PSDI, PLI
July 1973–Mar. 1974	Rumor IV (DC)	DC, PSI, PSDI, PRI
Mar. 1974–Nov. 1974	Rumor V (DC)	DC, PSI, PSDI
Nov. 1974–Feb. 1976	Moro IV (DC)	DC, PRI
Feb. 1976–July 1976	Moro V (DC)	DC
July 1976–Mar. 1978	Andreotti III (DC)	DC
Mar. 1978–Mar. 1979	Andreotti IV (DC)	DC
Mar. 1979–Aug. 1979	Andreotti V (DC)	DC, PSDI, PRI
Aug. 1979–Apr. 1980	Cossiga I (DC)	DC, PSDI, PLI
Apr. 1980–Oct. 1980	Cossiga II (DC)	DC, PSI (7), PRI
Oct. 1980–June 1981	Forlani (DC)	DC, PSI, PSDI, PRI
June 1981–Aug. 1982	Spadolini I (PRI)	DC, PSI, PSDI, PRI, PLI
Aug. 1982–Nov. 1982	Spadolini II (PRI)	DC, PSI, PSDI, PRI, PLI
Nov. 1982–Apr. 1983	Fanfani V (DC)	DC, PSI, PSDI, PLI
Apr. 1983–Aug. 1983	Fanfani VI (DC)	DC, PSI
Aug. 1983–Apr. 1987	Craxi (PSI)	DC, PSI, PSDI, PRI, PLI
Apr. 1987–July 1987	Fanfani VII (DC)	DC
July 1987–Apr. 1988	Goria (DC)	DC, PSI, PSDI, PRI, PLI
Apr. 1988–May 1989	De Mita (DC)	DC, PSI, PRI, PSDI, PLI
July 1989–Apr. 1991	Andreotti VI (DC)	DC, PSI, PRI, PSDI, PLI
Apr. 1991–July 1992	Andreotti VII (DC)	DC, PSI, PSDI, PLI
July 1992–Apr. 1993	Amato (PSI)	DC, PSI, PSDI, PLI
Apr. 1993–Apr. 1994	Ciampi (PSI)	DC, PSI, PSDI, PLI
Apr. 1994–	Berlusconi (LN)	FI, LN, AN

Regions (Regioni):

	Population (1990 figures)
Abruzzi	1 272 387
Basilicata	624 519
Calabria	2 153 656
Campania	5 853 902
Emilia-Romagna	3 928 744
Friuli-Venezia Giulia	1 201 027
Lazio	5 191 482
Liguria	1 719 202
Lombardia	8 939 429
Marche	1 435 574

Regions (Regioni): (*Contd.*)

	Population (1990 figures)
Molise	336 456
Piemonte	4 356 227
Puglia	4 081 542
Sardegna	1 664 373
Scilia	5 196 552
Toscana	3 562 525
Trentino-Alto Adige	891 421
Umbria	822 765
Valle d'Aosta	115 996
Veneto	4 398 114

Media:

(*a*) Major newspapers:

Name	Location	Circulation
Corriere della Sera	Milan	851 000
La Repubblica	Rome	775 000
La Stampa/Stampa Sera	Turin	571 000
Il Messaggero	Rome	390 000
II Sole/24 Ore	Milan	353 000
Il Resto del Carlino	Bologna	307 000
La Nazione	Florence	266 000
Il Giornale	Milan	247 000
Il Mattino	Naples	227 000
L'Unita	Rome	257 000

(*b*) Radio and television: *Radiotelevisione Italia* (RAI) is a government corporation broadcasting on three radio and three television networks. Until 1976 RAI had a broadcasting monopoly.

RAI still broadcasts its three major radio channels, but since 1975 has faced competition from private stations—a court case established the right for citizens to freely receive local information. In 1992 the government authorized certain national and local stations to broadcast, but demanded the closure of those 'illegal' stations not granted a licence—but these illegal stations continued to broadcast.

1989 saw the start of a Catholic TV network.

In addition to the three channels broadcast by RAI, there are now seven major private nationwide stations; Canale 5, Dee Jay TV, Video Music, Euro TV, Italia Uno, Rete A and Rete Quattro.

Education:

1990/91 figures	No. Schools	No. Teachers	No. Students
Pre-primary and primary	51 984	355 277	4 608 577
Secondary:			
Scuola Media	9 986	262 718	2 265 947
Secondaria Superiore	7 910	295 153	2 860 983
Higher	82	54 991	1 334 821

Economic Interest Organizations:

Employers' organization: Confederazione Generale dell'Industria Italiana (CONFINDUSTRIA).

Central trade union peak associations: Confederazione Generale Italiana del Lavoro (CGIL) (close to PCI, PSI), founded 1944; membership: 4,556,000; Confederazione Italiano dei Sindacati Lavoratori (CISL) (close to DC), founded 1948; membership: 3,080,000; Unione Italian dei Lavoro (UIL) (close to PSDI, PRI, PSI), founded 1950; membership: 1,541,404; Confederazione Italiana dei Sindacat: Nazionale dei Lavoratone (CISNAL) close to MSI), founded1950; membership: 1,969,635.

National or Central Bank: Banca d'Italia.

Central Statistical Office:
Istituto Centrale di Statistica
Via Cesare Balbo 16
I-00100 Roma

Budget: (1990)—in 1992 US dollars ($1 = 1,238.75 lire)—millions

Revenue	
Property and income taxes	148 771
Business taxation and duties	76 045
Customs and frontier charges, and taxes on manufacturing and consumption	29 050
Public lottery and sweepstakes	2 286
State monopolies	5 145
Other ordinary revenue	68 780
Total real revenue	330 087
Capital movements	995
General total	331 082

Budget, 1990—in 1992 (*Contd.*)

Expenditure	
Ministry of:	
Treasury	230 018
Finance	12 957
Justice	3 661
Education	33 026
Interior	44 921
Public Works	3 781
Agriculture and Forests	2 130
Defence	19 643
Labour and Social Welfare	41 422
Other Ministries	40 487
General Total	432 092

Further Information:

Clark, M. (1984), *Modern Italy, 1971–1982*. London: Longman.

The Economist. 26 May 1990. *Italy* [survey]. London.

Farneti, P. (1985), *The Italian Party System*. London: Pinter.

Financial Times. 7 July 1992. *Italy* [survey]. London.

Ginsborg, P. (1990), *A History of Contemporary Italy: Society and Politics 1943–1988*. London: Penguin.

Hine, D. (1993), *Governing Italy: The Politics of Bargained Pluralism*. Oxford: Oxford University Press.

LaPalombara, J. (1987), *Democracy: Italian Style*. New Haven, Conn.: Yale U.P.

Mack Smith, D. (1969), *Italy: A Modern History*. Ann Arbor, Mich.: University of Michigan Press.

Sassoon, D. (1986), *Contemporary Italy: Politics, Economics and Society since 1945*. London: Longman.

Spotts, F. and Weiser, T. (1986), *Italy, a Difficult Democracy*. Cambridge: Cambridge University Press.

11. Luxembourg

State Structure: Unitary.

Form of State: Constitutional monarchy.

Parliament (unicameral): Chambre des députés: 60 seats, 5 years.

Electoral System: Proportional representation: Hagenbach quota.

Main Languages: Luxembourgish (70%); Portuguese (8%); Italian (6%).

Population: 384,400 (1991 census).

Constitutional Development: The present constitution dates back to 1868 but important amendments were introduced in 1919 (universal suffrage) and 1956 (nationwide elections every five years).

Heads of State:

Grand Duchess Charlotte	Jan. 1919–Nov. 1964
Grand Duke Jean	Nov. 1964–

Capital City: Luxembourg-Ville (1981): 78,900.

Ministries:

Office of the Prime Minister and Ministry of State

Agriculture, Viticulture, and Rural Development	Health
Civil Service Communications	Interior, Housing, and Town Planning
Cultural Affairs and Scientific Research	Justice
Defence	Labour
Economy	Middle Classes and Tourism
Energy and Information Technology	National Education
Environment	Physical Education, Sport, and Youth
Family and Solidarity	Public Works
Finance	Social Security
Foreign Affairs, Foreign Trade and Co-operation	Territorial Administration
	Transport
	Treasury

Governments:

	Prime Minister	Parties represented in government
Mar. 1947–July 1951	Dupong I (CSP)	CSP, DP
July 1951–Dec. 1953	Dupong II (CSP)	CSP, SWP
Dec. 1953–Mar. 1958	Bech (CSP)	CSP, SWP
Mar. 1958–Feb. 1959	Frieden (CSP)	CSP, SWP
Feb. 1959–June 1964	Werner I (CSP)	CSP, DP
June 1964–Dec. 1966	Werner II (CSP)	CSP, SWP
Dec. 1966–Jan. 1969	Werner III (CSP)	CSP, SWP
Jan. 1969–June 1974	Werner IV (CSP)	CSP, DP
June 1974–July 1979	Thorn (DP)	DP, SWP
July 1979–July 1984	Werner V (CSP)	CSP, DP
July 1984–July 1989	Santer I (CSP)	CSP, SWP
July 1989–June 1994	Santer II (CSP)	CSP, SDP
June 1994–Dec. 1994	Santer III (CSP)	CSP, SDP

Districts:

	Population (1986)
Luxembourg	272 250
Diekirch	54 420
Grevenmacher	40 030

Media:
(*a*) Major newspapers:

Name	Location	Circulation
Luxemburger Wort	Luxembourg	85 000
Tageblatt	Luxembourg	26 000
La Républicain Lorrain	Luxembourg	15 000

(*b*) Radio and television: *Radio-Télé Luxembourg* (RTL) broadcast on five radio channels and two television channels.

CLT Multi Media (formerly RTL) now broadcasts seven stations.
Societé Européenne des Satellites (SES) is a Luxembourg-based consortium which operates the ASRTRA 1A and ASTRA 1B television satellites.

Education:

1990/91 figures	No. Students
Nursery and Primary	34 966
Secondary	7 594
Middle, vocational, and technical	11 207
Teacher training	223
University	4 957

NB: figures for number of institutions and staff were not available.

Economic Interest Organizations.

Employers' organization: Groupe de Liaison Patronal, with: Fédération des Industriels; Fédération des Artisans; Fédération du Commerce.

Central trade union peak association: Confédération Générale du Travail du Luxembourg (CGT), founded 1927; membership: 45,000 (1988).

National or Central Bank: The Banque Nationale de Belgique acts as Luxembourg's central bank.

Central Statistical Office:
Service Central de la Statistique et des Études Économiques
Ministère de l'Économie
19–21 boulevard Royal
2910 Luxembourg

Budget: (1990)—in 1992 US Dollars (1$ = 29.20 francs)—millions

Revenue	
Income tax	1 663 5
Other direct taxes	153 5
Turnover tax	542 7
Customs duties	353 5
Other indirect taxes	396 6
Other ordinary receipts	657 7
Other extraordinary receipts	7 8
Total	3 775 0

Expenditure	
Administration	265 5
Defence	109 9
Public order and foreign affairs	129 1
Education and arts	530 3

1990 general accounts (Contd.)

Expenditure		
Social security	990	1
Health, sport, and housing	233	1
Transport and power	562	9
Agriculture and economic affairs	203	5
War damage and national disasters	38	4
Public debt, subsidies etc.	383	5
Miscellaneous	314	5
Total	3 760	8

Further Information:

Als, G. (1982), *Le Luxembourg: Situation politique, économique et sociale.* Paris: La Documentation Française.

CRISP (1975) (1980) (1985), *Grand-Duché de Luxembourg: Système et comportements électoraux: Analyse et synthèse des scrutins de 1974, 1979 et 1984.* Bruxelles.

Department of Trade and Industry. (1992), *Country Profile: Luxembourg.* London.

Majerus, P. (1976), *The Institutions of the Grand Duchy of Luxembourg.* Luxembourg: Information and Press Service.

Newcomer, J. (1984), *The Grand Duchy of Luxembourg: The Evolution of Nationhood, 963 AD to 1983.* Lanham, MD: University Press of America.

12. The Netherlands

State Structure: Unitary.

Form of State: Constitutional monarchy.

Parliament (bicameral): Staten General Eerste Kamer (First chamber): 75 seats, 4 years; Tweede Kamer (Second chamber): 150 seats, 4 years.

Electoral System: Proportional representation: d'Hondt diviser.

Main Language: Dutch (96%).

Population: 15,183,700 (1992 official estimate).

Constitutional Development: Its present constitution only dates from 1983; its first constitution was adopted in 1814–15 and was subsequently revised and amended.

Heads of State:

Queen Wilhelmina	Nov. 1890–Sept. 1948
Queen Juliana	Sept. 1948–Apr. 1980
Queen Beatrix	Apr. 1980–

Capital Cities: Amsterdam (capital) (1986): 679,140; Gravenhage (seat of government) (1986): 443,961.

Ministries:

Office of the Prime Minister

Agriculture, Nature Conservation, and Fisheries
Defence
Development Co-operation
Economic Affairs
Education and Science
Finance
Foreign Affairs
Home Affairs
Housing, Physical Planning, and the Environment
Justice and Netherlands Antilles and Aruban Affairs
Social Affairs and Employment
Transport and Public Works
Welfare, Public Health, and Culture

Governments:

	Prime Minister	Parties represented in government
July 1946–Aug. 1948	Beel I (KVP)	KVP, PVDA
Aug. 1948–Mar. 1951	Drees I (PVDA)	KVP, PVDA, CHU, VVD
Mar. 1951–Sept. 1952	Drees II (PVDA)	KVP, PVDA, CHU, VVD
Sept. 1952–Oct. 1956	Drees III (PVDA)	KVP, PVDA, CHU, ARP
Oct. 1956–Dec. 1958	Drees IV (PVDA)	KVP, PVDA, CHU, ARP
Dec. 1958–May 1959	Beel II (KVP)	KVP, ARP, CHU
May 1959–Jan. 1961	De Quay I (KVP)	KVP, ARP, CHU, VVD
Jan. 1961–July 1963	De Quay II (KVP)	KVP, ARP, CHU, VVD
July 1963–Apr. 1965	Marijnen (KVP)	KVP, VVD, CHU, ARP
Apr. 1965–Nov. 1966	Cals (KVP)	KVP, PVDA, ARP
Nov. 1966–Apr. 1967	Zijlstra (ARP)	KVP, ARP
Apr. 1967–July 1971	De Jong (KVP)	KVP, VVD, ARP, CHU
July 1971–May 1973	Biesheuvel (ARP)	KVP, ARP, CHU, VVD, DS-70
May 1973–Dec. 1977	den Uyl (PVDA)	PVDA, KVP, ARP, PPR, D-66
Dec. 1977–Sept. 1981	van Agt I (CDA)	CDA, VVD
Sept. 1981–Oct. 1981	van Agt II (CDA)	CDA, PVDA, D-66
Oct. 1981–Nov. 1982	van Agt III (CDA)	caretaker
Nov. 1982–July 1986	Lubbers I (CDA)	CDA, VVD
July 1986–Nov. 1989	Lubbers II (CDA)	CDA, VVD
Nov. 1989–Aug. 1994	Lubbers III (CDA)	CDA, PVDA
Aug. 1994–	Kok	PVDA, VVD, D-66

Provinces:

	Population (1987)	Capital
Groningen	558 378	Groningen
Friesland	599 061	Leeuwarden
Drenthe	434 038	Assen
Overijssel	1 003 915	Zwolle
Flevoland (earlier Ijsselmeerpolders)	185 365	Lelystad
Gelderland	1 771 972	Arnhem
Utrecht	953 957	Utrecht
Noord-Holland	2 334 209	Haarlem
Zuid-Holland	3 186 249	's Gravenhage
Zeeland	335 434	Middelburg

Population (1987)		
Noord-Brabant	2 139 626	's Hertogenbosch
Limburg	1 091 553	Maastricht

Media:
(a) Major newspapers:

Name	Location	Circulation
De Telegraaf	Amsterdam	783 000
Algemeen Dagblad	Rotterdam	413 900
De Volkskrant	Amsterdam	342 100
NRC Handelsblad	Rotterdam	241 900
De Limburger	Maastricht	141 879
Het Parool	Amsterdam	100 800

(*b*) Radio and television: *Nederlandse Omroep Stichting*. The NOS no longer controls both radio and TV broadcasting since the 1988 Media Act. It was divided into two different organisations: Nederlandse Omroepprogramma Stichting (NOS) which concentrates on transmission and Nederlandse Omroepproductie Bedrijf (NOB) which is essentially a production company. (NOS) is the co-ordinating body for eight associate broadcasting companies transmitting programmes on radio and television. Among these the following may be named: *Algemene Omroepvereniging* (AVRO) (Independent); *Omroepvereniging Vara* (Socialist); *Katholicke Radio Omroep* (KRO) (Catholic); *Nederlands Christelijke Radio*; *Televisie Radio Omroep Stichting* (TROS) (Independent); *Vereniging* (NCRV) (Protestant); *Veronica Omroep Organisatie* (VOO) (Independent); *VPRO* (Independent).

Education:

1991/92 Full-time	No. Institutions	No. Students
Basic	8 435	1 408 000
Special	1 001	110 000
General secondary	1 211	673 000
Vocational	974	699 000
University status	22	175 000

Economic Interest Organizations:
Employers' organizations: Verbond van Nederlandse Ondernemingen (VNO); Nederlandse Christelijke Werkgeversorganisatie (NCW).

Central trade union peak associations: Federatie Nederlandse Vakbeweging (FNV), formed in 1976 as a confederation of the socialist Nederlands Verbond van Vakverenigingen (NVV) and the Catholic Nederlands Katholiek Vakverboend (NKV); membership: 1,030,000; Christelijk Nationaal Vakverbond in Nederland (CNV), formed 1909; membership. 308,000; Volkcentrale van Middelbaar en Hoger Personeel (MHP); membership: 117,000 (1988).

National or Central Bank: De Nederlandsche Bank NV.

Central Statistical Office:
Netherlands Central Bureau of Statistics
Prinses Beatrixlaan 428
POB 959
NL-2270 AZ Voorburg

Budget: (1992 provisional figures)—in 1992 US dollars ($1 = 1.5925 guilders)—millions

Revenue	
Income tax	41 680
Corporation tax	11 209
Import duties	2 141
Excise duties	7 105
Turnover tax	25 432
Motor vehicle tax	2 480
Tax on legal transactions	1 978
Other taxes	5 115
Shares in profit from Netherlands Bank	1 198
Interest from loans	2 330
Capital transfers, Postal and Telecom. Service	917
Natural gas revenue	4 710
Others	12 202
Total	118 497

Expenditure	
Social Security and public health	30 817
Education and culture	23 073
Defence	9 042
Transport and public works	8 031
Housing, town and country planning	7 970

Interest on public debt	16 781
Agriculture and fishery	5 319
Local authorities' shares in taxes	10 377
EC's shares in taxes	4 589
Public order and security	4 205
Foreign relations	922
Foreign aid	3 761
Trade and handicraft	2 849
Others	4 452
Total	132 189

Further Information:

Daalder, H., and Schuyt, C. (1986) (eds.), *Compendium voor Politiek en Samenleving*. Alphen aan den Rijn.

Daalder, H., and Irwin, D. (1989) (eds.), *Politics in the Netherlands: How much Change?* West European Politics, 12, London.

Gladdish, K. (1991), *Governing from the Centre: Politics and Policy-Making in the Netherlands*. London: C. Hurst and Co.

Griffiths, R. T. (1980) (ed.), *The Economy and Politics of the Netherlands since 1945*. Dordrecht: Martinus Nijhoff.

Lijphart, A. (1975), *The Politics of Accommodation*. Berkeley: University of California Press.

13. Norway

State Structure: Unitary.

Form of State: Constitutional monarchy.

Parliament (unicameral): Storting (divided into Lagting and Odelsting when it comes to legislation): 165 seats, 4 years.

Electoral System: Proportional representation: Sainte Lague, divisor 1, 4 + 8 seats to be distributed on nationwide result.

Main Language: Norwegian (98%).

Population: 4,274,030 (1992 official estimate).

Constitutional Development: The present constitution dates from 1814 but has been amended.

Heads of State:

King Haakon VII	Nov. 1905–Sept. 1957
King Olav V	Sept. 1957–Jan. 1991
King Harold V	Jan. 1991–

Capital City: Oslo (1986): 449,395.

Ministries:

Office of the Prime Minister

Agriculture	Fisheries
Children and Family Affairs	Foreign Affairs
Cultural Affairs	Government Administration
Defence	Health and Social Affairs
Education, Research and Church Affairs	Industry and Energy
	Justice
Environment	Local Government and Labour
Finance	Transport and Communications

Governments:

	Prime Minister	Parties represented in government
Nov. 1945–Nov. 1951	Gerhardsen II (DNA)	DNA
Nov. 1951–Jan. 1955	Torp (DNA)	DNA
Jan. 1955–Aug. 1963	Gerhardsen III (DNA)	DNA
Aug. 1963–Sept. 1963	Lyng (H)	H, V, SP, KRF
Sep. 1963–Oct. 1965	Gerhardsen IV (DNA)	DNA
Oct. 1965–Mar. 1971	Borten (SP)	SP, V, H, KRF
Mar. 1971–Oct. 1972	Bratteli I (DNA)	DNA
Oct. 1972–Oct. 1973	Korvald (KRF)	KRF, SP, V
Oct. 1973–Jan. 1976	Bratteli II (DNA)	DNA
Jan. 1976–Feb. 1981	Nordli (DNA)	DNA
Feb. 1981–Oct. 1981	Brundtland I (DNA)	DNA
Oct. 1981–June 1983	Willoch I (H)	H
June. 1983–Mar. 1986	Willoch II (H)	H, SP, KRF
Mar. 1986–Oct. 1989	Brundtland II (DNA)	DNA
Oct. 1989–Nov. 1990	Syse (H)	CON, CP, CPP
Nov. 1990–Sept. 1993	Brundtland III (DNA)	LAB
Sept. 1993–	Brundtland IV (DNA)	LAB

Counties (Fylker):

	Population (1992 official estimate)
Østfold	238 373
Akershus	421 510
Oslo	467 090
Hedmark	187 542
Oppland	182 479
Buskerud	225 712
Vestfold	199 553
Telemark	163 020
Aust-Agder	97 828
Vest-Agder	145 954
Rogaland	341 838
Hordaland	414 038
Sogn og Fjordane	106 834
Møre og Romsdal	238 810
Sør-Trøndelag	252 872
Nord-Trøndelag	127 491

	Population (1992 official estimate)
Nordland	239 856
Troms	147 979
Finnmark	75 251

Media:
(*a*) Major newspapers:

Name	Location	Circulation
Verdens Gang	Oslo	365 318
Aftenposten	Oslo	269 278 (morning)
		196 022 (afternoon)
Dagbladet	Oslo	220 000
Bergens Tidende	Bergen	98 175
Adresseavisen	Trondheim	89 734
Arbeiderbladet	Oslo	47 016

(*b*) Radio and television: *Norsk Rikskringkastning* (NRK) is the broadcasting board of the state. It has a monoply in radio broadcasting. It operates two main national stations and 17 regional ones. NRK also has a monopoly in TV broadcasting, although Norwegian viewers can recieve many foreign signals

Education:

1990/91 figures	No. Institutions	No. Teachers	No. of Students
Primary	3 406	32 869	309 432
Secondary and vocational	656	38 156	373 646
Special	39	897	912
Teacher training	30	1 049	16 468
Non-university	183	2 138	57 207
University	14	4 024	63 307

Economic Interest Organizations:
Employers' organization: As of 1988, NHO, Næringslivets Hovedorganisasjon (Confederation of Norwegian Business and Industry).

Central trade union peak associations: Landsorganisationen i Norge (LO), founded 1899; membership: 780,000; Confederation of Vocational Unions: Yrkesorganastioners Centralsörbund; membership: 131,739 (1986); Federation of Norwegian Professional Associations: Akaadaemikernas Sallasforbund; membership: 144,108 (1986). Other unions: 170,182 (1986).

National or Central Bank: Norges Bank (Bank of Norway).

Central Statistical Office:
Statistisk Sentralbyrå
POB 8131
N–0033 Oslo 1

Budget: (1991 estimates)—in 1992 US dollars ($1 = 5.745 kroner)—7millions

Revenue	
Income and property taxes	3 474
Tax and excise on petrol extraction	5 213
Customs and excise	244
Purchase tax	11 419
Tax on alcohol	1 072
Tobacco tax	729
Total (inc. others)	62 098

Expenditure	
Defence	3 904
Social services	16 184
Church and education	5 456
Communications	4 476
Aid to developing countries	1 297
Total (inc. others)	71 020

Further Information:
Allen, H. (1979), *Norway and Europe in the 1970s*. Oslo: Universitstsforlaget.
Brochmann, B. S., and Josefsen, D. (1984), *Fiskerinæringen*. Oslo: Tiden.
Derry, T. K. (1973), *A History of Modern Norway 1814–1972*. Oxford: Clarendon Press.
Eliassen, K. A., and Pederssen, M. N. (1986), *Nordiske politiske facta*. Oslo: Tiden.
Heidar, K. (1982), *Norske politiske fakta 1884–1982*. Oslo: Universitetsforlaget.
Kuhnle, S. (1983), *Velferdsstatens utvikling*. Oslo: Universitetsforlaget.
—— (1983), *Velferdsstaten*. Oslo: Tiden.
Lagreid, P., and Roness, P. (1983), *Sentraladministrasjonen*. Oslo: Tiden.
Listhaug, O. (1989), *Citizens, Parties and Norwegian Electoral Politics 1957–1985*. Trondheim: Tapir.

Olsen, J. P. (1983), *Organized Democracy: Political Institutions in a Welfare State: The Case of Norway.* Oslo: Universitetsforlaget.

Ostbye, H. (1984), *Massmedia.* Oslo: Tiden.

Rokkan, S. (1970), *Citizens, Elections, Parties.* Oslo: Universitetsforlaget.

Sather, L. B. (1986), *Norway,* Oxford: Clio Press, World Bibliographic Series, Vol. 67.

Svåsand, L. (1985), *Politiske partier.* Oslo: Tiden.

14. Portugal

State Structure: Unitary.

Form of State: Republic.

Parliament (unicameral): Assembleia da República: 250 seats, 4 years.

Electoral System: Proportional representation: d'Hondt divisor.

Main Language: Portuguese (99%).

Population: 9,853,100 (1991 provisional census results).

Constitutional Development: After the overthrow of the authoritarian regime the present constitution came into force on 25 April 1976. It was revised in 1982 and in 1989.

Heads of State:

A. de Spinola	May 1974–Sept. 1974
F. da Costa Gomes	Sep. 1974–June 1976
A. R. Eanes	July 1976–Mar. 1986
M. Soares	Mar. 1986–Jan. 1991
M. Soares	Jan. 1991–

Capital City: Lisboa (1981): 807, 937.

Ministries:

Office of the President
Office of the Prime Minister

Agriculture
Defence
Education
Employment and Social Security
Environment and Natural
   Resources
Finance
Foreign Affairs
Health
Industry and Energy

Internal Administration
Justice
Parliamentary Affairs
Planning and Territorial
   Administration
Public Works, Transport and
   Communications
Sea
Trade and Tourism

Country Tables

Governments:

	Prime Minister	Parties represented in government
May 1974–July 1974	Palma Carlos (Indep.)	Pro-communist
July 1974–Sept. 1974	Goncalves I (Indep.)	Pro-communist
Sept. 1974–Mar. 1975	Goncalves II (Indep.)	Pro-communist
Mar. 1975–Aug. 1975	Goncalves III (Indep.)	PS, PCP, PPD, MDP-CDE, Indep.
Aug. 1975–Sept. 1975	Goncalves IV (Indep.)	Pro-communist
Sept. 1975–July 1976	de Azevedo (Indep.)	PS, PCP, PPD, Indep.
July 1976–Jan. 1978	Soares I (PS)	PS, Indep.
Jan. 1978–Aug. 1978	Soares II (PS)	PS, CDS
Aug. 1978–Nov. 1978	Nobre da Costa (Indep.)	Indep.
Nov. 1978–July 1979	Mota Pinto (Indep.)	Indep.
July 1979–Jan. 1980	Pintasilgo (Indep.)	Indep.
Jan. 1980–Jan. 1980	Sa Carneiro (PSD)	PSD, CDS
Jan. 1980–Sept. 1981	Pinto Balsemao I (PSD)	PSD, CDS, PPM
Sept. 1981–Jan. 1983	Pinto Balsemao II (PSD)	PSD, CDS, PPM
Jan. 1983–June 1983	Pinto Balsemao III (PSD)	Caretaker
June 1983–June 1985	Soares III (PS)	PS, PSD
June 1985–Nov. 1985	Soares IV (PS)	PS
Nov. 1985–Aug. 1987	Cavaco Silva I (PSD)	PSD
Aug. 1987–Oct. 1991	Cavaco Silva II (PSD)	PSD, CDS
Oct. 1991–	Cavaco Silva III (PSD)	PSD

Districts:

Administrative division	Population (1991 provisional census results)
Aveiro	656 000
Beja	167 900
Braga	746 100
Bragança	158 300
Castelo Branca	214 700
Coimbra	427 600
Évora	173 500
Faro	340 100
Guarda	187 800

Administrative division	Population (1991 provisional census results)
Leiria	427 800
Lisbon	2 063 800
Portalegre	134 300
Pôrto	1 622 300
Santarém	442 700
Setúbal	713 700
Viana do Castelo	248 700
Vila Real	237 100
Viseu	401 000
Autonomous Regions:	
The Azores	236 700
Madeira	253 000

Media:
(*a*) Major newspapers:

Name	Location	Circulation
Correio da Manhā	Lisbon	85 000
Jornal de Notícias	Pôrto	70 000
Publico	Lisbon	64 000
Diário Popular	Lisbon	62 242
Diário de Notícias	Lisbon	58 898
A Capital	Lisbon	40 000

(*b*) Radio and television: *Radiodifusão Portuguesa* (RDP) is the state-controlled broadcasting company; in 1983 the establishment of private radio stations was permitted. *Radiotelevisão Portuguesa* (RTP) is the state-controlled television company; in 1987 private television channels were permitted. January 1991 saw the abolition of the TV licence fee.

February 1992 saw the birth of two new private stations: Sociedade Independente de Communicacao (SIC) and Televisao Independente (TVI).

Education:

1989/90 figures	No. Teachers	No. Students
Pre-primary and primary	42 310	1 208 000
Secondary	83 875	752 000
Higher	10 723	131 000

Economic Interest Organizations:
Employers' organizations: Confederação da Indústria Portuguesa (CIP), Confederação do Comércio Portuguesa (CCP), and Confederação dos Agricultores de Portugal (CAP).

Central trade union peak associations: Confederação Geral dos Trabalhadores Portugueses-Intersindical Nacional (CGTP-INTERSINDICAl) (close to PCP), founded secretly 1970, present name from 1978; membership: 1,186,000; União Geral dos Trabalhadores de Portugal (UGT) (close to PS and PSD), founded 1978; membership: 942,325.

National or Central Bank: Banco de Portugal.

Central Statistical Office:
Instituto Nacional de Estatistica
Av. António José de Almeida
P-1078 Lisboa Codex

Budget: (1989, provisional)—in 1992 US dollars ($1 = 125.65 escudos)—millions

Revenue	
Taxation	18 962
Other current revenue	748
Enterpreneurial and property income	
Capital revenue	53
Sub-total	20 579
Adjustment to total revenue	43
Total	20 622

Expenditure	
Current	21 196
Capital	2 556
Adjustment	177
Total	23 929

Further Information:
Baptista, C. (Co-ord.) (1989), *Portugal: O sistema politico e constitucional 1974/87*. Lisboa: IPS.
Bermeo, N. (1986), *Revolution Within the Revolution: Workers' Control in Rural Portugal*. Princeton: Princeton University Press.

Bruneau, T., and Macleod, A. (1986), *Politics in Contemporary Portugal.* Boulder, Colo.: Lynne Rienner.

Corkill, D. (1993), *An Economic History of Portugal.* Edinburgh: Edinburgh University Press.

Gallagher, T. (1983), *Portugal: A Twentieth Century Interpretation.* Manchester: Manchester University Press.

Graham, L. and Makler, H. (1979), *Contemporary Portugal: The Revolution and its Antecedents.* Austin, Tex.: University of Texas Press.

—— and Wheeler, D. (1984), *In Search of Portugal: The Revolution and its Antecedents.* Madison, Wis.: University of Wisconsin Press.

Harvey, R. (1978), *Portugal, Birth of a Democracy.* Basingstoke: Macmillan.

Kaplan, M. (1992), *The Portuguese.* London: Penguin.

Marques, A. (1975), *História de Portugal,* 2 vols. Lisboa: Palas Editores.

Maxwell, K. (1986), *Portugal in the 1980s.* Westport: Greenwood Press.

Robinson, R. A. H. (1979), *Contemporary Portugal: A History.* London: Allen & Unwin.

Unwin, P. T. H. (1987), *Portugal.* Oxford: Clio Press, World Bibliographical Series, Vol. 71.

15. Spain

State Structure: Unitary.

Form of State: Constitutional monarchy.

Parliament (bicameral): Cortes Senado: 257 seats, 4 years; Congreso de diputados: 350 seats, 4 years.

Electoral System: Proportional representation: d'Hondt divisor.

Main Languages: Castilian Spanish (73%); Catalan (16%); Galician (8%); Basque (2%).

Population: 38,872,268 (1991 census results).

Constitutional Development: The present constitution dates from 1978 and represents a definitive break with the Franco regime. There is a process of developing regional self-government.

Heads of State:

King Juan Carlos   Nov. 1975–

Capital City: Madrid (1981): 3,188,297.

Ministries:

Prime Minister's Chancellery

Agriculture, Fisheries and Food	Interior
Culture	Justice
Defence	Labour and Social Security
Economy and Finance	Public Administration
Education and Science	Public Works, Town Planning, and
Foreign Affairs	Transport
Health and Consumer Affairs	Relations with the Cortes
Industry, Trade and Tourism	Social Affairs

Governments:

	Prime Minister	Parties represented in government
July 1976–July 1977	Suarez I (UCD)	UCD
July 1977–Apr. 1979	Suarez II (UCD)	UCD
Apr. 1979–Feb. 1981	Suarez III (UCD)	UCD

Governments:

	Prime Minister	Parties represented in government
Feb. 1981–Dec. 1982	Calvo Sotelo (UCD)	UCD
Dec. 1982–July 1986	Gonzales I (PSOE)	PSOE, PSC
July 1986–Nov. 1989	Gonzales II (PSOE)	PSOE
Nov. 1989–June 1993	Gonzales III (PSOE)	PSOE
June 1993–	Gonzales IV (PSOE)	PSOE

Autonomous Communities:

	Population (1986)	Capital
Andalucía	6 735 600	Sevilla
Aragón	1 215 600	Zaragoza
Asturias	1 140 100	Oviedo
Baleares	675 400	Palma de Mallorca
Canarias	1 442 500	Santa Cruz de Tenerife
Cantabria	527 400	Santander
Castilla-La Mancha	1 670 100	Toledo
Extremadura	1 084 400	Mérida
Galicia	2 870 900	Santiago de Compostela
La Rioja	263 100	Logroño
Madrid	4 907 100	Madrid
Murcia	1 007 500	Murcia
Navarra	522 500	Pamplona
País Vasco	2 176 800	Vitoria
Valencia	3 790 200	Valencia

Media:
(*a*) Major newspapers:

Name	Location	Circulation
El Pais	Madrid	394 691
ABC	Madrid	298 000
Ya	Madrid	46 500

[NB: There are no truly national papers in Spain. The three above are the closest to nationals. There is a movement away from the local press towards the regional press.]

(*b*) Radio and television: *Radiotelevisión Española* (RTVE) controls and co-ordinates Spanish radio and television. There are in addition to the state-controlled radio many commercial and independent radio stations. Legislation aiming to end the monopoly of TVE was introduced in 1987. This legislation led to the granting of national licences for three new channels in 1989: Antena 3 de Television, SA; Canal +; Tele 5.

Education:

1987 figures	No. Teachers	No. Students
Pre-primary and primary	170 902	4 300 896
Secondary	229 145	4 798 337
Higher	52 206	1 009 521

Economic Interest Organizations:
Employers' organization: Confederación Española de Organizaciones Empresariales (CEOE).

Central trade union peak associations: Confederación Sindical de Comisiones Obreras (CSCO) (independent, but close to the communists), founded in the 1960s; membership: 988,615; Confederación Nacional de Trabajo (CNT), (anarchist), founded 1910; membership: N.A. (1984); Unión General de Trabajadores (UGT) (close to PSOE), founded 1888, reorganized 1977; membership: 700,000 (1984).

National or Central Bank: Banco de Espana.

Central Statistical Office:
Instituto Nacional de Estadística
Paseo Castellana 183
E-28071 Madrid

Budget: (1992, provisional)—in 1992 US Dollars ($1 = 99.05 pesetas)—millions

Revenue	
Direct taxation	63 255
Indirect taxation	49 548
Rates and other taxes	2 219
Current transfers	5 200
Estate taxes	5 654
Transfer of real investments	144
Capital transfers	1 615
Total (inc. others)	127 636

Expenditure

Justice	2 175
Defence	7 929
Interior	4 950
Public works and transport	10 792
Education and science	11 739
Agriculture, fisheries, and food	1 724
Industry, trade, and tourism	2 402
Health and consumer affairs	17 032
Labour and social security	12 551
Economy and finance	2 019
Territorial bodies	23 473
EC contributions	6 928
Public debt	19 578
Total (inc. others)	137 499

Further Information:

Carr, R. (1980), *Modern Spain 1875–1980*. Oxford: Oxford U.P.

Coverdale, J. F. (1979), *The Political Transformation of Spain after Franco*. New York: Praeger.

Donaghy, P. J., and Newton, M. Y. (1987), *Spain: A Guide to Political and Economic Institutions*. Cambridge: Cambridge U.P.

Gillespie, R. (1988), *The Spanish Socialist Party: A History of Factionalism*. Oxford: Oxford University Press.

Gilmour, D. (1985), *The Transformation of Spain: From Franco to the Constitutional Monarchy*. London: Quartet.

Gunther, R., *et al.* (1986), *Spain After Franco: The Making of a Competitive Party System*. Berkeley, Calif.: University of California Press.

Harrison, J. (1993), *The Spanish Economy from the Civil War to the Economic Community*. London: Macmillan.

Hooper, J. (1987), *The Spaniards: A Portrait of the New Spain*. London: Penguin.

Preston, P. (1986), *The Triumph of Democracy in Spain*. London: Methuen.

Share, D. (1987), *The Making of Spanish Democracy*. New York: Praeger.

Shields, G. (1985), *Spain*. Oxford: Clio Press, World Bibliographical Series, Vol. 60.

16. Sweden

State Structure: Unitary.

Form of State: Monarchy.

Parliament (unicameral since 1970): Riksdag: 349 seats, 3 years.

Electoral System: Proportional representation: Sainte Lague divisor; use of a national constituency for allocating 39 equalization seats.

Main Languages: Swedish (97%); Finnish (3%).

Population: 8,644,119 (official estimate 1991).

Constitutional Development: The present constitution dates from 1974 when the one from 1809 was replaced.

Heads of State:

King Gustav V	Dec. 1907–Oct. 1950
King Gustav VI	Dec. 1950–Sept. 1973
King Karl XVI Gustav	Sept. 1973–

Capital City: Stockholm (1985): 659,030.

Ministries:

Office of the Prime Minister

Agriculture	Foreign Affairs
Cultural Affairs	Health and Social Affairs
Defence	Industry and Commerce
Education	Justice
Environment and Natural	Labour
Resources	Public Administration
Finance	Transport and Communications

Governments:

	Prime Minister	Parties represented in government
Jan. 1945–Oct. 1946	Hansson (SAP)	SAP
Oct. 1946–Sep. 1951	Erlander I (SAP)	SAP
Sept. 1951–Oct. 1957	Erlander II (SAP)	SAP, BF
Oct. 1957–Oct. 1969	Erlander III (SAP)	SAP
Oct. 1969–Oct. 1976	Palme I (SAP)	SAP
Oct. 1976–Oct. 1978	Fälldin I (CP)	CP, M, FP
Oct. 1978–Oct. 1979	Ullsten (FP)	FP
Oct. 1979–May 1981	Fälldin II (CP)	CP, M, FP
May 1981–Oct. 1982	Fälldin III (CP)	CP, FP
Oct. 1982–Mar. 1986	Palme II (SAP)	SAP
Mar. 1986–Sept. 1988	Carlsson I (SAP)	SAP
Sept. 1988–Oct. 1991	Carlsson II (SAP)	SAP
Oct. 1991–Sept. 1994	Bildt (MOD)	MOD, FPL, CP, KrF
Oct. 1994–	Carlsson III (SAP)	SAP

Counties:

	Population (1991 official estimate)
Stockholms lan	1 654 511
Uppsalas lan	273 918
Södermanlands lan	256 818
Östergötlands lan	406 100
Jönköpings lan	309 738
Kronobergs lan	178 612
Kalmars lan	241 883
Gotlands lan	57 383
Blekinges	151 168
Kristianstads lan	291 468
Malmöhus lan	786 757
Hallands lan	257 874
Göteborgs o. Bohuslän	742 550
Älvsborgs lan	444 259
Skaraborgs lan	278 162
Värmlands lan	284 187
Orebros lan	273 608
Västmanlands lan	259 438
Kopparbergs lan	290 388
Gävleborgs lan	289 339

	Population (1991 official estimate)
Västernorrlands lan	261 280
Jämtlands lan	136 009
Västerbottens lan	253 835
Norrbottens lan	264 834

Media:
(a) Major newspapers:

Name	Location	Circulation
Expressen	Stockholm	558 913
Dagens Nyheter	Stockholm	393 829
Aftonbladet	Stockholm	364 808
Göteborgs-Posten	Gothenburg	275 315
Svenska Dagbladet	Stockholm	227 050
Sydsvenska Dagbladet Snallposten	Malmo	115 918
Arbetet	Malmo	114 675

(*b*) Radio and television: *Sveriges Radio* (Swedish Broadcasting Corporation) operates non-commercial radio and television under licence from the state. There are three radio and two television networks.
TV3, a satellite commercial TV channel, was launched in September 1990. Plans were introduced in 1991 to launch a new terrestrial commercial TV channel.

Education:

1990/91 figures	Institutions	Teachers	Students
Primary	n.a.	n.a.	578 359
Secondary	n.a.	n.a.	595 211
National higher	36	26 514	156 100
Municipal higher	34	n.a.	17 300
People's colleges	128	2 900	15 700
Municipal adult	397	6 550	125 200

Economic Interest Organizations:
Employers' organization: Svenska Arbetsgivareföreningen (SAF).

   Central trade union peak associations: Landsorganisationen i Sverige (LO) (Swedish Trade Union Confederation), founded 1898; membership: LO membership 2,246,166 (Dec. 1991); Tjänstemännens Centralorganisation (TCO) (Central Organization of Salaried Employees), present name 1944; membership: 1,300,000; Centralorganisation SACO/SR (Confederation of Professional Associations), present form 1975; membership: 325,000 (1991).

National or Central Bank: Sveriges Riksbank.

Central Statistical Office:
Statistiska Centralbyran
S-115 81 Stockholm

Budget: (1991/92)—in 1992 US dollars ($1 = 5.3075 kronor)—millions

Revenue	
Taxes on income, capital gains and profits	10 767
Statutory social security fees	16 095
Taxes on property	4 486
Taxes on goods and services	42 190
Regional discount tax	2 058
Total Revenue from Taxes	75 615
Non-tax revenue	10 324
Capital revenue	112
Loan repayment	1 339
Computed revenue	169
Total	87 543

Expenditure	
Royal households and residencies	10
Ministry of:	
Justice	1 343
Foreign affairs	2 907
Defence	7 123
Health and social affairs	23 685
Transport and communications	4 396
Finance	5 426
Education and cultural affairs	11 717
Agriculture	1 936
Labour	6 708
Housing and physical planning	6 126
Industry	1 200
Civil service affairs	2 883
Environment and energy	266
Parliament and its agencies	131

Expenditure	
Interest on the national debt	11 305
Unforseen expenditure	0.2
Estimated other expenditure	1 413
Total	88 574

Further Information:

Back, P. E., and Berglund, S. (1978), *Det svenska partiväsendet*. Stockholm: Almqvist & Wiksell.

Childs, M. W. (1980), *Sweden—The Middle Way on Trial*. New Haven, Conn.: Yale University Press.

Elder, N., Thomas, A., and Arter, D. (1987), *The Consensual Democracies? The Government and Politics of the Scandinavian States*. Oxford: Basil Blackwell.

Hancock, M. D. (1972), *The Politics of Post-industrial Change*. Hinsdale: Dryden Press.

Heclo, H., and Madsen, H. (1987), *Policy and Politics in Sweden*. Philadelphia: Temple University Press.

Holmberg, S., and Gilljam, M. (1987), *Väljare och val i Sverige*. Stockholm: Bonniers.

—— and Esaiasson, P. (1988), *De folkvalda: En bok om riksdagsledamöterna och den representativa demokratin i Sverige*. Stockholm: Bonniers.

Koblik, S. (1975) (ed.), *Sweden's Development from Poverty to Affluence 1750–1970*. Minneapolis: University of Minnesota Press.

Lane, J. E. (1991), (ed.), *Understanding the Swedish Model*. London: Frank Cass.

Lewin, L. (1989), *Ideology and Strategy: A Century of Swedish Politics*. Cambridge: Cambridge University Press.

Milner, H. (1989), *Sweden: Social Democracy in Practice*. Oxford: Oxford University Press.

17. Switzerland

State Structure: Federal.

Form of State: Republic.

Parliament (bicameral): Federal assembly (Bundesversammlung): Ständerat: 46 seats, 4 years; Nationalrat: 200 seats, 4 years.

Electoral System: Proportional representation: Hagenbach quota.

Main Languages: German (65%); French (18%); Italian (10%); Romansh (1%).

Population: 6,833,750 (1991 official estimate).

Constitutional Development: The present constitution dates from 1874. Attempts at drafting a new constitution in the 1980s were vetoed.

Heads of State:

The Presidents are elected on a yearly basis:

1945 E. von Steiger	1962 P. Chaudet	1979 H. Hürlimann
1946 K. Kobelt	1963 W. Spühler	1980 G. A. Chevallaz
1947 M. Petitpierre	1964 L. von Moos	1981 K. Furgler
1948 E. Celio	1965 H. Tschudi	1982 F. Honegger
1949 E. Nobs	1966 H. Schattner	1983 P. Aubert
1950 M. Petitpierre	1967 R. Bonvin	1984 L. Schlumpf
1951 E. von Steiger	1968 W. Spühler	1985 K. Furgler
1952 K. Kobelt	1969 L. von Moos	1986 A. Elgli
1953 P. Etter	1970 H. Tschudi	1987 P. Aubert
1954 R. Rubattel	1971 R. Gnägi	1988 O. Stich
1955 M. Petitpierre	1972 N. Celio	1989 J.-P. Pascal
1956 M. Feldmann	1973 R. Bonvin	1990 A. Koller
1957 H. Streuli	1974 E. Brugger	1991 F. Cotti
1958 T. Holenstein	1975 P. Graber	1992 R. Felber
1959 P. Chaudet	1976 R. Gnägi	1993 A. Ogi
1960 M. Petitpierre	1977 K. Furgler	
1961 F. T. Wahlen	1978 W. Ritschard	

Capital City: Bern (1985): 301,100.

Ministries:

	Federal Chancellery
Finance	Public Economy
Foreign Affairs	Transport, Communications, and
Home Affairs	Energy
Justice and Police	Military Department

Governments:

	Prime Minister	Parties represented in government
Oct. 1947–Oct. 1951	Petitpierre I (FDP)	FDP, CVP, SVP, SPS
Oct. 1951–Oct. 1953	Kobelt (FDP)	FDP, CVP, SVP, SPS
Oct. 1953–Oct. 1955	Rubattel (FDP)	FDP, CVP, SVP
Oct. 1955–Oct. 1959	Feldmann (SVP)	FDP, CVP, SVP
Oct. 1959–Oct. 1963	Petitpierre II (FDP)	FDP, CVP, SPS, SVP
Oct. 1963–Oct. 1967	von Moos (CVP)	FDP, CVP, SPS, SVP
Oct. 1967–Oct. 1971	Spühler (SPS)	FDP, CVP, SPS, SVP
Oct. 1971– Oct. 1975	Celio (FDP)	FDP, CVP, SPS, SVP
Oct. 1975–Oct. 1979	Gnägi (SVP)	FDP, CVP, SPS, SVP
Oct. 1979–Oct. 1983	Chevallaz (FDP)	FDP, CVP, SPS, SVP
Oct. 1983–Oct. 1987	Aubert (SPS)	FDP, CVP, SPS, SVP
Oct. 1987–	Stich (SPS)	FDP, CVP, SPS, SVP
Oct. 1987–Oct. 1991	Hurliman (CVP)	SVP, FDP, CVP, SP
Oct. 1991–Oct. 1995	Felber (SPS)	SVP, FDP, CVP, SP

Cantons:

	Population (1991)		Population (1991)
Solothurn	230 068	Neuchâtel	162 458
Basel-Stadt	193 512	Genève	378 849
Basel-Land	231 063	Jura	66 408
Zürich	1 159 080	Schaffhausen	72 454
Bern	952 595	Ausserhoden	52 346
Luzern	324 044	Innerrhoden	13 714
Uri	33 979	St. Gallen	426 689
Schwyz	112 986	Graubünden	173 028
Obwalden	29 478	Aargau	504 547
Nidwalden	33 285	Thurgau	210 237
Glarus	38 114	Ticino	290 001
Zug	86 357	Vaud	592 970
Fribourg	211 606	Valais	253 882

Media:

(*a*) Major newspapers:

	Location	Daily circulation
Blick	Zürich	382 275
Tages Anzeiger Zürich	Zürich	267 300
Neue Zürcher Zeitung	Zürich	151 470
Berner Zeitung	Berne	121 887
Basler Zeitung	Basel	114 413
24 heures	Havsanne	96 131
Journal de Genève	Genève	22 254

(*b*) Radio and television: *Schweizerische Radio-und Fernsehgesellschaft* (SRG) is an autonomous corporation under federal supervision responsible for the programme services. There are programmes on radio and television for the different language groups: Italian, French, German, and Romansh. Limited direct advertising is allowed.

Education:

1991/92 figures	No. Students
Primary	414 129
Secondary	390 537
Vocational	207 410
Higher	143 192

Economic Interest Organizations:

Employers' organization: Zentralverband Schweizerischer Arbeitgeber-Organisationen.

Central trade union peak associations: Schweizerischer Gewerkschaftsbund (SGB), founded 1880; membership: 444,000; Christlichnationaler Gewerkschaftsbund der Schweiz (CNG), founded 1907; membership: 112,332.

National or Central Bank: Schweizerische Nationalbank/Banque nationale suissse.

Central Statistical Office:
Federal Office of Statistics
Hallwylstr. 15
CH-3003 Bern

Federal Budget: (1991)—in 1992 US dollars ($1 = 1.2355 francs)–millions

Revenue	
Taxes on income and wealth	10 428
Taxes on consumption	13 179
Turnover tax	8 099
Tobacco tax	787
Customs duties	981
Total (inc. others)	27 106

Expenditure	
Foreign affairs	1 447
Defence	5 020
Education and research	2 149
Social welfare	6 549
Communications and energy	4 520
Agriculture	2 491
Financial services	3 712
Total (inc. others)	28 734

Further Information:

Blancpain, R. (1978) (ed.), *Almanach der Schweiz: Daten und Kommentare zu Bevölkerung, Gesellschaft und Politik*. Bern: Peter Lang.

Fleiner, T. (1989), 'Swiss Federalism: A Commentary', in *Forging Unity Out of Diversity*. Washington, DC.

Germann, R. (1992), 'Switzerland's Future in Europe', in *Gouvernance* 2: 224–34.

Gruner, E. (1971) (ed.), *Schweiz seit 1945*. Bern: Francke.

Katzenstein, P. (1980), *Capitalism in One Country? Switzerland in the International Economy*. Ithaca, NY: Cornell University Press.

Kerr, H. H. (1974), *Switzerland: Social Cleavages and Partisan Conflict*. London: Sage.

Linder, W. (1993), *Swiss Democracy*. Basingstoke: Macmillan.

McRae, K. D. (1983), *Conflict and Compromise in Multilingual Societies: Switzerland*. Waterloo, Ont.: Wilfrid Laurier University Press.

Schmidt, M. G. (1985), *Der Schweizerische Weg zur Vollbeschäftigung*. Frankfurt am Main: Campus.

Schwok, R. (1991), *Switzerland and the European Common Market*: New York: Praeger.

Sidjanski, D., *et al.* (1975), *Les Suisses et la politique*. Bern: Herbert Lang.

Steinberg, J. (1980), *Why Switzerland?* Cambridge: Cambridge University Press.

18. Turkey

State Structure: Unitary.

Form of State: Republic since 1922.

Parliament (unicameral): Grand national assembly (Turkiye Büjük Millet Meclisi): 400 seats, 5 years.

Electoral System: Plurality formula.

Main Languages: Turkish (86%); Kurdish (11%); Arabic 1(%).

Population: 56,473,035 (1990).

Constitutional Development: The present constitution dates from 1982 replacing the one from 1961. The military took over in October 1981 in the form of a National Security Council. More democratic measures were being introduced in the late 1980s.

Heads of State:

Ismet Inönü	Nov. 1938–May 1950
Celal Bayar	May 1950–May 1960
Cemal Gürsel	May 1960–Mar. 1966
Cevdet Sunay	Mar. 1966–Apr. 1973
Fahri Korüturk	Apr. 1973–Apr. 1980
Ihsan Sabri Caglayangil	Apr. 1980–Sept. 1980
Kenan Evren	Sept. 1980–Nov. 1989
Turgut Özal	Nov. 1989–

Capital City: Ankara (1980): 1,877,755.

Ministries:

President's Office
Prime Minister's Office
Deputy Prime Minister's Office

Health	Tourism
Industry and Commerce the Interior	Transport and Communications
Agriculture, Forestry, and Rural Affairs	Justice
Culture	Labour and Social Security
Energy and Natural Resources	National Defence
Finance and Customs	National Education
Foreign Affairs	Public Works and Housing

Governments:

	Prime Minister	Parties represented in government
Aug. 1946–Sept. 1947	Peker (People's)	People's
Sept. 1947–June 1948	Saka I (People's)	People's
June 1948–Jan. 1949	Saka II (People's)	People's
Jan. 1949–May 1950	Günaltay (People's)	People's
May 1950–Mar. 1951	Menderes I (Dem.)	Dem.
Mar. 1951–May 1954	Menderes II (Dem.)	Dem.
May 1954–Nov. 1955	Menderes III (Dem.)	Dem.
Nov. 1955–Nov. 1957	Menderes IV (Dem.)	Dem.
Nov. 1957–May 1960	Menderes V (Dem.)	Dem.
May 1960–Jan. 1961	Gürsel I	Military
Jan. 1961–Oct. 1961	Gürsel II	Military
Oct. 1961–June 1962	Ismet VI (RRP)	RRP, JP
June 1962–Dec. 1963	Ismet VII (RRP)	RRP, NTP, CNP
Dec. 1963–Feb. 1965	Ismet VIII (RRP)	RRP
Feb. 1965–Oct. 1965	Ürgüplü (JP)	JP, RRP, NTP, CNP
Oct. 1965–Nov. 1969	Demirel I (JP)	JP
Nov. 1969–Mar. 1970	Demirel II (JP)	JP
Mar. 1970–Mar. 1971	Demirel III (JP)	JP
Mar. 1971–Dec. 1971	Erim I (Indep.)	JP, RRP
Dec. 1971–May 1972	Erim II (Indep.)	JP, RRP
May 1972–Apr. 1973	Melen (NRP)	NRP, RRP, JP
Apr. 1973–Jan. 1974	Talu (Indep.)	RRP, JP
Jan. 1974–Mar. 1974	Ecevit I (RPP)	RPP, NSP
Nov. 1974–Mar. 1975	Irmak (Indep.)	RPP
Mar. 1975–June 1977	Demirel IV (JP)	JP, NSP, NAP
June 1977–July 1977	Ecevit II (RPP)	RPP
July 1977–Jan. 1978	Demirel V (JP)	JP, NSP, NAP
Jan. 1978–Nov. 1979	Ecevit III (RPP)	RPP, RRP, DP
Nov. 1979–Sept. 1980	Demirel VI (JP)	JP, HAP, NSP
Sept. 1980–Nov. 1983	Ülüsil	Military
Nov. 1983–Nov. 1989	Özal (ANAP)	ANAP
Nov. 1989–June 1991	Akbulut (ANAP)	ANAP
June 1991–Nov. 1991	Ylimaz (ANAP)	ANAP
Nov. 1991–June 1993	Demirel (DYP)	DYP, SHP
June 1993–	Ciller (DYP)	DYP, SHP

Regions:

	Population (1985)
Mediterranean Coast	4 653 426
West Anatolia	3 538 253
East Anatolia	6 290 086
South-east Anatolia	2 413 593
Central Anatolia	12 193 155
Black Sea Coast	6 652 172
Marmara and Aegean Coasts	9 834 576
Thrace	5 089 197

Media:
(*a*) Major newspapers:

Name	Location	Circulation
Hürriyet	Istanbul	600 000
Sabah	Istanbul	600 000
Milliyet	Istanbul	400 000
Gunaydin	Istanbul	300 000
Gunes	Istanbul	290 000
Cumhuriyet	Istanbul	139 000

(*b*) Radio and television: *Türkiye Radyo Televizyon Kurumu* (TRT) controls Turkish radio and television services. TRT is an autonomous public corporation funded by licence fees.

Education:

(1989/90 figures)	Institutions	Teachers	Students
Primary	51 170	221 000	6 767 000
Secondary:			
General	7 175	103 000	2 740 000
Technical and vocational	2 542	47 000	772 000
Higher	387	29 000	560 000

Economic Interest Organizations:
Employers' organization: Türkiye Isveren Sendikalari Konfederasyonu (TISK) (Turkish Confederation of Employers' Associations).

    Central trade union peak association: DISK (Confederation of Progressive Trade Unions of Turkey), founded 1967, suspended in September

1980; membership: 600,000 (1980); Türk-Is (Confederation of Turkish Trade Unions), founded 1952; membership: 1,947,000 (1985).

National or Central Bank: Turkiye Cumhuriyet Merkez Bankasi AS (Central Bank of the Republic of Turkey).

General Budget :(1989)—in 1991 US dollars ($1 = 5,079.9 liras)— millions

Revenue	
Taxation	5 034
Property income	121
Other current revenue	965
Capital revenue	33
Total	6 153

Expenditure	
General public services	2 367
Defence	888
Education	2 091
Health	220
Social security and welfare	125
Housing and community amenities	114
Other community and social services	0.69
Economic services	1 513
Other purposes	1 216
Total	7 646
Current	6 492
Capital	1 154

Further Information:

Caglar, Keyder (1987), *State and Class in Turkey*. London: Verso.

Dodd, C. H. (1969), *The Politics and Government of Turkey*. Manchester: Manchester University Press.

Heper, M., and Evin, A. (1988) (eds.), *State, Democracy and the Military: Turkey in the 1980s*. Berlin: de Gruyter.

19. United Kingdom

State Structure: Unitary.

Form of State: Constitutional monarchy.

Parliament (bicameral): House of Lords: 1,180 seats, continuous: House of Commons: 651 seats, 5 years (max).

Electoral System: Plurality formula.

Main Languages: English (99%); Welsh (1%).

Population: 57,649,200 (1991 official estimate).

Constitutional Development: There is no written constitution, but documents forming the core of a would-be constitution could be: Magna Carta of 1215, Bill of Rights of 1689, and the Reform Bill of 1832.

Heads of State:

King George VI	Dec. 1936–Feb. 1952
Queen Elizabeth II	Feb. 1952–

Capital City: London (1985): 6,767,500.

Ministries:

Prime Minister's Office

Agriculture, Fisheries and Food	Home Office
Office of the Chancellor of the Duchy of Lancaster (Office of Public Services and Science)	Lord Chancellor's Department
	National Heritage
	Northern Ireland Office
Defence	Scottish Office
Education and Science	Social Security
Employment	Trade and Industry
Environment	Transport
Foreign and Commonwealth Office	Treasury
Health	Welsh Office

Governments:

	Prime Minister	Parties represented in government
July 1945–Feb. 1950	Attlee I (Lab.)	Lab.
Feb. 1950–Oct. 1951	Attlee II (Lab.)	Lab.
Oct. 1951–Apr. 1955	Churchill (Con.)	Con.
Apr. 1955–Jan. 1957	Eden (Con.)	Con.
Jan. 1957–Oct. 1963	Macmillan (Con.)	Con.
Oct. 1963–Oct. 1964	Douglas-Home (Con.)	Con.
Oct. 1964–Apr. 1966	Wilson I (Lab.)	Lab.
Apr. 1966–June 1970	Wilson II (Lab.)	Lab.
June 1970–Mar. 1974	Heath (Con.)	Con.
Mar. 1974–Apr. 1976	Wilson III (Lab.)	Lab.
Apr. 1976–May 1979	Callaghan (Lab.)	Lab.
May 1979–June 1983	Thatcher I (Con.)	Con.
June 1983–June 1987	Thatcher II (Con.)	Con.
June 1987–Nov. 1990	Thatcher III (Con.)	Con.
Nov. 1990–Apr. 1992	Major I (Con.)	Con.
Apr. 1992–	Major II (Con.)	Con.

Countries of the UK:

	Population (1991 estimates)
Great Britain	56 054 800
England	48 068 400
Wales	2 886 400
Scotland	5 100 000
Northern Ireland	1 594 400

Media:

(*a*) Major newspapers:

Name	Location	Circulation
Sun	London	3 600 000
Daily Mirror	London	3 600 000
Daily Mail	London	1 739 756
Daily Express	London	1 570 365
Daily Telegraph	London	1 064 066
Daily Star	London	891 016

Name	Location	Circulation
Daily Record	Glasgow	800 000
Today	London	601 871
Evening Standard	London	518 789
The Times	London	450 626
The Guardian	London	418 000
The Independent	London	390 000
Manchester Evening News	Manchester	320 000
Financial Times	London	286 179

(*b*) Radio and television: *British Broadcasting Corporation* (BBC) formed in 1927 operates under Royal Charter and is financed by licence fees. BBC broadcasts two television channels. *Independent Broadcasting Authority* (IBA) is a commercial concern that provides television service additional to that of BBC. It runs one television channel and it supervises programmes produced by Channel Four.

Radio 5, (a BBC channel) began broadcasting in 1990, concentrating on sport and education.

British Sky Broadcasting, a satellite company, began broadcasting in 1990. An auction sale of regional commercial TV licences in 1991 led to a reorganisation of ITV companies.

Education:

1990/91 figures	No. Institutions	No. Staff	No. Students
Primary and nursery	n.a.	213 258	4 536 883
Secondary	n.a.	222 571	3 332 715
Special Schools	n.a.	n.a.	107 732
Independent	n.a.	n.a.	558 160
Further and higher education	n.a.	n.a.	1 194 027

Economic Interest Organizations:

Employers' organization: Confederation of British Industry (CBI).

Central trade union peak association: Trades Union Congress (TUC), founded 1868; membership: 7,786,885 (Jan. 1993).

National or Central Bank: Bank of England.

Central Statistical Office:
Central Statistical Office
HMSO

London

Budget: (1991)—in 1992 US dollars ($1 = 0.5613 pounds sterling)—millions

Revenue	
Current receipts	387 652
Taxes on income	133 806
Taxes on expenditure	147 912
National insurance	65 282
Community charge	14 541
Gross trading surpluses	212
Rents	7 664
Interest and dividends	10 645
Misc.	659
Non-trading capital imputed charge	6 930
Capital receipts	6 310
Total	393 962

Expenditure	
General public services	16 383
Defence	48 701
Public order and safety	22 804
Education	52 596
Health	55 111
Social security	131 605
Housing and community ammenities	16 225
Recreation and cultural affairs	6 916
Fuel and energy	−8 972
Agriculture forestry and fishing	4 326
Mining and mineral resources	2 941
Transport and communication	11 949
Other economic affairs	9 752
Other expenditure	35 022
Total	405 361

Further Information.

Arthur, P. (1980), *The Government and Politics of Northern Ireland*. London: Longman.

Balsom, D., and Burch, M. (1980), *A Political and Electoral Handbook for Wales*. Aldershot: Gower.

Budge, I., and McKay, D. (1991) (eds.), *The Changing British Political System: Into the 1990s*. London: Longman.

Curwen, P. (1990), *Understanding the UK Economy*. London: Macmillan.

Dunleavy, P. *et al.* 1995. *Developments in British Politics*. London: Macmillan Education, 3rd edition.

Kavanagh, D. (1990), *British Politics: Continuity and Change*. Oxford: Oxford University Press, 2nd edition.

Leys, C. (1989), *Politics in Britain: An Introduction*. London: Verso.

Parry, R. (1988), *Scottish Political Facts*. Edinburgh: T & T Clark.

Rose, R. (1989), *Politics in England*. Boston: Little, Brown.

—— and McAllister, I. (1982), *United Kingdom Facts*. London: Macmillan.

Sked, A., and Cook. C. (1990), *Post-War Britain: A Political History* London: Penguin, 3rd edition.

20. Canada

State Structure: Federal.

Form of State: Constitutional monarchy; acting Governor- General.

Parliament (bicameral): Federal parliament: Senate: 104 seats, until retirement. House of Commons: 195 seats, 5 years.

Electoral System: Plurality formula.

Main Languages: English (61%); French (26%).

Population: 27,408,900 (1992 official estimate).

Constitutional Development: Important acts passed by the British Parliament are: The Quebec Act of 1774, the Constitutional Act of 1791, the Act of Union of 1840, the British North America Act of 1867, the Canada Act of 1982.

Heads Of State:

King George VI	Dec. 1936–Feb. 1952
Queen Elizabeth II	Feb. 1952–

Governors-General:

Viscount Alexander of Tunis	Apr. 1946–Feb. 1952
Vincent Massey	Feb. 1952–Sept. 1959
Georges Philias Vanier	Sept. 1959–Mar. 1967
Roland Michener	Apr. 1967–Jan. 1974
Jules Léger	Jan. 1974–Jan. 1979
Edward Richard Schreyer	Jan. 1979–May 1984
Jeanne Sauvé	May 1984–

Capital City: Ottawa (1987): 301,000.

Ministries:

Office of the Prime Minister

Agriculture Canada	Health
Canadian Heritage	Human Resources and Labour
Citizenship	Indian Affairs and Northern
External Affairs	Development
Finance	Industry and Science
Fisheries and Oceans	International Trade
Government Services	Justice

National Defence
Natural Resources
Public Security
Westen Economic Diversification
Environment Canada
Environment Canada

Revenue Canada (Customs and
 Excise)
Revenue Canada (Taxation)
Treasury Board
Veteran's Affairs Canada

Governments:

	Prime Minister	Parties represented in government
June 1945–Nov. 1948	King III (Lib.)	Lib.
Nov. 1948–June 1957	St-Laurent (Lib.)	Lib.
June 1957–Apr. 1963	Diefenbaker (Prog. Con.)	Prog. Con.
Apr. 1963–Apr. 1968	Pearson (Lib.)	Lib.
Apr. 1968–Nov. 1972	Trudeau I (Lib.)	Lib.
Nov. 1972–Aug. 1974	Trudeau II (Lib.)	Lib.
Aug. 1974–June 1979	Trudeau III (Lib.)	'Lib.
June 1979–Mar. 1980	Clark (Prog. Con.)	Prog. Con.
Mar. 1980–June 1984	Trudeau IV (Lib.)	Lib.
June 1984–Sept. 1984	Turner (Lib.)	Lib.
Sept. 1984–Nov. 1988	Mulroney I (Prog. Con.)	Prog. Con.
Nov. 1988–June 1993	Mulroney II (Prog. Con.)	Prog. Con. (all)
June 1993–Nov. 1993	Campbell (Prog. Con.)	Prog. Con.
Nov. 1993–	Chretien (Lib.)	Lib.

Provinces:

	Population (1991 census figures)
Alberta	2 545 550
British Columbia	3 282 065
Manitoba	1 091 940
New Brunswick	723 900
Newfoundland	568 475
Northwest Territories	57 650
Nova Scotia	899 945
Ontario	10 084 855
Prince Edward Island	129 765
Quebec	6 895 960
Saskatchewan	988 930
Yukon Territory	27 795

Media:

(*a*) Major newspapers:

Name	Location	Circulation
Toronto Star	Toronto	543 000
Globe and Mail	Toronto	306 000
Le Journal de Montreal	Montreal	300 000
Toronto Sun	Toronto	273 000
La Presse	Quebec	214 000
Vancouver Sun	Vancouver	230 000
Ottawa Citizen	Ottawa	173 000
Gazette	Montreal	169 000

(*b*) Radio and television: *Canadian Broadcasting Corporation* (CBC) is the national, publicly owned, broadcasting service. Many privately owned television and radio stations have affiliation agreements with the CBC.
By 1992 74% of households had cable TV installed.

Education:

1990/91 figures	No. Institutions	No. Teachers	No. Students
Elementary-secondary	15 638	297 100	5 141 000
Community colleges	203	25 000	220 700
Universities	69	37 400	468 300

Economic Interest Organizations:
Employers' organization: Canadian Chamber of Commerce; Canadian Manufacturers' Association.

Central trade union peak association: Canadian Labour Congress, founded 1956; membership: 2,363,799 (1992).

National or Central Bank: The Bank of Canada.

Central Statistical Office:
Statistics Canada
Ottawa K1A OT6

Federal Budget: (1990/91 estimates)—in 1993 US dollars
($1 = C $1.2825)—millions

Revenue	
Tax revenue:	90 905
Personal income taxes	46 986
Corporation income taxes	9 669

Revenue

Taxes on payments to non-residents	1 158
Sales tax	12 663
Motive fuel taxes	2 772
Alcohol and tobacco tax	2 928
Air transportation tax	413
Custom duties	3 376
Other consumption taxes	282
Unemployment insurance	9 840
Petroleum and natural gas taxes	—
Miscellaneous	819
Non-tax revenues:	8 173
Natural resources revenue	39
Privileges, licences and permits	139
Sales of goods and services	2 206
Return on investments	4 940
Contributions to benefit plan	56
Bullion and coinage	125
Fines and penalties	31
Misceelaneous	563
Transfers from provincial govs.	74
Total gross revenue	99 078

Expenditure

General services	5 397
Protection of persons and property	11 532
Transport and communications	2 806
Health	5 804
Social services	37 168
Education	3 237
Resource conservation and industrial development	4 377
Environment	498
Recreation and culture	851
Labour, employment, and immigration	1 699
Housing	1 469
Foreign affairs and international assistance	2 677
Regional planning and development	390
Research establishments	972
General-purpose transfers to other governmental levels	7 832

Expenditure	
Transfers to own enterprises	1 634
Debt charges	31 979
Other	929
Total, gross expenditure	121 249

Further Information:

British Journal of Canadian Studies. Various issues. London.

Byron, R. J. (1986) (ed.), *Regionalism in Canada*. Toronto: Irwin Publishing.

Clarke, H. D., *et al.* (1979), *Political Choice in Canada*. Toronto: McGraw-Hill.

Engelman, F. C., and Schwartz, M. A. (1975), *Canadian Political Parties*. Scarborough: Prentice-Hall.

Hockin, T. A. (1976), *Government in Canada*. Toronto: McGraw-Hill.

McCann, L. D. (1987) (ed.), *Heartland and Hinterland: A Geography of Canada*. Scarborough, Ontario: Prentice-Hall Canada Inc., 2nd edition.

Meisel, J. (1973), *Working Papers on Canadian Politics*. Montreal: McGill-Queen's University Press.

Metcalfe, W. (1982) (ed.), *Understanding Canada: A Multidisciplinary Introduction to Canadian Studies*. New York and London: New York University Press.

Nossal, K. R. (1984), *The Politics of Canadian Foreign Policy*. Scarborough, Ontario: Prentice-Hall Canada Inc.

Savoie, D. J. (1986), *The Canadian Economy: A Regional Perspective*. Toronto: Methuen.

Verney, D. V. (1986), *Three Civilizations, Two Cultures, One State: Canada's Political Traditions*. Durham: Duke University Press.

Woodcock, C. (1989), *A Social History of Canada*. London: Viking.

21. USA

State Structure: Federal.

Form of State: Republic.

Parliament (bicameral): Congress: Senate: 100 seats, 6 years: House of representatives: 435 seats, 2 years.

Electoral System: Plurality formula.

Main Languages: English (89%); Spanish (6%).

Population: 252,177,000 (1991).

Constitutional Development: The constitution dates from 1787 and it was adopted in 1789. Twenty-six amendments made to the constitution, by 1991.

Heads of State:

H. S. Truman (Dem.)	Aug. 1945–Jan. 1949
H. S. Truman (Dem.)	Jan. 1949–Jan. 1953
D. D. Eisenhower (Rep.)	Jan. 1953–Jan. 1957
D. D. Eisenhower (Rep.)	Jan. 1957–Jan. 1961
J. F. Kennedy (Dem.)	Jan. 1961–Nov. 1963
L. B. Johnson (Dem.)	Nov. 1963–Jan. 1965
L. B. Johnson (Dem.)	Jan. 1965–Jan. 1969
R. M. Nixon (Rep.)	Jan. 1969–Jan. 1973
R. M. Nixon (Rep.)	Jan. 1973–Aug. 1974
G. R. Ford (Rep.)	Aug. 1974–Jan. 1977
J. E. Carter (Dem.)	Jan. 1977–Jan. 1981
R. Reagan (Rep.)	Jan. 1981–Jan. 1985
R. Reagan (Rep.)	Jan. 1985–Jan. 1989
G. Bush (Rep.)	Jan. 1989–Jan. 1993
W. Clinton (Dem.)	Jan. 1993–

Capital City: Washington (1984): 622,823.

Ministries:

The Executive Office of the President

The White House Office	Council on Environmental Quality
Office of the Vice-President	National Economic Council
Council of Economic Advisors	National Security Council

Office of Administration
Office of Management and Budget
Office of Federal Procurement Policy
Office of National Drug Control
  Policy
Office of Policy Development

Office of Science and Technology
  Policy
Office of the United States Trade
  Representative
United States Mission to the
  United Nations

Government Departments

Agriculture
Commerce
Defence
Education
Energy
Health and Human Services
Housing and Urban Development

Interior
Justice
Labor
State
Transportation
Treasury
Veterans Affairs

Governments:

	President	Parties represented in government
Aug. 1945–Jan. 1949	Truman I (Dem.)	Dem.
Jan. 1949–Jan. 1953	Truman II (Dem.)	Dem.
Jan. 1953–Jan. 1957	Eisenhower I (Rep.)	Rep.
Jan. 1957–Jan. 1961	Eisenhower II (Rep.)	Rep.
Jan. 1961–Nov. 1963	Kennedy (Dem.)	Dem.
Nov. 1963–Jan. 1965	Johnson I (Dem.)	Dem.
Jan. 1965–Jan. 1969	Johnson II (Dem.)	Dem.
Jan. 1969–Jan. 1973	Nixon I (Rep.)	Rep.
Jan. 1973–Aug. 1974	Nixon II (Rep.)	Rep.
Aug. 1974–Jan. 1977	Ford (Rep.)	Rep.
Jan. 1977–Jan. 1981	Carter (Dem.)	Dem.
Jan. 1981–Jan. 1985	Reagan I (Rep.)	Rep.
Jan. 1985–Jan. 1989	Reagan II (Rep.)	Rep.
Jan. 1989–Jan. 1993	Bush (Rep.)	Rep.
Jan. 1993–	Clinton (Dem.)	Dem.

States:

	Population–000s (1991)		Population–000s (1991)
Alabama	4 089	Missouri	5 158
Alaska	570	Montana	808
Arizona	3 750	Nebraska	1 593
Arkansas	2 372	Nevada	1 284
California	30 380	New Hampshire	1 105
Colorado	3 377	New Jersey	7 760
Connecticut	3 291	New Mexico	1 548
Delaware	680	New York	18 058
District of		North Carolina	6 737
Columbia	598	North Dakota	635
Florida	13 277	Ohio	10 939
Georgia	6 623	Oklahoma	3 175
Hawaii	1 135	Oregon	2 922
Idaho	1 039	Pennsylvania	11 961
Illinois	11 543	Rhode Island	1 004
Indiana	5 610	South Carolina	3 560
Iowa	2 795	South Dakota	703
Kansas	2 495	Tennessee	4 953
Kentucky	3 713	Texas	17 349
Louisiana	4 252	Utah	1 770
Maine	1 235	Vermont	567
Maryland	4 860	Virginia	6 286
Massachusetts	5 996	Washington	5 018
Michigan	9 368	West Virginia	1 801
Minnesota	4 432	Wisconsin	4 955
Mississippi	2 592	Wyoming	460

Media:

(*a*) Major newspapers:

Name	Location	Circulation
Wall Street Journal	New York, NY	1 795 206
USA Today	Arlington, VA	1 418 477
Los Angeles Times	Los Angeles, CA	1 146 631
New York Times	New York, NY	1 145 890
Washington Post	Washington, DC	802 057
Chicago Tribune	Chicago, IL	724 257
New York Post	New York, NY	437 962

(*b*) Radio and television: Major commercial networks: *Capital Cities/ABC* (ABC): *Columbia Broadcasting System* (CBS); *National Broadcasting Co.* (NBC).

Education:

1990 figures	No. Institutions	No. Teachers	No. Students
Grades 1–8:			
Public	59 757	1 379 000	29 742 000
Private	n.a.	253 000	4 066 000
Grades 9–12:			
Public	20 359	1 012 000	11 284 000
Private	n.a.	100 000	1 129 000
Post-secondary:			
Public	2 120	762 000*	10 912 000
Private	8 486		3 039 000

NB: * = figure for number of both Public and Private Teachers.

Economic Interest Organizations:
Employers' organization: US Chamber of Commerce; National Association of Manufacturers; The Business Round Table.

Central trade union peak association: American Federation of Labor and Congress of Industrial Organizations (AFL-CIO): AFL founded 1881, CIO founded 1938, AFL-CIO merged 1955; membership: 14,500,000 (1992); International Brotherhood of Teamsters, Chauffeurs, Warehousemen and Helpers of America (Teamsters), expelled from AFL-CIO 1957; membership: 1,600,000.

National or Central Bank: The Federal Reserve System has twelve Federal Reserve Banks (twenty-five branches) but a centralized Federal Reserve Board of Governors, who effectively influence the nation's credit and monetary affairs.

Central Statistical Office:
Bureau of the Census
US Department of Commerce
Washington, DC 20233

Federal Budget: (1994)—billions

Revenue	1 257
Individual income taxes	543
Corporation taxes	140

Revenue	
Social insurance and other contributions	462
Other	112

Expenditure	1 462
Defence	282
International affairs	17
Health	107
Medicare	145
Income security	214
Social security	320
Net interest	203
Other	174

Further Information:

Austin, E. W. (1986), *Political Facts of the United States since 1789*. New York: Columbia University Press.

Barone, M., *et al.* (1972–) (eds.), *The Almanac of American Politics*. Washington, DC: Barone & Co.

Brogan, H. (1990), *The Penguin History of the United States of America*. London: Penguin.

Dodd, L., and Oppenheimer, B. I. (1993) (eds.), *Congress Reconsidered*. Wasington DC: Congressional Quarterly Inc., 5th edition.

Janda, K., *et al.* (1987), *The Challenge of Democracy: Government in America*. Boston: Houghton Mifflin.

Maidment, R., and Tapin, M. (1989), *American Politics Today*. Manchester: Manchester University Press.

Mckay, D. (1993), *American Politics and Society*. Oxford: Blackwell, 3rd edition.

Peele, G., *et al.* (1994) (eds.), *Developments in American Politics 2*. Basingstoke: Macmillan.

Stanley, H. W., and Niemi, R. G. (1993), *Vital Statistics on American Politics*. Washington, DC: CQ Press.

22. Japan

State Structure: Unitary.

Form of State: Constitutional monarchy.

Parliament (bicameral): Kokkai (Diet): House of councillors: 252 seats, 6 years; House of representatives: 512 seats, 4 years.

Electoral System: Plurality formula; multi-member constituencies.

Main Language: Japanese (99%).

Population: 124,451,938 (1992 official estimate).

Constitutional Development: The present constitution dates from 1946.

Heads of State:

Emperor Hirohito	Dec. 1926–Jan. 1989
Emperor Akihito	Jan. 1989–

Capital City: Tokyo (1985): 8,353,674.

Ministries:

Prime Minister's Office
Imperial Household Agency

Agriculture, Forestry and Fisheries	Posts and Telecommunications
Construction	Transport
Education	Defence Agency
Finance	Economic Planning Agency
Foreign Affairs	Environment Agency
Health and Welfare	Hokkaido Development Agency
Home Affairs	Management and Co-ordination
International Trade and	Agency
Industry	National Land Agency
Justice	Okinawa Development Agency
Labour	Science and Technology Agency

Governments:

	Prime Minister	Parties represented in government
May 1946–May 1947	Yoshida I (Lib.)	Lib.
May 1947–Feb. 1948	Katayama (Lib.)	Lib.
Feb. 1948–Oct. 1948	Ashida (Lib.)	Lib.
Oct. 1948–Feb. 1949	Yoshida II (Lib.)	Lib.
Feb. 1949–Oct. 1952	Yoshida III (Lib.)	Lib., Prog.
Oct. 1952–May 1953	Yoshida IV (Lib.)	Lib.
May 1953–Dec. 1953	Yoshida V (Lib.)	Lib.-Yoshida
Dec. 1954–Mar. 1955	Hatoyama I (Lib.)	Lib.-Hatoyama
Mar. 1955–May 1955	Hatoyama II (Lib.)	Lib.
May 1955–Dec. 1956	Hatoyama III (LDP)	LDP
Dec. 1956–Feb. 1957	Ishibashi (LDP)	LDP
Feb. 1957–June 1958	Kishi I (LDP)	LDP
June 1958–July 1960	Kishi II (LDP)	LDP
July 1960–Dec. 1960	Ikeda I (LDP)	LDP
Dec. 1960–July 1962	Ikeda II (LDP)	LDP
July 1962–Dec. 1963	Ikeda III (LDP)	LDP
Dec. 1963–Nov. 1964	Ikeda IV (LDP)	LDP
Nov. 1964–Dec. 1968	Sato I (LDP)	LDP
Dec. 1968–Jan. 1970	Sato II (LDP)	LDP
Jan. 1970–July 1972	Sato III (LDP)	LDP
July 1972–Dec. 1972	Tanaka I (LDP)	LDP
Dec. 1972–Dec. 1974	Tanaka II (LDP)	LDP
Dec. 1974–Sept. 1976	Miki I (LDP)	LDP
Sept. 1976–Dec. 1976	Miki II (LDP)	LDP
Dec. 1976–Dec. 1978	Fukuda (LDP)	LDP
Dec. 1978–Nov. 1979	Ohira I (LDP)	LDP
Nov. 1979–July 1980	Ohira II (LDP)	LDP
July 1980–Nov. 1982	Suzuki (LDP)	LDP
Nov. 1982–Dec. 1983	Nakasone I (LDP)	LDP
Dec. 1983–July 1986	Nakasone II (LDP)	LDP-Nakasone (+NLC)
July 1986–Nov. 1987	Nakasone III (LDP)	LDP
Nov. 1987–May 1989	Takeshita (LDP)	LDP
May 1989–Aug. 1989	Uno (LDP)	LDP
Aug. 1989–Feb. 1990	Kaifu I (LDP)	LDP
Feb. 1990–Nov. 1991	Kaifu II (LDP)	LDP
Nov. 1991–Aug. 1993	Miyazama (LDP)	LDP

	Prime Minister	Parties represented in government
Aug. 1993–Apr. 1994	Hoskawa (JNP)	JRP, SDP, Komei, JNP, DSP, Sakigake, UDS
Apr. 1994–June 1994	Hata (Shinseito)	Shinseito, DSP, Komei, JNP, Kaikako
June 1994–	Murayama (SDJP)	SDJP, LDP, Sakigake

Regions:

	Population (1985)	Capital
Hokkaido	5 679 500	Sapporo
Tohoku	9 730 000	Sendai
Kanto	36 786 200	Tokyo
Chubu	20 595 000	Nagoya
Kinki	21 828 000	Osaka
Chugoku	7 748 500	Hiroshima
Shikoku	4 227 400	Matsuyama
Kyushu	13 276 000	Fukuoka
Ryukyu	1 179 000	Naha

Media:
(*a*) Major newspapers:

Name	Location	Circulation
Yomiuri Shimbun	Tokyo	10 000 000
Yomiuri Shimbun	Osaka	2 400 000
Asahi Shimbun	Tokyo	8 200 000
Asahi Shimbun	Osaka	2 300 000
Mainichi Shimbun	Tokyo	1 600 000
Mainichi Shimbun	Osaka	95 000
Nihon Keizai Shimbun	Tokyo	2 920 000
Chunichi Shimbun	Nagoya	2 200 000
Sankei Shimbun	Tokyo	818 848
Sankei Shimbun	Osaka	1 100 000

(*b*) Radio and television: *Nippon Hōsō Kyōkai*(NHK) (Japan Broadcasting Corporation) is the non-commercial public broadcasting corporation. National Association of Commercial Broadcasters in Japan (MINPOREN) is the association of the commercial broadcasting corporations.

Education:

(1992 figures)	Institutions	Teachers	Students
Primary Schools	24 730	440 769	8 947 226
Lower Secondary Schools	11 300	282 737	5 036 840
High Schools	5 501	284 409	5 218 497
Technological Colleges	62	6 439	54 786
Junior Schools	591	56 974	524 538
Graduate Schools and Universities	523	227 697	2 293 269

Economic Interest Organizations:

Employers' organization: Nihon Keieisha Dantai Renmei (NIK- KEIREN) (Japan Federation of Employers' Associations).

Trade union central peak associations: As of November 1989, the three major union federations merged to form the Nihon Rōdō Kumiai Sōrengōkai, which has about 8 million members (acronym SHINREN-GO—English translation 'General Federation of Japanese Labour Unions'). There is a JCP-orientated federation Zenkoku Rōdō Kumiai Sōrengō, which claims 1.4 million members (acronym ZENROREN—English translation 'National Federation of Labour Unions'). There is a group of left-wing socialists, who used to belong to Sōhyō and refused to join the new federation: Kyōtō Soshiki Zenkoku Rō do Kumiai Renraku Kyōgikai, with 500,000 members (acronym ZENRŌKYŌ—National Labour Union Federation Co-ordinating Council Joint Struggle Organization). SOHYO and RENGO—the two largest confederations–merged in November 1989 to form the Japan Trade Union Confederation (JTUC-RENGO), with 9 million members.

National or Central Bank: Nippon Ginko.

Central Statistical Office:
Statistics Bureau
Management and Co-ordination
19-1 Wakamatsucho
Shinjuku-ku
Tokyo 162

Budget: (1993/4 estimates)—in 1994 US dollars ($1 = 98.645 yen)—million

Revenue	
Taxes and stamps	621 450

Revenue	
Public bonds	76 395
Others	35 643
Total	733 489

Expenditure	
Social Security	133 256
Education and science	59 010
Government debt servicing	156 541
Defence	47 048
Public works	88 337
Local finance	158 315
Pensions	18 014
Total (inc. others)	733 489

Further Information:

Baerwald, H. (1986), *Party Politics in Japan*. Boston: Little, Brown.

Buckley, R. (1986), *Japan Today*. Cambridge: Cambridge University Press.

Curtis, G. L. (1989), *The Japanese Way of Politics*. Irvington, New York: Columbia University Press.

Francks, P. (1992), *Japanese Economic Development: Theory and Practice*. London: Routledge.

Giffard, S. (1994), *Japan Among the Powers: 1890–1990*. New Haven, Conn: Yale University Press.

Hrebenar, R. J. (1986), *The Japanese Party System: From One-Party Rule to Coalition Government*. Boulder, Colo.: Westview Press.

Morishima, M. (1984), *Why has Japan 'Succeeded'?* Cambridge: Cambridge U.P.

Upham, F. K. (1990), *Law and Social Change in Postwar Japan*. Cambridge, MA: Harvard University Press.

Ward, R. E. (1978), *Japan's Political System*. Englewood Cliffs, NJ: Prentice-Hall.

23. Australia

State Structure: Federal.

Form of State: Constitutional monarchy; acting Governor-General.

Parliament (bicameral): Federal parliament: Senate: 76 seats, 6 years; House of representatives: 148 seats, 3 years.

Electoral System: Majority formula with alternative vote; single member constituencies.

Main Language: English (99%).

Population: 17,657,400 (1993 official estimate).

Constitutional Development: The federal constitution dates from 1900.

Heads of State:

King George VI	Dec. 1936–Feb. 1952
Queen Elizabeth II	Feb. 1952–

Governors-General:

Duke of Gloucester	1945–1947
William McKell	1947–1953
Viscount Slim	1953–1960
Viscount Dunrossil	1960–1961
Viscount De L'Isle	1961–1965
Lord Casey	1965–1969
Paul Hasluck	1969–1974
John Kerr	1974–1977
Zelman Cowen	1977–1982
Ninian Stephen	1982–1989
Bill Hayden	1989–

Capital City: Canberra (1989): 277,100.

Ministries:

Department of the Prime Minister and Cabinet

Aboriginal and Torres Strait Islander Commission

Attorney-General's Department

Department of Administrative Services

Department of Defence

Department of Employment, Education and Training

Department of the Environment, Sport and Territories

Department of Finance
Department of Foreign Affairs and Trade
Department of Health, Housing, Local Government, and Human Services
Department of Immigration and Ethnic Affairs
Department of Industrial Relations
Department of Industry, Science and Technology
Department of Primary Industries and Energy
Department of Social Security
Department of Transport and Communications
Department of the Treasury
Department of Veterans' Affairs

Governments:

	Prime Minister	Parties represented in government
July 1945–Nov. 1946	Chifley I (ALP)	ALP
Nov. 1946–Dec. 1949	Chifley II (ALP)	ALP
Dec. 1949–May 1951	Menzies I (Lib.)	Lib., Nat.
May 1951–Jan. 1956	Menzies II (Lib.)	Lib., Nat.
Jan. 1956–Dec. 1958	Menzies III (Lib.)	Lib., Nat.
Dec. 1958–Dec. 1963	Menzies IV (Lib.)	Lib., Nat.
Dec. 1963–Jan. 1966	Menzies V (Lib.)	Lib., Nat.
Jan. 1966–Dec. 1966	Holt I (Lib.)	Lib., Nat.
Dec. 1966–Dec. 1967	Holt II (Lib.)	Lib., Nat.
Dec. 1967–Jan. 1968	McEwen (Lib.)	Lib., Nat.
Jan. 1968–Feb. 1968	Gorton I (Lib.)	Lib., Nat.
Feb. 1968–Nov. 1969	Gorton II (Lib.)	Lib., Nat.
Nov. 1969–Mar. 1971	Gorton III (Lib.)	Lib., Nat.
Mar. 1971–Dec. 1972	McMahon (Lib.)	Lib., Nat.
Dec. 1972–Nov. 1975	Whitlam (ALP)	ALP
Nov. 1975–Dec. 1975	Fraser I (Lib.)	Lib., Nat.
Dec. 1975–Dec. 1977	Fraser II (Lib.)	Lib., Nat.
Dec. 1977–Nov. 1980	Fraser III (Lib.)	Lib., Nat.
Nov. 1980–Mar. 1983	Fraser IV (Lib.)	Lib., Nat.
Mar. 1983–Dec. 1984	Hawke I (ALP)	ALP
Dec. 1984–July 1987	Hawke II (ALP)	ALP
July 1987–Apr. 1990	Hawke III (ALP)	ALP
Apr. 1990–Dec. 1991	Hawke IV (ALP)	ALP
Dec. 1991–Mar. 1993	Keating I (ALP)	ALP
Mar. 1993–	Keating II (ALP)	ALP

States and Territories:

	Population
New South Wales	6 023 500
Victoria	4 468 300
Queensland	3 115 400
South Australia	1 466 500
Western Australia	1 687 300
Tasmania	4 721 000
Northern Territory	170 500
Australian Capital Territory	299 400

Media:

(*a*) Major newspapers:

Name	Location	Circulation
Herald Sun News Pictorial	Melbourne	600 000
Daily Telegraph Mirror	Surrey Hills	442 980
The Sydney Morning Herald	Sydney	266 000
The Western Australian	Perth	262 556
Courier-Mail	Brisbane	250 875
The Age	Melbourne	227 787
Advertiser	Adelaide	220 174
The Australian	Sydney	153 000
Australian Financial Review	Sydney	78 000

(*b*) Radio and television: *Australian Broadcasting Corporation* (ABC) operates a nationwide non-commercial radio and television service: National Broadcasting Service and National Television and SBS (multicultural broadcasting channel). Federation of Australian Radio Broadcasters and Federation of Australian Commercial Television represents privately-owned commercial radio and television stations.

Education:

(1991 figures)	Institutions	Teaching Staff	Students
Government schools	7 470	145 985	2 217 226
Non-gov. schools	2 510	53 673	857 911
Higher educational establishments	44	48 772	534 538

Economic Interest Organizations:
Employers' organization: Confederation of Australian Industries (CAI).
Central trade union peak association: Australian Council of Trade Unions
(ACTU), founded 1927; membership: 2,250,000 (1984).

National or Central Bank: Reserve Bank of Australia.

Central Statistical Office:
Australian Bureau of Statistics
POB 10
Belconnen
Australian Capital Territory 2616

Budget: (1993/4)—in 1994 US dollars ($1 = $A 1.3687)—millions

Revenue	
Tax revenue	67 731
Non-tax revenue	
Interest, rent, dividends, royalties	5 046
Total	72 778

Expenditure	
Final consumption expenditure	17 978
Requited and unrequited current transfer payments	64 843
Contingency service	−172
Capital outlays	1 573
Total	84 223

Further Information:

Aitkin, D. (1977), *Stability and Change in Australian Politics*. Canberra:
Australian National University Press.

Aitkin, Jinks, and Warhurst (1989), *Australian Political Institutions*. Melbourne: Longman Cheshire.

Australian Bureau of Statistics. *Year Book Australia*

Brynes, M. (1994), *Australia and the Asia Game*. St. Leonards, NSW: Allen and Unwin.

Clark, M. (1986), *A Short History of Australia*. Melbourne: Macmillan.

Hughes, C. A., and Graham, B. D. (1968), *A Handbook of Australian Government and Politics 1890–1964*. Canberra: Australian National University Press.

Jupp, J. (1968), *Australian Party Politics*. 2nd edn. Melbourne: Melbourne University Press.

Kelly, P. (1993), *The End of Certainty: The Story of the 1980s*. Sydney: Allen & Unwin.

—— (1982), *Party Politics Australia (1966–81)*. Sydney: Allen & Unwin.

Sharp, C. A. (1963), *The Discovery of Australia*. Oxford: Oxford University Press.

Shaw, A. G. L. (1980), *The Economic Development of Australia*. Melbourne: 7th edn.

Starr, G., *et al.* (1978), *Political Parties in Australia*. Melbourne: Heinemann.

24. New Zealand

State Structure: Unitary

Form of State: Constitutional monarchy; acting Governor-General.

Parliament (unicameral): House of Representatives: 97 seats, 3 years.

Electoral System: Plurality formula.

Main Languages: English (100%); Maori (1.6%).

Population: 3,541,700 (1994 official estimate).

Constitutional Development: As in the United Kingdom constitutional practice is predominantly an accumulation of convention, precedent, and tradition.

Heads of State:

King George VI	Dec. 1936–Feb. 1952
Queen Elizabeth II	Feb. 1952—

Governors-General:

Lord Freyberg	1946–1952
Lord Norrie	1952–1957
Viscount Cobham	1957–1962
Bernard Fergusson	1962–1967
Arthur Porrit	1967–1972
Denis Blundell	1972–1977
Keith Holyoake	1977–1980
David Beattie	1980–1985
Paul Reeves	1985–1990
Dame Catherine Tizard	1990–

Capital City: Wellington (1986): 325,693.

Ministries:

Department of the Prime Minister and Cabinet

Ministry of Agriculture and Fisheries	Customs Department
Ministry of Civil Defence	Ministry of Defence
Ministry of Commerce	Ministry of Education
Department of Conservation	Ministry for the Environment
Ministry of Consumer Affairs	Ministry of Foreign Affairs and
Ministry of Cultural Affairs	Trade

Ministry of Forestry
Ministry of Health
Department of Internal Affairs
Department of Justice
Department of Labour
Ministry of Maori Development
Minstry of Pacific Island Affairs
Ministry of Research, Science and
    Development

Department of Social Welfare
State Services Commission
Statistics New Zealand
Department of Survey and Land
    Information
Ministry of Transport
Treasury
Ministry of Women's Affairs
Ministry of Youth Affairs

Governments:

	Prime Minister	Parties represented in government
Apr. 1940–Sept. 1943	Fraser I (LP)	LP
Sept. 1943–Nov. 1946	Fraser II (LP)	LP
Nov. 1946–Dec. 1949	Fraser III (LP)	LP
Dec. 1949–Sept. 1951	Holland I (NP)	NP
Sept. 1951–Nov. 1954	Holland II (NP)	NP
Nov. 1954–Sept. 1957	Holland III (NP)	NP
Sept. 1957–Dec. 1957	Holyoake I (NP)	NP
Dec. 1957–Dec. 1960	Nash (LP)	LP
Dec. 1960–Dec. 1963	Holyoake II (NP)	NP
Dec. 1963–Nov. 1966	Holyoake III (NP)	NP
Nov. 1966–Nov. 1969	Holyoake IV (NP)	NP
Nov. 1969–Feb. 1972	Holyoake V (NP)	NP
Feb. 1972–Dec. 1972	Marshall (NP)	NP
Dec. 1972–Aug. 1974	Kirk (LP)	LP
Aug. 1974–Dec. 1975	Rowling (LP)	LP
Dec. 1975–Dec. 1978	Muldoon I (NP)	NP
Dec. 1978–Dec. 1981	Muldoon II (NP)	NP
Dec. 1981–July 1984	Muldoon III (NP)	NP
July 1984–Aug. 1987	Lange I (LP)	LP
Aug. 1987–Aug. 1989	Lange II (LP)	LP
Aug. 1989–Nov. 1990	Palmer (LP)	NAT
Nov. 1990–Nov. 1993	Bolger I (LP)	NAT
Nov. 1993–	Bolger II (LP)	NAT

Principle Cities	Population (1993 official estimate)
Auckland	910 200
Wellington	326 900
Christchurch	312 600
Homilton	151 800
Napier-Hastings	111 200
Dunedin	110 800
Palmerston North	74 100
Tauranga	73 800

Media:
(*a*) Major newspapers:

Name	Location	Circulation
New Zealand Herald	Auckland	250 000
The Press	Christchurch	102 066
Evening Post	Wellington	72 000
The Dominion	Wellington	64 296
Otago Daily News	Dunedin	51 113

(*b*) Radio and television: *Broadcasting Corporation of New Zealand* (BCNZ) is the public broadcasting corporation. Its operating services are Radio New Zealand (RNZ) and Television New Zealand (TVNZ). Commercial radio has been operating since 1936.
There are three major private TV broadcasters:
Canterbury Television, a regional operator, began transmission in June 1991.
TV3 Network Holdings, a national private TV service, began broadcasting in November 1989.
Sky Network Television Ltd. was granted its licence in February 1990.

Education:

(1993 figures)	Institutions	Teachers	Students
Pre-school	3 640	6 428	148 239
Primary	2 329	19 730	401 681
Composite schools	83	1 517	32 637
Secondary	339	14 946	230 132
Special Schools	50	578	2 120
Polytechnic	25	5 092	88 427
Colleges of education	5	642	10 872
University	7	4 088	97 835

Economic Interest Organizations:
Employers' organization: New Zealand Employers' Federation.

Central trade union peak association: The New Zealand Council of Trade Unions, formed 1987 from a merger of the Combined State Unions and the former Federation of Labour (NCTU), founded 1937; membership: 357 000

National or Central Bank: Reserve Bank of New Zealand.

Central Statistical Office:
Department of Statistics
Private Bag
Wellington 1

Budget: (1992/3)—in 1994 US dollars ($1 = $NZ 1.6798)—millions

Revenue	
Income tax (inc. Corporation tax)	9 473
Other direct taxation	53
Excise duty	1 106
Goods and services tax	3 896
Other indirect taxation	806
Interest, profit, and misc.	44
Total	16 276

Expenditure	
Administration	1 891
Foreign relations	921
Development of industry	671
Education	2 708
Social services	6 398
Health	2 321
Transport	432
Debt services	2 329
Other expenditure	—
Total	17 670

Further Information:
Birks, S. (1992), *The New Zealand Economy, Issues and Policies*. Palmerston North: Dunmore Press.
Jackson, K. (1988), *The Dilemmas of Parliament*. Auckland: Allen & Unwin.

McLauchlan, G. (1987), *New Zealand Encyclopedia*, Auckland: David Bateman Ltd.

New Zealand Official Yearbook.

Palmer, G. (1988), *Unbridled Power*. 2nd edn. Oxford: Oxford University Press.

Rice, G. R. (1992) (ed.), *The Oxford History of New Zealand*. Auckland: University Press.

Statistics New Zealand. *New Zealand Official Yearbook*. Wellington.

Data Archives for the Social Sciences

Austria: WISDOM
                 Maria-Theresienstrasse 9
                 A–1090 Wien
                 Austria

Belgium: Belgian Archives for the Social Sciences (BASS)
                 Bâtiment SH 2 J. Leclerc
                 Place Montesquieu 1
                 B–1348 Louvain-la-Neuve
                 Belgium

Denmark: Danish Data Archives (dda)
                 Islandgade 10
                 DK-5000 Odense C
                 Denmark

Finland: No data archive

France: BDSP/C.E.R.A.T.
                 Institut d'Etudes Politiques
                 B.P 45
                 38402 Saint Martin d'Heres
                 France

Germany: Zentralarchiv für empirische
                 Sozialforschung (ZA)
                 Bachemer Str. 40
                 50931 Köln
                 Germany

Greece: No data archive

Iceland: No data archive

Ireland: Centre for the Study of Irish Elections
                 University College
                 Galway
                 Ireland

Italy: Archivo Dati e Programmi per le Scienze Sociali (ADPSS)
                 Istituto Superiore di Sociologica
                 Via G. Cantoni 4
                 I–20144 Milano
                 Italy

Luxembourg: No data archive

The Netherlands:	SWIDOC Steinmetz Archive Herengracht 410–412 1017 BX Amsterdam The Netherlands
Norway:	Norwegian Social Science Data Services (NSD) Hans Holmboesgate 22 5007 Bergen Norway
Portugal:	No data archive
Spain:	No data archive
Sweden:	Swedish Social Science Data Service (SSD) Göteborgs Universitet Pilgatan 19A 41122 Göteborg Sweden
Switzerland:	SIDOS ruelle Vaucher 13 CH-2000 Neuchatel Switzerland
Turkey:	No data archive
United Kingdom:	Economic and Social Research Council Data Archive University of Essex Wivenhoe Park Colchester Essex CO4 3SQ England
Canada:	Leisure Studies Data Bank (LSDB) Department of Recreation University of Waterloo Waterloo, Ontario Canada N2L 3G1 Machine Readable Archives—Public Archives Canada Public Archives Canada 395 Wellington Ottawa, Ontario Canada K1A 0N3 Social Science Data Library (SSDL) Department of Sociology Carleton Drive Colonel By Drive Ottawa, Ontario Canada K1S 5B6

	University Data Library (UDL)
	University of British Columbia
	Room 206
	6356 Agricultural Road
	Vancouver, British Columbia
	Canada V6T 1W5
USA:	Data and Program Library Service (DPLS)
	University of Wisconsin
	4452 Social Science Building
	Madison, Wisconsin 53706
	USA
	Inter-University Consortium for Political and Social Research (ICPSR)
	University of Michigan
	PO Box 1248
	Ann Arbor, Michigan 48106
	USA
	National Opinion Research Center (NORC)
	University of Chicago
	6030 South Ellis Avenue
	Chicago, Illinois 60637
	USA
	The Roper Center (RC)
	University of Connecticut
	Box U–164
	Storrs, Connecticut 06268
	USA
	Social Science Data Library (SSDL)
	Institute for Research in Social Science
	University of North Carolina
	Chapel Hill, North Carolina 27514
	USA
Japan:	No data archive
Australia:	Social Science Data Archive (SSDA)
	Australian National University
	PO Box 4
	Canberra ACT 2600
	Australia
New Zealand:	No data archive

Official Sources of National Statistics

Austria:	Austrian Central Statistical Office, 1033 Vienna Hintere zollamtsstr. 2B.
Belgium:	Institut National de Statistique, 44 rue de Louvain, 1000 Brussels.
Denmark:	Danmarks Statistik, Serjrogade 11, POB 2250, Copenhagen.
Finland:	Central Statistical Office of Finland, POB 504, Annankatu 44, 00101 Helsinki.
France:	Institut national de la statistique et des etudes economiques, 18 boulevard Adolphe-Pinard, 75675 Paris.
Germany:	Statistisches Bundesamt, 6200 Weisbaden 1, Gustavstresemann-Ring 11, Postfach 5528.
Iceland:	Statistical Bureau of Iceland, Hverfisgata 8–10, 150 Reykjavik.
Ireland:	Central Statistical Office, St Stephen's Green House, Earlsfort Terrace, Dublin 2.
Italy:	Instituto Nazionale di Statistica, Via Cesare Blabo 16, 00100 Rome.
Luxembourg:	Service Central de la Statistique et des Etudes Economiques (STATEC), Ministere de l' Economie, 19–21 blvd Royal, BP 304, 2013 Luxembourg.
Netherlands:	Central Bureau of Statistics, Princes Beatrixlaan 428, POB 959, 2270 AZ Voorburg.
Norway:	Statistisk Sentralbyra, Skippergt 15, POB 8131 Dep., 0030 Oslo 1.
Portugal:	Instituto Nacional de Estatistica (INE), Av Antonio Jose de Almeida 5, 1078 Lisbon Codex.
Spain:	Instituto Nacional de Estadistica, Paseo de la Castellana 183, 28046, Madrid.
Sweden:	Statistics Sweden, Karlavagen 100, 115 81 Stockholm.
Switzerland:	Federal Office of Statistics, 3003 Berne, Hallwylstr 15.
Turkey:	Turkiye Is Bankasi AS, Economic Research Department, Ataturk Bul. 191, 06684 Kavaklidere, Ankara.
United Kingdom:	Office of Population Census and Surveys, HMSO Publications Centre, PO Box 276, London, SW8 5DT.
Canada:	Statistics Canada, Ottawa, ONKIA OT6.
U.S.A:	Economics and Statistics Administration, Bureau of Census, US Department of Commerce, Washington, DC. 20230.
Japan:	Japan Center for Economic Research (JCER), 6–1 Nihombashi Kayabacho 2-chome, Chuo-ku, Tokyo 103.

Australia: Australian Bureau of Statistics, P.O. Box 10, Belconnen, ACT
                 2616.
New Zealand: Department of Statistics, Aorangi House, 85 Molesworth
                 Street, POB 2922, Wellington 1.

Source: *Europa World Yearbook 1992* (1992). London: Europa
                 Publications.

Bibliography

AHLUWALIA, M. S. (1976), 'Inequality Poverty and Development', *Journal of Development Economics*, 3: 307–42.

ARMINGEON, K. (1989), Arbeitsbeziehungen und Gewerkschaftsentwicklung in den achtziger Jahren: Ein Vergleich der OECD—Länder.' *Politische Viertalsjahrschrift* 30, 603–28.

BANKS, R. S. (1993) (ed.), *Political Handbook of the World*. Binghampton University: CSA Publications.

BARRETT, D. B. (1982) (ed.), *World Christian Encyclopedia*. Oxford: Oxford University Press.

BARTOLINI, S., and MAIR, P. (1990), *Identity Competition and Electoral Availability: the Stabilisation of European Electorates 1885–1985*. Cambridge: Cambridge University Press.

BOLLEN, K. (1980), 'Issues in the Comparative Measurement of Political Democracy', *American Sociological Review*, 45: 370–90.

—— (1993), 'Liberal Democracy: Validity and Method Factors in Cross-National Measures', *American Journal of Political Science*, 37: 1207–1230.

BORNISCHER, V. (1978), Einkommensungleichheit innerhalb von Landern in komparativer Sicht', *Schweizerischer Zeitschrift für Soziologie*, 4: 3–45.

CASTLES, S. (1984), *Here for Good: Western Europe's New Ethnic Minorities*. London: Pluto Press.

—— and KOSACK, G. (1973), *Immigrant Workers and Class Structure in Western Europe*. Oxford: Oxford University Press.

CHURCH, C. H., and PINNEMORE, D. (1994), *European Union and the European Community*. London: Harvester Wheatsheaf.

COMMISSION OF THE EUROPEAN COMMUNITIES (1991 Dec.), 'Annual Report of the Court of Auditors Concerning the Financial Year 1991', *Official Journal of the European Communities*, C330.

COMMISSION OF THE EUROPEAN COMMUNITY (1992 Nov.), 'Final Adoption of Amending and Supplementary Budget No 3 of the European Communities for the Financial Year 1992', *Official Journal of the European Communities*, L349.

CURTICE, J. (1989), '1989 European Elections: Protest or Green Tide?', *Electoral Studies*, 8: 217–30.

DAY, A. (1993) (ed.), *Political Parties of the World*. Harlow: Longman International Reference.

Encyclopaedia Britannica (1988), *Britannica Book of the Year*. Chicago: Encyclopaedia Britannica.

—— (1993), *Britannica Book of the Year*. Chicago: Encyclopaedia Britannica.

ESTES, R. J. (1984), *The Social Progress of Nations*. New York: Praeger.

FASSMANN, H., and MÜNZ, R. (1992), 'Patterns and Trends of International Migration in Western Europe, *Population and Development Review* 18, 460.

GASTIL, R. D. (1987) (ed.), *Political Rights and Civil Liberties 1986–87*. New York: Greenwood Press.

HARTMANN, J. (1984), *Politische Prole der westeuropaischen industriegesellschaft: Ein vergleichendes Handbuch*. Frankfurt am Main: Campus.

HUMANA, C. (1983), *World Human Rights Guide*. London: Hutchinson.

ILO (1985), *The Cost of Social Expenditure*. Geneve: ILO.

—— (various years), *World Labour Report*. Geneve: ILO.

—— (various years), *Yearbook of Labour Statistics*. Geneve: ILO.

IMF (various years), *Government Finance Statistical Yearbook*. Washington, DC: International Monetary Fund.

—— (various years), *International Financial Statistics Yearbook*. Washington, DC: International Monetary Fund.

Interparliamentary Union (1986), *Parliaments of the World: A Comparative Reference Compendium*. 2nd edn. Aldershot: Gower.

ISSP (various years), *The Role of Government*. Zentralarchiv für Empirische Sozial forschung an der Universität Zur Köln.

JACOBS, F. (1989) (ed.), *Western European Political Parties: A Comprehensive Guide*. Harlow: Longman International Reference.

JANOVA, M., and SINEAU, M. (1992), 'Women's Participation in Political Power in Europe: An Essay in East-West Comparrison', *Women's Studies International Forum*, 15: 115–28.

Keesing's Contemporary Archives (various years). Harlow: Longman.

Keesing's Record of World Events (various years). Harlow: Longman.

KJELLBERG, A. (1983), *Facklig organisering i tolv lander*. Lund: Arkiv.

KOOLE, R., and MAIR, P. (1992) (eds.), Political Data Yearbook. (special issue). *European Journal of Political Research*. 22: 4.

—— —— (1993), Special Issue: Political Data Yearbook, 1993, *European Journal of Political Research*, 24: 4.

KORPI, W. (1983), *The Democratic Class Struggle*. London: Routledge.

KOSACK, G. (1973), *Immigrant Workers and Class Structure in Western Europe*. Oxford: Oxford University Press.

LAAKSO, M., and TAAGEPERA, R. (1979), 'Effective Number of Parties: A Measure with Application to West Europe', *Comparative Political Studies*, 12: 3–27.

LAUNDY, P. (1989), *Parliaments in the Modern World*. Aldershot: Dartmouth.

LAWSON, E. H. (1990), *Encyclopedia of Human Rights*. Basingstoke: Taylor & Francis.

LIJPHART, A. (1984), *Democracies*. New Haven, Conn.: Yale University Press.

—— (1994), *Electoral Systems and Party Systems*. Oxford: Oxford University Press.

MACKIE, T. T. (various years), 'General Elections in Western Nations during (the year in question)', *European Journal of Political Research*.

—— and ROSE, R. (1982), *The International Almanac of Electoral History*. 2nd edn. London: Macmillan.

MADSEN, E. S., and PALDAM, M. (1978), *Economic and Political Data for the Main OECD Countries 1948–1975*. Arhus University: Institute of Economics.

MAIR, P., and KATZ, R. S. (1992) (eds.), *Party Organisations: A Data Handbook of Party Organisations in Western Democracies 1960–1990*. London: Sage Publications.

MATHESON, D. K. (1979), *Ideology, Political Action and the Finnish Working Class: A Survey Study of Political Behaviour*. Helsinki: Societas Scientiarium Fennica.

MIELKE, S. (1983) (ed.), *Internationales Gewerkschaftshandbuch*. Opladen: Leske & Budrich.

MITCHELL, B. R. (1981), *European Historical Statistics 1750–1975*. London: Macmillan.

—— (1982), *International Historical Statistics: Africa and Asia*. London: Macmillan.

—— (1983), *International Historical Statistics: The Americas and Australasia*. London: Macmillan.

MULLER, E. N. (1985), 'Income inequality, regime repressiveness, and political violence', *American Sociological Review*, 50: 47–61.

—— (1988), 'Democracy, Economic Development, and Income Inequality', *American Sociological Review*, 53: 50–68.

MUSGRAVE, R. A., and JARRETT, P. (1979), 'International Redistribution', *Kyklos* 32: 541–58.

NOHLEN, D. (1978), *Wahlsysteme der Welt: Daten und Analysen*. Munich: Piper.

Nordic Council (1984), *Yearbook of Nordic Statistics 1983*. Stockholm: Nordic Council.

NORTON, A. (1994), *International Handbook of Local and Regional Government: A Comparative Analysis of Advanced Democracies*. Aldershot: Edward Elgar Publishing.

OECD (1979), *OECD Observer*, 97. Paris: OECD.

—— (1985*a*), *Labour Force Statistics 1963–1983*. Paris: OECD.

—— (1985*b*), *Employment Outlook*. Paris: OECD.

—— (1985*c*), *Social Expenditure 1960–1990: Problems of Growth and Control*. Paris: OECD.

—— (1985*d*), *Measuring Health Care 1960–1983: Expenditure, Costs and Performance*. Paris: OECD.

—— (1986), *Living Conditions in OECD Countries: A Compendium of Social Indicators*. Paris: OECD.

—— (1987), *OECD Observer*, 145. Paris: OECD.

—— (1988), *Labour Force Statistics 1966–1986*. Paris: OECD.

—— (1992), *OECD In Figures*. Paris: OECD.

—— (1993), *OECD In Figures*. Paris: OECD.

—— (1993), *Education at a Glance: OECD Indicators*. Paris: OECD.

—— (1993), *Labour force Statistics 1971–1991*. Paris: OECD.

—— (1993), *OECD Health Systems: Facts and Trends 1960–1991*. Paris: OECD.

—— (various years), *Economic Outlook*. Paris: OECD.

—— (various years), *Economic Outlook: Historical Statistics*. Paris: OECD.

—— (various years), *National Accounts*. Paris: OECD.

—— (various years), *Revenue Statistics*. Paris: OECD.

OSMANCZYK, E. J. (1990), *Encyclopedia of the United Nations and International Agreements*. London: Taylor & Francis.

PALOHEIMO, H. (1986), *Governments in Democratic Capitalist States 1950–1983: A Data Handbook*. University of Turku, Department of Sociology and Political Science.

PATHIRANE, L., and BLADES, D. W. (1982), 'Defining and Measuring the Public Sector: Some International Comparisons', *Review of Income and Wealth*, 28: 261–89.

PAUKERT, F. (1973), 'Income Distribution at Different Levels of Development: A Survey of Evidence', *International Labour Review*, 108: 97–125.

PEDERSEN, M. (1979), 'The Dynamics of European Party Systems: Changing Patterns of Electoral Volatility', *European Journal of Political Research*, 7: 1–26.

—— (1983), 'Changing Patterns of Electoral Volatility in European Party Systems, 1948–1977: Explorations in Explanation', in Daadler, H., and Mair, P. (eds.), *West European Party Systems: Continuity and Change*. London: Sage.

RUSTOW, D. A. (1967), *A World of Nations: Problems of Political Modernisation*. Washington, DC: The Brookings Institution.

SAWYER, M. (1976), 'Income Distribution in OECD Countries', *OECD Economic Outlook: Occasional Studies*, July: 3–36.

SIPRI, (1980), *World Armaments and Disarmament*. London: Taylor & Francis.

—— (1988), *World Armaments and Disarmament*. Oxford: Oxford University Press.

—— (1992), *World Armaments and Disarmament*. London: Taylor & Francis.

SMITH, G. (1984), *Politics in Western Europe: A Comparative Analysis*. 4th edn. London: Heinemann.

The Statesman's Year-Book, 1989–1990 (1989) London: Macmillan.

STEPHENS, M. (1976), *Linguistic Minorities in Western Europe*. Llandysul: Gomer Press.

SUMMERS, R., and HESTON, A. (1988), 'A New Set of International Comparisons of Real Product and Price Levels Estimates for 130 Countries, 1950–1985', *Review of Income and Wealth*, 34: 1–25.

—— —— (1991), 'The Penn World Table (Mark 5): An Expanded Set of International Comparisons, 1950–1988', *Quarterly Journal of Economics*, 332–68.

TAYLOR, C. L., and JODICE, D. A. (1983), *World Handbook of Political and Social Indicators*. 3rd edn. New Haven, Conn. and London: Yale University Press.

—— —— and HUDSON, M. (1972), *World Handbook of Political and Social Indicators*. 2nd edn. New Haven, Conn: Yale University Press.

TESNIÈRE, L. (1928), 'Statistiques des langues de l'Europe', in A. Meillet, *Les Langues dans l'Europe nouvelle*. Paris: Payot.

The Economist, April 15th 1995. London.

The Europa World Yearbook (various years). London: Europa Publications.

The International Institute for Strategic Studies. (1993), *The Military Balance 1993–1994*. London: Brassey's.

THERBORN, G. (1984), 'The Prospects of Labour and the Transformation of Advanced Capitalism', *New Left Review*, 145: 5–38.

Trade Unions of the World, 1989–1990 (1989). Harlow: Longman International Reference.

UNDP (various years), *Human Development Report*. New York: Oxford University Press.

UNESCO (various years), *Statistical Yearbook*. Paris: UNESCO.

United Nations (1991), *The World's Women 1970–1990*. New York: United Nations.

—— (1992), *World Economic Survey 1992: Current Trends and Policies in the World Economy*. New York: United Nations.

—— (various years), *Demographic Yearbook*. New York: United Nations.

—— (various years), *National Accounts Statistics: Main Aggregates and Detailed Tables*. New York: United Nations.

—— (various years), *Statistical Yearbook*. New York: United Nations.

UPHAM, M. (1994), *Trade Unions and Employers' Organisations of the World*. Harlow: Longman International Reference.

URWIN, D. W., and PATERSON, W. E. (1990) (eds.), *Politics in Western Europe Today: Perspectives, Policies and Problems Since 1980*. Harlow: Longman.

UUSITALO, H. (1975), *Income and Welfare: A Study of Income as a Component of Welfare in Scandinavian Countries in the 1970's*. Helsinki: Research Group for Comparative Sociology.

VANHANEN, T. (1984), *The Emergence of Democracy: A Comparative Study of 119 States, 1850–1979*. Helsinki: Societas Scientiarum Fennica.

VISSER, J. (1992), 'Trends in Trade Union Membership'. *OECD Employment Outlook*: Paris: OECD.

WALLECHINSKY, D., WALLACE, I., and WALLACE, A. (1980), *The Book of Lists*. London: Corgi.

WESTERN, B. (1993), 'Postwar Unionization in Eighteen Advanced Capitalist Countries', *American Sociological Review* 58, 226–82.

WOLDENDORP, J., KEMAN, H., and BUDGE, I. (1993) (eds.), Special Issue: Political Data 1945–1990: Party Government in 20 Democracies, *European Journal of Political Research*, 24: 1.

World Bank (1984), *World Tables. i: Economic Data ii: Social Data*. 3rd edn. Baltimore, Md: Johns Hopkins University Press.

—— (1988), *World Tables 1987*. 4th edn. Washington, DC: World Bank.

—— (1989), *The 1988 Update of the World Bank Atlas*. Washington, DC: World Bank.

—— (1989), *Social Indicators of Development*. Baltimore and London: Johns Hopkins University Press.

—— (various years), *The World Bank Atlas*. Washington, DC: World Bank.

—— (various years), *World Development Report*. New York: Oxford University Press.

The World Directory of Diplomatic Representation (1992). London: Europa Publications.

Worldmark (1984), *Worldmark Encyclopedia of Nations*. New York: John Wiley.